W9-BPR-950

HOW TO KNOW THE WILD FLOWERS

A Guide

TO THE NAMES, HAUNTS, AND HABITS OF OUR COMMON WILD FLOWERS

BY

MRS. WILLIAM STARR DANA

ILLUSTRATED BY

MARION SATTERLEE

"The first conscious thought about wild flowers was to find out their names—the first conscious pleasure—and then I began to see so many that I had not previously noticed. Once you wish to identify them, there is nothing escapes, down to the little white chickweed of the path and the moss of the wall."

—RICHARD JEFFERIES

REVISED EDITION

BY

CLARENCE J. HYLANDER

DOVER PUBLICATIONS, INC.

NEW YORK

Published in Canada by General Publishing Company, Ltd., 30 Lesmill Road, Don Mills, Toronto, Ontario.

Published in the United Kingdom by Constable and Company Limited, 10 Orange Street, London W.C.2.

This new Dover edition, first published in 1963, is a revised and enlarged version of the last revised (1900) edition of the work first published by Charles Scribner's Sons in 1893.

Standard Book Number: 486-20332-8

Library of Congress Catalog Card Number: 63-3428

Manufactured in the United States of America
Dover Publications, Inc.
180 Varick Street
New York, N.Y. 10014

CONTENTS

This New Edition is Dedicated
to the Memory of

MRS. WILLIAM STARR DANA
(MRS. JAMES RUSSELL PARSONS)
1862-1952

PREFACE TO THE DOVER EDITION

"How to Know the Wild Flowers" is a classic among American nature books. It first appeared some seventy years ago; during the first decades of the twentieth century it was the leading popular flower guide, introducing to thousands of readers the pleasures of an acquaintance with the flowers of New England. Few recent books on wild flowers have had such widespread acceptance and appeal. Its reprinting will revive many nostalgic memories in the older generations, and will reveal to younger generations a strikingly different approach to nature from that of a matter-of-fact flower guide.

Mrs. Dana's book includes a minimum of botanical terminology; it is not burdened by a technical arrangement into plant families, with the resulting complicated classification of plants. The flowers are arranged in groups by colors, a system which (although it has its scientific limitations) serves the beginner very adequately. The customary and necessary botanical features of stem, foliage, flowers, and fruits are neatly disposed of in fine type under each species, for use of the reader who wishes to identify his flower specimen accurately.

The real contribution of the book, however, lies in the comments and supplementary information found in the body of the text. This is a refreshing and illuminating discourse on a variety of topics associated with the flower under consideration. How did the flower get its common name? Does the scientific name have any significance? What uses, if any, have been made of the plant? Was the flower known to the ancient Greeks or the contemporaries of the Biblical writers, and if so what role if any did it play in their lives? Is the flower a "native American" or an "immigrant"; if the latter, how did it get to our shores? Has the flower become part of our heritage in poetry and art?

Thus we discover that "the derivation of marigold is somewhat obscure. In the 'Grete Herball' of the sixteenth century the flower is spoken of as *Mary Gowles*, and by the early English poets as *gold* simply . . . it seems possible that the entire name may signify *marsh-gold*. . . ." Or that "The *Kalmia* was named by Linnaeus after Peter Kalm, one of his pupils who travelled in this country, who was, perhaps, the first to make known the shrub to his great master." Or, in reference to mullein, that "The Romans called it 'candelaria,' from their custom of dipping the long, dried stalk in suet and using it as a funeral torch. . . ." Or, in reference to witch-hazel, that "*wych*-hazel, as it was called after the wych-elm, whose leaves it resembles, and which was so named because the chests termed in old times 'wyches' were made of its wood. . . ." Or that the flower Oswego-tea was known to the American Indians, who "named the flower *O-gee-chee*—flaming flower, and are said to have made a tea-like decoction from the blossoms."

From the above it can be seen that an unusual, and delightful aspect of Mrs. Dana's book is the introduction of much relevant material gleaned from a lifetime of reading and delving into the literature, history, and folklore of the past. Charming as a period piece is her constant interweaving of passages from Bryant, Emerson, Longfellow, Thoreau, and Burroughs with references to Linnaeus and Wallace. This mingling of botanical and literary ingredients makes the flower become more than a combination of pistils, stamens, and petals; it brings to mind past customs, a poem, or a picture.

The botanical sciences dealing with the identification and naming of plants has brought many changes in usage of both common and scientific names since Mrs. Dana's day. Thus all the nomenclature has had to be carefully revised to conform with the Eighth Edition (1950) of *Gray's Manual of Botany*. As a result, all common and scientific names have been checked and now agree with those used in recent flower field guides.

PREFACE TO THE DOVER EDITION

The text of this new Dover edition is basically that of the last revised and enlarged edition of 1900, the only changes being the complete updating of nomenclature, as explained above, and the revision of a very few passages which had become obsolete.

This edition contains 174 plates. These represent all the black and white plates from the 1900 edition plus almost all the plates from the earlier editions that were dropped in 1900 in favor of color plates. (The only plates from earlier editions not restored are three or four of which the identification is now considered dubious.) We have chosen to reproduce the black and white plates instead of the color plates because the color plates, being over fifty years old, would be considered unsatisfactory when compared with color illustrations now produced with modern reproduction techniques. Also, the black and white illustrations afford the reader the opportunity of coloring the illustrations by hand, an enjoyable exercise which helps one become well acquainted with a flower's appearance.

With this revision and updating, "How to Know the Wild Flowers" now makes an excellent companion volume to newer guides which may present more "meat" in a more scientific package, but which lack the style and spirit of Mrs. Dana's work. "How to Know the Wild Flowers" remains an excellent introduction to the five hundred species of native and introduced wild flowers in the northeastern United States.

CLARENCE J. HYLANDER

BAR HARBOR, MAINE
1962

PREFACE TO THE NEW EDITION

In offering the public an edition of "How to Know the Wild Flowers," containing colored reproductions from the charming and faithful sketches in water color of Miss Elsie Louise Shaw, we feel sure that we are adding materially to the book's actual value as well as to its attractiveness.

As color plates replace, in this edition, certain of the black and white illustrations, these, with a few others have been omitted and Miss Satterlee has added a number of new drawings. Some of these black and white plates are of flowers not before figured in the book, while others present in fresh forms subjects already illustrated in it.

Quite a large number of flowers not found in previous editions are now described, and advantage has been taken of the opportunity which the entire resetting of the book afforded for a careful revision of the text. This amplification has seemed advisable in view of the fact that, during the five years which have elapsed since the publication of a thoroughly revised edition, the peculiar charm or importance of certain plants has so forced itself upon the author's consciousness, or else been brought to her notice so emphatically by others, as to persuade her that their inclusion would not transgress the restrictions originally laid down in the chapter "How to Use the Book," restrictions which still seem indispensable if the volume is to be kept small enough to be a convenient companion in the woods and fields, and simple enough to appeal to the unbotanical flower lover.

It is hoped that these additions will meet with the approval of the public, which has already attested so generously its eagerness to know the wild flowers.

ALBANY April 25, 1900.

PREFACE TO THE FIRST EDITION

THE pleasure of a walk in the woods and fields is enhanced a hundredfold by some little knowledge of the flowers which we meet at every turn. Their names alone serve as a clew to their entire histories, giving us that sense of companionship with our surroundings which is so necessary to the full enjoyment of outdoor life. But if we have never studied botany it has been no easy matter to learn these names, for we find that the very people who have always lived among the flowers are often ignorant of even their common titles, and frequently increase our eventual confusion by naming them incorrectly. While it is more than probable that any attempt to attain our end by means of some "Key," which positively bristles with technical terms and outlandish titles, has only led us to replace the volume in despair, sighing, with Emerson, that these scholars

> "Love not the flower they pluck, and know it not,
> And all their botany is Latin names!"

So we have ventured to hope that such a book as this will not be altogether unwelcome, and that our readers will find that even a bowing acquaintance with the flowers repays one generously for the effort expended in its achievement. Such an acquaintance serves to transmute the tedium of a railway journey into the excitement of a tour of discovery. It causes the monotony of a drive through an ordinarily uninteresting country to be forgotten in the diversion of noting the wayside flowers, and counting a hundred different species where formerly less than a dozen would have been detected. It invests each boggy meadow and bit of rocky woodland with almost irresistible charm.

Surely Sir John Lubbock is right in maintaining that "those who love nature can never be dull," provided that love be expressed by an intelligent interest rather than by a purely sentimental rapture.

The "Flower Descriptions" should be consulted in order to learn the actual dimensions of the different plants, as it has not always been possible to preserve their relative sizes in the illustrations. The aim in the drawings has been to help the reader to identify the flowers described in the text, and to this end they are presented as simply as possible, with no attempt at artistic arrangement or grouping.

We desire to express our thanks to Miss Harriet Procter, of Cincinnati, for her assistance and encouragement. Acknowledgment of their kind help is also due to Mrs. Seth Doane, of Orleans, Mass., and to Mr. Eugene P. Bicknell, of Riverdale, N. Y. To Dr. N. L. Britton, of Columbia College, we are indebted for permission to work in the College Herbarium.

NEW YORK, March 15, 1893.

HOW TO USE THE BOOK

Many difficulties have been encountered in the arrangement of this guide to the flowers. To be really useful such a guide must be of moderate size, easily carried in the woods and fields; yet there are so many flowers, and there is so much to say about them, that we have been obliged to control our selection and descriptions by certain regulations which we hope will commend themselves to the intelligence of our readers and secure their indulgence should any special favorite be conspicuous by its absence.

These regulations may be formulated briefly as follows:

1. Flowers so common as to be generally recognized are omitted, unless some peculiarity or fact in their history entitles them to special mention.

2. Flowers so inconspicuous as generally to escape notice are usually omitted.

3. Rare flowers and escapes from gardens are usually omitted.

4. Those flowers are chosen for illustration which seem entitled to prominence on account of their beauty, interest, or frequent occurrence.

5. Flowers which have less claim upon the general public than those chosen for illustration and full description, yet which are sufficiently common or conspicuous to arouse occasional curiosity, are necessarily dismissed with as brief a description as seems compatible with their identification.

In parts of New England, New York, New Jersey, Pennsylvania and in the vicinity of Washington, I have been enabled to describe many of our wild flowers from personal observation; and I have endeavored to increase the usefulness of the book by including as well those comparatively few flowers not found within the range mentioned, but commonly encountered at some point this side of Chicago.

The grouping according to color was suggested by a passage in one of Mr. Burroughs's "Talks about Flowers." It seemed, on careful consideration, to offer an easier identification than any other arrangement. One is constantly asked the name of some "little blue flower," or some "large pink flower," noted by the wayside. While both the size and color of a flower fix themselves in the mind of the casual observer, the color is the more definitely appreciated characteristic of the two and serves far better as a clew to its identification.

When the flowers are brought in from the woods and fields they should be sorted according to color and then traced to their proper places in the various sections. As far as possible the flowers have been arranged according to the seasons' sequence, the spring flowers being placed in the first part of each section, the summer flowers next, and the autumn flowers last.

It has sometimes been difficult to determine the proper position of a flower—blues, purples, and pinks shading so gradually one into another as to cause difference of opinion as to the color of a blossom among the most accurate. So if the object of our search is not found in the first section consulted, we must turn to that other one which seems most likely to include it.

It has seemed best to place in the White section those flowers which are so faintly tinted with other colors as to give a white effect in the mass, or when seen at a distance. Some flowers are so green as to seem almost entitled to a section of their own, but if closely examined the green is found to be so diluted with white as to render them describable by the term *greenish-white*. A white flower veined with pink will also be described in the White section, unless its general effect should be so pink as to entitle it to a position in the pink section. Such a flower again as the Painted Cup is placed in the Red section because its floral leaves are so red that probably none but the botanist would appreciate that the actual flowers were yellow. Flowers which fail to suggest any definite color are relegated to the Miscellaneous section.

With the description of each flower is given—

1. Its common English name—if one exists. This may be looked upon as its "nickname," a title attached to it by chance, often endeared to us by long association, the name by which it may be known in one part of the country but not necessarily in another, and about which, consequently, a certain amount of disagreement and confusion often arises.

2. Its scientific name. This compensates for its frequent lack of euphony by its other advantages. It is usually composed of two Latin—or Latinized—words, and is the same in all parts of the world (which fact explains the necessity of its Latin form). Whatever confusion may exist as to a flower's English name, its scientific one is an accomplished fact—except in those rare cases where an undescribed species is encountered—and rarely admits of dispute. The first word of this title indicates the *genus* of the plant. It is a substantive, answering to the last or family name of a person, and shows the relationship of all the plants which bear it. The second word indicates the *species*. It is usually an adjective, which betrays some characteristic of the plant, or it may indicate the part of the country in which it is found, or the person in whose honor it was named.

3. The English title of the larger Family to which the plant belongs. All flowers grouped under this title have in common certain important features which in many cases are too obscure to be easily recognized; while in others they are quite obvious. One who wishes to identify the flowers with some degree of ease should learn to recognize at sight such Families as present conspicuously characteristic features.

For fuller definitions, explanations, and descriptions than are here given, Gray's text-books and "Manual" should be consulted. After some few flowers have been compared with the partially technical description which prefaces each popular one, little difficulty should be experienced in the use of a botanical key. Many of the measurements and technical descriptions have been based upon Gray's "Manual." It has been thought best to omit any mention of species and varieties not included in the latest edition of that work.

An ordinary magnifying-glass (such as can be bought for seventy-five cents), a sharp penknife, and one or two dissecting-needles will be found useful in the examination of the smaller flowers. The use of a note-book, with jottings as to the date, color, surroundings, etc., of any newly identified flower, is recommended. This habit impresses on the memory easily forgotten but important details. Such a book is also valuable for further reference, both for our own satisfaction when some point which our experience had already determined has been forgotten, and for the settlement of the many questions which are sure to arise among flower-lovers as to the localities in which certain flowers are found, the dates at which they may be expected to appear and disappear, and various other points which even the scientific books sometimes fail to decide.

Some of the flowers described are found along every country highway, and it is interesting to note that these wayside plants may usually be classed among the foreign population. They have been brought to us from Europe in ballast and in loads of grain, and invariably follow in the wake of civilization. Many of our most beautiful native flowers have been crowded out of the hospitable roadside by these aggressive, irresistible, and mischievous invaders; for Mr. Burroughs points out that nearly all of our troublesome weeds are emigrants from Europe. We must go to the more remote woods and fields if we wish really to know our native plants. Swamps especially offer an eagerly sought asylum to our shy and lovely wild flowers.

LIST OF PLATES

LIST OF PLATES

LIST OF PLATES

LIST OF PLATES

LIST OF PLATES

"MOST young people find botany a dull study. So it is, as taught from the text-books in the schools; but study it yourself in the fields and woods, and you will find it a source of perennial delight."

"One of these days some one will give us a hand-book of our wild flowers, by the aid of which we shall all be able to name those we gather in our walks without the trouble of analyzing them. In this book we shall have a list of all our flowers arranged according to color, as white flowers, blue flowers, yellow flowers, pink flowers, etc., with place of growth and time of blooming."

JOHN BURROUGHS

INTRODUCTORY CHAPTER

UNTIL a comparatively recent period the interest in plants centred largely in the medicinal properties, and sometimes in the supernatural powers, which were attributed to them.

> "— O who can tell
> The hidden power of herbes and might of magick spell ?—"

sang Spenser in the "Faerie Queene;" and to this day the names of many of our wayside plants bear witness, not alone to the healing properties which their owners were supposed to possess, but also to the firm hold which the so-called "doctrine of signatures" had upon the superstitious mind of the public. In an early work on "The Art of Simpling," by one William Coles, we read as follows: "Yet the mercy of God which is over all his works, maketh-Grasse to grow upon the Mountains and Herbes for the use of men, and hath not only stamped upon them a distinct forme, but also given them particular signatures, whereby a man may read, even in legible characters, the use of them." Our hepatica or liverleaf, owes both its generic and English titles to its leaves, which suggested the form of the organ after which the plant is named, and caused it to be considered "a sovereign remedy against the heat and inflammation of the liver." *

Although his once-renowned system of classification has since been discarded on account of its artificial character, it is probably to Linnæus that the honor is due of having raised the

* Lyte.

study of plants to a rank which had never before been accorded it. The Swedish naturalist contrived to inspire his disciples with an enthusiasm, and to invest the flowers with a charm and personality which awakened a wide-spread interest in the subject. It is only since his day that the unscientific nature-lover, wandering through those woods and fields where

> "—wide around, the marriage of the plants
> Is sweetly solemnized—"

has marvelled to find the same laws in vogue in the floral as in the animal world.

To Darwin we owe our knowledge of the significance of color, form, and fragrance in flowers. These subjects have been widely discussed during the last twenty-five years, because of their close connection with the theory of natural selection; they have also been more or less enlarged upon in modern text-books. Nevertheless, it seems wiser to repeat what is perhaps already known to the reader, and to allude to some of the interesting theories connected with these topics, rather than to incur the risk of obscurity by omitting all explanation of facts and deductions to which it is frequently necessary to refer.

It is agreed that the object of a flower's life is the making of seed, *i.e.*, the continuance of its kind. Consequently its most essential parts are its reproductive organs, the stamens, and the pistil or pistils.

The stamens (p. xxxi) are the fertilizing organs. These produce the powdery, quickening material called pollen, in little sacs which are borne at the tips of their slender stalks.

The pistil (p. xxxii) is the seed-bearing organ. The pollen-grains which are deposited on its roughened summit throw out minute tubes which penetrate the style, reaching the little ovules in the ovary below, and quickening them into life.

These two kinds of organs can easily be distinguished in any large, simple, complete flower (p. xxx). The pollen of the stamens, and the ovules which line the base of the pistil, can also be detected with the aid of an ordinary magnifying-glass.

Now, we have been shown that nature apparently prefers that the pistil of a flower should not receive its pollen from the stamens in the same flower-cup with itself. Experience teaches that sometimes when this happens no seeds result. At other times the seeds appear, but they are less healthy and vigorous than those which are the outcome of *cross-fertilization*—the term used by botanists to describe the quickening of the ovules in one blossom by the pollen from another.

But perhaps we hardly realize the importance of abundant health and vigor in a plant's offspring.

Let us suppose that our eyes are so keen as to enable us to note the different seeds which, during one summer, seek to secure a foothold in some few square inches of the sheltered roadside. The neighboring herb-roberts and jewelweeds discharge—catapult fashion—several small invaders into the very heart of the little territory. A battalion of silky-tufted seeds from the cracked pods of the milkweed float downward and take lazy possession of the soil, while the heavy rains wash into their immediate vicinity those of the violet from the overhanging bank. The hooked fruit of the stick-tight is finally brushed from the hair of some exasperated animal by the jagged branches of the neighboring thicket and is deposited on the disputed ground, while a bird passing just overhead drops earthward the seed of the partridge-berry. The ammunition of the witch-hazel, too, is shot into the midst of this growing colony ; to say nothing of a myriad more little squatters that are wafted or washed or dropped or flung upon this one bit of earth, which is thus transformed into a bloodless battle-ground, and which is incapable of yielding nourishment to one-half or one-tenth or even one hundredth of these tiny strugglers for life !

So, to avoid diminishing the vigor of their progeny by *self-fertilization* (the reverse of cross-fertilization), various species take various precautions. In one species the pistil is so placed that the pollen of the neighboring stamens cannot reach it. In others one of these two organs ripens before the other, with the result that the contact of the pollen with the stigma of the pistil would be ineffectual. Often the stamens and pistils are in different flowers, sometimes on different plants. But these pistils must, if possible, receive the necessary pollen in some way and fulfil their destiny by setting seed. And we have been shown that frequently it is brought to them by insects, occasionally by birds, and that sometimes it is blown to them by the winds.

Ingenious devices are resorted to in order to secure these desirable results. Many flowers make themselves useful to the insect world by secreting somewhere within their dainty cups little glands of honey, or, more properly speaking, nectar, for honey is the result of the bees' work. This nectar is highly prized by the insects, and is in many cases the only object which attracts them to the flowers, although sometimes the pollen, which Darwin believes to have been the only inducement offered formerly, is sought as well.

But of course this nectar fails to induce visits unless the bee's attention is first attracted to the blossom, and it is tempted to explore the premises ; and we now observe the interesting fact that those flowers which depend upon insect-agency for their pollen, usually advertise their whereabouts by wearing bright colors or by exhaling fragrance. It will also be noticed that a flower sufficiently conspicuous to arrest attention by its appearance alone is rarely fragrant.

When, attracted by either of these significant characteristics—color or fragrance—the bee alights upon the blossom, it is sometimes guided to the very spot where the nectar lies hidden by markings of some vivid color. Thrusting its head into the heart of the flower for the purpose of extracting the secret treasure, it unconsciously strikes the stamens with sufficient force to cause them to powder its body with pollen. Soon it flies away to another plant *of the same kind*, where, in repeating the process just described, it unwittingly brushes some of the pollen from the first blossom upon the pistil of the second, where it helps to make new seeds. Thus these busy bees which hum so restlessly through the long summer days are working better than they know and are accomplishing more important feats than the mere honey-making which we usually associate with their ceaseless activity.

Those flowers which are dependent upon night-flying insects for their pollen contrive to make themselves noticeable by wearing white or pale yellow—red, blue, and pink being with difficulty detected in the darkness. They, too, frequently indicate their presence by exhaling perfume, which in many cases increases in intensity as the night falls and a clew to their whereabouts becomes momentarily more necessary. This fact partially accounts for the large proportion of fragrant white flowers. Darwin found that the proportion of sweet-scented white flowers to sweet-scented red ones was 14.6 per cent. of white to 8.2 of red.

We notice also that some of these night-fertilized flowers close during the day, thus insuring themselves against the visits of insects which might rob them of their nectar or pollen, and yet be unfitted by the shape of their bodies to accomplish their fertilization. On the other hand, many blossoms which are dependent upon the sun-loving bees close at night, securing the same advantage.

Then there are flowers which close in the shade, others at the approach of a storm, thus protecting their pollen and nectar from the dissolving rain; others at the same time every day. Linnæus invented a famous "flower-clock," which indicated the hours of the day by the closing of different flowers. This habit of closing has been called the "sleep of flowers."

There is one far from pleasing class of flowers which entices insect-visitors—not by attractive colors and alluring fragrance—but "by deceiving flies through their resemblance to putrid meat—imitating the lurid appearance as well as the noisome smell of carrion." Our common carrion-flower (Plate LV.), which covers the thickets so profusely in early summer that Thoreau complained that every bush and copse near the river emitted an odor which led one to imagine that all the dead dogs in the neighborhood had drifted to its shore, is probably an example of this class, without lurid color, but certainly with a sufficiently noisome smell! Yet this foul odor seems to answer the plant's purpose as well as their delicious aroma does that of more refined blossoms, if the numberless small flies which it manages to attract are fitted to successfully transmit its pollen.

Certain flowers are obviously adapted to the visits of insects by their irregular forms. The fringed or otherwise conspicuous lip and long nectar-bearing spur of many orchids point to their probable dependence upon insect agency for perpetuation; while the papilionaceous blossoms of the Pulse family also betray interesting adaptations for cross-fertilization by the same means. Indeed it is believed that irregularity of form is rarely conspicuous in a blossom that is not visited by insects.

The position of a nodding flower, like the harebell, protects its pollen and nectar from the rain and dew; while the hairs in the throat of many blossoms answer the same purpose and exclude useless insects as well.

Another class of flowers which calls for special mention is that which is dependent upon the wind for its pollen. It is interesting to observe that this group expends little effort in useless adornment. "The wind bloweth where it listeth" and takes no note of form or color. So here we find those

"Wan flowers without a name,"

which, unheeded, line the way-side. The common plantain of the country dooryard, from whose long tremulous stamens the light, dry pollen is easily blown, is a familiar example of this usually ignored class. Darwin first observed, that "when a flower is fertilized by the wind it never has a gayly colored corolla." Fragrance and nectar as well are usually denied these sombre blossoms. Such is the occasional economy of that at times most reckless of all spendthrifts—nature!

Some plants—certain violets and the jewelweeds among others—bear small inconspicuous blossoms which depend upon no outside agency for fertilization. These never open, thus effectually guarding their pollen from the possibility of being blown away by the wind, dissolved by the rain, or stolen by insects. They are called *cleistogamous* flowers.

Nature's clever devices for securing a wide dispersion of seeds have been already hinted at. One is tempted to dwell at length upon the ingenious mechanism of the elastically bursting capsules of one species, and the deft adjustment of the silky sails which waft the seeds of others ; on the barbed fruits which have pressed the most unwilling into their prickly service, and the bright berries which so temptingly invite the hungry winter birds to peck at them till their precious contents are released, or to devour them, digesting only the pulpy covering and allowing the seeds to escape uninjured into the earth at some conveniently remote spot.

Then one would like to pause long enough to note the slow movements of the climbing plants and the uncanny ways of the insect-devourers. At our very feet lie wonders for whose elucidation a lifetime would be far too short. Yet if we study for ourselves the mysteries of the flowers, and, when daunted, seek their interpretation in those devoted students who have made this task part of their life-work, we may hope finally to attain at least a partial insight into those charmed lives which find

> "—tongues in trees, books in the running brooks,
> Sermons in stones, and good in everything."

EXPLANATION OF TERMS

THE comprehension of the flower descriptions and of the opening chapters will be facilitated by the reading of the following explanation of terms. For words or expressions other than those which are included in this section, the Index of Technical Terms at the end of the book should be consulted.

The **Root** of a plant is the part which grows downward into the ground and absorbs nourishment from the soil. True roots bear nothing besides root-branches or **rootlets.**

"The **Stem** is the axis of the plant, the part which bears all the other organs." (Gray.)

A **Rootstock** is a creeping stem which grows beneath the surface of the earth. (See Solomon's-seal. Pl. LXII.)

A **Tuber** is a thickened end of a rootstock, bearing buds, —"eyes,"—on its sides. The common Potato is a familiar example of a tuber, being a portion of the stem of the potato plant.

A **Corm** is a short, thick, fleshy underground stem which sends off roots from its lower surface. (See Jack-in-the-Pulpit, Pl. CLXXII.)

A **Bulb** is an underground stem, the main body of which consists of thickened scales, which are in reality leaves or leaf bases, as in the onion.

A **Simple Stem** is one which does not branch.

A **Stemless** plant is one which bears no obvious stem, but only leaves and flower-stalks, as in the Common Blue Violet and Hepatica (Pl. CXLI.).

A **Scape** is the leafless flower-stalk of a stemless plant. (See Hepatica, Pl. CXLI.)

An **Entire Leaf** is one the edge of which is not cut or lobed in any way. (See Great Laurel, Pl. XXIV.)

A **Simple Leaf** is one which is not divided into leaflets; its edges may be either lobed or entire. (See Great Laurel, Pl. XXIV.; also Fig. 1.)

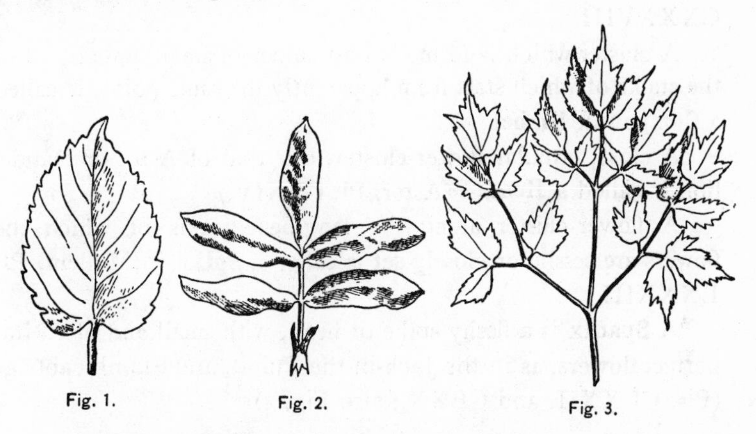

Fig. 1. Fig. 2. Fig. 3.

A **Compound Leaf** is one which is divided into leaflets, as in Wild Rose, Pink Clover, and Virgin's-bower (Pl. XLVII.; also Fig. 2).

A **Much-divided Leaf** is one which is several times divided into leaflets (Fig. 3).

The **Axil** of a leaf is the upper angle formed by a leaf or leaf-stalk and the stem.

Flowers which grow from the axils of the leaves are said to be **Axillary**.

When leaves or flowers are arranged in a circle around the stem they are said to be **Whorled**, or to form a **Whorl**. (See Indian Cucumber-root, Pl. LXIX.; Whorled Loosestrife, Pl. LXXVII.)

A cluster in which the flowers are arranged—each on its own stalk—along the sides of a common stem or stalk is called a **Raceme**. (See Shinleaf, Pl. XXIX.)

A **Corymb** is the same as a raceme, except that it is flat and broad, a raceme becoming a **Corymb** if the stalks of its lower flowers are lengthened while those of the upper remain shorter.

A cluster in which the flower-stalks all spring from apparently the same point, as in the Milkweeds, somewhat suggesting the spreading ribs of an umbrella, is called an **Umbel** (Pl. CXXXVIII.).

A cluster which is formed of a number of small umbels, all of the stalks of which start from apparently the same point, is called a **Compound Umbel.**

A close, circular flower-cluster, like that of Aster or Dandelion is called a **Head.** (Aster, Pl. CLXIV.)

A flower-cluster along the lengthened axis of which the flowers are sessile or closely set is called a **Spike.** (Mullein, Pl. LXXXIII.)

A **Spadix** is a fleshy spike or head, with small and often imperfect flowers, as in the Jack-in-the-Pulpit, and Skunk-cabbage (Pls. CLXXII. and CLXX.; also Fig. 4).

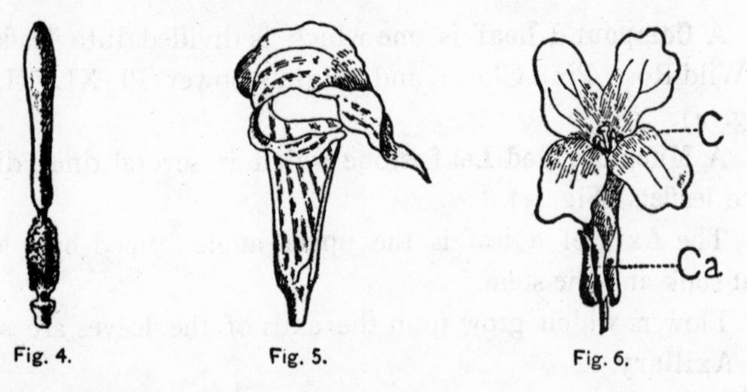

Fig. 4. Fig. 5. Fig. 6.

A **Spathe** is the peculiar leaf-like bract which usually envelops a spadix. (See Jack-in-the-Pulpit and Skunk-cabbage, Pls. CLXXII. and CLXX.; also Fig. 5.)

A **Bract** is a leaf belonging to or subtending a flower-cluster or a flower. It differs from the ordinary leaves usually in shape or size, sometimes in texture and color. The flower of an orchid is always subtended by a bract. (See Rose Pogonia, Pl. CX.)

Involucre is the name given to the circle or spiral collection of bracts around a flower-cluster. (See Elecampane, Pl.

XC., where the involucre surrounds what is probably considered a single flower, but what is actually a cluster of ray- and disk-flowers; also bunchberry, Pl. XXVI.; where the involucre consists of the four showy white leaves which are usually supposed to be petals, while the greenish centre is actually a cluster of inconspicuous flowers.)

A leaf or flower which is set so close in the stem as to show no sign of a separate leaf or flower-stalk, is said to be **Sessile.**

A **Complete Flower** (Fig. 6) is "that part of a plant which subserves the purpose of producing seed, consisting of stamens and pistils, which are the essential organs, and the calyx and corolla, which are the protecting organs." (Gray.)

The green outer flower-cup, or outer set of green parts, which we notice at the base of many flowers, is the **Calyx** (Fig. 6 Ca). At times this part is brightly colored and may be the most conspicuous feature of the flower.

When the calyx is divided into separate parts, these parts are called **Sepals.**

The inner flower-cup or the inner set of parts is the **Corolla** (Fig. 6, C).

When the corolla is divided into separate parts, these parts are called **Petals.**

We can look upon calyx and corolla as the natural tapestry which protects the delicate organs of the flower, and serves as well, in many cases, to attract the attention of passing insects. In some flowers only one of these two parts is present; in such a case the single cup or set of floral leaves is generally considered to be the calyx.

The floral leaves may be spoken of collectively as the **Perianth.** This word is used especially in describing members of families where there might be difficulty in deciding as to whether the single set of floral leaves present should be considered calyx or corolla (see Lilies, Pls. LXXXI. and CXXXIV.); or where the petals and sepals can only be distinguished with difficulty, as with the Orchids.

The **Stamens** (Fig. 7) are the fertilizing organs of the flower.

A stamen usually consists of two parts, its **Filament** (F), or stalk, and its **Anther** (A), the little sac at the tip of the filament which produces the dust-like, fertilizing substance called **Pollen** (p).

The **Pistil** (Fig. 8) is the seed-bearing organ of the flower. When complete it consists of **Ovary** (O), **Style** (Sty), and **Stigma** (Stg).

The **Ovary** is the hollow portion at the base of the pistil. It contains the ovules or rudimentary seeds which are quickened into life by the pollen.

The **Style** is the slender tapering stalk above the ovary.

The **Stigma** is usually the tip of the style. The pollen-grains which are deposited upon its moist roughened surface throw out

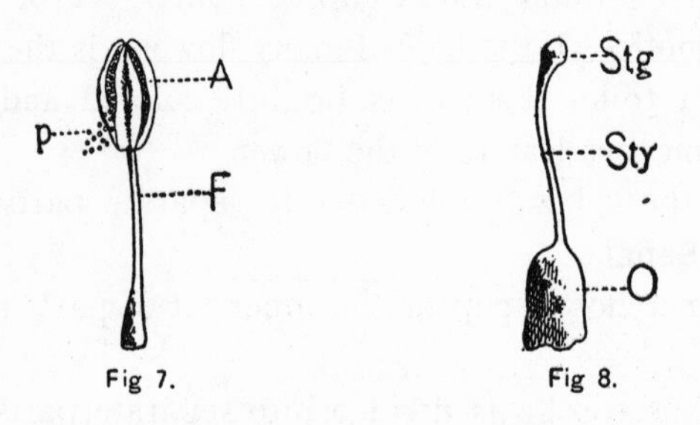

Fig 7. Fig 8.

minute tubes which penetrate to the little ovules of the ovary and cause them to ripen into seeds.

A flower which has neither stamens nor pistils is described as **Neutral.**

A flower with only one kind of these organs is termed **Unisexual.**

A **Male** or **Staminate** flower is one with stamens but without pistils.

A **Female** or **Pistillate** flower is one with pistils but without stamens.

The **Fruit** of a plant is the ripened seed-vessel or seed-vessels, including the parts which are intimately connected with it or them.

NOTABLE PLANT FAMILIES

Although the great majority of plant families can only be distinguished by a combination of characteristics which are too obscure to obtain any general recognition, there are some few instances where these family traits are sufficiently conspicuous to be of great assistance in the ready identification of flowers.

If, for instance, we recognize at sight a papilionaceous blossom and know that such an one only occurs in the Pulse family, we save the time and energy which might otherwise have been expended on the comparison of a newly found blossom of this character with the descriptions of flowers of a different lineage. Consequently it has seemed wise briefly to describe the marked features of such important families as generally admit of easy identification.

Composite Family.—It is fortunate for the amateur botanist that the plant family which usually secures the quickest recognition should also be the largest in the world. The members of the Composite family attract attention in every quarter of the globe, and make themselves evident from early spring till late autumn, but more especially with us during the latter season.

The most notable characteristic of the Composites is the crowding of a number of small flowers into a close cluster or *head*, which head is surrounded by an involucre, and has the effect of a single blossom. Although this grouping of small flowers in a head is not peculiar to this tribe, the same thing being found in the clovers, the milkworts, and in various other plants—still a little experience will enable one to distinguish a Composite without any analysis of the separate blossoms which form the head.

These heads vary greatly in size and appearance. At times they are large and solitary, as in the dandelion. Again they are small and clustered, as in the yarrow.

In some genera they are composed of flowers which are all similar in form and color, as in the dandelion, where all the corollas are *strap-shaped* and yellow; or, as in the common thistle, where they are all *tubular-shaped* and pinkish-purple.

In others they are made up of both kinds of flowers, as in the daisy, where only the yellow central or *disk-flowers* are tubular-shaped, while the white outer or *ray-flowers* are strap-shaped. The flower-heads of the well-known asters and goldenrods are composed of both ray and disk-flowers also; but while the ray-flowers of the aster, like those of the daisy, wear a different color from the yellow disk-flowers, both kinds are yellow in the goldenrod.

If the dandelion or the chicory (Pl. CLXII.) is studied as an example of a head which is composed entirely of strap-shaped blossoms; the common thistle or the stick-tight (Pl. XCII.) as an example of one which is made up of tubular-shaped blossoms; and the daisy or the aster (Pl. CLXIV.) as an example of one which combines ray and disk-flowers—as the strap-shaped and tubular blossoms are called when both are present—there need be little difficulty in the after recognition of a member of this family. The identification of a particular species or even genus will be a less simple matter; the former being a task which has been known to tax the patience of even advanced botanists.

Mr. Grant Allen believes that the Composites largely owe their universal sway to their "co-operative system." He says: "If we look close into the Daisy we see that its centre comprises a whole mass of little yellow bells, each of which consists of corolla, stamens, and pistil. The insect which alights on the head can take his fill in a leisurely way, without moving from his standing-place; and meanwhile he is proving a good ally of the plant by fertilizing one after another of its numerous ovaries. Each tiny bell by itself would prove too inconspicuous to attract much attention from the passing bee; but union is strength for the Daisy as for the State, and the little composites have found their co-operative system answer so well, that late as was their appearance upon the earth they are generally considered at the present day to be the most numerous family both in species and individuals of all flowering plants." While those of us who know the country lanes at that season when

"—ranks of seeds their witness bear,"

feel that much of their omnipresence is due to their unsurpassed facilities for globe-trotting. Our roadsides every autumn are lined with tall goldenrods, whose brown velvety clusters are compossed of masses of tiny seeds whose downy sails are set for their aërial voyage; with asters, whose myriad flower-heads are transformed into little puff-balls which are awaiting dissolution by the November winds, and with others of the tribe whose hooked seeds win a less ethereal but equally effective transportation.

Parsley Family.—The most familiar representative of the Parsley family is the wild carrot (p. 104), which so profusely decks the highways throughout the summer with its white, lace-like clusters; while the meadow-parsnip is perhaps the best known of its yellow members (p. 152).

This family can usually be recognized by the arrangement of its minute flowers in umbels, which umbels are again so clustered as to form a compound umbel whose radiating stalks suggest the ribs of an umbrella, and give this Order its Latin name of *Umbelliferae*.

A close examination of the tiny flowers which compose these umbrella-like clusters discovers that each one has five white or yellow petals, five stamens, and a two-styled pistil. Sometimes the calyx shows five minute teeth. The leaves are usually divided into leaflets or segments which are often much toothed or incised.

The Parsleys are largely distinguished from one another by differences in their fruit, which can only be detected with the aid of a microscope. It is hoped, however, that the more common and noticeable species will be recognized by means of descriptions which give their general appearance, season of blooming, and favorite haunts.

Pulse Family.—The Pulse family includes many of our common wood and field flowers. The majority of its members are easily distinguished by those irregular, butterfly-shaped blossoms which are described as *papilionaceous*. The sweet pea is a familiar example of such a flower, and a study of its curious structure renders easy the after-identification of a papilionaceous blossom, even if it be as small as one of the many which make up the head of the common pink clover.

The calyx of such a flower is of five more or less—and sometimes unequally—united sepals. The corolla consists of five irregular petals, the upper one of which is generally wrapped about the others in bud, while it spreads or turns backward in flower. This petal is called the *standard*. The two side petals are called *wings*. The two lower ones are usually somewhat united and form a sort of pouch which encloses the stamens and style; this is called the *keel*, from a fancied likeness to the prow of an ancient vessel. There are usually ten stamens and one pistil.

These flowers are peculiarly adapted to cross-fertilization through insect agency, although one might imagine the contrary to be the case from the relative positions of stamens and pistil. In the pea-blossom, for example, the hairy portion of the style receives the pollen from the early maturing stamens. The weight of a visiting bee projects the stigma and the pollen-laden style against the insect's body. But it must be observed that in this action the *stigma first brushes against the bee*, while the *pollen-laden style touches him later*, with the result that the bee soon flies to another flower on whose fresh stigma the detached pollen is left, while a new cargo of this valuable material is unconsciously secured, and the same process is indefinitely repeated.

Mint Family.—A member of the Mint family usually exhales an aromatic fragrance which aids us to place it correctly. If to this characteristic is added a square stem, opposite leaves, a two-lipped corolla, four stamens in pairs—two being longer than the others—or two stamens only, and a pistil whose style (two-lobed at the apex) rises from a deeply four-lobed ovary which splits apart in fruit into four little seed-like nutlets, we may feel sure that one of the many Mints is before us.

Sometimes we think we have encountered one of the family because we find the opposite leaves, two-lipped corolla, four stamens, and an ovary that splits into four nutlets in fruit; but unless the ovary was also deeply four-lobed in the flower, the plant is probably a Vervain, a tribe which greatly resembles the Mints. The Figworts, too, might be confused with the Mints did we not always keep in mind the four-lobed ovary.

In this family we find the common catnip and pennyroyal, the pretty ground-ivy, and the handsome Oswego-tea (p. 311).

Mustard Family.—The Mustard family is one which is abundantly represented in waste places everywhere by the little shepherd's-purse or pickpocket, and along the roadsides by the yellow mustard, and wild radish. (See Crinkleroot, Pl. IV.)

Its members may be recognized by their alternate leaves, their biting, harmless juice, and by their white, yellow, or purplish flowers, the structure of which at once betrays the family to which they belong.

The calyx of these flowers is divided into four sepals. The four petals are placed opposite each other in pairs, their spreading blades forming a cross which gives the Order its Latin name *Cruciferæ*. There are usually six stamens, two of which are inserted lower down than the others. The single pistil becomes in fruit a pod. Many of the Mustards are difficult of identification without a careful examination of their pods and seeds.

Orchis Family.—To the minds of many the term orchid only suggests a tropical air-plant, which is rendered conspicuous either by its beauty or by its unusual and noticeable structure.

This impression is, perhaps, partly due to the rude print in some old text-book which endeared itself to our childish minds by those startling and extravagant illustrations which are responsible for so many shattered illusions in later life; and partly to the various exhibitions of flowers in which only the exotic members of this family are displayed.

Consequently, when the dull clusters of the ragged fringed orchids, or the muddy racemes of the coral-root, or even the slender, graceful spires of the ladies'-tresses are brought from the woods or roadside and exhibited as one of so celebrated a tribe, they are usually viewed with scornful incredulity, or, if the authority of the exhibitor be sufficient to conquer disbelief, with unqualified disappointment. The marvellous mechanism which is exhibited by the humblest member of the Orchis family, and which suffices to secure the patient scrutiny and wondering admiration of the scientist, conveys to the uninitated as little of interest or beauty as would a page of Homer in the original to one without scholarly attainments.

The uprooting of a popular theory must be the work of years, especially when it is impossible to offer as a substitute one which is equally capable of being tersely defined and readily apprehended; for many seem to hold it a righteous principle to cherish even a delusion till it be replaced by a belief which affords an equal amount of satisfaction. It is simpler to describe an orchid as a tropical air-plant which apes the appearance of an insect and never roots in the ground than it is to master by patient study and observation the various characteristics which so combine in such a plant as to make it finally recognizable and describable. Unfortunately, too, the enumeration of these unsensational details does not appeal to the popular mind, and so fails to win by its accuracy the place already occupied by the incorrect but pleasing conception of an orchid.

For the benefit of those who wish to be able correctly to place these curious and interesting flowers, as brief a description as seems compatible with their recognition is appended.

Leaves.—Alternate, parallel-veined.

Flowers.—Irregular in form, solitary or clustered, each one subtended by a bract.

Perianth.—Of six divisions in two sets. The three outer

divisions are sepals, but they are usually petal-like in appearance. The three inner are petals. By a twist of the ovary what would otherwise be the upper petal is made the lower. This division is termed the *lip;* it is frequently brightly colored or grotesquely shaped, being at times deeply fringed or furrowed; it has often a spur-like appendage which secretes nectar; it is an important feature of the flower and is apparently designed to attract insects for the purpose of securing their aid in the cross-fertilization which is usually necessary for the perpetuation of the different species of this family, all of which give evidence of great modification by means of insect-selection.

In the heart of the flower is the *column;* this is usually composed of the stamen (of two in the *Cypripediums*), which is confluent with the *style* or thick, fleshy *stigma.* The two *cells* of the *anther* are placed on either side of and somewhat above the stigma; these cells hold the two pollen masses.

Darwin tells us that the flower of an orchid originally consisted of fifteen different parts, three petals, three sepals, six stamens, and three pistils. He shows traces of all these parts in the modern orchid.

FLOWER DESCRIPTIONS

"A fresh footpath, a fresh flower, a fresh delight"
RICHARD JEFFERIES

I

WHITE

[White or occasionally White Flowers not described in White Section.]

Hepatica. *Hepatica americana.* April and May.
(Blue and Purple Section, p. 319.)

Trailing Arbutus. *Epigaea repens.* April and May.
(Pink Section, p. 228.)

Dog's-tooth-Violet. *Erythronium americanum.* April and May.
(Yellow Section, p. 144.)

Bluets. *Houstonia caerulea.* May and June.
(Blue and Purple Section, p. 324.)

Beard-tongue. *Penstemon hirsutus and Penstemon Digitalis.* June.
(Blue and Purple Section, p. 344)

Wild Morning-glory. *Convolvulus sepium.* Summer.
(Pink Section, p. 262.)

Moth-Mullein. *Verbascum Blattaria.* Later Summer.
(Yellow Section, p. 196.)

Bouncing-Bet. *Saponaria officinalis.* Later Summer.
(Pink Section, p. 290.)

NOTE.—Occasional white varieties of other flowers may be found.
In this section also are placed flowers so pale as to give a white effect.

I

WHITE

BLOODROOT.

Sanguinaria canadensis. Poppy Family.

Rootstock.—Thick; charged with a crimson juice. *Scape.*—Naked; one-flowered. *Leaves.*—Rounded; deeply lobed. *Flower.*—White; terminal. *Calyx.*—Of two sepals falling early. *Corolla.*—Of eight to twelve snow-white petals. *Stamens.*—About twenty-four. *Pistil.*—One; short.

In early April the curled-up leaf of the bloodroot, wrapped in its papery bracts, pushes its firm tip through the earth and brown leaves, bearing within its carefully shielded burden, the young erect flower-bud. When the perils of the way are passed and a safe height is reached, this pale, deeply lobed leaf resigns its precious charge and gradually unfolds itself; meanwhile the bud slowly swells into a blossom.

Surely no flower of the year can vie with this in spotless beauty. Its very transitoriness enhances its charm. The snowy petals fall from about their golden centre before one has had time to grow satiated with their perfection. Unless the rocky hillsides and wood-borders are jealously watched it may escape us altogether. One or two warm sunny days will hasten it to maturity, and a few more hours of wind and storm shatter its loveliness.

Care should be taken in picking the flower—if it must be picked—as the red liquid which oozes blood-like from the wounded stem makes a lasting stain. This crimson juice was prized by the Indians as a decoration for their faces and tomahawks.

BLOODROOT.—*Sanguinaria canadensis.*

SHADBUSH. JUNEBERRY. SERVICEBERRY.

Amelanchier canadensis. Rose Family.

A tall shrub or small tree found in low ground. *Leaves.*—Oblong; acutely pointed; finely toothed; mostly rounded at base. *Flowers.*—White; growing in racemes. *Calyx.*—Five-cleft. *Corolla.*—Of five rather long petals. *Stamens.*—Numerous; short. *Pistils.*—With five styles. *Fruit.*—Round; red; sweet and edible; ripening in June.

Down in the boggy meadow, in early March, we can almost fancy that from beneath the solemn purple cowls of the skunk-cabbage brotherhood comes the joyful chorus—

"For lo, the winter is past!"

but we chilly mortals still find the wind so frosty and the woods so unpromising that we return shivering to the fireside, and refuse to take up the glad strain till the feathery clusters of the shadbush droop from the pasture thicket. Then only are we ready to admit that

"The flowers appear upon the earth,
The time of the singing of birds is come."

Even then, search the woods as we may, we shall hardly find thus early in April another shrub in blossom, unless it be the spicebush, whose tiny honey-yellow flowers escape all but the careful observer. The shadbush has been thus named because of its flowering at the season when shad "run;" Juneberry, because the shrub's crimson fruit surprises us by gleaming from the copses at the very beginning of summer; serviceberry, because of the use made by the Indians of this fruit, which they gathered in great quantities, and, after much crushing and pounding, made into a sort of cake.

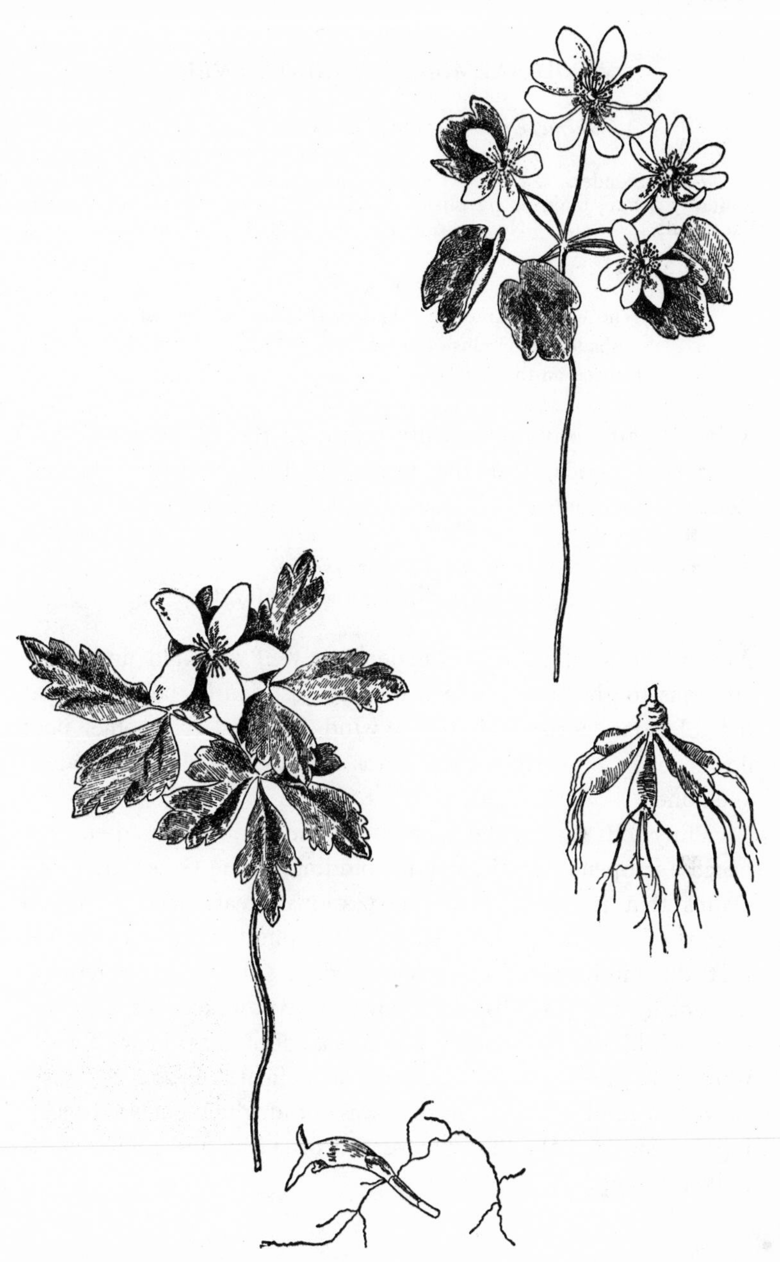

WOOD-ANEMONE.—*Anemone quinquefolia.* **RUE-ANEMONE.**—*Anemonella thalictroides.*

WOOD-ANEMONE. WIND-FLOWER.

Anemone quinquefolia. Crowfoot Family.

Stem.—Slender. *Leaves.*—Divided into delicate leaflets. *Flower.*—Solitary; white, pink, or purplish. *Calyx.*—Of from four to seven petal-like sepals. *Corolla.*—None. *Stamens and Pistils.*—Numerous.

"—Within the woods,
Whose young and half transparent leaves scarce cast
A shade, gay circles of anemones
Danced on their stalks;"

writes Bryant, bringing vividly before us the feathery foliage of the spring woods, and the tremulous beauty of the slender-stemmed anemones. Whittier, too, tells how these

"—wind-flowers sway
Against the throbbing heart of May."

And in the writings of the ancients as well we could find many allusions to the same flower, were we justified in believing that the blossom christened the "wind-shaken," by some poet flower-lover of early Greece, was identical with our modern anemone.

Pliny tells us that the anemone of the classics was so entitled because it opened at the wind's bidding. The Greek tradition claims that it sprang from the passionate tears shed by Venus over the body of the slain Adonis. At one time it was believed that the wind which had passed over a field of anemones was poisoned, and that disease followed in its wake. Perhaps because of this superstition the flower was adopted as the emblem of illness by the Persians. Surely our delicate blossom is far removed from any suggestion of disease or unwholesomeness, seeming instead to hold the very essence of spring and purity in its quivering cup.

RUE-ANEMONE.

Anemonella thalictroides. Crowfoot Family.

Stem.—Six to twelve inches high. *Leaves.*—Divided into rounded leaflets. *Flowers.*—White or pinkish; clustered. *Calyx.*—Of five to ten petal-like sepals. *Corolla.*—None. *Stamens.*—Numerous. *Pistils.*—Four to fifteen.

The rue anemone seems to linger especially about the spreading roots of old trees. It blossoms with the wood anemone, from which it differs in bearing its flowers in clusters.

STAR-FLOWER.

Trientalis borealis. Primrose Family.

Stem.—Smooth; erect. *Leaves.*—Thin; pointed; whorled at the summit of the stem. *Flowers.*—White; delicate; star-shaped. *Calyx.*—Generally seven-parted. *Corolla.*—Generally seven-parted; flat; spreading. *Stamens.*—Four or five. *Pistil.*—One.

Finding this delicate flower in the May woods, one is at once reminded of the anemone. The whole effect of plant, leaf, and snow-white blossom is starry and pointed. The frosted tapering petals distinguish it from the rounded blossoms of the wild strawberry, near which it often grows.

CANADA MAYFLOWER. WILD LILY-OF-THE-VALLEY.

Maianthemum canadense. Lily Family.

Stem.—Three to six inches high; with two or three leaves. *Leaves.*—Lance-shaped to oval; heart-shaped at base. *Flowers.*—White or straw-color; growing in a raceme. *Perianth.*—Four-parted. *Stamens.*—Four. *Pistil.*—One, with a two-lobed stigma. *Fruit.*—A red berry.

This familiar and pretty little plant, long without any homely English name, is now known as "Canada Mayflower," but while undoubtedly it grows in Canada and flowers in May, the name is not a happy one, for it abounds as far south as North Carolina, and is not the first blossom to be entitled "Mayflower."

In late summer the red berries are often found in close proximity to the fruit of the shin-leaf and pipsissewa.

PLATE III

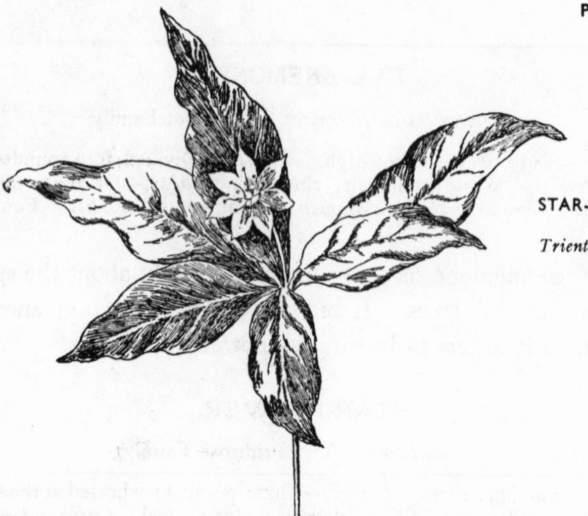

STAR-FLOWER

Trientalis borealis.

CANADA MAYFLOWER

Fruit.

Maianthemum canadense.

Flower.

M.S.

GOLDTHREAD.

Coptis groenlandica. Crowfoot Family.

Scape.—Slender; three to five inches high. *Leaves.*—Evergreen; shining; divided into three leaflets. *Flowers.*—White; solitary. *Calyx.*—Of five to seven petal-like sepals which fall early. *Corolla.*—Of five to seven club-shaped petals. *Stamens.*—Fifteen to twenty-five. *Pistils.*—Three to seven. *Root.*—Of long, bright yellow fibres.

This decorative little plant abundantly carpets the northern bogs and extends southward over the mountains. Its delicate flowers appear in May, but its shining, evergreen leaves are noticeable throughout the year. The bright yellow thread-like roots give it its common name.

EARLY EVERLASTING. PLANTAIN-LEAVED EVERLASTING.

Antennaria plantaginifolia. Composite Family.

Stems.—Downy or woolly, three to eighteen inches high. *Leaves.*—Silky, woolly when young; those from the root, oval, three-nerved; those on the flowering stems, small, lance-shaped. *Flower-heads.*—Crowded; clustered; small; yellowish-white; composed entirely of tubular flowers.

In early spring the hillsides are whitened with this, the earliest of the everlastings.

RED CHOKEBERRY.

Pyrus arbutifolia. Rose Family.

A shrub from one to three feet high. *Leaves.*—Oblong or somewhat lance-shaped; finely toothed; downy beneath. *Flowers.*—White or pinkish; rather small; clustered. *Calyx.*—Five-cleft. *Corolla.*—Of five petals. *Stamens*—Numerous. *Pistil.*—One, with two to five styles. *Fruit.*—Small, pear-shaped or globular, dark red or blackish.

Among the earliest shrubs of the year to flower is the chokeberry. Its white or pink blossoms, despite their smaller size, indicate a close kinship to those of the apple-tree. They are found during the spring months in swamps and thickets, and

CRINKLEROOT.—*Dentaria diphylla.*

also on the mountain sides all along the Atlantic coast, as well as farther inland. The red or blackish fruit suggests superficially a huckleberry.

PYXIE. FLOWERING-MOSS.

Pyxidanthera barbulata. Order *Diapensiaceae.*

Stems.—Prostrate and creeping; branching. *Leaves.*—Narrowly lance-shaped; awl-pointed. *Flowers.*—White or pink; small; numerous. *Calyx.*—Of five sepals. *Corolla.*—Five-lobed. *Stamens.*—Five. *Pistil.*—One, with a three-lobed stigma.

In early spring we may look for the dainty white flowers of this delicate moss-like plant in the sandy pine-woods of New Jersey and southward. At Lakewood they appear even before those of the trailing arbutus which grows in the same localities. The generic name is from two Greek words which signify a *small box* and *anther*, and refers to the anthers, which open as if by a lid.

CRINKLEROOT. PEPPERROOT.

Dentaria diphylla. Mustard Family.

Rootstock.—Five to ten inches long; wrinkled; crisp; of a pleasant, pungent taste. *Stem.*—Leafless below: bearing two leaves above. *Leaves.*—Divided into three toothed leaflets. *Flowers.*—White; in a terminal cluster. *Calyx.*—Of four early-falling sepals. *Corolla.*—Of four petals. *Stamens.*—Six; two shorter than the others. *Pistil.*—One. *Pod.*—Flat and lance-shaped.

The crinkleroot has been valued, not so much on account of its pretty flowers which may be found in the rich May woods, but for its crisp, edible root, which has lent savor to many a simple luncheon in the cool shadows of the forest.

TOOTHWORT.

Dentaria laciniata. Mustard Family.

Rootstock.—Tuberous; sometimes more or less bead-like. *Stem-leaves.*—Deeply parted; the divisions gash-toothed. *Flowers.*—White or pink; in a terminal cluster; otherwise as in above, but usually appearing somewhat earlier in the spring.

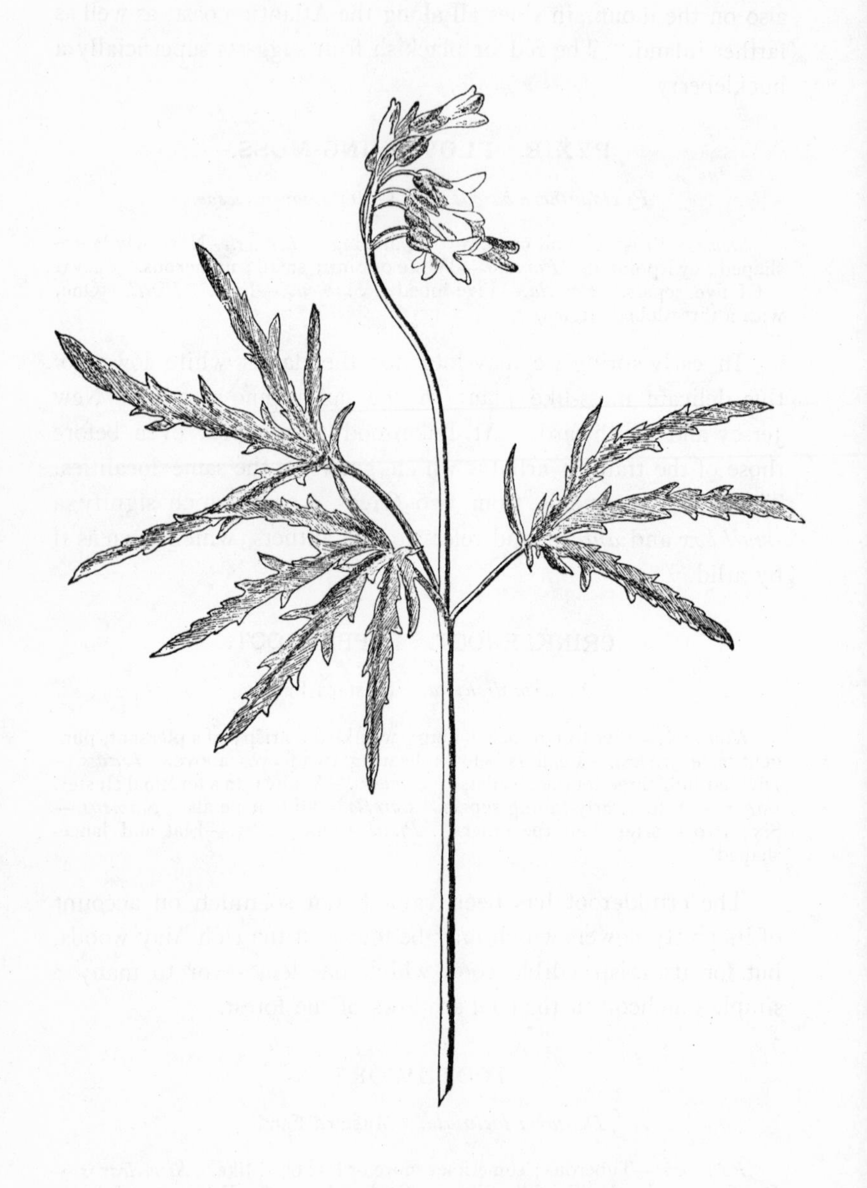

TOOTHWORT.—*Dentaria laciniata.*

SPRING-CRESS.

Cardamine bulbosa. Mustard Family.

Rootstock.—Slender; bearing small tubers. *Stem.*—From a tuberous base; upright; slender. *Root-leaves.*—Round and often heart-shaped. *Stem-leaves.*—The lower rounded, the upper almost lance-shaped. *Flowers.*—White; large; clustered. *Calyx.*—Of four early-falling sepals. *Corolla.*—Of four petals. *Stamens.*—Six; two shorter than the others. *Pistil.*—One. *Pod.*—Flat; lance-shaped; pointed with a slender style tipped with a conspicuous stigma; smaller than that of the crinkle-root.

The spring-cress grows abundantly in the wet meadows and about the borders of springs. Its large white flowers appear as early as April, lasting until June.

WHITLOW-GRASS.

Draba verna. Mustard Family.

Scapes.—One to three inches high. *Leaves.*—All from the root; oblong or lance-shaped. *Flowers.*—White; with two-cleft petals; clustered. *Calyx.*—Of four early-falling sepals. *Corolla.*—Of four petals. *Stamens.*—Six; two shorter than the others. *Pistil.*—One. *Pod.*—Flat; varying from oval to oblong-lance-shaped.

This little plant may be found flowering along the roadsides and in sandy places during April and May. It has come to us from Europe.

WATERCRESS.

Nasturtium officinale. Mustard Family.

Leaves.—Divided into roundish segments. *Flowers.*—White, clustered. *Calyx.*—Of four early-falling sepals. *Corolla.*—Of four petals, twice the length of the sepals. *Stamens.*—Six; two shorter than the others. *Pistil.*—One. *Pod.*—Linear.

Although the watercress is not a native of North America it has made itself so entirely at home in many of our streams that we hardly look upon it as a stranger. Whoever, after a long ramble through the woods on a summer morning, has plucked its fresh, pungent leaves from some sparkling stream and added them to his frugal sandwich, looks upon the little plant with a sense of familiar gratitude, which we rarely feel toward an alien.

The name *nasturtium*, signifying twisted nose, is said to be given to this genus on account of the effect supposedly produced on the nose by eating the acrid leaves.

SHEPHERD'S-PURSE.

Capsella Bursa-pastoris. Mustard Family.

Stem.—Low; branching. *Root-leaves.*—Clustered; incised or toothed *Stem-leaves.*—Arrow-shaped; set close to the stem. *Flowers.*—White; clustered. *Calyx.*—Of four early-falling sepals. *Corolla.*—Of four petals. *Stamens.*—Six; two shorter than the others. *Pistil.*—One. *Pod.*—Triangular, heart-shaped.

This is one of the commonest of our wayside weeds, working its way everywhere with such persistency and appropriating other people's property so shamelessly, that it has won for itself the nickname of pickpocket. Its popular title arose from the shape of its little seed-pods.

ROCK-CRESS.

Arabis hirsuta. Mustard Family.

Erect; one to two feet high. *Stem-leaves.*—Oblong or lance-shaped; sometimes toothed; partly clasping by a somewhat heart-shaped base. *Flowers.*—Small; greenish white; clustered. *Calyx.*—Of four early-falling sepals. *Corolla.*—Of four petals. *Stamens.*—Six; two shorter than the others. *Pistil.*—One. *Fruit.*—A long, narrow, flattened pod.

During May and June in rocky places, especially northward, we find this flower in abundance.

SMALL BITTER CRESS.

Cardamine hirsuta. Mustard Family.

Stem.—Three inches to two feet high; springing from a spreading cluster of root-leaves. *Leaves.*—Pinnate. *Flowers.*—Small; white; clustered. *Calyx.*—Of four early-falling sepals. *Corolla.*—Of four petals. *Stamens.*—Six, two shorter than the others. *Pistil.*—One. *Pod.*—Linear. Very narrow; erect or ascending.

The small bitter cress is a plant found in flower from May to July. Its spreading cluster of pinnately divided root-leaves is specially noticeable near the rocky banks of streams.

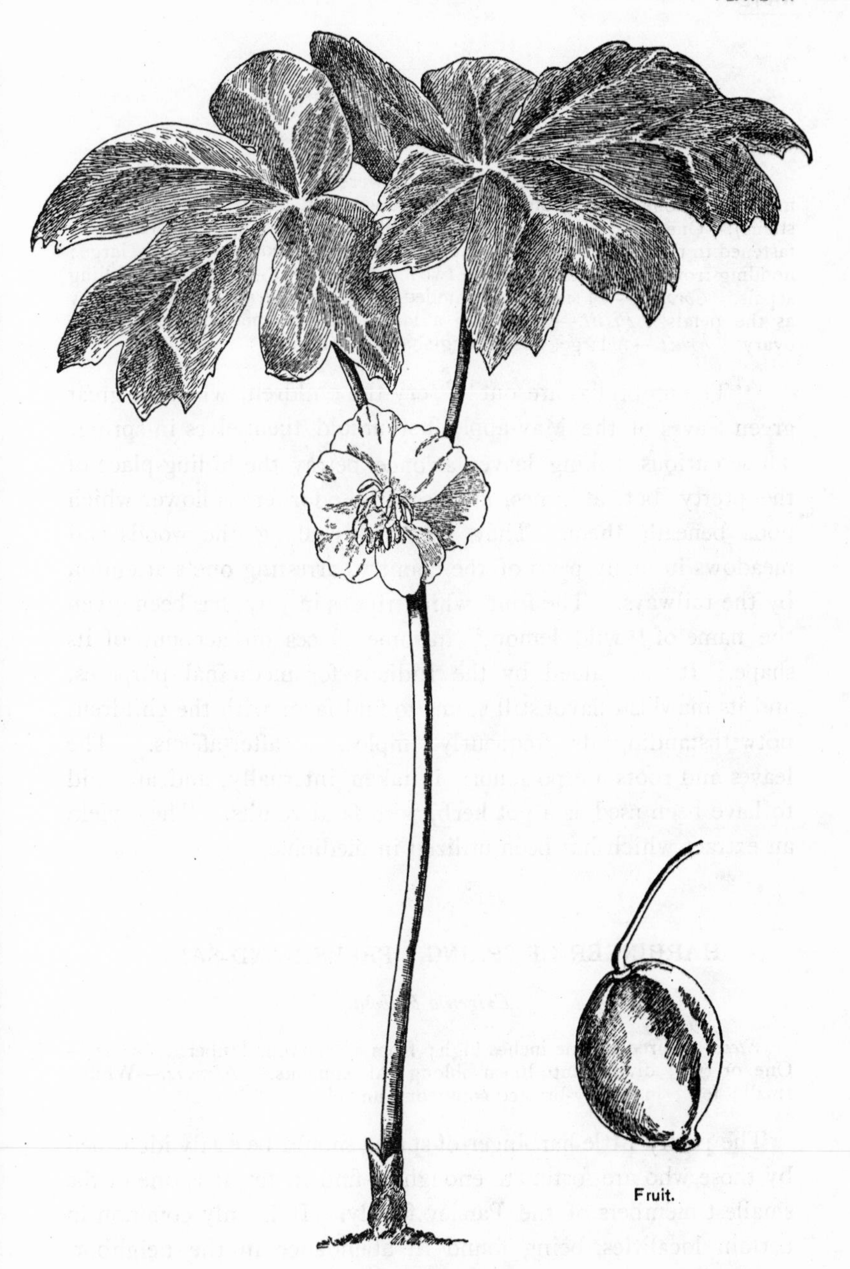

MAY-APPLE.—*Podophyllum peltatum.*

MAY-APPLE. MANDRAKE.

Podophyllum peltatum. Barberry Family.

Flowering-stem.—Two-leaved ; one-flowered. *Flowerless-stems.*—Terminated by one large, rounded, much-lobed leaf. *Leaves* (of flowering-stems).—One-sided ; five to nine-lobed, the lobes oblong ; the leaf-stalks fastened to their lower side near the inner edge. *Flower.*—White ; large ; nodding from the fork made by the two leaves. *Calyx.*—Of six early-falling sepals. *Corolla.*—Of six to nine rounded petals. *Stamens.*—Twice as many as the petals. *Pistil.*—One, with a large, thick stigma set close to the ovary. *Fruit.*—A large, fleshy, egg-shaped berry.

"The umbrellas are out!" cry the children, when the great green leaves of the May-apple first unfold themselves in spring. These curious-looking leaves at once betray the hiding-place of the pretty, but, at times, unpleasantly odoriferous flower which nods beneath them. They lie thickly along the woods and meadows in many parts of the country, arresting one's attention by the railways. The fruit, which ripens in July, has been given the name of "wild lemon," in some places on account of its shape. It was valued by the Indians for medicinal purposes, and its mawkish flavor still seems to find favor with the children, notwithstanding its frequently unpleasant after-affects. The leaves and roots are poisonous if taken internally, and are said to have been used as a pot herb, with fatal results. They yield an extract which has been utilized in medicine.

HARBINGER-OF-SPRING. PEPPER-AND-SALT.

Erigenia bulbosa.

Stem.—Three to nine inches high ; from a deep round tuber. *Leaves.*—One or two ; divided into linear-oblong leaf-segments. *Flowers.*—White ; small ; few ; in a leafy-bracted compound umbel.

The pretty little harbinger-of-spring should be easily identified by those who are fortunate enough to find it, for it is one of the smallest members of the Parsley family. It is only common in certain localities, being found in abundance in the neighborhood of Washington, where its flowers appear as early as March.

DUTCHMAN'S-BREECHES.—*Dicentra Cucullaria.*

DUTCHMAN'S-BREECHES. WHITE-HEARTS.

Dicentra Cucullaria. Fumitory Family.

Scape.—Slender. *Leaves.*—Thrice-compound. *Flowers.*—White and yellow; growing in a raceme. *Calyx.*—Of two small, scale-like sepals. *Corolla.*—Closed and flattened; of four somewhat cohering white petals tipped with yellow; the two outer—large, with spreading tips and deep spurs; the two inner—small, with spoon-shaped tips uniting over the anthers and stigma. *Stamens.*—Six. *Pistil.*—One.

There is something singularly fragile and spring-like in the appearance of this plant as its heart-shaped blossoms nod from the rocky ledges where they thrive best. One would suppose that the firmly closed petals guarded against any intrusion on the part of insect visitors and indicated the flower's capacity for self-fertilization; but it is found that when insects are excluded by means of gauze no seeds are set, which goes to prove that the pollen from another flower is a necessary factor in the continuance of this species. The generic name, *Dicentra,* is from the Greek and signifies *two-spurred.* The flower, when seen, explains its two English titles. It is accessible to every New Yorker, for in early April it whitens many of the shaded ledges in the upper part of the Central Park.

SQUIRREL-CORN.

Dicentra canadensis. Fumitory Family.

The squirrel-corn closely resembles the Dutchman's-breeches. Its greenish or pinkish flowers are heart-shaped, with short, rounded spurs. They have the fragrance of hyacinths, and are found blossoming in early spring in the rich woods of the North.

EARLY SAXIFRAGE.

Saxifraga virginiensis. Saxifrage Family.

Scape.—Four to nine inches high. *Leaves*—Clustered at the root; somewhat wedge-shaped; narrowed into a broad leaf-stalk. *Flowers.*—White; small; clustered. *Calyx.*—Five-cleft. *Corolla.*—Of five petals. *Stamens.*—Ten. *Pistil.*—One, with two styles.

In April we notice that the seams in the rocky cliffs and hillsides begin to whiten with the blossoms of the early saxifrage.

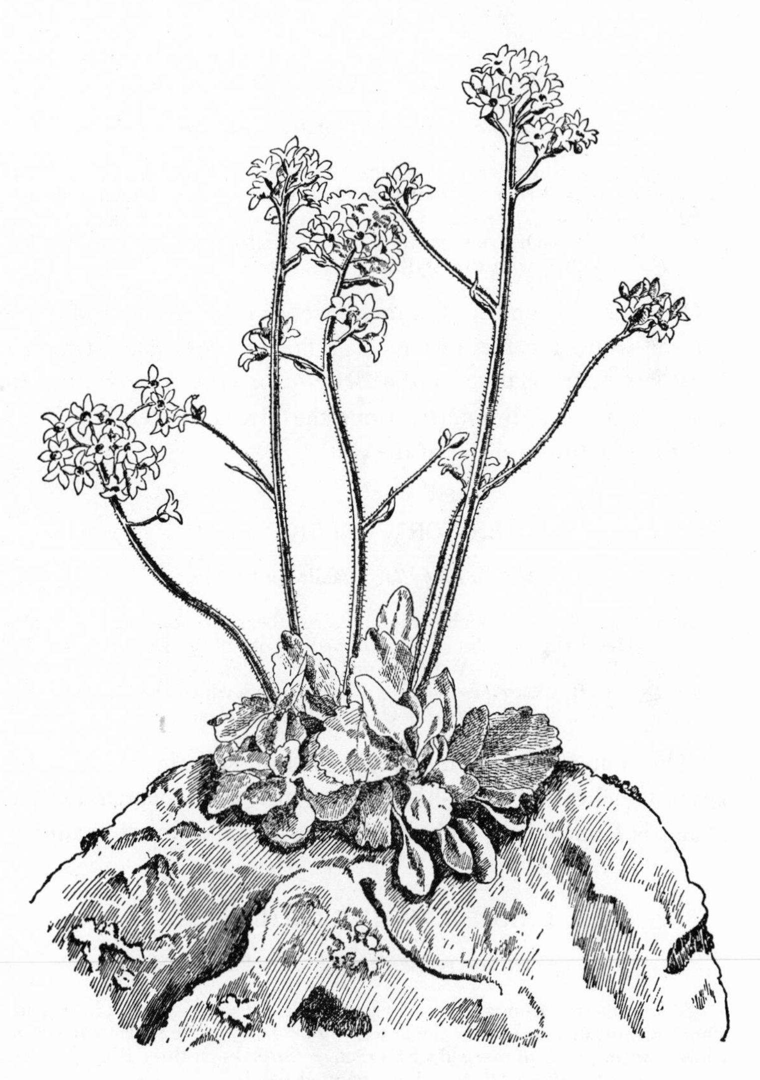

EARLY SAXIFRAGE.—*Saxifraga virginiensis.*

Steinbrech—stonebreak—the Germans appropriately entitle this little plant, which bursts into bloom from the minute clefts in the rocks and which has been supposed to cause their disintegration by its growth. The generic and common names are from *saxum*—a rock, and *frangere*—to break.

FOAMFLOWER. FALSE MITERWORT

Tiarella cordifolia. Saxifrage Family.

Stem.—Five to twelve inches high; leafless, or rarely with one or two leaves. *Leaves.*—From the rootstock or runners; heart-shaped; sharply lobed. *Flowers.*—White; in a full raceme. *Calyx.*—Bell-shaped; five-parted. *Corolla.*—Of five petals on claws. *Stamens.*—Ten; long and slender. *Pistil.*—One, with two styles.

Over the hills and in the rocky woods of April and May the graceful white racemes of the foam-flower arrest our attention. This is a near relative of the *Mitella* or true miterwort. Its generic name is a diminutive from the Greek for *turban*, and is said to refer to the shape of the pistil.

MITERWORT. BISHOP'S-CAP.

Mitella diphylla. Saxifrage Family.

Stem.—Six to twelve inches high; hairy; bearing two opposite leaves. *Leaves.*—Heart-shaped; lobed and toothed; those of the stem opposite and nearly sessile. *Flowers.*—White; small; in a slender raceme. *Calyx.*—Short; five-cleft. *Corolla.*—Of five slender petals which are deeply incised. *Stamens.*—Ten; short. *Pistil.*—One, with two styles.

The miterwort resembles the foamflower in foliage, but bears its delicate, crystal-like flowers in a more slender raceme. It also is found in the rich woods, blossoming somewhat later.

LARGER WHITE TRILLIUM.

Trillium grandiflorum. Lily Family.

Stem.—Stout; from a tuber-like root stock. *Leaves.*—Ovate; three in a whorl, a short distance below the flower. *Flower.*—Single; terminal; large; white, turning pink or marked with green. *Calyx.*—Of three green, spreading sepals. *Corolla.*—Of three long pointed petals. *Stamens.*—Six. *Pis-*

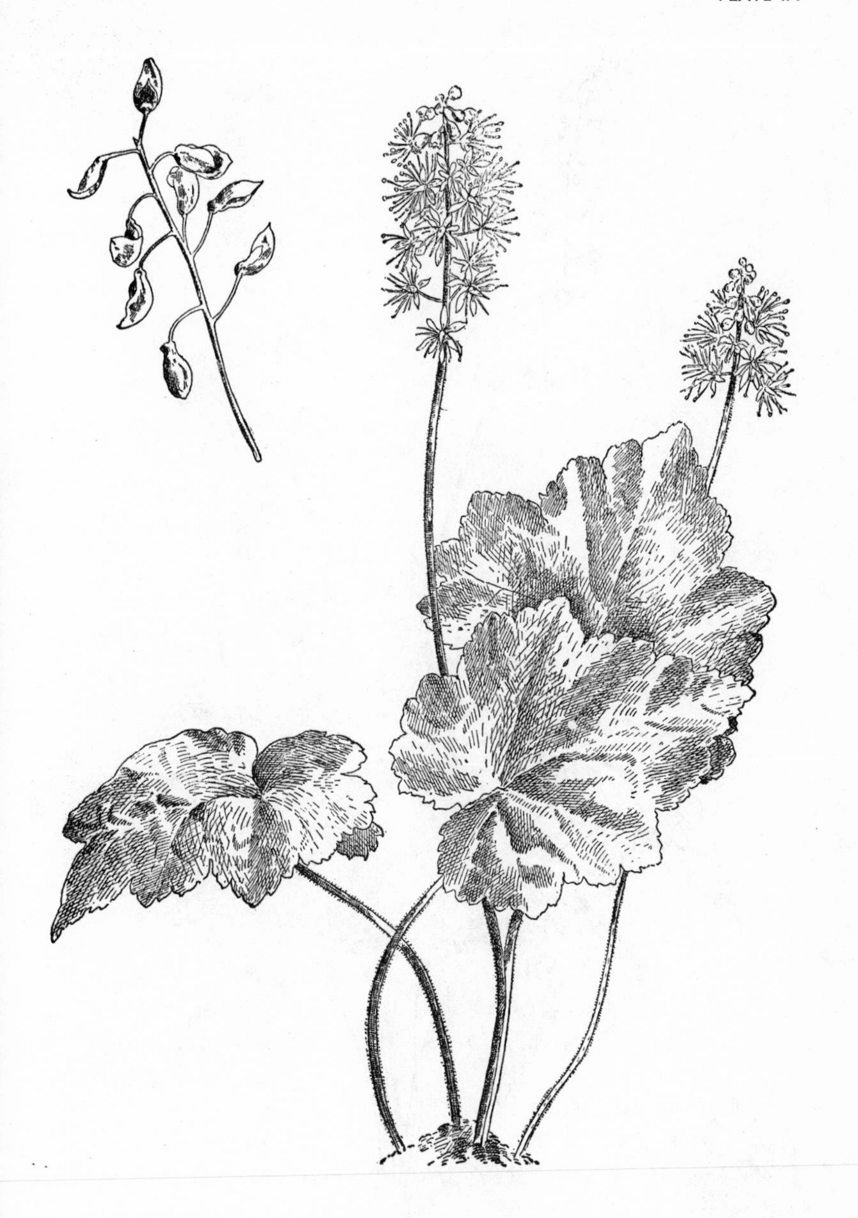

Fruit.

FOAMFLOWER.—*Tiarella cordifolia.*

Flower enlarged.

MITERWORT.—*Mitella diphylla.*

til.—One, with three spreading stigmas. *Fruit.*—A large ovate, somewhat angled, dark purple berry.

This singularly beautiful flower is found during April and May. Its great white stars gleam from shaded wood borders or from the banks of swift-flowing streams.

The nodding trillium, *T. cernuum*, bears its smaller white or pinkish blossom in a manner which suggests the may apple, on a stalk so curved as sometimes quite to conceal the flower beneath the leaves. This is a fragrant and attractive blossom, which may be found in the early year in moist shaded places.

The painted trillium, *T. undulatum*, is also less large and showy than the great white trillium, but it is quite as pleasing. Its white petals are painted at their base with red stripes. This species is very plentiful in the Adirondack and Catskill Mountains.

TWINLEAF. RHEUMATISM-ROOT.

Jeffersonia diphylla. Barberry Family.

A low plant. *Leaves.*—From the root; long-stalked; parted into two rounded leaflets. *Scape.*—One flowered. *Flower.*—White; one inch broad. *Sepals.*—Four, falling early. *Petals.*—Eight; flat, oblong. *Stamens.*—Eight. *Pistil.*—One, with a two-lobed stigma.

The twinleaf is often found growing with the bloodroot in the woods of April or May. It abounds somewhat west and southward.

CHOKE-CHERRY.

Prunus virginiana. Rose Family.

A shrub two to ten feet high. *Leaves.*—Oval or oblong; abruptly pointed; sharply toothed. *Flowers.*—White, in erect or spreading racemes terminating leafy branches. *Calyx.*—Five cleft. *Corolla.*—Of five spreading petals. *Stamens.*—Fifteen to twenty. *Pistil.*—One. *Fruit.*—Round, red or almost black, in drooping clusters.

In April or May, along the country lane where the oriole flashes in and out among the blossoms, and the blue-bird "with the earth tinge on his breast and the sky tinge on his back,"

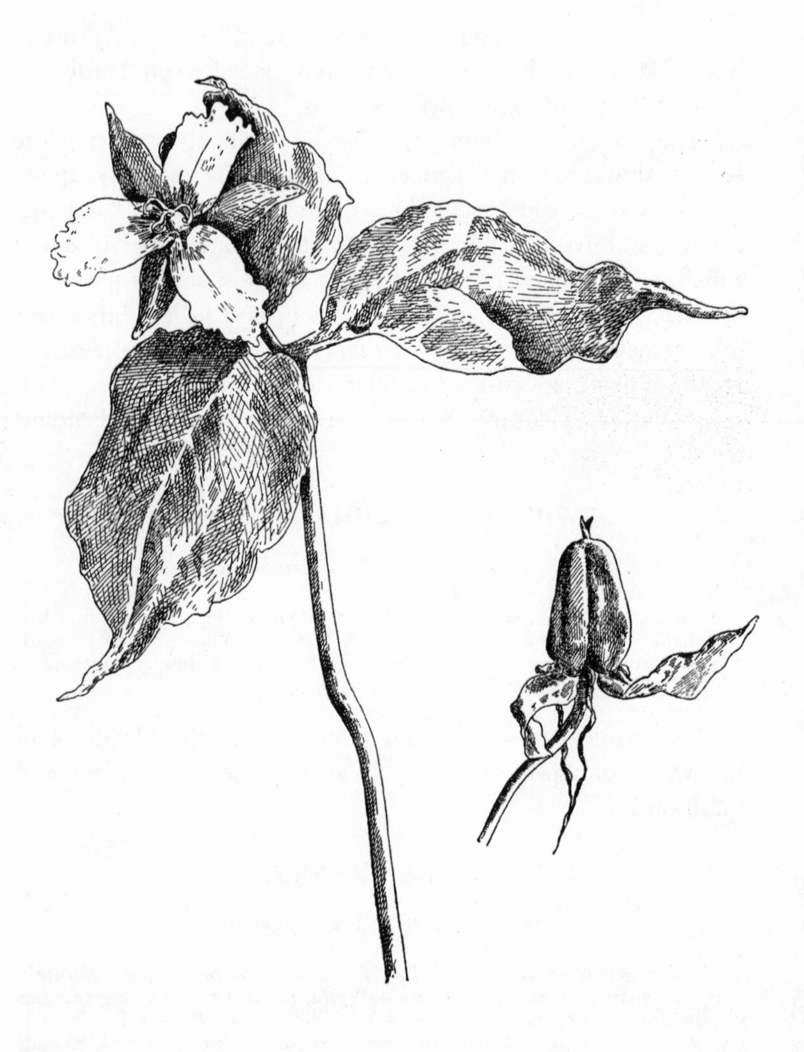

Fruit.

PAINTED TRILLIUM.—*Trillium undulatum.*

is resting on the fence rail, singing his simple song of joy in the perfect season, the long white flower-clusters of the choke-cherry arrest our attention. In August, or sometimes late in July, these same lanes are decorated by drooping clusters of the dark red acid fruit, well known to the country children, who perhaps gave the shrub its peculiar name.

WILD SARSAPARILLA.

Aralia nudicaulis. Ginseng Family.

Stem.—Bearing a single large, long-stalked, much-divided leaf, and a shorter naked scape which bears the rounded flower-clusters. *Flowers.*—Greenish-white; in umbels. *Calyx.*—With short or obsolete teeth. *Corolla.*—Of five petals. *Stamens.*—Five. *Fruit.*—Black or dark-purple; berry-like.

In the June woods the much-divided leaf and rounded flower-clusters of the wild sarsaparilla are frequently noticed, as well as the dark berries of the later year. The long aromatic roots of this plant are sold as a substitute for the genuine sarsaparilla. The rice-paper plant of China is a member of this genus.

GROUND-NUT. DWARF GINSENG.

Panax trifolius. Ginseng Family.

Stem.—Four to eight inches high. *Leaves.*—Three in a whorl; divided into from three to five leaflets. *Flowers.*—White; in an umbel. *Fruit.*—Yellowish; berry-like. *Root.*—A globular tuber.

The tiny white flowers of the dwarf ginseng are so closely clustered as to make "one feathery ball of bloom," to quote Mr. Hamilton Gibson. This little plant resembles its larger relative the true ginseng. It blossoms in our rich open woods early in spring, and hides its small round tuber so deep in the earth that it requires no little care to uproot it without breaking the slender stem. This tuber is edible and pungent tasting, giving the plant its name of ground-nut.

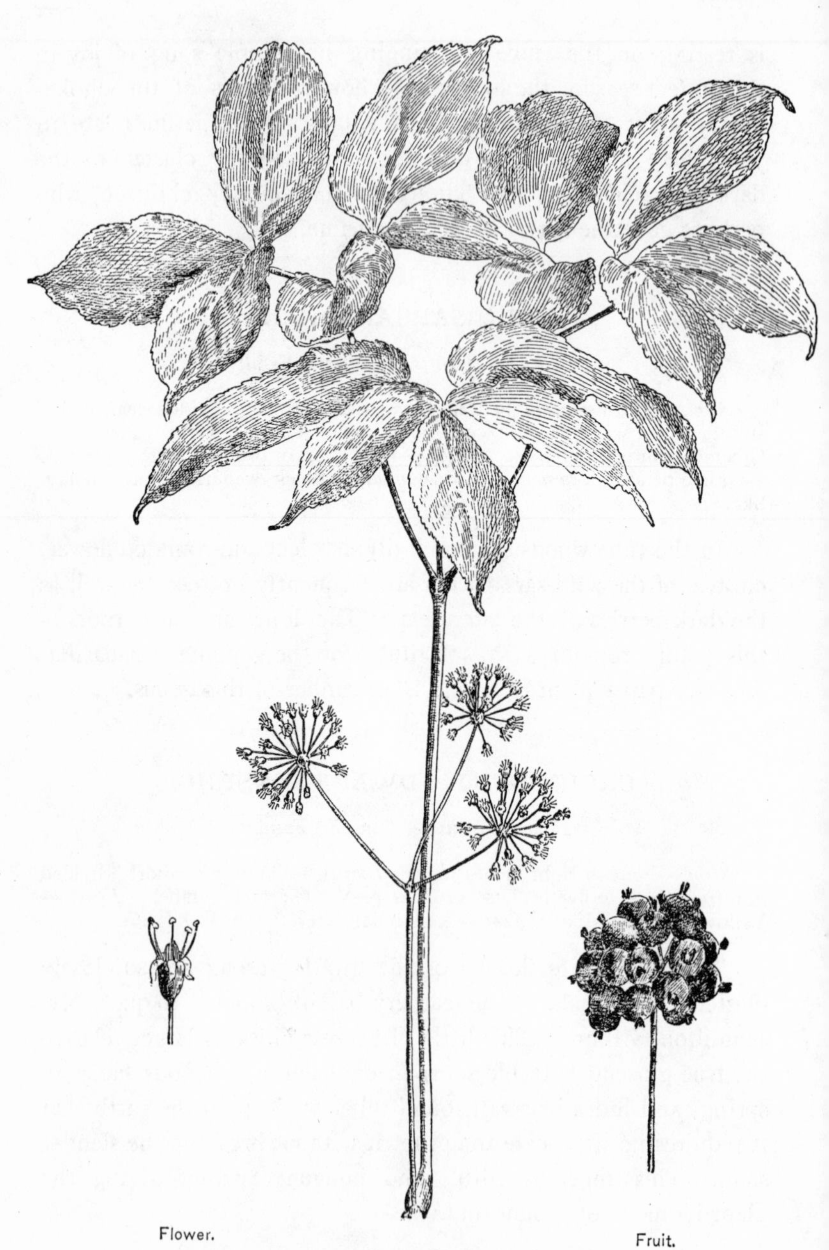

WILD SARSAPARILLA.—*Aralia nudicaulis.*

GINSENG.

Panax quinquefolius. Ginseng Family.

Root.—Large and spindle-shaped; often forked. *Stem.*—About one foot high. *Leaves.*—Three in a whorl; divided into leaflets. *Flowers.*—Greenish-white; in a simple umbel. *Fruit.*—Bright red; berry-like.

This plant is well known by name, but is yearly becoming more scarce. The aromatic root was so greatly valued in China for its supposed power of combating fatigue and old age that it could only be gathered by order of the emperor. The forked specimens were believed to be the most powerful, and their fancied likeness to the human form obtained for the plant the Chinese title of *Jin-chen* (from which ginseng is a corruption), and the Indian one of *Garan-toguen,* both which, strangely enough, are said to signify, *like a man.* The Canadian Jesuits first began to ship the roots of the American species to China. where they sold at about five dollars a pound. In 1900 they commanded about one-fifth of that price in the home market.

SPIKENARD.

[Pl. X

Aralia racemosa. Ginseng Family.

Root.—Large and aromatic. *Stem.*—Often tall and widely branched, leafy. *Leaves.*—Large; divided into somewhat heart-shaped, toothed, and pointed leaflets. *Flowers.*—Greenish-white; small; in clusters in early summer. *Fruit.*—Dark purple, red, or black; berry-like.

The spikenard is conspicuous chiefly in autumn, when its partially ripened clusters of glass-like fruit are sure to excite, by their rich beauty, the curiosity of the passer-by.

BRISTLY SARSAPARILLA.

Aralia hispida. Ginseng Family.

Stem.—One to two feet high; bristly, leafy, terminating in a stalk bearing several umbels of small white flowers. *Leaves.*—Divided into ovate or oval leaflets. *Flowers.*—White, small, in roundish clusters.

In June or July, in open, somewhat rocky or sandy places, the bristly sarsaparilla is conspicuous by reason of its pretty

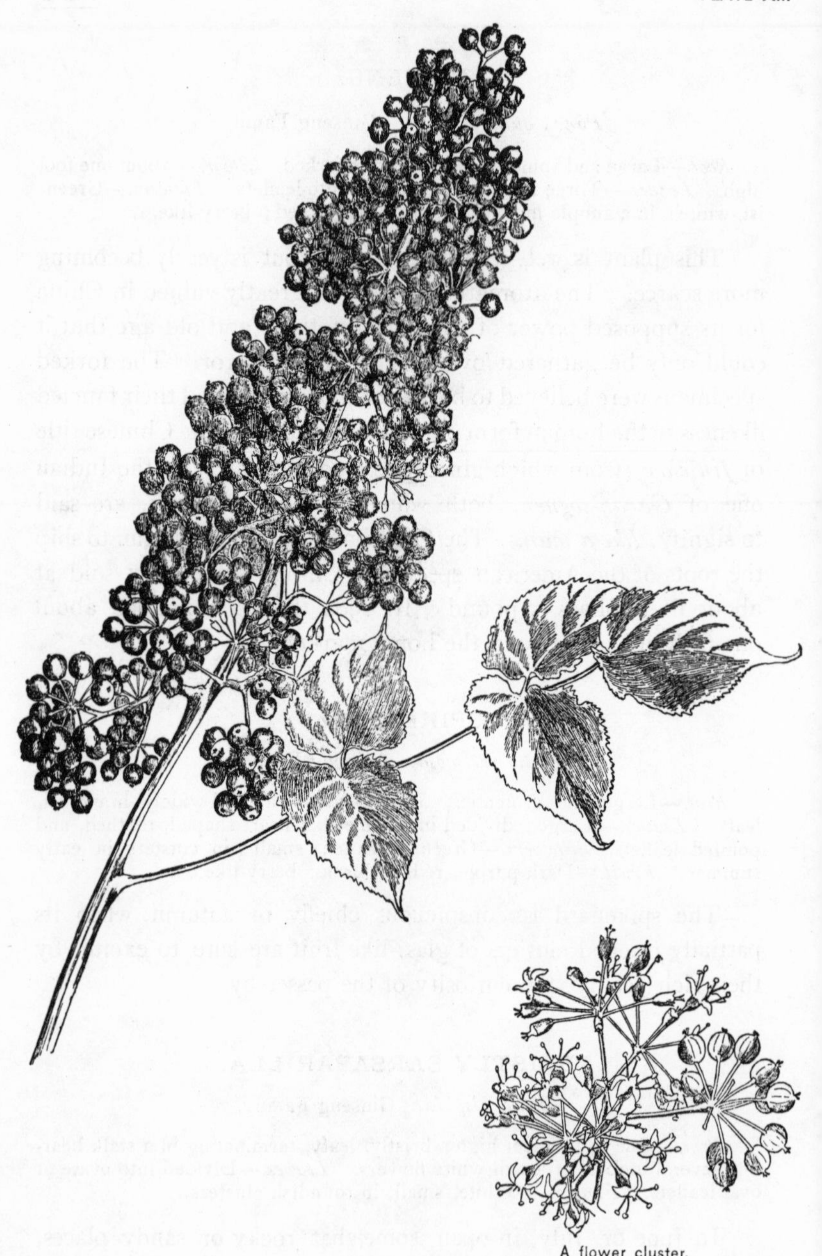

SPIKENARD.—*Aralia racemosa.*

rounded flower clusters. Later in the year its umbels of dark blue or purple fruit are even more noticeable than were the blossoms.

CANADA VIOLET.

Viola canadensis. Violet Family.

Stem.—Leafy; upright; one to two feet high. *Leaves.*—Heart-shaped; pointed; toothed. *Flowers.*—White, veined with purple, violet beneath, otherwise greatly resembling the common blue violet.

We associate the violet with the early year, but I have found the delicate fragrant flowers of this species blossoming high up on the Catskill Mountains late into September; and have known them to continue to appear in a New York city-garden into November. They are among the loveliest of the family, having a certain sprightly self-assertion which is peculiarly charming, perhaps because so unexpected.

The tiny sweet white violet, *V. blanda*, with brown or purple veins, which is found in nearly all low, wet, woody places in spring, is perhaps the only uniformly fragrant member of the family, and its scent, though sweet, is faint and elusive.

The lance-leaved violet, *V. lanceolata*, is another white species which is easily distinguished by its smooth lance-shaped leaves, quite unlike those of the common violet. It is found in damp soil, especially eastward.

CREEPING SNOWBERRY.

Gaultheria hispidula. Heath Family.

Stem.—Slender; trailing and creeping. *Leaves.*—Evergreen; small; ovate; pointed. *Flowers.*—Small; white; solitary from the axils of the leaves. *Calyx.*—Four-parted; with four large bractlets beneath. *Corolla.*—Deeply four-parted. *Stamens.*—Eight. *Pistil.*—One. *Fruit.*—A pure white berry.

One must look in May for the flower of this plant; but it is late in the summer when the beautiful little creeper especially challenges our admiration. Studded with snow-white berries, it nearly covers some decaying log which has fallen into a lonely

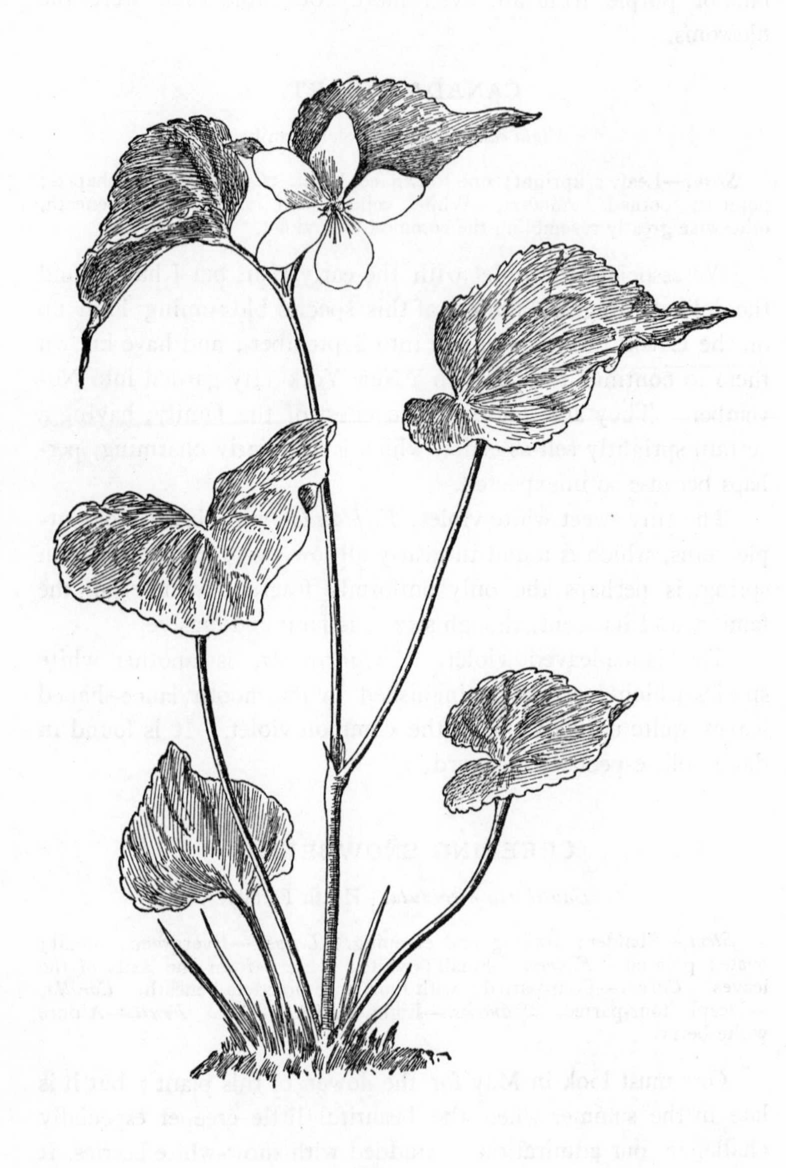

CANADA VIOLET.—*Viola canadensis.*

Adirondack stream. Or else it thickly carpets the peat-bog where we are hunting cranberries, or brightens the moist mossy woods which earlier in the year were redolent with the breath of the twin-flower. Its aromatic flavor suggests the wintergreen and sweet birch.

FALSE SOLOMON'S-SEAL.

Smilacina racemosa. Lily family.

Stems.—Usually curving; one to three feet long. *Leaves.*—Oblong; veiny. *Flowers.*—Greenish-white; small; in a terminal raceme. *Perianth.*—Six-parted. *Stamens.*—Six. *Pistil.*—One. *Fruit.*—A pale red berry speckled with purple.

A singular lack of imagination is betrayed in the common name of this plant. Despite a general resemblance to the true Solomon's-seal, and the close proximity in which the two are constantly found, *S. racemosa* has enough originality to deserve an individual title. The position of the much smaller flowers is markedly different. Instead of drooping beneath the stem they terminate it, having frequently a pleasant fragrance, while the berries of late summer are pale red, flecked with purple. It puzzles one to understand why these two plants should so constantly be found growing side by side—so close at times that they almost appear to spring from one point. The generic name is from *smilax*, on account of a supposed resemblance between the leaves of this plant and those which belong to that genus.

BLACK-HAW.

Viburnum prunifolium. Honeysuckle Family.

A tall shrub or small tree. *Leaves.*—Oval; finely and sharply toothed. *Flowers.*—White; small; in flat-topped clusters. *Calyx*—Five-toothed. *Corolla.*—Wheel-shaped; five-lobed. *Stamens.*—Five. *Pistil.*—One. *Fruit.*—Berry-like; oval; black, or with bluish bloom.

In May one of the most beautiful and noticeable of our white-flowered shrubs or trees is the black-haw. Its flat, circular flower-clusters are usually very perfect and spotless. They are massed abundantly along the country lanes.

PLATE XV

FALSE SOLOMON'S-SEAL.—*Smilacina racemosa.*

MAPLE-LEAVED VIBURNUM.—*Viburnum acerifolium.*

HOBBLEBUSH. AMERICAN WAYFARING-TREE.

Viburnum alnifolium. Honeysuckle Family.

Leaves.—Rounded; pointed; closely toothed; heart-shaped at the base; the veins beneath as well as the stalks and small branches being covered with a rusty scurf. *Flowers.*—White; small; in flat-topped clusters; appearing in April and May. *Calyx, Corolla, etc.*—As in above. *Fruit.*—Coral-red; berry-like.

The marginal flowers of the flat-topped clusters of the hobblebush, like those of the hydrangea, are much larger than the inner ones, and usually are without either stamens or pistils; their only part in the economy of the shrub being to form an attractive setting for the cluster, and thus to allure the insect visitors that are usually so necessary to the future well-being of the species. The shrub is a common one in our northern woods and mountains, its coral-red, berry-like fruit and brilliant leaves making it especially attractive in the later year. Its straggling growth, and the reclining branches which often take root in the ground, have suggested the popular names of hobblebush and wayfaring-tree.

MAPLE-LEAVED VIBURNUM. DOCKMACKIE.

Viburnum acerifolium. Honeysuckle Family.

A shrub from three to six feet high. *Leaves.*—Somewhat three-lobed, resembling those of the maple; downy underneath. *Flowers.* — White; small; in flat-topped clusters. *Calyx.*—Five-toothed. *Corolla.*—Spreading; five-lobed. *Stamens.*—Five. *Pistil.*—One. *Fruit.*—Berry-like; crimson turning purple.

Our flowering shrubs contribute even more to the beauty of the June woods and fields than the smaller plants. The viburnums and dogwoods especially are conspicuous at this season, abundantly lining the roadsides with their snowy clusters. When the blossoms of the maple-leaved viburnum or dockmackie have passed away we need not be surprised if we are informed that this shrub is a young maple. There is certainly a resemblance between its leaves and those of the maple, as the specific

Flower enlarged.

ARROW-WOOD.—*Viburnum dentatum.*

name indicates. To be sure, the first red, then purple berries, can scarcely be accounted for, but such a trifling incongruity would fail to daunt the would-be wiseacre of field and forest. With Napoleonic audacity he will give you the name of almost any shrub or flower about which you may inquire. Seizing upon some feature he has observed in another plant, he will immediately christen the one in question with the same title—somewhat modified, perhaps—and in all probability his authority will remain unquestioned. There is a marvellous amount of inaccuracy afloat in regard to the names of even the commonest plants, owing to this wide-spread habit of guessing at the truth and stating a conjecture as a fact.

WITHEROD.

Viburnum cassinoides. Honeysuckle Family.

A shrub five to twelve feet high. *Leaves.*—Ovate or oval, thick, smooth. *Flowers.*—White, much as in above. *Fruit.*—First pink, then turning dark blue or blackish with a bloom.

The witherod blossoms in early summer. The first pink, then dark blue fruit, is noticeable and very decorative in August in wet or sandy places.

ARROW-WOOD.

Viburnum dentatum. Honeysuckle Family.

A shrub from five to fifteen feet high. *Leaves.*—Broadly egg-shaped; sharply toothed; strongly veined. *Flowers.*—White; small; in flat-topped clusters. *Calyx, etc.*—As in above. *Fruit.*—Dark blue.

This is a not uncommon shrub in wet places. Its white flower-clusters are noticeable in June along the wooded roadsides. There are many other species of viburnums which are common in certain localities. If an analysis of the flower shows it to belong to this genus, Gray's "Manual" should be consulted for further identification.

ROUND-LEAVED DOGWOOD.

Cornus rugosa. Dogwood Family.

A shrub six to ten feet high. *Leaves.*—Rounded; abruptly pointed. *Flowers.*—Small; white; in flat, spreading clusters. *Calyx.*—Minutely four-toothed. *Corolla.*—Of four white, oblong, spreading petals. *Stamens.*—Four. *Pistil.*—One. *Fruit.*—Light blue; berry-like.

The different members of the Dogwood family are important factors in the lovely pageant which delights our eyes along the country lanes every spring. Oddly enough, only the smallest and largest representative of the tribe (the little bunchberry, and the flowering dogwood, which is sometimes a tree of goodly dimensions), have in common the showy involucre which is usually taken for the blossom itself; but which instead only surrounds the close cluster of inconspicuous greenish flowers.

The other members of the genus are all comprised in the shrubby dogwoods; many of these are very similar in appearance, bearing their white flowers in flat, spreading clusters, and differing chiefly in their leaves and fruit.

The branches of the round-leaved dogwood are greenish and warty-dotted. Its fruit is light blue, and berry-like.

The bark of this genus has been considered a powerful tonic, and an extract entitled "cornine," is said to possess the properties of quinine less strongly marked. The Chinese peel its twigs, and use them for whitening their teeth. It is said that the Creoles also owe the dazzling beauty of their teeth to this same practice.

ALTERNATE-LEAVED DOGWOOD.

Cornus alternifolia. Dogwood Family.

A shrub or tree eight to twenty-five feet high. *Branches.*—Greenish streaked with white. *Leaves.*—Alternate; clustered at the ends of the branches; oval; long-pointed. *Flowers.*—White; small; in broad, open clusters. *Calyx, Corolla, etc.*—As in above. *Fruit.*—Deep blue on reddish stalks.

In copses on the hillsides we find this shrub flowering in May or June. Its deep blue, red-stalked fruit is noticeable in late summer.

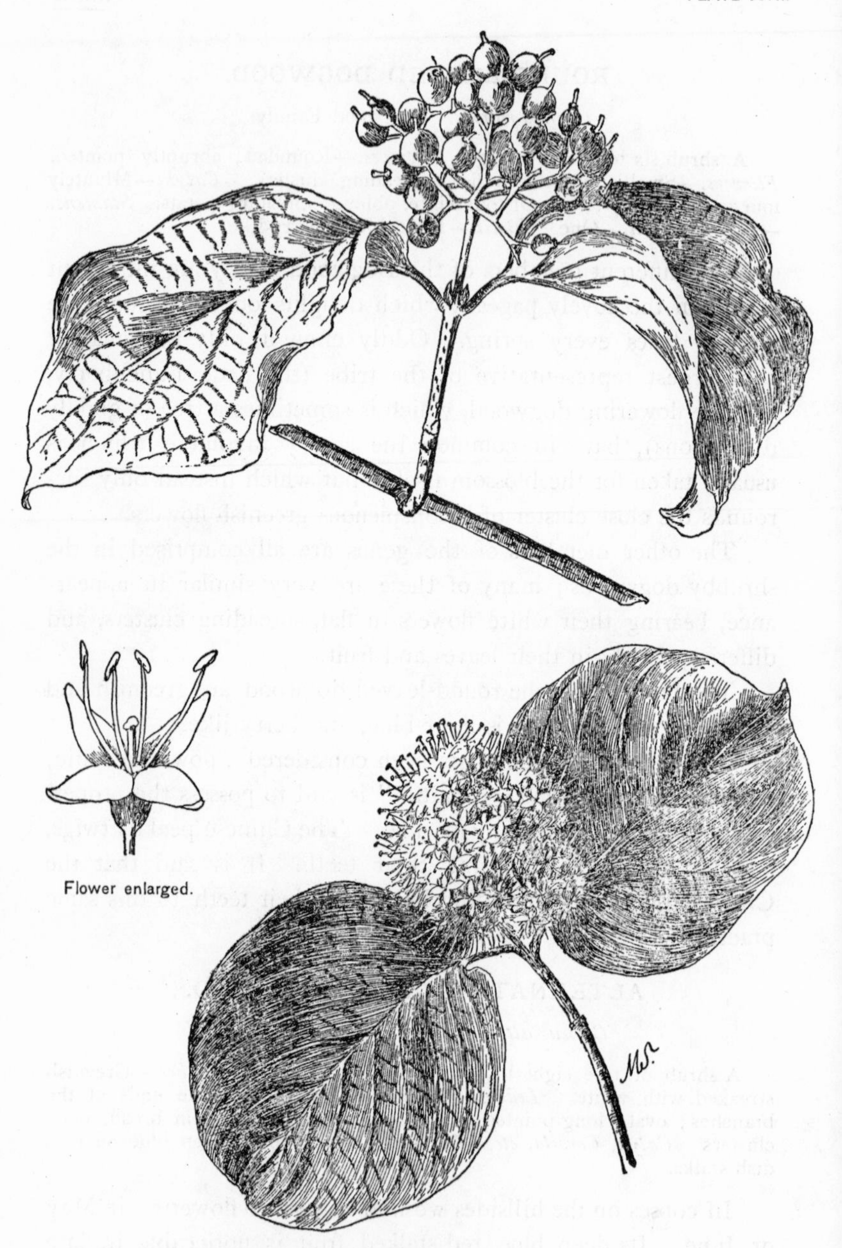

ROUND-LEAVED DOGWOOD.—*Cornus rugosa.*

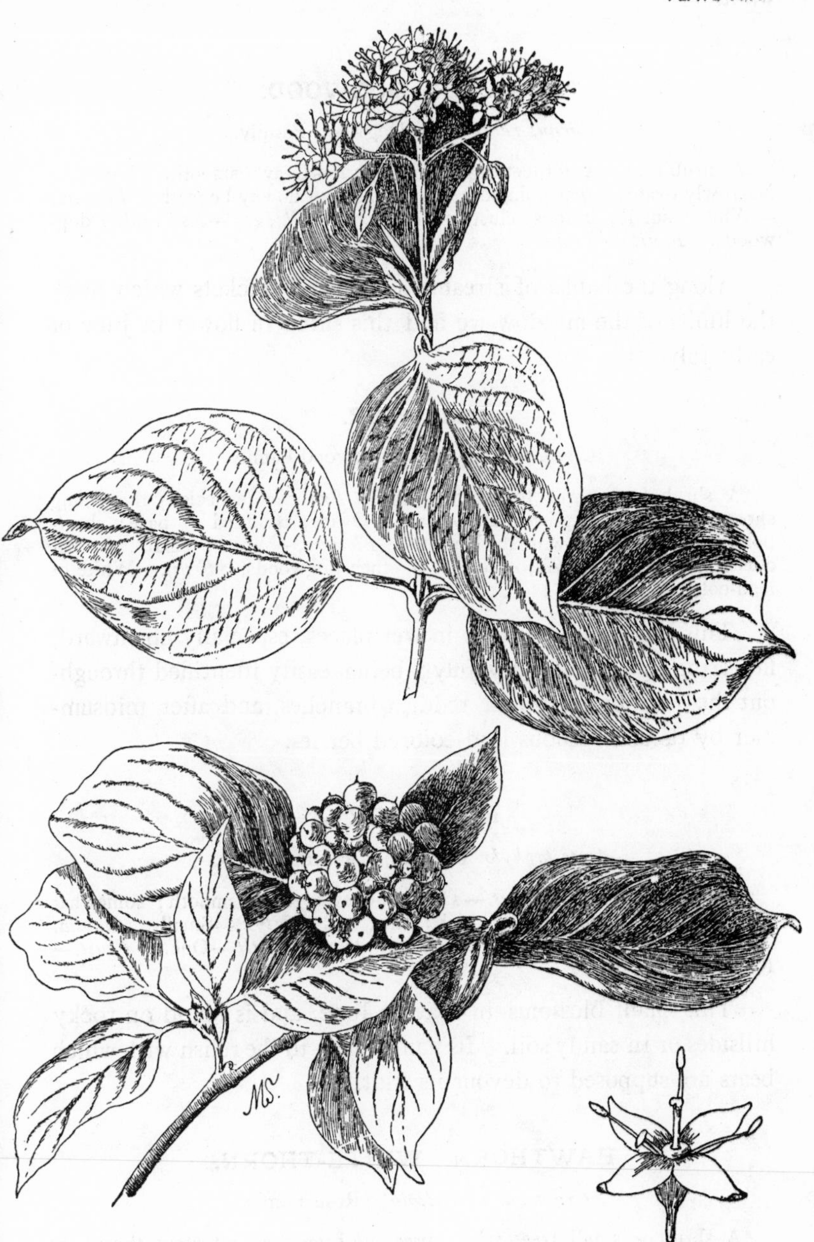

Flower enlarged.

RED OSIER.—*Cornus stolonifera.*

PANICLED DOGWOOD.

Cornus racemosa. Dogwood Family.

A shrub four to eight feet high. *Branches.*—Gray; smooth. *Leaves.*—Narrowly ovate; taper-pointed; whitish but not downy beneath. *Flowers.*—White; small; in loose clusters. *Calyx, Corolla, etc.*—As in other dogwoods. *Fruit.*—White.

Along the banks of streams and in the thickets which mark the limits of the meadow we find this shrub in flower in June or early July.

RED OSIER.

Cornus stolonifera. Dogwood Family.

A shrub from three to six feet high. *Branches* (especially the young shoots).—Bright purplish-red. *Leaves.*—Ovate; rounded at base; short-pointed; roughish; whitish beneath. *Flowers.*—White; small; in flat clusters. *Calyx, Corolla, etc.*—As in other dogwoods. *Fruit.*—White or lead-color.

This is a common shrub in wet places, especially northward, flowering in June or early July; being easily identified throughout the year by its bright reddish branches, and after midsummer by its conspicuous lead-colored berries.

BEARBERRY.

Arctostaphylos Uva-ursi. Heath Family.

A trailing shrub. *Leaves.*—Thick and evergreen; smooth; somewhat wedge-shaped. *Flowers.*—Whitish; clustered. *Calyx.*—Small. *Corolla.*—Urn-shaped; five-toothed. *Stamens.*—Ten. *Pistil.*—One. *Fruit.*—Red; berry-like.

This plant blossoms in May or June, and is found on rocky hillsides or in sandy soil. Its name refers to the relish with which bears are supposed to devour its fruit.

HAWTHORN. WHITE-THORN.

Crataegus pedicellata. Rose Family.

A shrub or small tree, with spreading branches, and stout thorns or spines. *Leaves.*—On slender leaf-stalks; thin; rounded; toothed, sometimes lobed. *Flowers.*—White or sometimes reddish; rather large; clustered; with a somewhat disagreeable odor. *Calyx.*—Urn-shaped; five-cleft. *Corolla.*—Of five broad, rounded petals. *Stamens.*—Five to ten or many. *Pistil.*—One with one to five styles. *Fruit.*—Coral-red.

The flowers of the white-thorn appear in spring, at the same time with those of many of the dogwoods. Its scarlet fruit gleams from the thicket in September.

COCKSPUR-THORN.

Crataegus crus-galli. Rose Family.

A shrub or low tree. *Thorns.*—Smooth; slender; often four inches long. *Leaves.*—Thick; dark green; shining above; somewhat wedge-shaped; toothed above the middle; tapering into a very short leaf-stalk. *Flowers.*—White; fragrant; in clusters on short side branches. *Calyx, Corolla, etc.*—As in above. *Fruit.*—Globular; red, in late summer or autumn.

The cockspur-thorn flowers in June. Its red fruit, somewhat suggesting a crab-apple, is conspicuous throughout the autumn and winter.

There are several other species of thorn, and if a flower be found which proves, on analysis, to belong to this genus, a reference to Gray's "Manual" will lead to its farther identification.

BEACH-PLUM.

Prunus maritima. Rose Family.

A low straggling shrub. *Leaves.*—Ovate or oval, finely toothed. *Flowers.*—White; showy; clustered, appearing before the leaves. *Calyx.*—Five-lobed. *Corolla.*—Of five obovate petals. *Stamens.*—Numerous. *Pistil.*—One. *Fruit.*—Roundish, purple, with a bloom.

During the months of April and May the flowers of the beach-plum are conspicuous on the sand-hills of our coast. The fruit ripens in the fall.

MOUNTAIN-HOLLY.

Nemopanthus mucronata. Holly Family.

A much-branched shrub ; with ash-gray bark. *Leaves.*—Alternate ; oblong ; smooth ; on slender leaf-stalks. *Flowers.*—White ; some perfect ; others unisexual ; solitary or clustered in the axils of the leaves on long, slender flower-stalks. *Calyx.*—Minute or obsolete. *Corolla.*—Of four or five spreading petals. *Stamens.*—Four or five. *Pistil.*—One. *Fruit.*—Coral-red ; berry-like.

The flowers of this shrub appear in the damp woods of May. Its light red berries on their slender stalks are noticed in late summer when its near relation, the black alder or winterberry, is also conspicuous. Its generic name signifies *flower with a thread-like stalk.*

WINTERBERRY. BLACK ALDER.

Ilex verticillata. Holly Family.

A shrub, common in low grounds. *Leaves.*—Oval or lance-shaped ; pointed at apex and base ; toothed. *Flowers.*—White ; some perfect, others unisexual ; clustered on very short flower-stalks in the axil of the leaves ; appearing in May or June. *Calyx.*—Minute. *Corolla.*—Of four to six petals. *Stamens.*—Four to six. *Pistil.*—One. *Fruit.*—Coral-red ; berry-like.

The year may draw nearly to its close without our attention being arrested by this shrub. But in September it is well-nigh impossible to stroll through the country lanes without pausing to admire the bright red berries clustered so thickly among the leaves of the black alder. The American holly, *I. opaca*, is closely related to this shrub, whose generic name is the ancient Latin title for the holly-oak.

WHITE BANEBERRY.

Actaea pachypoda. Crowfoot Family.

Stem.—About two feet high. *Leaves.*—Twice or thrice-compound ; leaflets incised and sharply toothed. *Flowers.*—Small ; white ; in a thick, oblong, terminal raceme. *Calyx.*—Of four to five tiny sepals which fall as the flower expands. *Corolla.*—Of four to ten small flat petals with slender claws. *Stamens.*—Numerous, with slender white filaments. *Pistil*—One,

PLATE XX

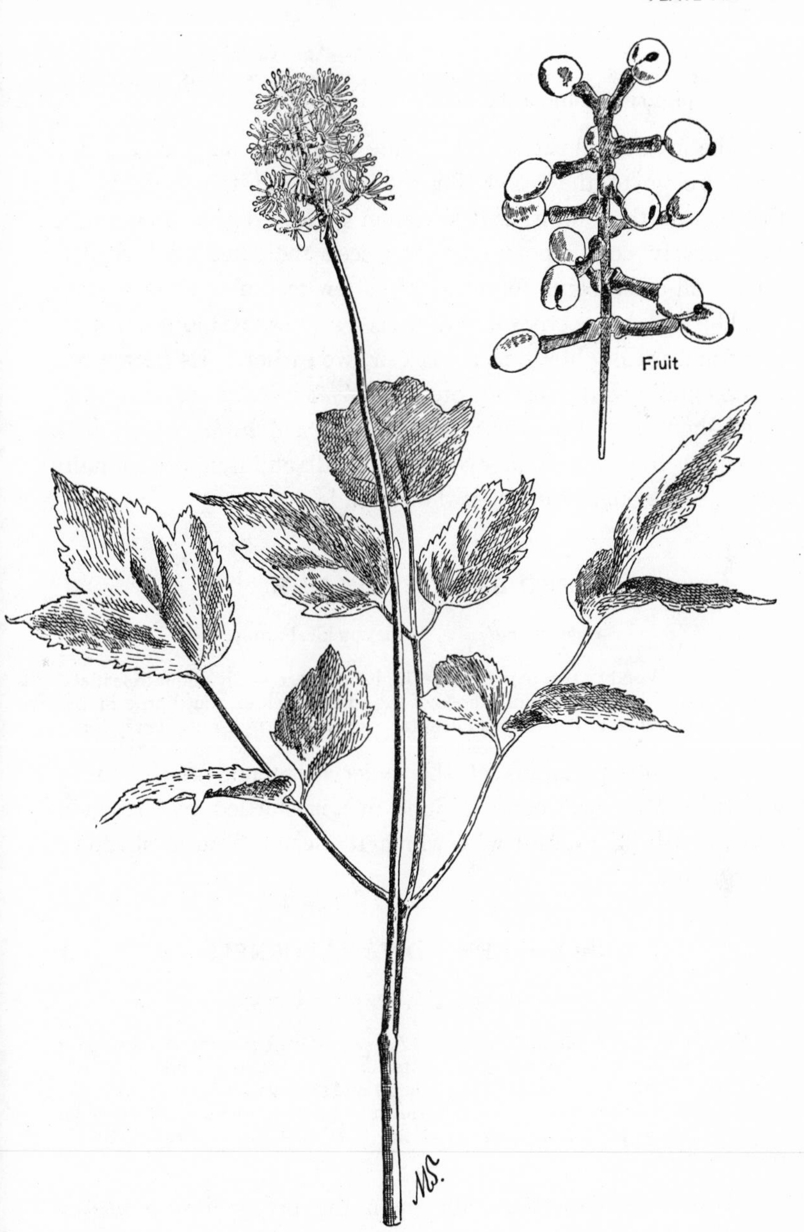

WHITE BANEBERRY.—*Actaea pachypoda.*

with a depressed, two-lobed stigma. *Fruit.*—An oval white berry, with a dark spot, on a *thick red stalk*, growing in a cluster, which is sometimes a very conspicuous feature of the woods of midsummer.

The feathery clusters of the white baneberry may be gathered when we go to the woods for the columbine, the wild ginger, the Jack-in-the-Pulpit, and Solomon's-seal. These flowers are very nearly contemporaneous and seek the same cool shaded nooks, all often being found within a few feet of one another.

The red baneberry, *A. rubra*, is a somewhat more northern plant and usually blossoms a week or two earlier. Its cherry-red (occasionally white) berries on their *slender stalks* are easily distinguished from the white ones of *A. pachypoda*, which look strikingly like the china eyes that small children occasionally manage to gouge from their dolls' heads.

RED-BERRIED ELDER.

Sambucus pubens. Honeysuckle Family.

Stems.—Woody; two to twelve feet high. *Leaves.*—Divided into leaflets. *Flowers.*—White; resembling those of the common elder, but borne in pyramidal instead of in flat-topped clusters. *Fruit.*—Bright red; berry-like.

The white pyramids of this elder are found in the rocky woods of May. As early as June one is startled by the vivid clusters of brilliant fruit with which it gleams from its shadowy background.

BUNCHBERRY. DWARF CORNEL.

Cornus canadensis. Dogwood Family.

Stem.—Five to seven inches high. *Leaves.*—Ovate; pointed; the upper crowded into an apparent whorl of four to six. *Flowers.*—Greenish; small; in a cluster which is surrounded by a large and showy four-leaved, petal-like white or pinkish involucre. *Calyx.*—Minutely four-toothed. *Corolla.*—Of four spreading petals. *Stamens.*—Four. *Pistil.*—One, *Fruit.*—Bright red; berry-like.

When one's eye first falls upon the pretty flowers of the bunchberry in the June woods, the impression is received that each low stem bears upon its summit a single large white blos-

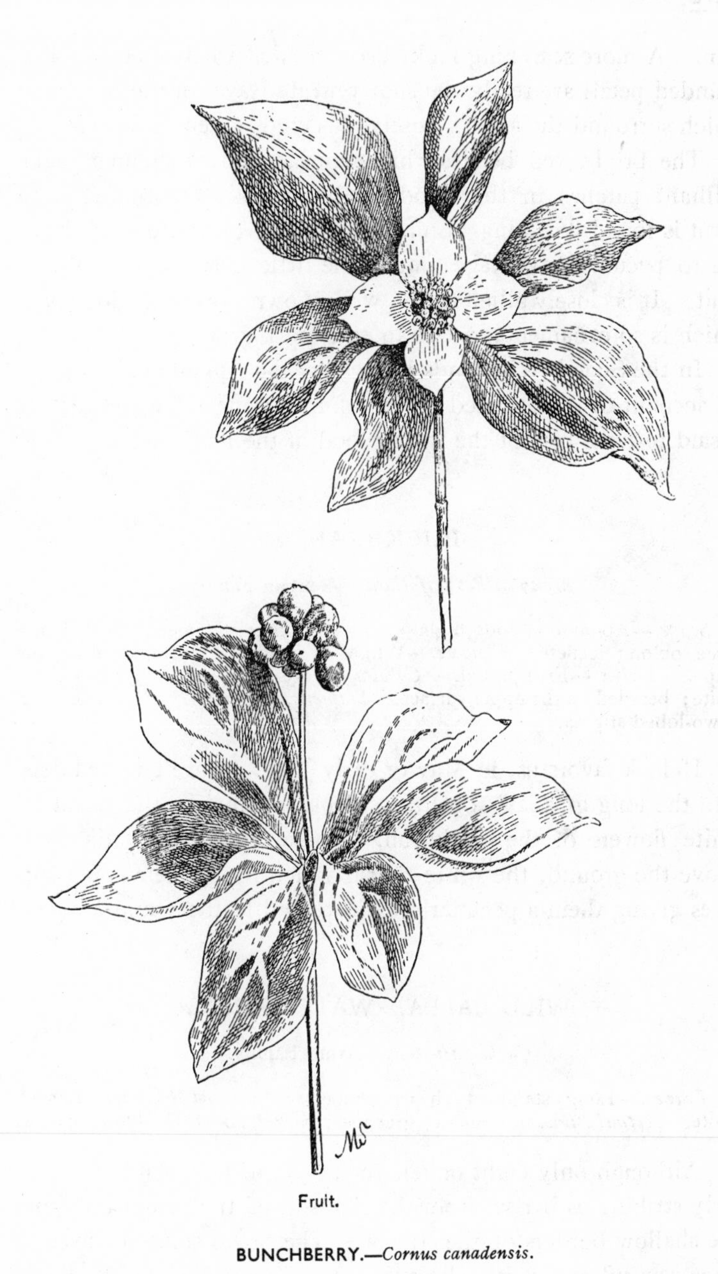

Fruit.

BUNCHBERRY.—*Cornus canadensis.*

som. A more searching look discovers that what appeared like rounded petals are really the showy white leaves of the involucre which surround the small, closely clustered, greenish flowers.

The bright red berries which appear in late summer make brilliant patches in the woods and swamps. Occasionally the plant is found flowering also at this season, its white stars showing to peculiar advantage among the little clusters of coral-like fruit. It is closely allied to the well-known flowering dogwood, which is so ornamental a tree in early spring.

In the Scotch Highlands it is called the "plant of gluttony," on account of its supposed power of increasing the appetite. It is said to form part of the winter food of the Esquimaux.

BUCKBEAN.

Menyanthes trifoliata. Gentian Family.

Scape.—About one foot high. *Leaves.*—Long stemmed; divided into three oblong leaflets. *Flowers.*—White or reddish; clustered along the scape. *Calyx.*—Five-parted. *Corolla.*—Five-cleft; short funnel-form; white; bearded on the upper surface. *Stamens.*—Five. *Pistil.*—One, with a two-lobed stigma.

If luck favors us, in May or early June, we are tempted deep into the long grass of some treacherous swamp by the beautiful white flowers of the buckbean. These grow about one foot above the ground, the white beards which fringe their upper surfaces giving them a peculiarly delicate and feathery appearance.

WILD CALLA. WATER-ARUM.

Calla palustris. Arum Family.

Leaves.—Long-stemmed; heart-shaped. *Apparent Flower.*—Large; white. *Actual Flowers.*—Small; greenish; packed about the oblong spadix.

Although only eight or ten inches high, this plant is peculiarly striking as it rises from the rich soil of the swamp, or from the shallow borders of the stream. The broad smooth leaves at once remind one of its relationship to the so-called "calla-lily"

WATER-ARUM.—*Calla palustris.*

of the greenhouses, a native of the Cape of Good Hope; and the likeness is still more apparent in the white, petal-like (although flat and open) spathe which tops the scape; so that even one knowing nothing of botanical families would naturally christen the plant "wild calla." The first sight of these white spathes gleaming across a wet meadow in June, and the closer inspection of the upright, vigorous little plants, make an event in the summer. None of our aquatics is more curious and interesting, more sturdy, yet dainty and pure, than the wild calla.

LIZARD'S-TAIL.

Saururus cernùus. Pepper Family.

Stem.—Jointed; often tall. *Leaves.*—Alternate; heart-shaped. *Flowers.*—White; without calyx or corolla; crowded into a slender, wand-like terminal spike which nods at the end. *Stamens.*—Usually six or seven. *Pistils.*—Three or four, united at their base.

The nodding, fragrant spikes of the lizard's-tail abound in certain swamps from June till August. While the plant is not a common one, it is found occasionally in great profusion, and is sure to arrest attention by its odd appearance.

MOONSEED.

Menispermum canadense. Moonseed Family.

Stem.—Woody; climbing. *Leaves.*—Three to seven-angled or lobed; their stalks fastened near the edge of the lower surface. *Flowers.*—White or yellowish; in small loose clusters; unisexual. *Calyx.*—Of four to eight sepals. *Corolla.*—Of six to eight short petals. *Stamens and Pistils.*—Occurring on different plants. *Fruit.*—Berry-like; black, with a bloom.

Clambering over the thickets which line the streams, we notice in September the lobed or angled leaves and black berries of the moonseed, the small white or yellowish flowers of which were, perhaps, overlooked in June.

CLOUDBERRY. BAKED-APPLE-BERRY.

Rubus Chamæmorus. Rose Family.

Stem.—Low, simple. *Leaves.*—Two or three; roundish kidney-shaped; usually somewhat five-lobed, finely toothed, wrinkled. *Flower.*—Solitary; white. *Calyx.* — Five-parted. *Corolla.*—Of five white obovate petals. *Fruit.*—A berry of a few reddish or amber-colored grains; edible.

This quaint pretty little plant I have found springing from beds of golden brown sphagnum, on one of the Cranberry Islands, off Mount Desert. Gray [early editions] assigned it to the "highest peaks of White Mountains, coast of eastern Maine, and north and west to the Arctic regions." It is one of the plants which is found in Alaska, as well as along our own coast.

COMMON BLACKBERRY. HIGH BLACKBERRY.

Rubus flagellaris. Rose Family.

A shrub one to six feet high, armed with stout prickles. *Leaves.*—Divided into three to five leaflets. *Flowers.*—With five-parted calyx; five petals; numerous stamens and pistils. *Fruit.*—Black.

Though the common blackberry seems almost too well known to need description, yet occasionally its flowers arouse some doubt and curiosity in the mind of the wanderer along those country lanes, where its blossoming branches form so beautiful and luxuriant a border.

RUNNING SWAMP BLACKBERRY.

Rubus hispidus. Rose Family.

Stems.—Slender; creeping; beset with small, weak prickles. *Leaves.*—Divided into three, or rarely five, leaflets. *Flowers.*—With five-parted calyx; five white petals; numerous stamens and pistils. *Fruit.*—Nearly black when ripe, of few grains.

Over the mosses in the swamp the running swamp blackberry trails its reddish stems with their thick, smooth, shining leaves, and in early summer their white flowers. A few weeks later we find the first, red, then blackish berries. It is a charming plant, and one is tempted to carry home, for decorative purposes, a few of its long lithe strands.

LOW BLACKBERRY. DEWBERRY.

Rubus canadensis. Rose Family.

A trailing shrub, armed with scattered prickles or nearly naked; branches erect or ascending. *Leaves.*—Divided into three ovate or oval leaflets. *Flowers.*—With five-parted calyx; five white petals; numerous stamens and pistils. *Fruit.*—Black, edible, delicious.

The dewberry is found in dry ground, trailing along the roadside, or in dry, perhaps rocky fields. It ripens earlier than the common blackberry.

MOUNTAIN-LAUREL. SPOONWOOD. CALICO-BUSH.

Kalmia latifolia. Heath Family.

An evergreen shrub. *Leaves.*—Oblong; pointed; shining; of a leathery texture. *Flowers.*—White or pink; in terminal clusters. *Calyx.*—Five-parted. *Corolla.*—Marked with red; wheel-shaped; five-lobed; with ten depressions. *Stamens.*—Ten; each anther lodged in one of the depressions of the corolla. *Pistil.*—One.

The shining green leaves which surround the white or rose-colored flowers of the mountain-laurel are familiar to all who have skirted the west shore of the Hudson River, wandered across the hills that lie in its vicinity, or clambered across the mountains of Pennsylvania, where the shrub sometimes grows to a height of thirty feet. Not that these localities limit its range; for it abounds more or less from Canada to Florida, and far inland, especially along the mountains, whose sides are often clothed with an apparent mantle of pink snow during the month of June, and whose waste places are, in very truth, made to blossom like the rose at this season.

The shrub is highly prized and carefully cultivated in England. Barewood Gardens, the beautiful home of the editor of

MOUNTAIN-LAUREL.—*Kalmia latifolia.*

the London *Times*,* is celebrated for its fine specimens of mountain-laurel and American rhododendron. The English papers advertise the approach of the flowering season, the estate is thrown open to the public, and the people for miles around flock to see the radiant strangers from across the water. The shrub is not known there as the laurel, but by its generic title, *Kalmia*. The head gardener of the place received with some incredulity my statement that in parts of America the waste hill-sides were brilliant with its beauty every June.

The ingenious contrivance of these flowers to secure cross-fertilization is most interesting. The long filaments of the stamens are arched by the fact that each anther is caught in a little pouch of the corolla; the disturbance caused by the sudden alighting of an insect on the blossom, or the quick brush of a bee's wing, dislodges the anthers from their niches, and the stamens spring upward with such violence that the pollen is jerked from its hiding-place in the pore of the anther-cell on to the body of the insect-visitor, who straightway carries it off to another flower upon whose protruding stigma it is sure to be inadvertently deposited. In order to see the working of this for one's self, it is only necessary to pick a fresh blossom and either brush the corolla quickly with one's finger, or touch the stamens suddenly with a pin, when the anthers will be dislodged and the pollen will be seen to fly.

This is not the laurel of the ancients—the symbol of victory and fame—notwithstanding some resemblance in the form of the leaves. The classic shrub is supposed to be identical with the *Laurus nobilis*, which was carried to our country by the early colonists, but which did not thrive in its new environment.

The leaves of our species are supposed to possess poisonous qualities, and are said to have been used by the Indians for suicidal purposes. There is also a popular belief that the flesh of a partridge which has fed upon its fruit becomes poisonous. The clammy exudation about the flower-stalks and blossoms may serve the purpose of excluding from the flower such small insects as would otherwise crawl up to it, dislodge the stamens, scatter

* [1900].

GREAT LAUREL.—*Rhododendron maximum.*

the pollen, and yet be unable to carry it to its proper destination on the pistil of another flower.

The *Kalmia* was named by Linnæus after Peter Kalm, one of his pupils who travelled in this country, who was, perhaps, the first to make known the shrub to his great master.

The popular name spoonwood grew from its use by the Indians for making eating-utensils. The wood is of fine grain and takes a good polish.

The title calico-bush probably arose from the marking of the corolla, which, to an imaginative mind, might suggest the cheap cotton-prints sold in the shops.

AMERICAN RHODODENDRON. GREAT LAUREL.

Rhododendron maximum. Heath Family.

A shrub from six to thirty-five feet high. *Leaves.*—Thick and leathery; oblong; entire. *Flowers.*—White or pink; clustered. *Calyx.*—Minute; five-toothed. *Corolla.*—Somewhat bell-shaped; five-parted; greenish in the throat; with red, yellow, or green spots. *Stamens.*—Usually ten. *Pistil.*—One.

This beautiful native shrub is one of the glories of our country when in the perfection of its loveliness. The woods which nearly cover many of the mountains of our Eastern States hide from all but the bold explorer a radiant display during the early part of July. Then the lovely waxy flower-clusters of the American rhododendron are in their fulness of beauty. As in the laurel, the clammy flower-stalks seem fitted to protect the blossom from the depredations of small and useless insects, while the markings on the corolla attract the attention of the desirable bee.

In those parts of the country where it flourishes most luxuriantly, veritable rhododendron jungles, termed "hells" by the mountaineers, are formed. The branches reach out and interlace in such a fashion as to be almost impassable.

The nectar secreted by the blossoms is popularly supposed to be poisonous. We read in Xenophon that during the retreat of the Ten Thousand the soldiers found a quantity of honey, of which they freely partook, with results that proved almost fatal.

WOOD-SORREL.—*Oxalis montana*

This honey is said to have been made from a rhododendron which is still common in Asia Minor, and which is believed to possess intoxicating and poisonous properties.

Comparatively little attention had been paid to this superb flower until the Centennial Celebration at Philadelphia, when some fine exhibits attracted the admiration of thousands. The shrub has been carefully cultivated in England, having been brought to great perfection on some of the English estates. It is yearly winning more notice in this country.

The generic name is from the Greek for *rose-tree*.

WOOD-SORREL.

Oxalis montana. Geranium Family.

Scape.—One-flowered; two to five inches high. *Leaves*.—Divided into three clover-like leaflets. *Flower*.—White, veined with red; solitary. *Calyx*.—Of five sepals. *Corolla*.—Of five petals. *Stamens*.—Ten. *Pistil*.—One with five styles.

Surely nowhere can be found a daintier carpeting than that made by the clover-like foliage of the wood-sorrel, when studded with its rose-veined blossoms, in the northern woods of June. At the very name comes a vision of mossy nooks where the sunlight only comes on sufferance, piercing its difficult path through the tent-like foliage of the forest, resting only long enough to become a golden memory.

The early Italian painters availed themselves of its chaste beauty. Mr. Ruskin says: "Fra Angelico's use of the *Oxalis Acetosella** is as faithful in representation as touching in feeling. The triple leaf of the plant and white flower stained purple probably gave it strange typical interest among the Christian painters."

Throughout Europe it bears the odd name of "Hallelujah" on account of its flowering between Easter and Whitsuntide, the season when the Psalms sung in the churches resound with that word. There has been an unfounded theory that this title sprang from St. Patrick's endeavor to prove to his rude audience the

* [*montana*].

possibility of a Trinity in Unity from the three-divided leaves. By many this ternate leaf has been considered the shamrock of the ancient Irish.

The English title, "cuckoo-bread," refers to the appearance of the blossoms at the season when the cry of the cuckoo is first heard.

Our name sorrel is from the Greek for *sour* and has reference to the acrid juice of the plant. The delicate leaflets "sleep" at night. That is, they droop and close one against another.

SWEET CICELY.

Osmorhiza longistylis. Parsley Family.

One to three feet high. *Root.*—Thick; aromatic; edible. *Leaves.*—Twice or thrice-compound. *Flowers.*—White; small; growing in a somewhat flat-topped cluster.

This is one of the earliest-flowering of the white Parsleys. Its roots are prized by country children for their pleasant flavor. Great care should be taken not to confound this plant with the water-hemlock, which is very poisonous, and which it greatly resembles, although flowering earlier in the year. The generic name is from two Greek words which signify *scent* and *root.*

WHITE SWAMP-HONEYSUCKLE. CLAMMY AZALEA.

Rhododendron viscosum. Heath Family.

A shrub from three to ten feet high. *Leaves.*—Oblong. *Flowers.*—White; clustered; appearing after the leaves. *Calyx-lobes.*—Minute. *Corolla.*—White; five-lobed; the clammy tube much longer than the lobes. *Stamens.*—Usually five; protruding. *Pistil.*—One; protruding.

The fragrant white flowers of this beautiful shrub appear in early summer along the swamps which skirt the coast, and occasionally farther inland. The close family resemblance to the pink azalea (Pl. CV.) will be at once detected. On the branches of both species will be found those abnormal fleshy growths, called variously "swamp apples" and "May apples," which

WHITE SWAMP-HONEYSUCKLE.—*Rhododendron viscosum.*

are so relished by the children. Formerly these growths were attributed to the sting of an insect, as in the "oak apple;" now they are generally believed to be modified buds.

SWEET BAY. LAUREL-MAGNOLIA.

Magnolia virginiana. Magnolia Family.

A shrub from four to twenty feet high. *Leaves.*—Oval to broadly lance-shaped; from three to six inches long. *Flowers.*—White; two inches long; growing singly at the ends of the branches. *Calyx.*—Of three sepals. *Corolla.*—Globular; with from six to nine broad petals. *Stamens.*—Numerous; with short filaments and long anthers. *Pistils.*—Many; packed so as to make a sort of cone in fruit. *Fruit.*—Cone-like; red; fleshy when ripe; the pistils opening at maturity and releasing the scarlet seeds which hang by delicate threads.

The beautiful fragrant blossoms of the sweet bay may be found from June till August, in swamps along the coast from Cape Ann southward. This is one of the shrubs whose beauty bids fair to be its own undoing. The large flowers are sure to attract the attention of those ruthless destroyers who seem bent upon the final extermination of our most pleasing and characteristic plants.

COMMON BLACK HUCKLEBERRY.*

Gaylussacia baccata. Heath Family.

One to three feet high. *Stems.*—Shrubby; branching. *Leaves.*—Oval or oblong; sprinkled more or less with waxy resinous atoms. *Flowers.*—White, reddish, or purplish; bell-shaped; growing in short, one-sided clusters. *Calyx.*—With five short teeth. *Corolla.*—Bell-shaped, with a five-cleft border. *Stamens.*—Ten. *Pistil.*—One. *Fruit.*—A black, bloomless, edible berry.

The flowers of the common huckleberry appear in May or June; the berries in late summer. The shrub abounds in rocky woods and swamps.

* There is a great similarity between many of the Heaths. For more accurate identification than can be here given, Gray's Manual should be consulted.

DANGLEBERRY.

Gaylussacia frondosa. Heath Family.

A loosely branched shrub; from three to six feet high. *Leaves.*—Oblong; blunt; pale beneath. *Flowers.*—Much as in above, but borne in loose, slender clusters. *Fruit.*—A large blue berry with a whitish bloom; sweet and edible.

The dangleberry is found along the coast of New England and in the mountains farther south. It flowers in May or June.

HIGHBUSH-BLUEBERRY.

Vaccinium corymbosum. Heath Family.

A tall shrub (from five to ten feet high). *Flowers.*—White or reddish; very similar to those in above (*Gaylussacia*), but borne in *short* clusters; appearing in spring or early summer. *Fruit.*—A sweet edible berry; blue or black, with a bloom; in late summer.

The highbush-blueberry is found in swamps and low thickets.

LOW SWEET BLUEBERRY.

Vaccinium angustifolium. Heath Family.

Six inches to three feet high. *Flowers.*—White or reddish-white; appearing in spring or early summer. *Calyx, Corolla, etc.*—As in other members of this genus. *Fruit.*—A large blue berry; sweet.

The low sweet blueberries usually ripen in July or August. They are found on dry hills from New Jersey northward, being especially abundant in New England.

SQUAW-HUCKLEBERRY.

Vaccinium stamineum.—Heath Family.

Two or three feet high. *Stems.*—Diffusely branched. *Flowers.*—Greenish-white or purplish; suggesting somewhat those of the blueberry and huckleberry, but noticeable especially for their protruding stamens. *Fruit.*—A globular or pear-shaped, few-seeded berry.

This large greenish or yellowish berry is hardly edible. The pretty, fragrant flowers appear in June, and are easily recognized by their protruding stamens. The leaves are pale green above and whitish underneath.

Fruit.

SQUAW-HUCKLEBERRY.—*Vaccinium stamineum.*

ALPINE BILBERRY.

Vaccinium uliginosum. Heath Family.

Low; spreading; tufted; from four inches to two feet high. *Leaves.*—Oblong; pale; not toothed. *Flowers.*—White or reddish; solitary, or two or three together, set close to the stem. *Corolla.*—Usually four-toothed; short; urn-shaped. *Fruit.*—A sweet berry; black with a bloom.

The bog bilberry is found blossoming in early summer on the high mountain-tops of New England and New York, also farther west and northward.

BOG-ROSEMARY.

Andromeda glaucophylla. Heath Family.

An evergreen shrub from six to eighteen inches high. *Leaves.*—Thick; long and narrow; smooth; with rolled edges; dark green above, white beneath. *Flowers.*—White or pinkish; crowded in drooping clusters at the ends of the branches. *Calyx.*—Of five sepals. *Corolla.*—Five-toothed, urn-shaped. *Stamens.*—Ten. *Pistil.*—one.

This pretty evergreen is found in boggy places from Pennsylvania and New Jersey northward, flowering in June. It was named Andromeda by Linnæus because he found it "always fixed on some little turfy hillock in the midst of the swamps, as Andromeda herself was chained to a rock in the sea." Before expansion the flowers are usually bright red.

STAGGER-BUSH.

Lyonia mariana. Heath Family.

Two to four feet high. *Leaves.*—Thin; oblong. *Flowers.*—White or reddish. *Calyx, Corolla, etc.*—Much as in above.

The nodding flowers of the stagger-bush appear in early summer. They are clustered on leafless shoots or branches, and are usually in low, dry places, from Rhode Island southward. The English name refers to the supposition that the foliage is poison ous to sheep.

FETTER-BUSH.

Leucothoë racemosa. Heath Family.

Four to ten feet high. *Leaves.*—Narrowly oblong; acute. *Flowers.*—White and fragrant. *Calyx, Corolla, etc.*—Much as in above.

In moist thickets, usually near the coast, we find in May and June the long, dense, usually erect, one-sided flower-clusters of the Leucothoë.

LEATHER-LEAF.

Chamaedaphne calyculata. Heath Family.

A much-branched shrub from two to four feet high. *Leaves.*—Oblong; nearly evergreen; leathery and shining above; rusty beneath. *Flowers.*—White; in the axils of the small upper leaves, forming one-sided, leafy clusters which are less dense than those of the *Leucothoë.*

In April or May the leather-leaf is found flowering in wet places.

CASSIOPE.

Cassiope hypnoides. Heath Family.

One to four inches high. *Stems.*—Tufted; procumbent. *Leaves.*—Needle-shaped; evergreen. *Flowers*—White or rose-colored; solitary; nodding from erect, slender stalks. *Calyx.*—Of four or five sepals. *Corolla.*—Deeply four or five cleft. *Stamens.*—Eight or ten. *Pistil.*—One.

This pretty moss-like little plant is found on the mountain summits of New York and New England. Its delicate nodding flowers usually appear in June.

LABRADOR-TEA.

Ledum groenlandicum. Heath Family.

An erect shrub from one to three feet high. *Leaves.*—Thickly clothed beneath with a rusty wool; edges rolled; narrowly oblong. *Flowers.*—White, small; in clusters at the ends of the branches. *Calyx.*—Very small; five-toothed. *Corolla.*—Of five petals. *Stamens.*—Five or ten. *Pistil.*—One.

The dense woolliness which clothes the lower side of the leaves of Labrador-tea easily identifies it. It is found upon the mountains, and in boggy places, from Pennsylvania north and westward.

ONE-FLOWERED WINTERGREEN.

Moneses uniflora. Heath Family.

Scape.—Two to four inches high. *Leaves.*—Rounded; thin; veiny; toothed; from the roots. *Flower.*—White or rose-colored; solitary; half an inch broad. *Calyx.*—Five-parted. *Corolla.*—Of five rounded widely spreading petals. *Stamens.*—Ten. *Pistil.*—One; protruding; with a large five-rayed stigma.

This lovely little plant is found in flower in the deep pine woods of June or July. It has all the grace and delicacy of its kinsman, the shinleaf and pipsissewa, but, if possible, is even more daintily captivating. The generic name is from two Greek words signifying *single* and *delight*, in reference to the "beauty which is a joy" of the solitary flower, and betraying the always pleasing fact that the scientist who christened it was fully alive to its peculiar charm.

SHINLEAF.

Pyrola elliptica. Heath Family.

Scape.—Upright; scaly; terminating in a many-flowered raceme. *Leaves.*—From the root; thin and dull; somewhat oval. *Flowers.*—White; nodding. *Calyx.*—Five-parted. *Corolla.*—Of five rounded, concave petals. *Stamens.*—Ten. *Pistil.*—One, with a long curved style.

In the distance these pretty flowers suggest the lilies-of-the-valley. They are found in the woods of June and July, often in close company with the pipsissewa. The ugly common name of shinleaf arose from an early custom of applying the leaves of this genus to bruises or sores; the English peasantry being in the habit of calling any kind of plaster a "shin-plaster" without regard to the part of the body to which it might be applied. The old herbalist, Salmon, says that the name *Pyrola* was given to the genus by the Romans on account of the fancied resemblance of its leaves and flowers to those of a pear-tree. The English also call the plant "wintergreen," which name we usually reserve for *Gaultheria procumbens*.

P. rotundifolia is a species with thick, shining, rounded leaves. It is the tallest of the genus, its scape standing, at times, one foot

Flower.

ONE-FLOWERED WINTERGREEN.—*Moneses uniflora.*

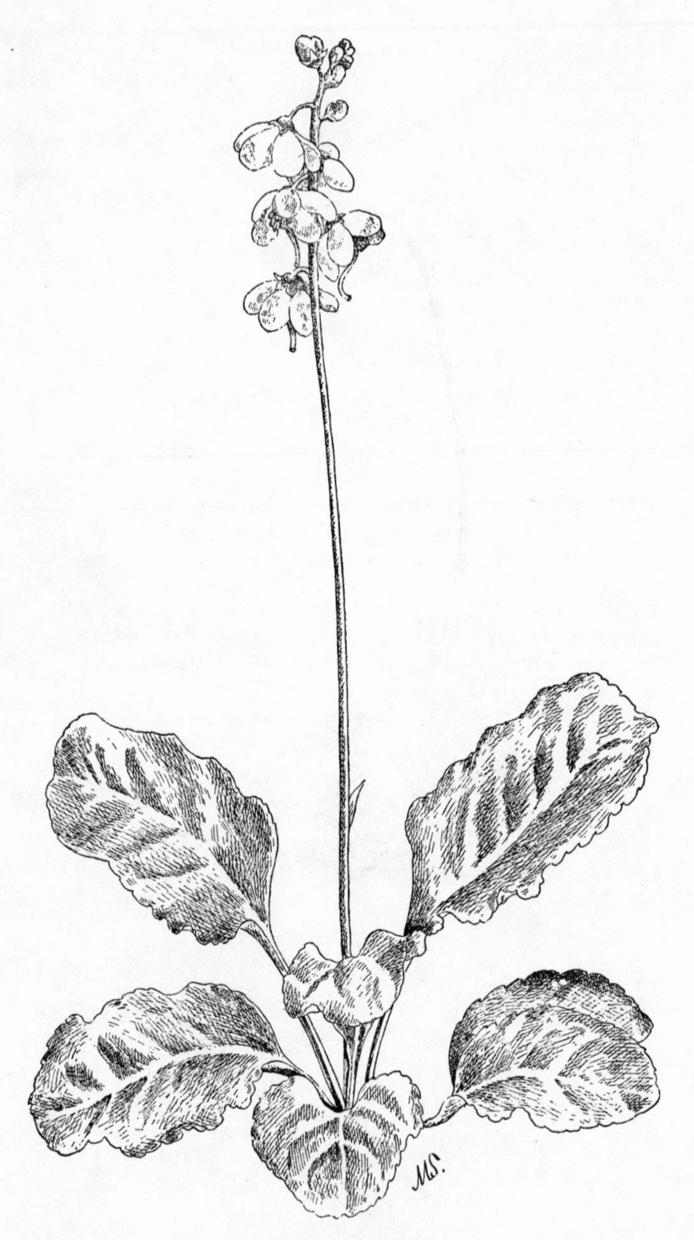

SHINLEAF.—*Pyrola elliptica.*

above the ground. This species exhibits several varieties with rose-colored flowers.

The smallest member of the group, *P. secunda,* is only from three to six inches high. Its numerous small, greenish flowers are turned to one side, and are scarcely nodding. They are clustered in spike-like fashion along the scape.

P. minor can be distinguished from all other *Pyrolas* by the short style which does not protrude from the globular blossom. This is a retiring little plant which is only found in our northern woods and mountains.

Many of these flowers are fragrant.

PIPSISSEWA. PRINCE'S PINE.

Chimaphila umbellata. Heath Family.

Stem.—Four to ten inches high; leafy. *Leaves.*—Somewhat whorled or scattered; evergreen; lance-shaped; with sharply toothed edges. *Flowers.*—White or pinkish: fragrant; in a loose terminal cluster. *Calyx.*—Five-lobed. *Corolla.*—With five rounded, widely spreading petals. *Stamens.*—Ten, with violet anthers *Pistil.*—One; with a short top-shaped style and disk-like stigma.

When strolling through the woods in summer one is apt to chance upon great patches of these deliciously fragrant and pretty flowers. The little plant, with its shining evergreen foliage, flourishes abundantly among decaying leaves in sandy soil, and puts forth its dainty blossoms late in June. It is one of the latest of the fragile wood-flowers which are so charming in the earlier year, and which have already begun to surrender in favor of their hardier, more self-assertive brethren of the fields and roadsides. The common name, pipsissewa, is evidently of Indian origin, and perhaps refers to the strengthening properties which the red men ascribed to it.

SPOTTED WINTERGREEN.

Chimaphila maculata. Heath Family.

The spotted wintergreen blossoms a little later than its twin-sister, the pipsissewa. Its slightly toothed leaves are conspicuously marked with white.

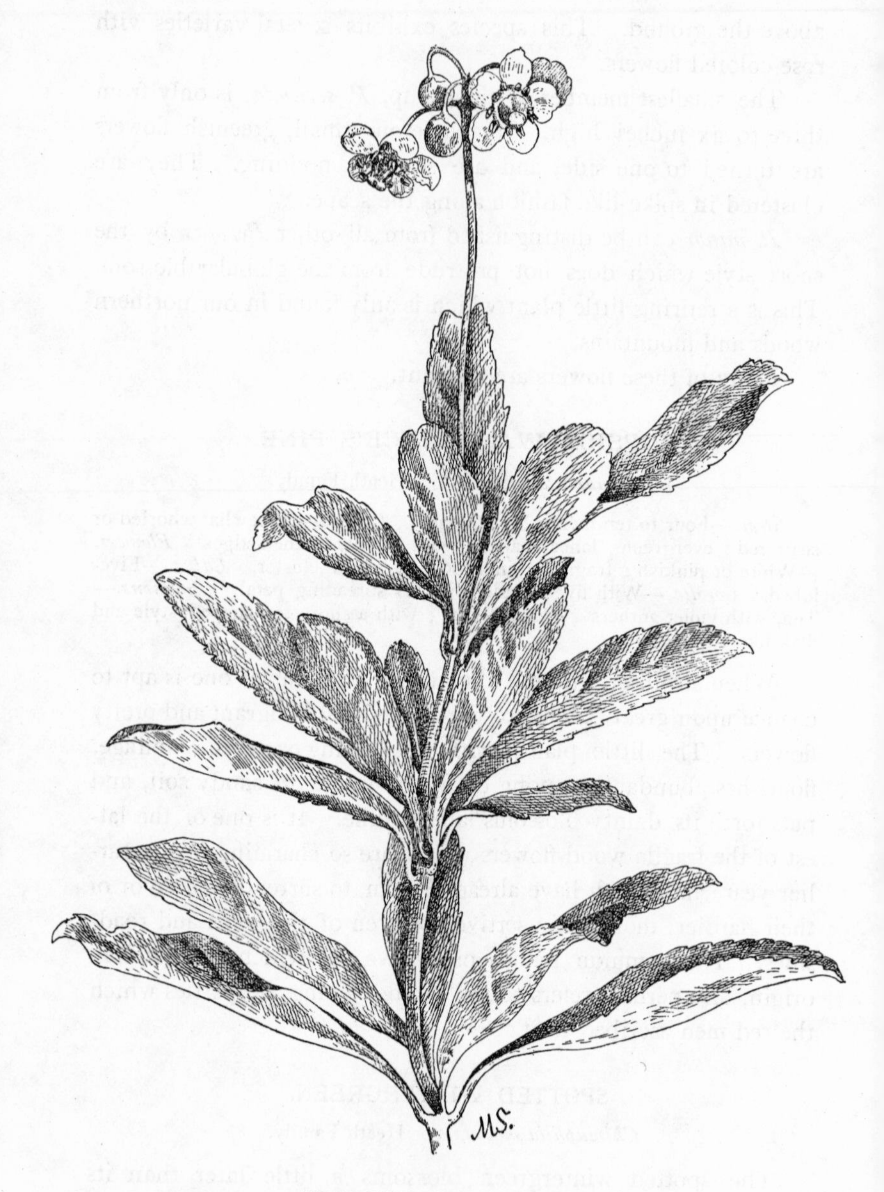

PIPSISSEWA.—*Chimaphila umbellata.*

WHITE DAISY. WHITEWEED. OX-EYE-DAISY.

Chrysanthemum Leucanthemum. Composite Family.

The common white daisy stars the June meadows with those gold-centred blossoms which delight the eyes of the beauty-lover while they make sore the heart of the farmer, for the "whiteweed," as he calls it, is hurtful to pasture land and difficult to eradicate.

The true daisy is the *Bellis perennis* of England,—the

> "Wee, modest crimson-tippit flower"

of Burns. This was first called "day's eye," because it closed at night and opened at dawn,—

> "That well by reason men it call may,
> The Daisie, or else the eye of the day,"

sang Chaucer nearly five hundred years ago. In England our flower is called "ox-eye" and "moon daisy;" in Scotland, "dog-daisy."

The plant is not native to this country, but was brought from the Old World by the early colonists.

DAISY-FLEABANE. SWEET-SCABIOUS.

Erigeron annuus. Composite Family.

Stem.—Stout; from three to five feet high; branched; hairy. *Leaves.*—Coarsely and sharply toothed; the lowest ovate, the upper narrower. *Flower-heads.*—Small; clustered; composed of both ray and disk-flowers, the former white, purplish, or pinkish, the latter yellow.

During the summer months the fields and waysides are whitened with these very common flowers which look somewhat like small white daisies or asters.

Another common species is *E. strigosus*, a smaller plant, with smaller flower-heads also, but with the white ray-flowers longer. The generic name is from two Greek words signifying

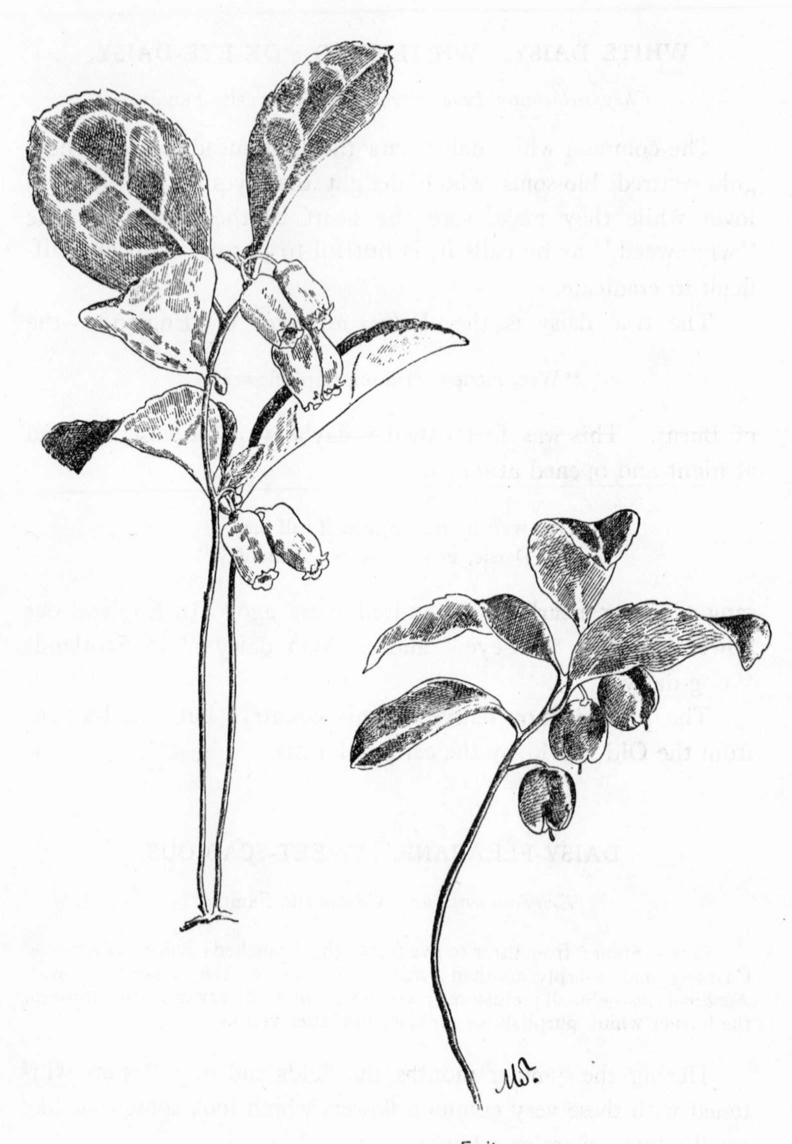

Fruit.

CHECKERBERRY.—*Gaultheria procumbens.*

spring and *an old man*, in allusion to the hoariness of certain species which flower in the spring. The fleabanes were so named from the belief that when burned they were objectionable to insects. They were formerly hung in country cottages for the purpose of excluding such unpleasant intruders.

WINTERGREEN. CHECKERBERRY. MOUNTAIN-TEA.

Gaultheria procumbens. Heath Family.

Stem.—Three to six inches high; slender; leafy at the summit. *Leaves.*—Oval; shining; evergreen. *Flowers.*—White, growing from the axils of the leaves. *Calyx.*—Five-lobed. *Corolla.*—Urn-shaped; with five small teeth. *Stamens.*—Ten. *Pistil.*—One. *Fruit.*—A globular red berry.

He who seeks the cool shade of the evergreens on a hot July day is likely to discover the nodding wax-like flowers of this little plant. They are delicate and pretty, with a background of shining leaves. These leaves when young have a pleasant aromatic flavor similar to that of the sweet birch; they are sometimes used as a substitute for tea. The bright red berries are also edible and savory, and are much appreciated by the hungry birds and deer during the winter. If not thus consumed they remain upon the plant until the following spring, when they either drop or rot upon the stem, thus allowing the seeds to escape.

INDIAN-PIPE. CORPSE-PLANT. GHOST-FLOWER.

Monotropa uniflora. Heath Family.

A low fleshy herb from three to eight inches high; without green foliage; of a wax-like appearance; with colorless bracts in the place of leaves. *Flower.*—White or pinkish; single; terminal; nodding. *Calyx.*—Of two to four bract-like scales. *Corolla.*—Of four or five wedge-shaped petals. *Stamens.*—Eight or ten; with yellow anthers. *Pistil.*—One, with a disk-like, four or five-rayed stigma.

"In shining groups, each stem a pearly ray,
Weird flecks of light within the shadowed wood,
They dwell aloof, a spotless sisterhood.
No Angelus, except the wild bird's lay,

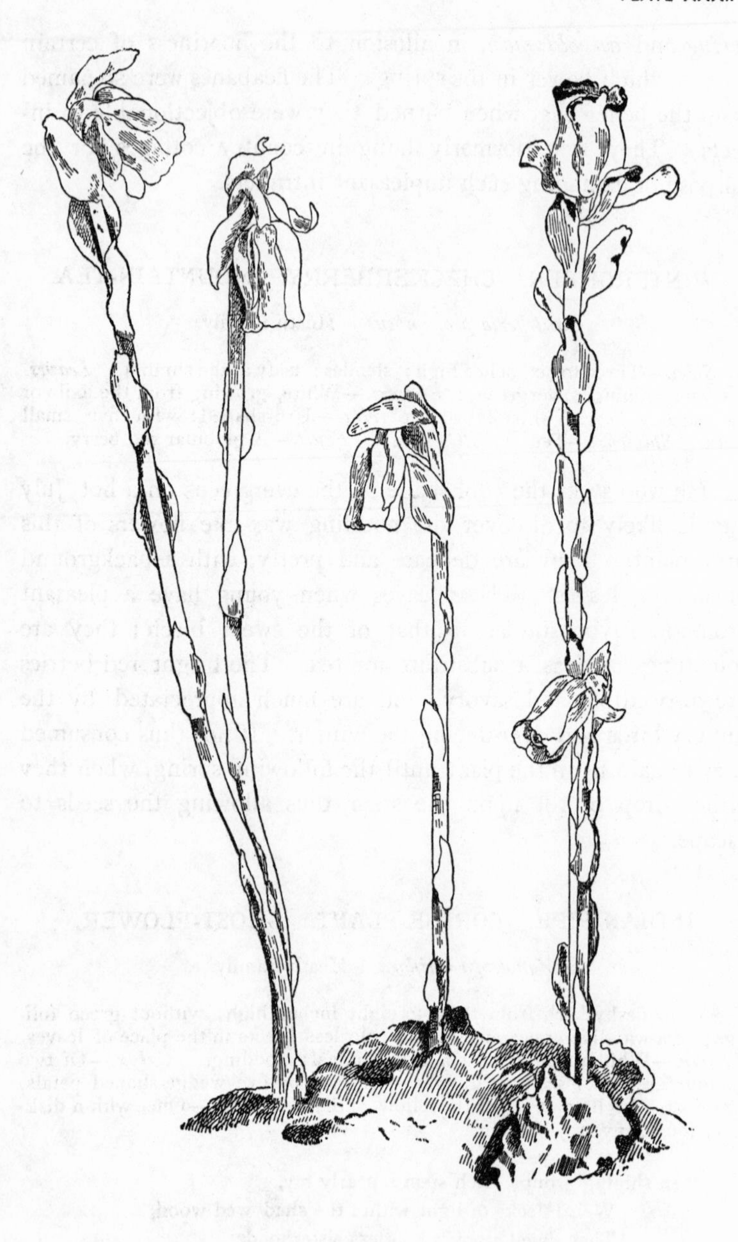

INDIAN-PIPE.—*Monotropa uniflora.*

Awakes these forest nuns; yet, night and day,
Their heads are bent, as if in prayerful mood.
A touch will mar their snow, and tempests rude
Defile; but in the mist fresh blossoms stray
From spirit-gardens, just beyond our ken.
Each year we seek their virgin haunts, to look
Upon new loveliness, and watch again
Their shy devotions near the singing brook;
Then, mingling in the dizzy stir of men,
Forget the vows made in that cloistered nook." *

The effect of a cluster of these nodding, wax-like flowers in the deep woods of summer is singularly fairy-like. They spring from a ball of matted rootlets, and are parasitic, drawing their nourishment from decaying vegetable matter. In fruit the plant erects itself and loses its striking resemblance to a pipe. Its clammy touch, and its disposition to decompose and turn black when handled, has earned it the name of corpse-plant. It was used by the Indians as an eye-lotion, and is still believed by some to possess healing properties.

MAYWEED. CHAMOMILE.

Anthemis Cotula. Composite Family.

Stem.—Branching. *Leaves.*—Finely dissected. *Flower-heads.*—Composed of white ray and yellow disk-flowers, resembling the common white daisy.

In midsummer the pretty daisy-like blossoms of this strong-scented plant are massed along the roadsides. So nearly a counterpart of the common daisy do they appear that they are constantly mistaken for that flower. The smaller heads, with the yellow disk-flowers crowded upon a receptable which is much more conical than that of the daisy, and the finely dissected, feathery leaves, serve to identify the mayweed. The country-folk brew "chamomile tea" from these leaves, and through their agency raise painfully effective blisters in an emergency.

* Mary Thacher Higginson.

NEW JERSEY TEA. REDROOT.

Ceanothus americanus. Buckthorn Family.

Root.—Dark red. *Stem.*—Shrubby; one to three feet high. *Flowers.*—White; small; clustered. *Calyx.*—White; petal-like; five-lobed; incurved. *Corolla.*—With five long-clawed hooded petals. *Stamens.*—Five. *Pistil.*—One, with three stigmas.

This shrubby plant is very common in dry woods. In July its white feathery flower-clusters brighten many a shady nook in an otherwise flowerless neighborhood. During the Revolution its leaves were used as a substitute for tea.

BASTARD TOADFLAX.

Comandra umbellata. Sandalwood Family.

Stem.—Eight to ten inches high; branching; leafy. *Leaves.*—Alternate; oblong; pale. *Flowers.*—Greenish-white; small; clustered. *Calyx.*—Bell or urn-shaped; five-cleft. *Corolla.*—None. *Stamens.*—Five; inserted on the edge of a disk which lines the calyx, to the middle of which the anthers are connected by a tuft of thread-like hairs. *Pistil.*—One; slender. *Fruit.*—Nut-like; crowned by the lobes of the calyx.

In May or June we often find masses of these little flowers in the dry, open woods. The root of the bastard toadflax forms parasitic attachments to the roots of trees.

WHITE SWEET CLOVER. WHITE MELILOT.

Melilotus alba. Pulse Family.

Stem.—Two to four feet high. *Leaves.*—Divided into three-toothed leaflets. *Flowers.*—Papilionaceous; white; growing in spike-like racemes.

Like its yellow sister, *M. officinalis*, this plant is found blossoming along the roadsides throughout the summer. The flowers are said to serve as flavoring in Gruyère cheese, snuff, and smoking-tobacco, and to act like camphor when packed with furs to preserve them from moths, besides imparting a pleasant fragrance.

PLATE XXXIII

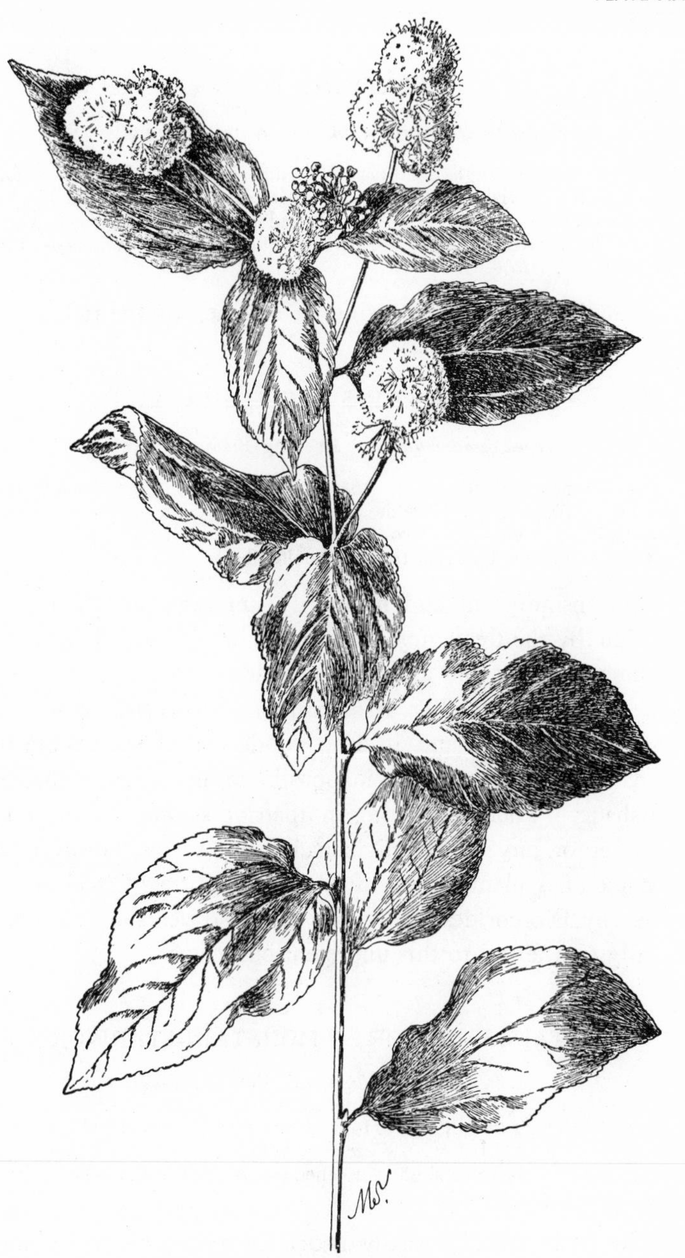

NEW JERSEY TEA.—*Ceanothus americanus.*

WATERLEAF.

Hydrophyllum virginianum. Waterleaf Family.

One to two feet high. *Leaves.*—Divided into five to seven oblong, pointed, toothed divisions. *Flowers.*—White or purplish; in one-sided raceme-like clusters which are usually coiled from the apex when young. *Calyx.*—Five-parted. *Corolla.*—Five-cleft; bell-shaped. *Stamens.*—Five; protruding. *Pistil.*—One.

This plant is found flowering in summer in the rich woods.

ENCHANTER'S NIGHTSHADE.

Circaea quadrisulcata. Evening-Primrose Family.

Stem.—One or two feet high. *Leaves.*—Opposite; thin; ovate; slightly toothed. *Flowers.*—Dull white; small; growing in a raceme. *Calyx.*—Two-lobed. *Corolla.*—Of two petals. *Stamens.*—Two. *Pistil.*—One. *Fruit.*—Small; bur-like; bristly with hooked hairs.

This insignificant and ordinarily uninteresting plant arrests attention by the frequency with which it is found flowering in the summer woods and along shady roadsides.

C. alpina is a smaller, less common species, which is found along the mountains and in deep woods. Both species are burdened with the singularly inappropriate name of enchanter's nightshade. There is nothing in their appearance to suggest an enchanter or any of the nightshades. It seems, however, that the name of a plant called after the enchantress Circe, and described by Dioscorides nearly two thousand years ago, was accidentally transferred to this unpretentious genus.

MOUNTAIN-SANDWORT. MOUNTAIN-STARWORT.

Arenaria groenlandica. Pink Family.

Stems.—Densly tufted, two to four inches high. *Leaves.*—Linear, scattered above, matted below. *Flowers.*—White. *Calyx.*—Of five sepals. *Corolla.*—Of five entire or slightly notched petals. *Stamens.*—Ten. *Pistil.*—One, with three styles.

This little plant is usually associated with some rocky mountain summit from whose crevices the slender tufted stems and

ENCHANTER'S NIGHTSHADE.—*Circaea quadrisulcata.*

pretty white flowers spring in dainty contrast to their rugged surroundings. But occasionally the mountain-sandwort is found in the lowlands close to the river bank, or on the rocks that rise from the sea.

GROVE-SANDWORT.

Arenaria lateriflora. Pink Family.

Four to six inches high. *Leaves.*—Thin; oval or oblong. *Flowers.*—White, their parts sometimes in fours.

The grove-sandwort abounds in moist places along the seashore in parts of the country. Its little white flowers gleaming through the grasses are almost too small to be noticed by the unobservant pedestrian.

FIELD-CHICKWEED.

Cerastium arvense. Pink Family.

Four to eight inches high. *Stems.*—Slender. *Leaves.*—Linear or narrowly lance-shaped. *Flowers.*—White; large; in terminal clusters. *Calyx.*—Usually of five sepals. *Corolla.*—Usually of five two-lobed petals which are more than twice the length of the calyx. *Stamens.*—Twice as many, or fewer than the petals. *Pistil.*—One, with as many styles as there are sepals.

This is one of the most noticeable of the chickweeds. Its starry flowers are found in dry or rocky places, blossoming from May till July.

The common chickweed, which besets damp places everywhere, is *Stellaria media;* this is much used as food for song birds.

The long-leaved stitchwort, *S. longifolia*, is a species which is common in grassy places, especially northward. It has linear leaves, unlike those of *S. media*, which are ovate or oblong.

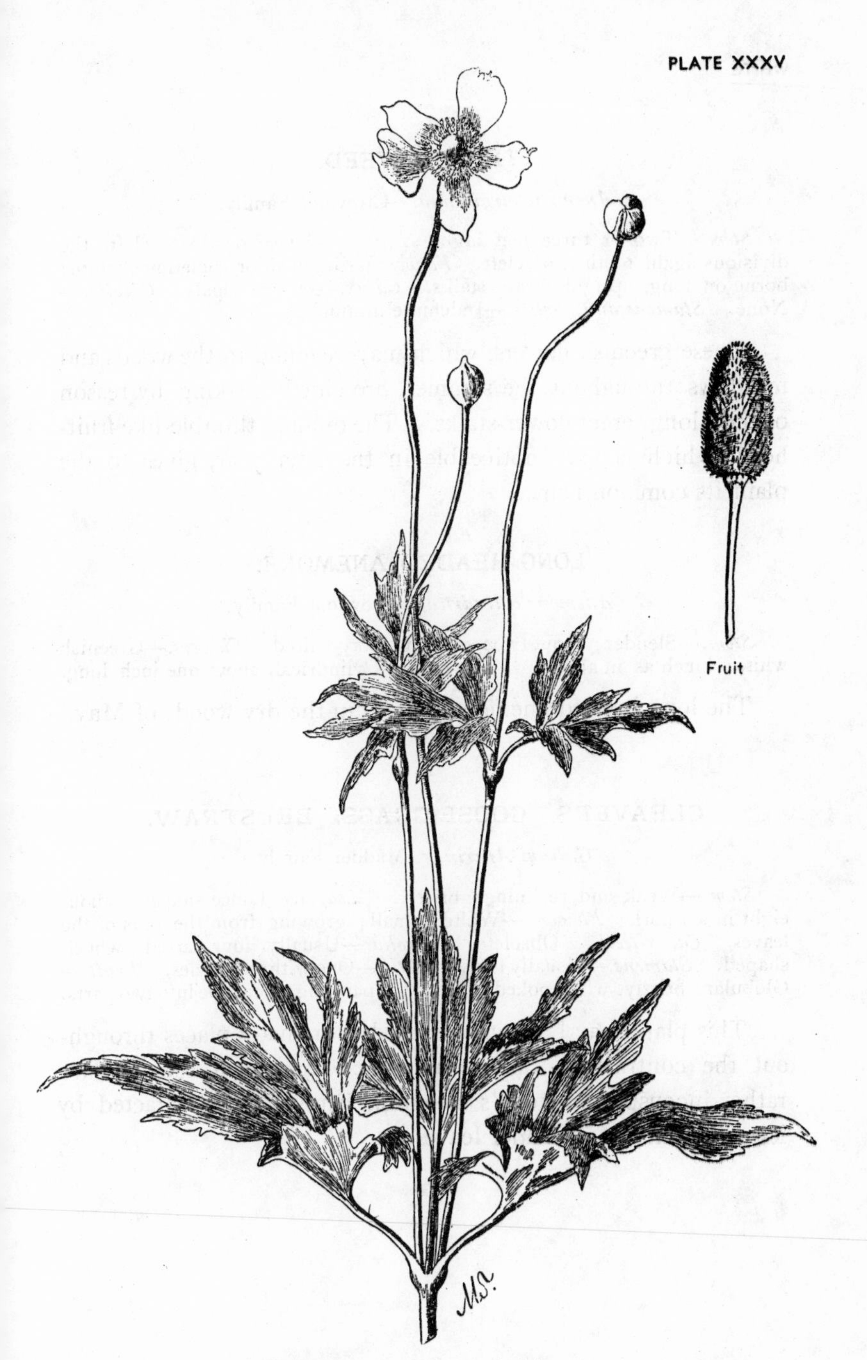

THIMBLEWEED.—*Anemone virginiana.*

THIMBLEWEED.

Anemone virginiana. Crowfoot Family.

Stem.—Two or three feet high. *Leaves.*—Twice or thrice cleft, the divisions again toothed or cleft. *Flowers.*—Greenish or sometimes white; borne on long, upright flower-stalks. *Calyx.*—Of five sepals. *Corolla.*—None. *Stamens and Pistils.*—Indefinite in number.

These greenish flowers, which may be found in the woods and meadows throughout the summer, are chiefly striking by reason of their long, erect flower-stalks. The oblong, thimble-like fruit-head, which is very noticeable in the later year, gives to the plant its common name.

LONG-HEADED ANEMONE.

Anemone cylindrica. Crowfoot Family.

Stem.—Slender; about two feet high; silky-haired. *Flowers.*—Greenish white; much as in above. *Fruit-head.*—Cylindrical, about one inch long.

The long-headed anemone flowers in the dry woods of May.

CLEAVERS. GOOSE-GRASS. BEDSTRAW.

Galium Aparine. Madder Family.

Stem.—Weak and reclining; bristly. *Leaves.*—Lance-shaped; about eight in a whorl. *Flowers.*—White; small; growing from the axils of the leaves. *Calyx-teeth.* Obsolete. *Corolla.*—Usually four-parted; wheel-shaped. *Stamens.*—Usually four. *Pistil.*—One with two styles. *Fruit.*—Globular; bristly, with hooked prickles; separating when ripe into two parts.

This plant may be found in wooded or shady places throughout the continent. Its flowers, which appear in summer, are rather inconspicuous, one's attention being chiefly attracted by its many whorls of slender leaves.

SMALL BEDSTRAW.

Galium trifidum. Madder Family.

Stems.—Weak; five to twenty inches high; rough. *Leaves.*—In whorls of four to six. *Flowers.*—White; small; one to seven in a cluster. *Calyx-teeth.*—Obsolete. *Corolla.*—Three or four-parted. *Stamens.*—Three or four. *Pistil.*—One, with two styles. *Fruit.*—Globular; smooth; separating when ripe into two parts.

Very common in wet places is the small bedstraw. From its relative, cleavers or goose-grass, it may be distinguished by its smooth fruit, and by the number of leaves in a whorl.

ROUGH BEDSTRAW.

Galium asprellum. Madder Family.

Stem.—Much branched; rough with crooked prickles; leaning on bushes; three to four feet high. *Leaves.*—In whorls of four to six; with almost prickly margins; sharply-pointed at tip; oval. *Flowers.*—As in small bedstraw.

This larger bedstraw is common and noticeable in New England, as well as farther south and west. All three species of *Galium* are conspicuous chiefly on account of their pretty foliage.

BLACK COHOSH. BUGBANE. BLACK SNAKEROOT.

Cimicifuga racemosa. Crowfoot Family.

Stem.—Three to eight feet high. *Leaves.*—Divided, the leaflets toothed or incised. *Flowers.*—White; growing in elongated wand-like racemes. *Calyx.*—Of four or five white petal-like sepals; falling early. *Corolla.*—Of from one to eight white petals or transformed stamens. *Stamens.*—Numerous, with slender white filaments. *Pistils.*—One to three.

The tall white wands of the black cohosh shoot up in the shadowy woods of midsummer like so many ghosts. A curious-looking plant it is, bearing aloft the feathery flowers which have such an unpleasant odor that even the insects are supposed to

BLACK COHOSH.—*Cimicifuga racemosa.*

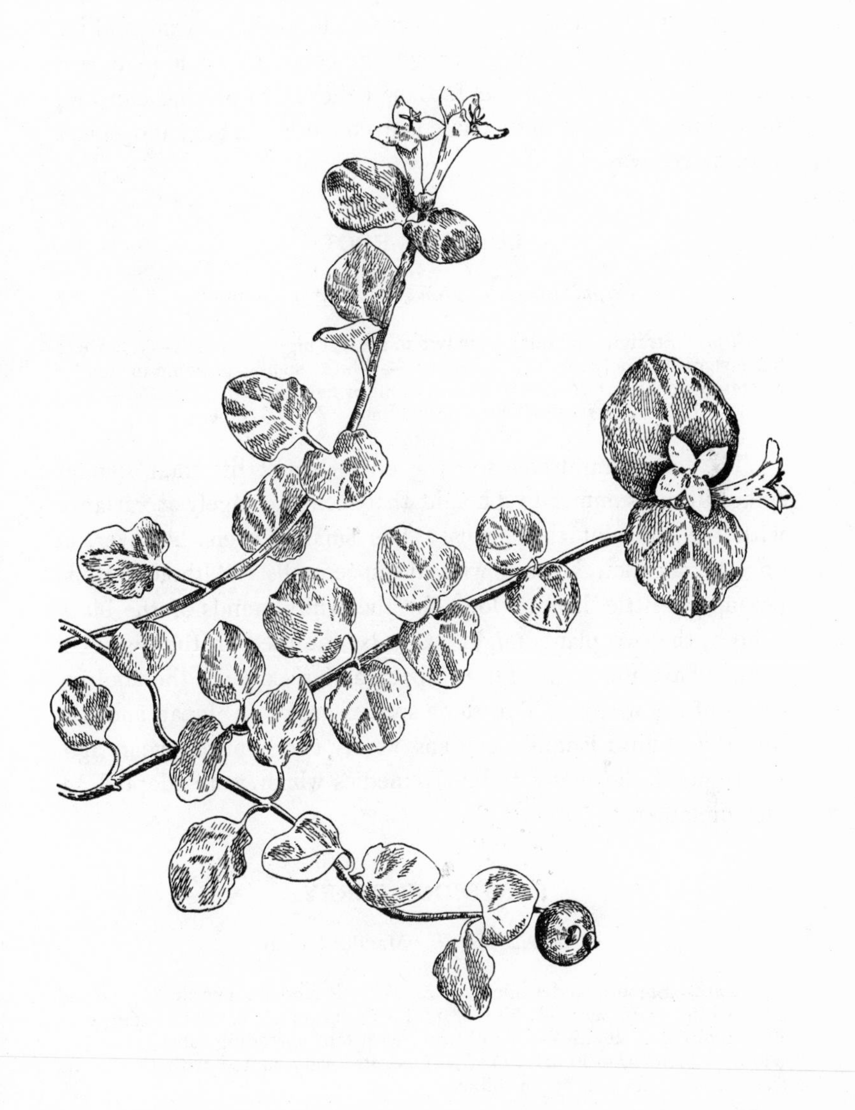

PARTRIDGE-BERRY.—*Mitchella repens.*

avoid them. Fortunately they are sufficiently conspicuous to be admired at a distance, many a newly cleared hill-side and wood-border being lightened by their slender, torch-like racemes which flash upon us as we travel through the country. The plant was one of the many which the Indians believed to be efficacious for snake-bites. The generic name is from *cimex*—a bug, and *fugare* —to drive away.

CULVER'S-ROOT.

Veronicastrum virginicum. Figwort Family.

Stem.—Straight and tall; from two to six feet high. *Leaves.*—Whorled; lance-shaped; finely toothed. *Flowers.*—White; small; growing in slender clustered spikes. *Calyx.*—Irregularly four or five-toothed. *Corolla.*—Four or five-lobed. *Stamens.*—Two; protruding. *Pistil.*—One.

The tall straight stems of the culver's-root lift their slender spikes in midsummer to a height that seems strangely at variance with the habit of this genus. The small flowers, however, at once betray their kinship with the speedwells. Although it is, perhaps, a little late to look for the white wands of the black cohosh, the two plants might easily be confused in the distance, as they have much the same aspect and seek alike the cool recesses of the woods. This same species grows in Japan and was introduced into English gardens nearly two hundred years ago. It is one of the many Indian remedies which were adopted by our forefathers.

PARTRIDGE-BERRY.

Mitchella repens. Madder Family.

Stems.—Smooth and trailing. *Leaves.*—Rounded; evergreen; veined with white. *Flowers.*—White or pinkish; fragrant; in pairs. *Calyx.*—Four-toothed. *Corolla.*—Funnel-form, with four spreading lobes; bearded within. *Stamens.*—Four. *Pistil.*—One, its ovary united with that of its sister flower; its four stigmas linear.

At all times of the year this little evergreen plant fulfils its mission of adorning that small portion of the earth to which it finds itself rooted. But only the early summer finds the partridge-berry exhaling its delicious fragrance from the delicate sister blossoms which are its glory. Among the waxy flowers will be found as many of the bright red berries of the previous year as have been left unmolested by the hungry winter birds. This plant is found not only in the moist woods of North America, but also in the forests of Mexico and Japan. It is a near relative of the dainty bluets or Quaker ladies, and has the same peculiarity of dimorphous flowers (p. 324).

COMMON ELDER.

Sambucus canadensis. Honeysuckle Family.

Stems.—Scarcely woody; five to ten feet high. *Leaves.*—Divided into toothed leaflets. *Flowers.*—White; small; in flat-topped clusters. *Calyx.*—Lobes minute or none. *Corolla.*—With five spreading lobes. *Stamens.*—Five. *Pistil.*—One, with three stigmas. *Fruit.*—Dark-purple.

The common elder borders the lanes and streams with its spreading flower-clusters in early summer, and in the later year is noticeable for the dark berries from which "elderberry wine" is brewed by the country people. The fine white wood is easily cut and is used for skewers and pegs. A decoction of the leaves serves the gardener a good purpose in protecting delicate plants from caterpillars. Evelyn wrote of it: "If the medicinal properties of the leaves, berries, bark, etc., were thoroughly known, I cannot tell what our countrymen could ail for which he might not fetch from every hedge, whether from sickness or wound."

The white pith can easily be removed from the stems, hence the old English name of bore-wood.

The name elder is probably derived from the Anglo-Saxon *aeld*—a fire—and is thought to refer to the former use of the hollow branches in blowing up a fire.

SPURGE.

Euphorbia corollata. Spurge Family.

Stem.—Two or three feet high. *Leaves.*—Ovate; lance-shaped or linear. *Flowers.*—Clustered within the usually five-lobed, cup-shaped involucre, which was formerly considered the flower itself; the male flowers numerous and lining its base, consisting each of a single stamen; the female flower solitary in the middle of the involucre, consisting of a three-lobed ovary with three styles, each style being two-cleft. *Pod.*—On a slender stalk; smooth.

In this plant the showy white appendages of the clustered cup-shaped involucres are usually taken for the petals of the flower; only the botanist suspecting that the minute organs within these involucres really form a cluster of separate flowers of different sexes. While the most northerly range in the Eastern States of this spurge is usually considered to be New York, we are told that it has been recently naturalized in Massachusetts. It blossoms from July till October.

CANADIAN BURNET.

Sanguisorba canadensis. Rose Family.

One to six feet high. *Leaves.*—Divided into numerous ovate or oblong leaflets. *Flowers.*—White; small. *Calyx.*—White; corolla-like, four-lobed. *Corolla.*—None. *Stamens.*—Four, long-exserted, club-shaped, white. *Pistil.*—One.

A conspicuous midsummer arrival in many of our wet meadows, more especially perhaps in those near the sea, is the Canadian burnet. This is a tall showy plant, with foliage suggestive of the Rose family to which it belongs, and long-stalked spikes of feathery white flowers, the lower ones opening first, leaving the upper part of the spike in bud. These flowers owe their feathery appearance to the long white stamens, of which each blossom seems chiefly to consist, the four petal-like lobes of the calyx falling early, and the pistil being inconspicuous.

PLATE XXXVIII

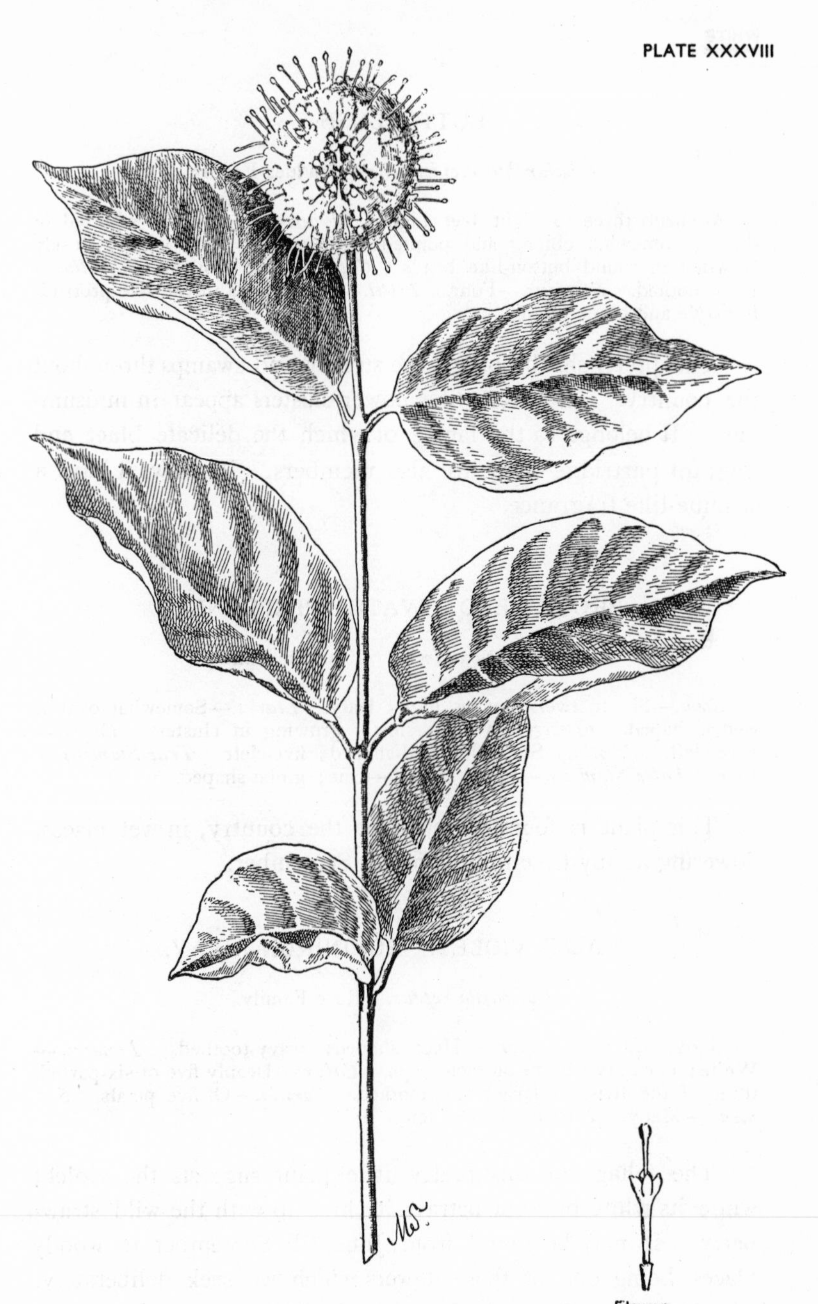

BUTTONBUSH.—*Cephalanthus occidentalis.*

BUTTONBUSH.

Cephalanthus occidentalis. Madder Family.

A shrub three to eight feet high. *Leaves.*—Opposite or whorled in threes; somewhat oblong and pointed. *Flowers.*—Small; white; closely crowded in round button-like heads. *Calyx.*—Four-toothed. *Corolla.*—Four-toothed. *Stamens.*—Four. *Pistil.*—One, with a thread-like protruding style and blunt stigma.

This pretty shrub borders the streams and swamps throughout the country. Its button-like flower-clusters appear in midsummer. It belongs to the family of which the delicate bluet and fragrant partridge-berry are also members. Its flowers have a jasmine-like fragrance.

BROOKWEED. WATER-PIMPERNEL.

Samolus parviflorus. Primrose Family.

Stem.—Six to twelve inches high; leafy. *Leaves.*—Somewhat oval or wedge-shaped. *Flowers.*—White; small; growing in clusters. *Calyx.*—Five-cleft. *Corolla.*—Somewhat bell-shaped; five-cleft. *True Stamens.*—Five. *False Stamens.*—Five. *Pistil.*—One; globe-shaped.

This plant is found throughout the country, in wet places, flowering at any time from June till September.

FALSE VIOLET. ROBIN-RUN-AWAY.

Dalibarda repens. Rose Family.

Scape.—Low. *Leaves.* — Heart-shaped; wavy-toothed. *Flowers.* — White; one or two borne on each scape. *Calyx.*—Deeply five or six-parted, three of the divisions larger and toothed. *Corolla.*—Of five petals. *Stamens.*—Many. *Pistils.*—Five to ten.

The foliage of this pretty little plant suggests the violet; while its white blossom betrays its kinship with the wild strawberry. It may be found from June till September in woody places, being one of those flowers which we seek deliberately, whose charm is never decreased by its being thrust upon us in-

FALSE VIOLET.—*Dalibarda repens.*

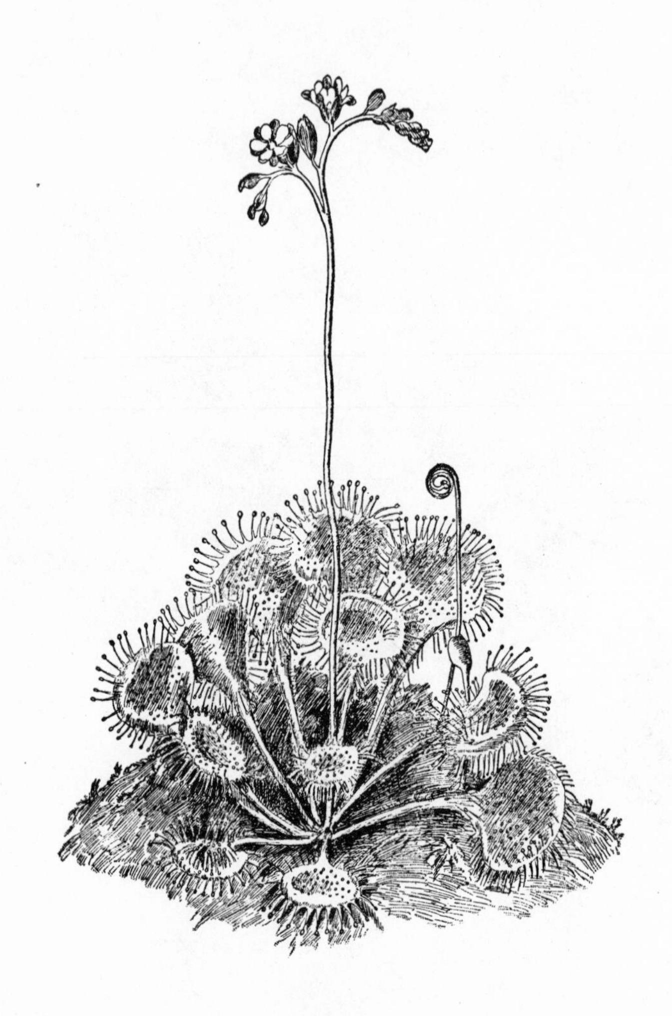

ROUND-LEAVED SUNDEW.—*Drosera rotundifolia.*

opportunely. Who can tell how much the attractiveness of the wild carrot, the dandelion, or butter-and-eggs would be enhanced were they so discreet as to withdraw from the common haunts of men into the shady exclusiveness which causes us to prize many far less beautiful flowers?

ROUND-LEAVED SUNDEW.

Drosera rotundifolia. Sundew Family.

Scape.—A few inches high. *Leaves.*—Rounded, abruptly narrowed into spreading, hairy leaf-stalks; beset with reddish, gland-bearing bristles. *Flowers.*—White; growing in a one-sided raceme, which so nods at its apex that the fresh-blown blossom is always uppermost. *Calyx.*—Of five sepals. *Corolla.*—Of five petals. *Pistil.*—One, with three or five styles, which are sometimes so deeply two-parted as to be taken for twice as many.

"What's this I hear
About the new carnivora?
Can little plants
Eat bugs and ants
And gnats and flies?
A sort of retrograding:
Surely the fare
Of flowers is air,
Or sunshine sweet;
They shouldn't eat,
Or do aught so degrading!"

But by degrees we are learning to reconcile ourselves to the fact that the more we study the plants the less we are able to attribute to them altogether unfamiliar and ethereal habits. We find that the laws which control their being are strangely suggestive of those which regulate ours, and after the disappearance of the shock which attends the shattered illusion, their charm is only increased by the new sense of kinship.

The round-leaved sundew is found blossoming in many of our marshes in midsummer. When the sun shines upon its leaves they look as though covered with sparkling dewdrops, hence its common name. These drops are a glutinous exudation, by means of which insects visiting the plant are first captured; the reddish bristles then close tightly about them, and it is supposed that their juices are absorbed by the plant. At all events the rash visitor rarely escapes. In many localities it is easy to secure any number of these little plants and to try for one's self the rather grewsome experiment of feeding them with small insects. Should the tender-hearted recoil from such reckless slaughter, they might confine their offerings on the altar of science to mosquitoes, small spiders, and other deservedly unpopular creatures.

The dew-thread, *D. filiformis*, has fine, thread-like leaves and pink flowers, and is found in wet sand along the coast.

> "A little marsh-plant, yellow green,
> And pricked at lip with tender red.
> Tread close, and either way you tread
> Some faint black water jets between
> Lest you should bruise the curious head.
>
> . . . .
>
> You call it sundew: how it grows,
> If with its color it have breath,
> If life taste sweet to it, if death
> Pain its soft petal, no man knows:
> Man has no sight or sense that saith."

—SWINBURNE.

POKEWEED. GARGET. PIGEONBERRY.

Phytolacca americana. Pokeweed Family.

Stems.—At length from six to ten feet high; purple-pink or bright red; stout. *Leaves.*—Large; alternate; veiny. *Flowers.*—White or pinkish; the green ovaries conspicuous; growing in racemes. *Calyx.*—Of five rounded or petal-like sepals, pinkish without. *Corolla.*—None. *Stamens.*—Ten. *Pistil.*—One, with ten styles. *Fruit.*—A dark purplish berry.

There is a vigor about this native plant which is very pleasing. In July it is possible that we barely notice the white flow-

PLATE XLI

Fruit.

POKEWEED.—*Phytolacca americana.*

ers and large leaves; but when in September the tall purple stems rear themselves above their neighbors in the roadside thicket, the leaves look as though stained with wine, and the long clusters of rich dark berries hang heavily from the branches, we cannot but admire its independent beauty. The berries serve as food for the birds. A tincture of them at one time acquired some reputation as a remedy for rheumatism. In Pennsylvania they have been used with whiskey to make a so-called "port-wine." From their dark juice arose the name of "red-ink plant," which is common in some places. The large roots are poisonous, but the acrid young shoots are rendered harmless by boiling, and are eaten like asparagus, being quite as good, I have been told by country people.

Despite the difference in the spelling of the names, it has been suggested that the plant was called after President Polk. This is most improbable, as it was common throughout the country long before his birth, and its twigs are said to have been plucked and worn by his followers during his campaign for the presidency.

BUNCHFLOWER.

Melanthium virginicum. Lily Family.

Stem.—Three to five feet high; rather slender; leafy. *Leaves.*—Linear. *Flowers.*—Greenish yellow turning brown; in a rather dense panicle. *Perianth.*—Of six somewhat heart-shaped, petal-like sepals raised on slender claws, each one bearing two dark glands at base. *Stamens.*—Six. *Pistil.*—One, with three styles.

This plant derives its name from the way in which the small flowers are bunched or crowded together on top of the tall stems. Usually the lower flowers are staminate; the upper pistillate.

It grows in wet meadows from Rhode Island to Florida, and blossoms from June to August.

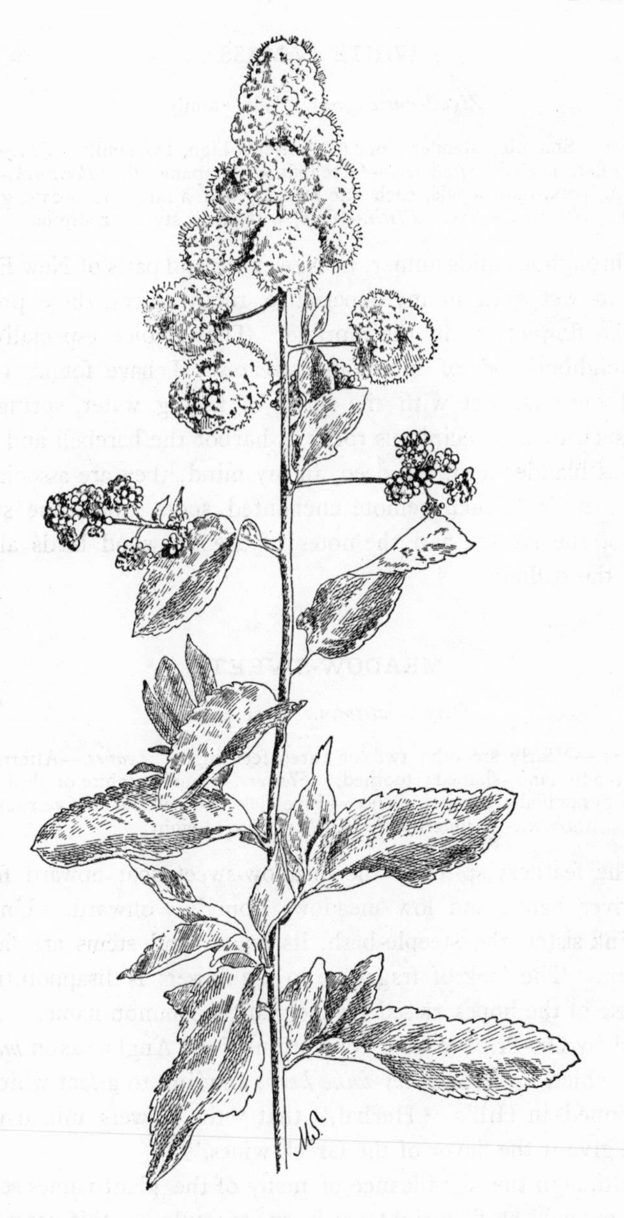

MEADOW-SWEET.—*Spiraea latifolia.*

WHITE CAMASS.

Zigadenus elegans. Lily Family.

Stem.—Smooth; slender; one to three feet high, from bulb. *Leaves.*—Linear, flat, keeled. *Flowers.*—Greenish-white, panicled. *Perianth.*—Of six, thin, petal-like sepals, each one marked with a large obcordate gland at base. *Stamens.*—Six. *Pistil.*—One, with three styles or stigmas.

Throughout midsummer, in New York and parts of New England, in wet and, in my experience, rocky places, these pretty lily-like flowers are in their prime. They rejoice especially in the neighborhood of mountain streams. I have found their tufted clusters, wet with the spray of falling water, springing from such moist precipitous rocks as harbor the harebell and the bulbous bladder fern. Indeed, in my mind, they are associated altogether with such remote enchanted spots, where the swift rush of the stream and the notes of the shy wood birds alone break the stillness.

MEADOW-SWEET.

Spiraea latifolia. Rose Family.

Stem.—Nearly smooth; two or three feet high. *Leaves.*—Alternate; very broadly lance-shaped; toothed. *Flowers.*—Small; white or flesh-color; in pyramidal clusters. *Calyx.*—Five-cleft. *Corolla.*—Of five rounded petals. *Stamens.*—Numerous. *Pistils.*—Five to eight.

The feathery spires of the meadow-sweet soar upward from the river banks and low meadows from July onward. Unlike its pink sister, the steeple-bush, its leaves and stems are fairly smooth. The lack of fragrance in the flowers is disappointing, because of the hopes raised by the plant's common name. This is said by Dr. Prior to be a corruption of the Anglo-Saxon *mead-wort,* which signifies *honey-wine herb*, alluding to a fact which is mentioned in Hill's "Herbal," that "the flowers mixed with mead give it the flavor of the Greek wines."

Although the significance of many of the plant-names seems clear enough at first sight, such an example as this serves to show how really obscure it often is.

WHITE AVENS.

Geum canadense. Rose Family.

Stem.—Slender; about two feet high. *Root-leaves.*—Divided into from three to five leaflets, or entire. *Stem-leaves.*—Three-lobed or divided, or only toothed. *Flowers.*—White. *Calyx.*—Deeply five-cleft, usually with five small bractlets alternating with its lobes. *Corolla.*—Of five petals. *Stamens.*—Numerous. *Pistils.*—Numerous, with hooked styles which become elongated in fruit.

The white avens is one of the less noticeable plants which border the summer woods, blossoming from May till August. Later the hooked seeds which grow in round bur-like heads secure wide dispersion by attaching themselves to animals or clothing. Other species of avens have more conspicuous golden-yellow flowers.

THREE-TOOTHED CINQUEFOIL.

Potentilla tridentata. Rose Family.

Stems.—Low; one to ten inches high; rather woody at base; tufted. *Leaves.*—Divided into three oblong leaflets, which are thick, and coarsely three-toothed at their apex. *Flowers.*—White; clustered. *Calyx.*—Five-cleft. *Corolla.*—Of five petals. *Stamens.*—Many. *Pistils.*—Many in a head.

The strawberry-like blossoms of this pretty little plant appear in summer. They are found on the mountain-tops of the Alleghanies, and also along the New England coast, and the shores of the Great Lakes.

RATTLESNAKE-PLANTAIN.

Goodyera pubescens. Orchis Family.

Scape.—Six to twelve inches high. *Leaves.*—From the root in a sort of flat rosette; conspicuously veined with white; thickish; evergreen. *Flowers.*—Small; greenish-white; crowded in a close spike.

The flowers of the rattlesnake-plantain appear in late summer and are less conspicuous than the prettily tufted, white-veined leaves which may be found in the rich woods throughout

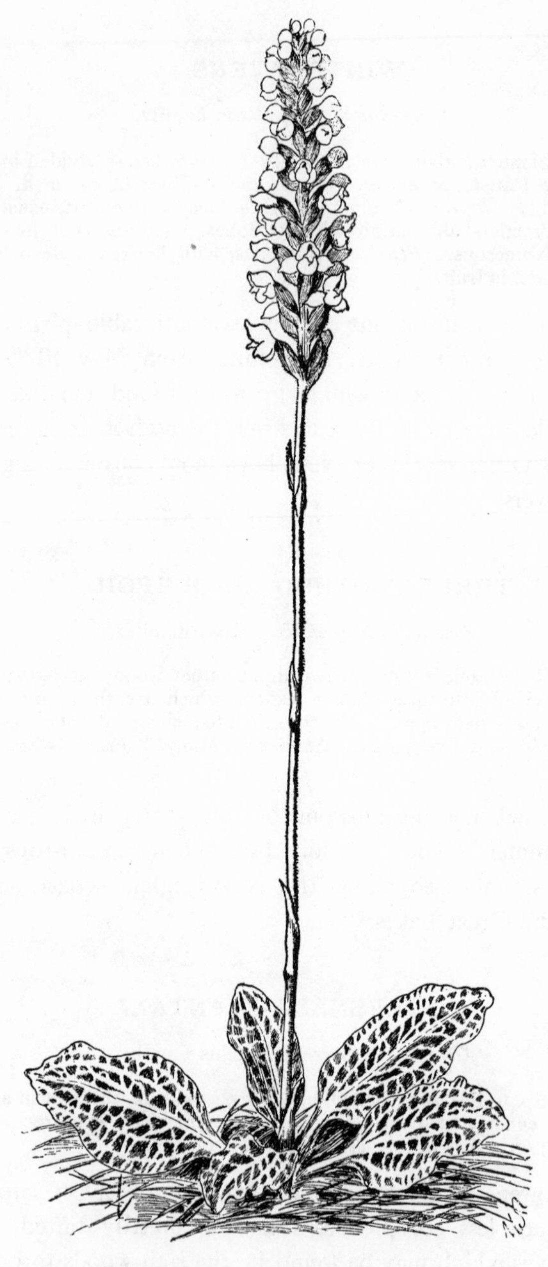

RATTLESNAKE-PLANTAIN.—*Goodyera pubescens.*

the year. The plant has been reputed an infallible cure for hydrophobia and snake-bites. It is said that the Indians had such faith in its remedial virtues that they would allow a snake to drive its fangs into them for a small sum, if they had these leaves on hand to apply to the wound.

WHITE FRINGED ORCHIS.

Habenaria blephariglottis. Orchis Family.

About one foot high. *Leaves.*—Oblong or lance-shaped; the upper passing into pointed bracts. *Flowers.*—Pure white; with a slender spur and fringed lip; growing in an oblong spike.

This seems to me the most exquisite of our native orchids. The fringed lips give the snowy, delicate flowers a feathery appearance as they gleam from the shadowy woods of midsummer, or from the peat-bogs where they thrive best; or perhaps they spire upward from among the dark green rushes which border some lonely mountain lake. Like the yellow fringed orchis, which they greatly resemble in general structure, they may be sought for in vain many seasons and then will be discovered, one midsummer day, lavishing their spotless loveliness upon some unsuspected marsh which has chanced to escape our vigilance.

LEAFY WHITE ORCHIS.

Habenaria dilatata. Orchis Family.

Stem.—Slender; leafy. *Leaves.*—Long and narrow. *Flowers.*—Small; white; with an incurved spur; growing in a slender spike.

The mention of the leafy white orchis recalls to my mind one midsummer morning in a New England swamp, where tangles of sheep-laurel barred the way, branches of dogwood and azalea snapped into my eyes, while patches of fragrant adder's-mouth and fragile *Calopogon* just escaped being trodden underfoot, and exacted, by way of compensation, a breathless but delighted homage at their lovely shrines. Among tall-growing ferns, springing from elastic beds of moss, here I first found the slender, fragrant wands of this pretty orchid.

LARGE ROUND-LEAVED ORCHIS.

Habenaria orbiculata. Orchis Family.

Scape.—Stout, bracted, one to two feet high. *Basal leaves.*—Two, very large, orbicular, spreading flat on the ground, shining above, silvery beneath. *Flowers.*—Greenish-white, spreading in a loose raceme, with linear and slightly wedge-shaped lips and curved, slender spurs about an inch and a half long.

The peculiar charm of this orchid lies in its great flat rounded shining leaves, which spread themselves over the ground in an opulent fashion that seems to accord with the spirit of the deep pine woods where they are most at home. The tall scape with its many greenish-white flowers reaches maturity in July or August.

SWEET PEPPERBUSH. WHITE ALDER.

Clethra alnifolia. Heath Family.

A shrub from three to ten feet high. *Leaves.*—Alternate; ovate; sharply toothed. *Flowers.*—White; growing in clustered finger-like racemes. *Calyx.*—Of five sepals. *Corolla.*—Of five oblong petals. *Stamens.*—Ten; protruding. *Pistil.*—One; three-cleft at apex.

Nearly all our flowering shrubs are past their glory by midsummer, when the fragrant blossoms of the sweet pepperbush begin to exhale their perfume from the cool thickets which line the lanes along the New England coast. There is a certain luxuriance in the vegetation of this part of the country in August which is generally lacking farther inland, where the fairer flowers have passed away, and the country begins to show the effects of the long days of heat and drought. The moisture of the air, and the peculiar character of the soil near the sea, are responsible for the freshness and beauty of many of the late flowers which we find in such a locality.

Clethra is the ancient Greek name for the alder, which this plant somewhat resembles in foliage.

SWEET PEPPERBUSH,—*Clethra alnifolia.*

WILD CUCUMBER.

Echinocystis lobata. Gourd Family.

Stem.—Climbing; nearly smooth; with three-forked tendrils. *Leaves.*—Deeply and sharply five-lobed. *Flowers.*—Numerous; small; greenish-white; unisexual; the staminate ones growing in long racemes, the pistillate ones in small clusters or solitary. *Fruit.*—Fleshy; oval; green; about two inches long; clothed with weak prickles.

This is an ornamental climber which is found bearing its flowers and fruit at the same time. It grows in rich soil along rivers in parts of New England, Pennsylvania, and westward; and is often cultivated in gardens, making an effective arbor-vine. The generic name is from two Greek words which signify *hedgehog* and *bladder*, in reference to the prickly fruit.

COLICROOT. STARGRASS.

Aletris farinosa. Bloodwort Family.

Leaves.—Thin; lance-shaped; in a spreading cluster from the root. *Scape.*—Slender; two to three feet high. *Flowers.*—White; small, growing in a wand-like, spiked raceme. *Perianth.*—Six-cleft at the summit; oblong-tubular. *Stamens.*—Six, orange-colored. *Pistil.*—One, with style three-cleft at apex.

In low wet meadows and in grassy woods the tall white wands of the colicroot shoot above its companion plants. At the first glance one might confuse its long clusters with the twisted spikes of ladies'-tresses, but a closer examination reveals no real likeness between the blossoms of the two plants. Then, too, the flat rosette of lance-shaped leaves from which springs the white wand of flowers is a distinguishing feature of the colicroot.

Its blossoms are wrinkled and rough outside, with a look of being dusted with white meal, whence springs its generic title, the Greek word for "a female slave who grinds corn." They have a faint raspberry-like fragrance. This is really a striking and interesting plant.

PLATE XLV

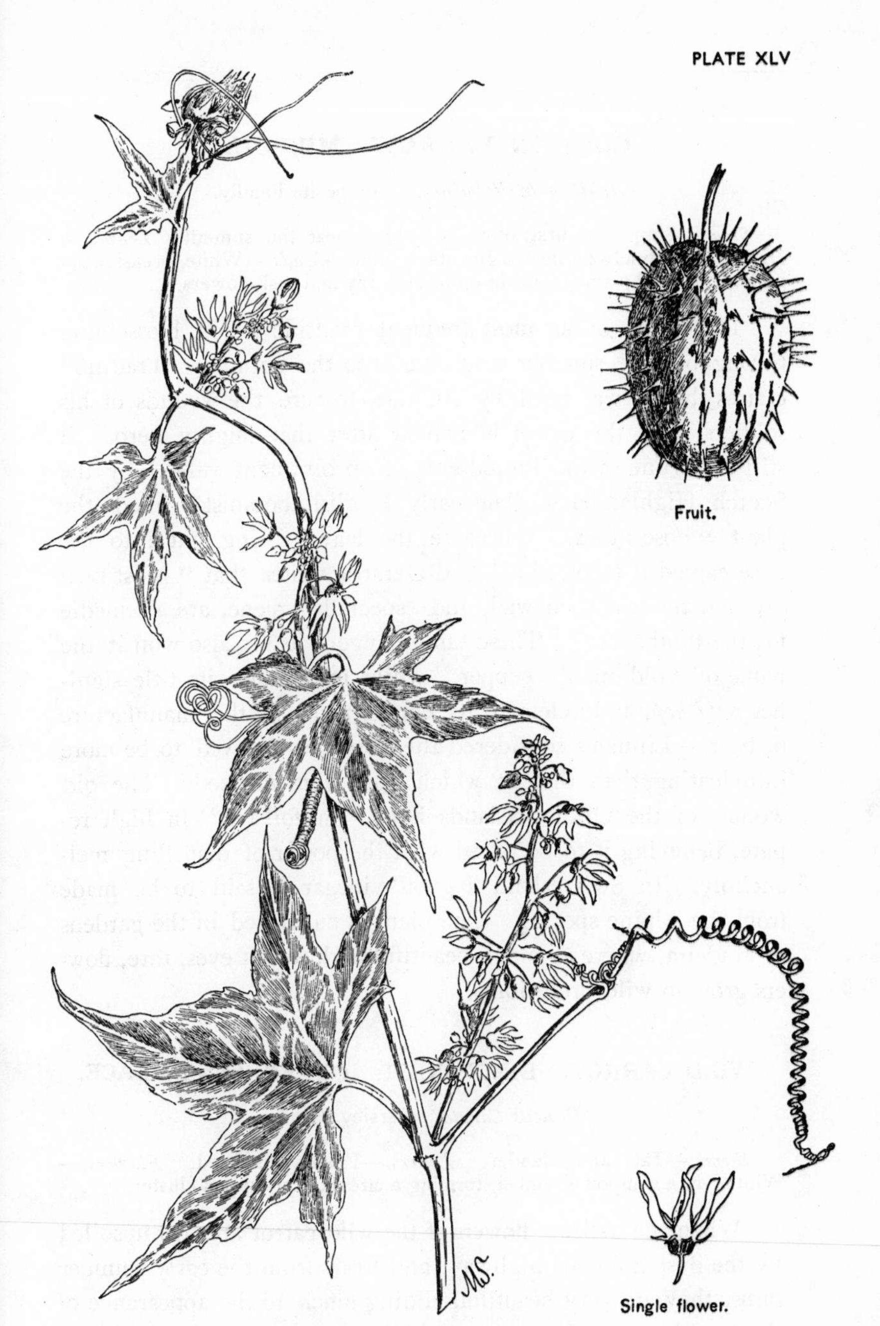

WILD CUCUMBER.—*Echinocystis lobata.*

COMMON YARROW. MILFOIL.

Achillea Millefolium. Composite Family.

Stem.—Simple at first, often branching near the summit. *Leaves.*—Divided into finely toothed segments. *Flower-heads.*—White, occasionally pink; clustered; small; made up of both ray and disk-flowers.

This is one of our most frequent roadside weeds, blossoming throughout the summer and late into the autumn. Tradition claims that it was used by Achilles to cure the wounds of his soldiers, and the genus is named after that mighty hero. It still forms one of the ingredients of an ointment valued by the Scotch Highlanders. The early English botanists called the plant "nose-bleed," "because the leaves being put into the nose caused it to bleed;" and Gerarde writes that "Most men say that the leaves chewed, and especially greene, are a remedie for the toothache." These same pungent leaves also won it the name of "old man's pepper," while in Sweden its title signifies *field hop*, and refers to its employment in the manufacture of beer. Linnæus considered the beer thus brewed to be more intoxicating than that in which hops were utilized. The old women of the Orkney Islands hold "milfoil tea" in high repute, believing it to be gifted with the power of dispelling melancholy. In Switzerland a good vinegar is said to be made from the Alpine species. The plant is cultivated in the gardens of Madeira, where so many beautiful and, in our eyes, rare, flowers grow in wild profusion.

WILD CARROT. BIRD'S-NEST. QUEEN ANNE'S-LACE.

Daucus Carota. Parsley Family.

Stems.—Tall and slender. *Leaves.*—Finely dissected. *Flowers.*—White; in a compound umbel, forming a circular flat-topped cluster.

When the delicate flowers of the wild carrot are still unsoiled by the dust from the highway, and fresh from the early summer rains, they are very beautiful, adding much to the appearance of the roadsides and fields along which they grow so abundantly as

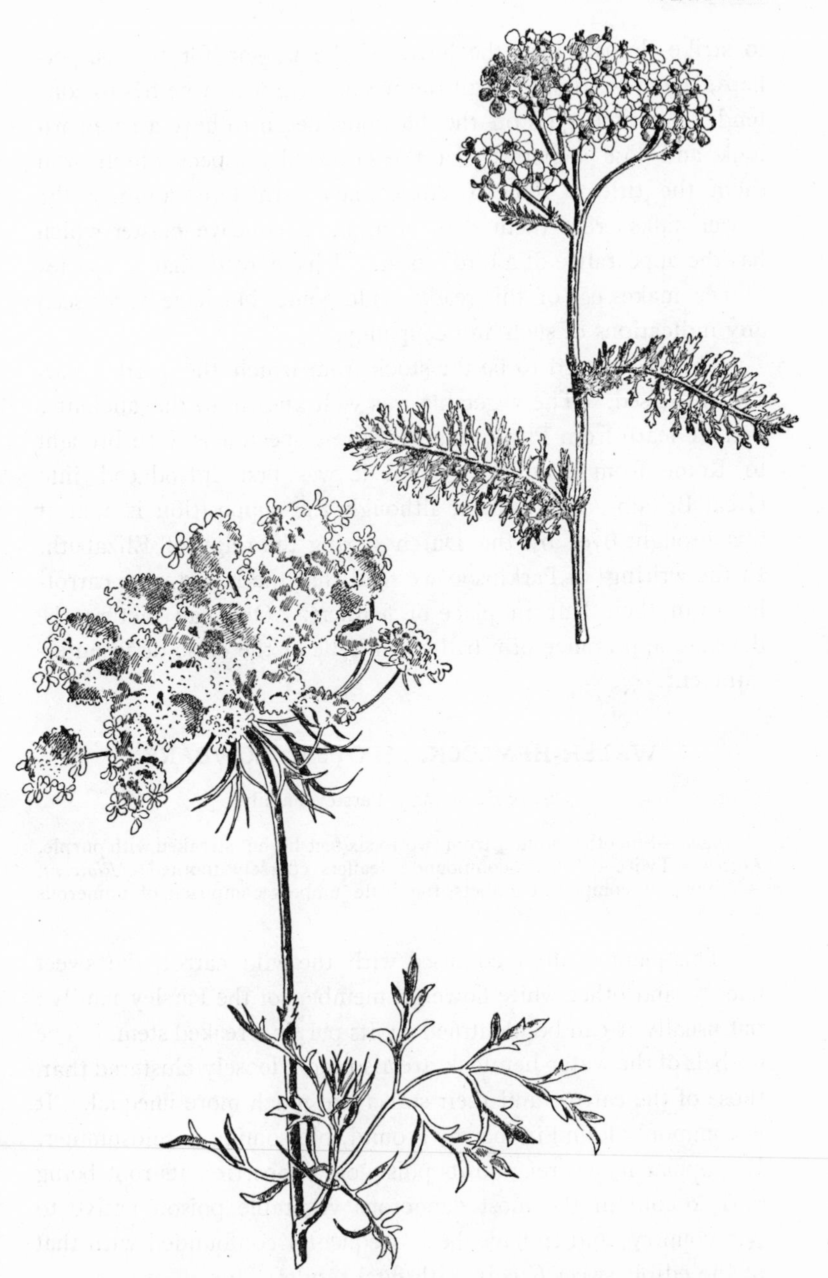

WILD CARROT.—*Daucus Carota.* YARROW.—*Achillea Millefolium.*

to strike despair into the heart of the farmer, for this is, perhaps, the "peskiest" of all the weeds with which he has to contend. As time goes on the blossoms begin to have a careworn look and lose something of the cobwebby aspect which won them the title of Queen Anne's-lace. In late summer the flower-stalks erect themselves, forming a concave cluster which has the appearance of a bird's nest. I have read that a species of bee makes use of this ready-made home, but have never seen any indications of such an occupancy.

This is believed to be the stock from which the garden carrot was raised. The vegetable was well known to the ancients, and we learn from Pliny that the finest specimens were brought to Rome from Candia. When it was first introduced into Great Britain is not known, although the supposition is that it was brought over by the Dutch during the reign of Elizabeth. In the writings of Parkinson we read that the ladies wore carrot-leaves in their hair in place of feathers. One can picture the dejected appearance of a ball-room belle at the close of an entertainment.

WATER-HEMLOCK. SPOTTED COWBANE.

Cicuta maculata. Parsley Family.

Stem.—Smooth; stout; from two to six feet high; streaked with purple. *Leaves.*—Twice or thrice-compound; leaflets coarsely toothed. *Flowers.*—White; in compound umbels, the little umbels composed of numerous flowers.

This plant is often confused with the wild carrot, the sweet Cicely, and other white-flowered members of the Parsley family; but usually it can be identified by its purple-streaked stem. The umbels of the water-hemlock are also more loosely clustered than those of the carrot, and their stalks are much more unequal. It is commonly found in marshy ground, blossoming in midsummer. Its popular names refer to its poisonous properties, its root being said to contain the most dangerous vegetable poison native to our country, and to have been frequently confounded with that of the edible sweet Cicely with fatal results.

COW-PARSNIP.

Heracleum maximum. Parsley Family.

Stem.—Stout, often two inches thick at base, four to eight feet high, ridged, hollow, green. *Leaves.*—The lower large, compound in three divisions, leaflets lobed and sharply notched; on short leaf-stems which are much inflated and clasp the stalk; rank-smelling. *Flowers.*—In spreading, flat-topped clusters, white, with heart-shaped, notched petals; outer flowers larger than inner ones, and with irregular petals.

In swampy places this great vigorous looking plant, which blossoms in early summer, is often a conspicuous, and despite its coarseness, not altogether an unpleasing feature.

PURPLE-STEMMED ANGELICA.

Angelica atropurpurea. Parsley Family.

Stem.—Stout, four to six feet high, smooth, dark purple. *Leaves.*—The lower very large, with inflated leaf-stems; compound in two or three divisions, these divided into lance-shaped or ovate sharply-toothed leaflets. *Flowers.*—White or greenish, in large spreading more or less flat-topped clusters.

In early summer, especially along the banks of streams and rivers, the great purple-stemmed angelica may be found spreading its flat-topped clusters of small greenish flowers. This plant may be distinguished from the cow-parsnip by its purple stem, and by its numerous pinnately-arranged leaflets.

SANICLE. BLACK SNAKEROOT.

Sanicula marilandica. Parsley Family.

Stem.—One to four feet high. *Leaves.*—Three to seven-parted; the divisions sharply cut. *Flowers.*—Greenish-white or yellowish, small; borne in small button-like heads in a two to four-rayed umbel which tops the stem; some perfect, others staminate only. *Fruit.*—Round and prickly.

This plant, which is uninteresting in appearance and hardly suggestive of the Parsley family, blossoms in our wet woods during the summer.

WATER-PARSNIP.

Sium suave. Parsley Family.

Two to six feet high. *Stem.*—Stout. *Leaves.*—Divided into from three to eight pairs of sharply toothed leaflets. *Flowers.*—White, in compound umbels.

This plant grows in water or wet places throughout North America. I have found it in great abundance both in swamps along the coast, and bordering mountain streams far inland. Its Parsley-like flower-clusters at once indicate the family of which it is a member.

MOCK BISHOP'S-WEED.

Ptilimnium capillaceum. Parsley Family.

One or two feet high, occasionally much taller. *Stems.*—Branching. *Leaves.*—Dissected into fine, thread-like divisions. *Flowers.*—White; very small; growing in compound umbels with thread-like bracts.

This plant blossoms all summer in wet meadows, both inland and along the coast; but it is especially common in the salt-marshes near New York City. It probably owes its English name to the fancied resemblance between the bracted flower-clusters and a bishop's cap. Its effect is feathery and delicate.

WATER-HOREHOUND.

Lycopus americanus. Mint Family.

Stem.—Erect; one to three feet high; acutely four-angled *Leaves*—Opposite; oblong or lance-shaped; pointed; irregularly toothed or deeply parted, or some of the upper merely wavy-margined. *Flowers.*—Small; mostly white; in close whorls in the axils of the leaves. *Calyx-teeth.*—Usually five; with short, sharp points. *Corolla.*—Bell-shaped; nearly equally four-lobed. *Stamens.*—Four (the upper pair slender and conspicuous but sterile). *Pistil.*—One, with a two-lobed style. *Ovary.*—Deeply four-lobed; splitting when ripe into four little nutlets.

This plant abounds in wet places, flowering throughout the summer.

BUGLEWEED.

Lycopus virginicus. Mint Family.

Stem.—Six inches to two feet high; *obtusely four-angled.* *Flowers.*—Much as in above. *Calyx-teeth.*—Usually only four; barely pointed.

The bugleweed is found in wet places across the continent.

WHITE VERVAIN.

Verbena urticifolia. Verbena Family.

Three to five feet high. *Leaves.*—Oval; coarsely toothed. *Flowers.*—Small; white; in slender spikes.

It almost excites one's incredulity to be told that this uninteresting-looking plant, which grows rankly along the highways, is an importation from the tropics, yet for this statement the botany is responsible.

TRAVELLER'S-JOY. VIRGIN'S-BOWER.

Clematis virginiana. Crowfoot Family.

Stem.—Climbing; somewhat woody. *Leaves.*—Opposite; three-divided. *Flowers.*—Whitish; in clusters; unisexual. *Calyx.*—Of four petal-like sepals. *Corolla.*—None. *Stamens and Pistils.*—Indefinite in number; occurring on different plants.

In July and August this beautiful plant, covered with its white blossoms and clambering over the shrubs which border the country lanes, makes indeed a fitting bower for any maid or traveller who may chance to be seeking shelter. Later in the year the seeds with their silvery plumes give a feathery effect, which is very striking.

This graceful climber works its way by means of its bending or clasping leaf-stalks. Darwin has made interesting experiments regarding the movements of the young shoots of the *Clematis.* He discovered that, "one revolved, describing a broad oval, in five hours, thirty minutes; and another in six hours, twelve minutes; they follow the course of the sun."

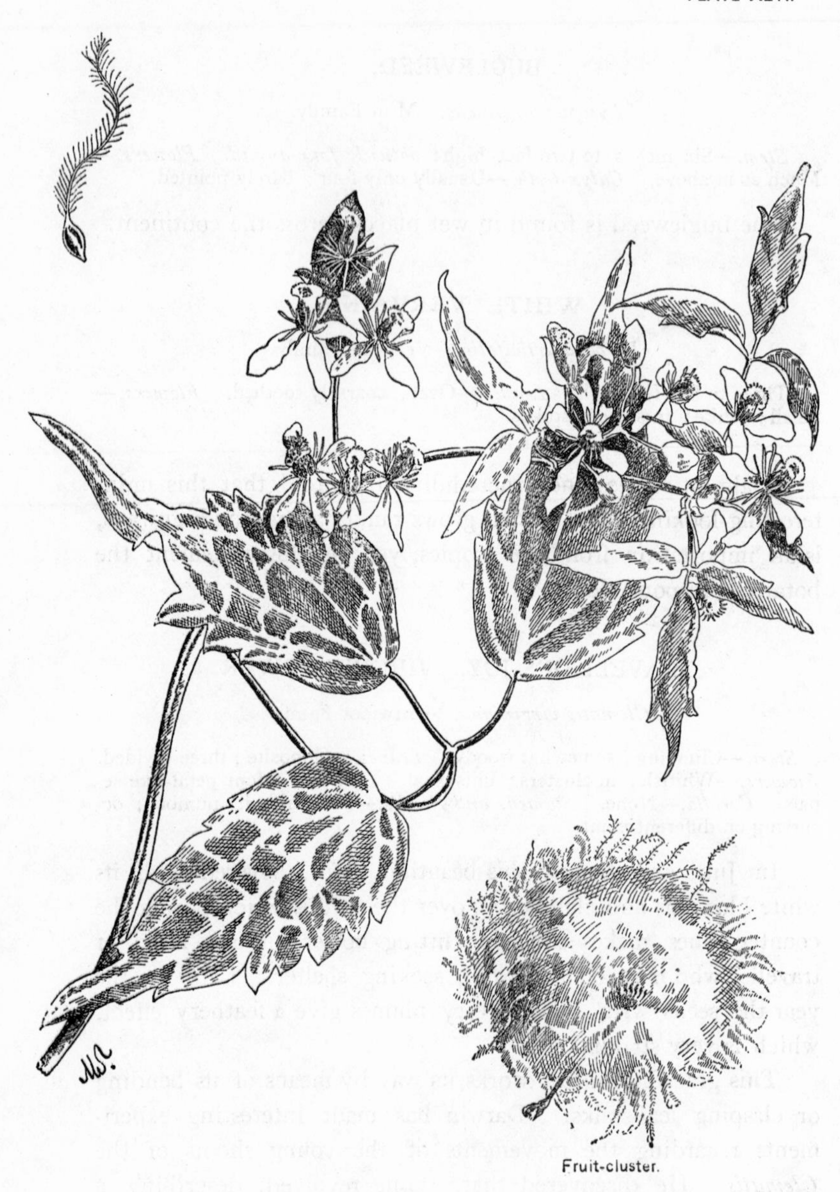

VIRGIN'S-BOWER.—*Clematis virginiana.*

GROUND-CHERRY.

Physalis virginiana. Nightshade Family.

A strong-scented, low, much-branched and spreading herb. *Leaves.*—Somewhat oblong or heart-shaped; wavy-toothed. *Flowers.*—Greenish or yellowish-white; solitary on nodding flower-stalks. *Calyx.*—Five-cleft; enlarging and much inflated in fruit, loosely enclosing the berry. *Corolla.*—Between wheel-shaped and funnel-form. *Stamens.*—Five; erect; with yellow anthers. *Pistil.*—One. *Fruit.*—A green or yellow edible berry which is loosely enveloped in the much-inflated calyx.

We find the ground-cherry in light sandy soil, and are more apt to notice the loosely enveloped berry of the late year than the rather inconspicuous flowers which appear in summer.

TURTLEHEAD.

Chelone glabra. Figwort Family.

One to seven feet high. *Stem.*—Smooth; upright; branching. *Leaves.*—Opposite; lance-shaped; toothed. *Flowers.*—White or pinkish; growing in a spike or close cluster. *Calyx.*—Of five sepals. *Corolla.*—Two-lipped; the upper lip broad and arched, notched at the apex; lower lip three-lobed at the apex, woolly bearded in the throat. *Stamens.*—Four perfect ones, with woolly filaments and very woolly, heart-shaped anthers, and one small sterile one. *Pistil.*—One.

It seems to have been my fate to find the flowers which the botany relegates to "dry, sandy soil" flourishing luxuriantly in marshes; and to encounter the flowers which by right belong to "wet woods" flaunting themselves in sunny meadows. This cannot be attributed to the natural depravity of inanimate objects, for what is more full of life than the flowers?—and no one would believe in their depravity except perhaps the amateur-botanist who is endeavoring to master the different species of golden-rods and asters. Therefore it is pleasant to record that I do not remember ever having met a turtlehead, which is assigned by the botany to "wet places," which had not gotten as close to a stream or a marsh or a moist ditch as it well could without actually wetting its feet. The flowers of this plant are more odd and striking than pretty. Their appearance is such

TURTLEHEAD.—*Chelone glabra.*

that their common name seems fairly appropriate. I have heard unbotanical people call them "white closed gentians."

COMMON DODDER. LOVE-VINE.

Cuscuta Gronovii. Convolvulus Family.

Stems.—Yellow or reddish; thread-like; twining; leafless. *Flowers*.—White; in close clusters. *Calyx*.—Five-cleft. *Corolla*.—With five spreading lobes. *Stamens*.—Five. *Pistil*.—One, with two styles.

Late in the summer perhaps we are tempted deep into some thicket by the jasmine-scented heads of the buttonbush or the fragrant spikes of the *Clethra*, and note for the first time the tangled golden threads and close white flower-clusters of the dodder. If we try to trace to their source these twisted stems, which the Creoles know as "angels' hair," we discover that they are fastened to the bark of the shrub or plant about which they are twining by means of small suckers; but nowhere can we find any connection with the earth, all their nourishment being extracted from the plant to which they are adhering. Originally this curious herb sprang from the ground which succored it until it succeeded in attaching itself to some plant; having accomplished this it severed all connection with mother-earth by the withering away or snapping off of the stem below.

The flax-dodder, *C. Epilinum*, is a very injurious plant in European flax-fields. It has been sparingly introduced into this country with flax-seed.

THORN-APPLE. JIMSONWEED.

Datura Stramonium. Nightshade Family.

Stem.— Smooth and branching. *Leaves*.—Ovate; wavy toothed or angled. *Flowers*.—White; large and showy; on short flower-stalks from the forks of the branching stem. *Calyx*.—Five-toothed. *Corolla*.—Funnel-form; the border five-toothed. *Stamens*.—Five. *Pistils*.—One. *Fruit*.—Green; globular; prickly.

The showy white flowers of the thorn-apple are found in waste places during the summer and autumn, a heap of rubbish forming their usual unattractive background. The plant is a rank, ill-scented one, which was introduced into our country from Asia. It was so associated with civilization as to be called the "white man's plant" by the Indians.

Its purple-flowered relative, *D. Tatula*, is an emigrant from the tropics. This genus possesses narcotic-poisonous properties.

WHITE ASTERS.

Aster. Composite Family.

Flower-heads.—Composed of white or sometimes purplish ray-flowers with a centre of yellow disk-flowers.

While we have far fewer species of white than of blue or purple asters, some of these few are so abundant in individuals as to hold their own fairly well against their bright-hued rivals.

The smooth, slender, somewhat zigzag stem of the white wood aster, *A. corymbosus*,* is green or purple, with reddish streaks. Its leaves are thin, the lower ones large, heart-shaped, and somewhat coarsely toothed, the uppermost small, oval, and tapering. The white flower-heads are borne in loose leafy clusters. The plant is found blossoming during the month of August in open woods and along the shaded roadsides.

Bordering the dry fields at this same season and later, we notice the spreading wand-like branches, thickly covered on their upper sides with tiny flower-heads, as with snow-flakes, of the white heath aster, *A. ericoides*. This plant is easily distinguished by its small rigid linear leaves. The lower leaves, however, are much larger and somewhat wedge-shaped.

The pointed-leaved aster, *A. acuminatus*, is easily identified by means of the oblong-pointed leaves, which are crowded so close to the top of the stem as to give often the effect of being whorled just below the white, or sometime purplish, flower-clusters. This is peculiarly a wood-loving plant.

A. umbellatus is the tall white aster of the swamps and moist thickets. It sometimes reaches a height of seven feet, and can

* Obsolete scientific name.

be identified by its long tapering leaves and large, flat flower-clusters.

A beautiful and abundant seaside species is *A. multiflorus*.* Its small flower-heads are closely crowded on the low, bushy, spreading branches; its leaves are narrow, rigid, crowded, and somewhat hoary. The whole effect of the plant is heath-like; it also somewhat suggests an evergreen.

MILD WATER-PEPPER.

Polygonum hydropiperoides. Buckwheat Family.

Stem.—One to three feet high; smooth; branching. *Leaves.*—Alternate; narrowly lance-shaped or oblong. *Flowers.*—White or flesh-color; small; growing in erect, slender spikes. *Calyx.*—Five-parted. *Corolla.*—None. *Stamens.*—Eight. *Pistil.*—One, usually with three styles.

These rather inconspicuous but very common flowers are found in moist places and shallow water.

The common knotweed, *P. aviculare*, which grows in such abundance in country door-yards and waste places, has slender, often prostrate, stems, and small greenish flowers, which are clustered in the axils of the leaves or spiked at the termination of the stems. This is perhaps the "hindering knotgrass" to which Shakespeare refers in the "Midsummer Night's Dream," so terming it, not on account of its knotted trailing stems, but because of the belief that it would hinder the growth of a child. In Beaumont and Fletcher's "Coxcomb" the same superstition is indicated:

"We want a boy
Kept under for a year with milk and knotgrass."

It is said that many birds are nourished by the seeds of this plant.

* Now generally *A. ericoides*.

CLIMBING FALSE BUCKWHEAT.

Polygonum scandens. Buckwheat Family.

Stem.—Smooth; twining, and climbing over bushes; eight to twelve feet high. *Leaves.*—Heart or arrow shaped; pointed; alternate. *Flowers.*—Greenish or pinkish; in racemes. *Calyx.*—Five-parted; with colored margins. *Corolla.*—None. *Stamens.*—Usually eight. *Pistil.*—One, with three styles. *Seed-vessel.*—Green; three-angled; winged; conspicuous in autumn.

In early summer this plant, which clambers so perseveringly over the moist thickets which line our country lanes, is comparatively inconspicuous. The racemes of small greenish flowers are not likely to attract one's attention, and it is late summer or autumn before the thick clusters of greenish fruit, composed of the winged seed-vessels, arrest one's notice. At this time the vine is very beautiful and striking, and one wonders that it could have escaped detection in the earlier year.

BONESET. THOROUGHWORT.

Eupatorium perfoliatum. Composite Family.

Stem.—Stout and hairy; two to four feet high. *Leaves.*—Opposite; widely spreading; lance-shaped; united at the base around the stem. *Flower-heads.*—Dull white; small; composed entirely of tubular blossoms borne in large clusters.

To one whose childhood was passed in the country some fifty years ago the name or sight of this plant is fraught with unpleasant memories. The attic or wood-shed was hung with bunches of the dried herb, which served as so many grewsome warnings against wet feet, or any over-exposure which might result in cold or malaria. A certain Nemesis, in the shape of a nauseous draught which was poured down the throat under the name of "boneset tea," attended such a catastrophe. The Indians first discovered its virtues, and named the plant ague-weed. Possibly this is one of the few herbs whose efficacy has not been overrated. Dr. Millspaugh says: "It is prominently adapted

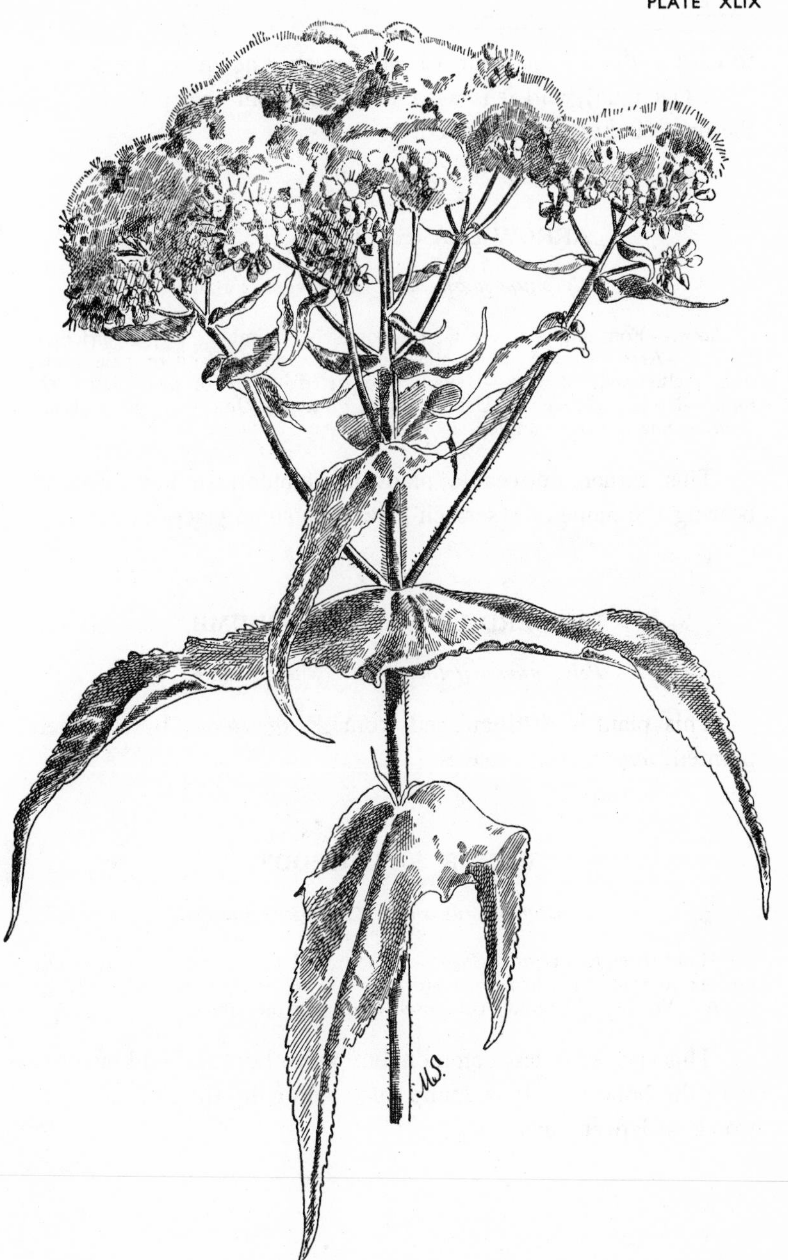

BONESET.—*Eupatorium perfoliatum.*

to cure a disease peculiar to the South, known as break-bone fever (Dengue), and it is without doubt from this property that the name boneset was derived."

ARROW-LEAVED TEARTHUMB.

Polygonum sagittatum. Buckwheat Family.

Stem.—Four-angled; erect, or somewhat climbing by its prickles. *Leaves.*—Arrow-shaped; short-stemmed. *Flowers.*—White or pale pink; small; clustered. *Calyx.*—Usually five-parted; white or pale pink. *Corolla.*—None. *Stamens.*—Usually eight. *Pistil.*—One, with three styles. *Fruit.*—Sharply three-angled.

This rather noticeable plant is common in low grounds, bearing the name of "scratch-grass" in some places.

HALBERD-LEAVED TEARTHUMB.

Polygonum arifolium. Buckwheat Family.

This plant is distinguished from *P. sagittatum* by its taper-pointed, *long-stemmed* leaves.

WHITE SNAKEROOT.

Eupatorium rugosum. Composite Family.

About three feet high. *Stem.*—Smooth and branching. *Leaves.*—Opposite; long-stalked; broadly ovate; coarsely and sharply toothed. *Flower-heads.*—White; clustered; composed of tubular blossoms.

This species is less common but more beautiful and effective than the boneset. It is found blossoming in the rich northern woods of late summer.

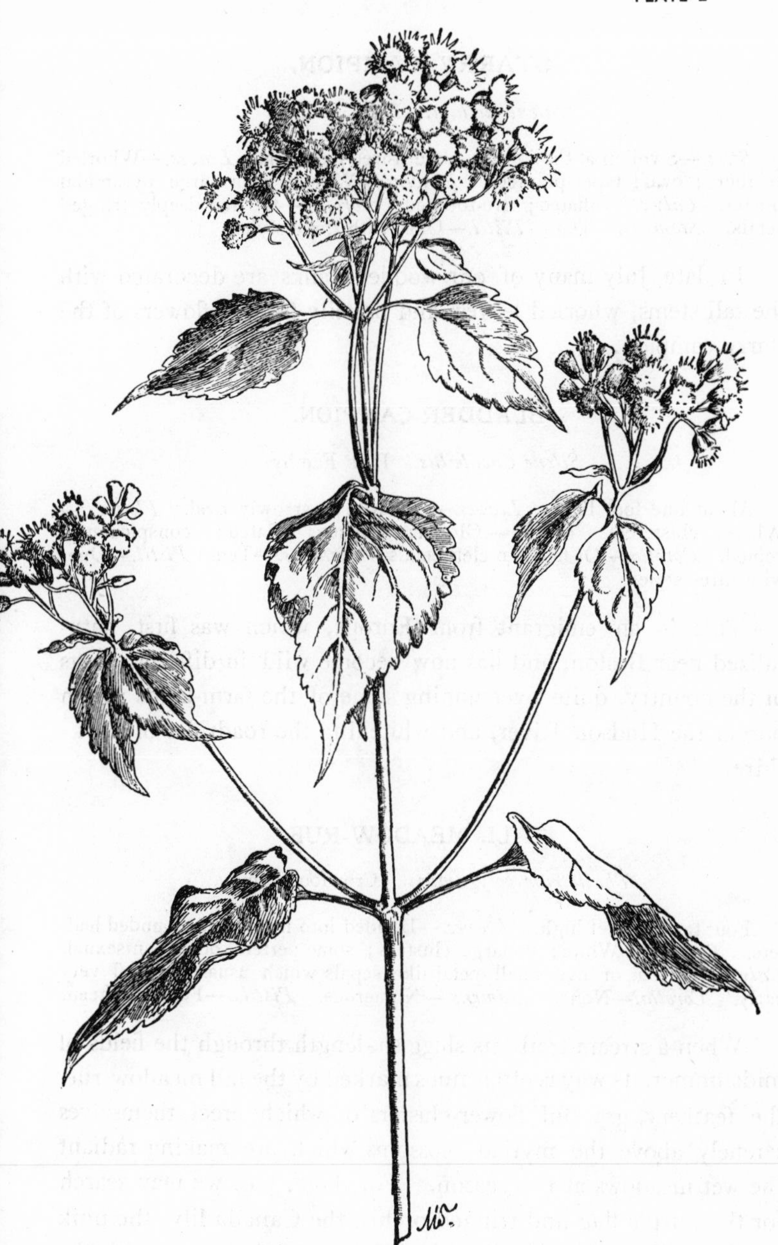

WHITE SNAKEROOT.—*Eupatorium rugosum.*

STARRY CAMPION.

Silene stellata. Pink Family.

Stem.—Swollen at the joints; about three feet high. *Leaves.*—Whorled in fours; oval; taper-pointed. *Flowers.*—White; in a large pyramidal cluster. *Calyx.*—Inflated; five-toothed. *Corolla.*—Of five deeply fringed petals. *Stamens.*—Ten. *Pistil.*—One, with three styles.

In late July many of our wooded banks are decorated with the tall stems, whorled leaves, and prettily fringed flowers of the starry campion.

BLADDER-CAMPION.

Silene Cucubalus. Pink Family.

About one foot high. *Leaves.*—Opposite; narrowly oval. *Flowers.*—White; clustered. *Calyx.*—Globular; much inflated; conspicuously veined. *Corolla.*—Of five two-cleft petals. *Stamens.*—Ten. *Pistil.*—One, with three styles.

This is an emigrant from Europe, which was first naturalized near Boston, and has now become wild in different parts of the country, quite overrunning some of the farm-lands which border the Hudson River, and whitening the roadsides of Berkshire.

TALL MEADOW-RUE.

Thalictrum polygamum. Crowfoot Family.

Four to eight feet high. *Leaves.*—Divided into many firm, rounded leaflets. *Flowers.*—White; in large clusters; some perfect, others unisexual. *Calyx.*—Of four or five small petal-like sepals which usually fall off very early. *Corolla.*—None. *Stamens.*—Numerous. *Pistils.*—Four to fifteen.

When a stream trails its sluggish length through the fields of midsummer, its way is oftentimes marked by the tall meadow-rue, the feathery, graceful flower-clusters of which erect themselves serenely above the myriad blossoms which are making radiant the wet meadows at this season. For, here, too, we may search for the purple flag and fringed orchis, the Canada lily, the pink swamp-milkweed, each charming in its way, but none with the

TALL MEADOW-RUE.—*Thalictrum polygamum.*

cool chaste beauty of the meadow-rue. The staminate flowers of this plant are especially delicate and feathery.

LADIES'-TRESSES.

Spiranthes cernua. Orchis Family.

Stem.—Leafy below, leafy-bracted above; six to twenty inches high. *Leaves.*—Linear-lance-shaped; the lowest elongated. *Flowers.*—White; fragrant; the lips wavy or crisped; growing in slender spikes.

This pretty little orchid is found in great abundance in September and October. The botany relegates it to "wet places," but I have seen dry upland pastures as well as low-lying swamps profusely flecked with its slender, fragrant spikes. The braided appearance of these spikes would easily account for the popular name of ladies'-tresses; but we learn that the plant's English name was formerly "ladies' *traces*," from a fancied resemblance between its twisted clusters and the lacings which played so important a part in the feminine toilet. I am told that in parts of New England the country people have christened the plant "wild hyacinth."

The flowers of *S. gracilis* are very small, and grow in a much more slender, one-sided spike than those of *S. cernua.* They are found in the dry woods and along the sandy hill-sides from July onward.

DEVIL'S-BIT. BLAZING-STAR.

Chamaelirium luteum. Lily Family.

One to four feet high, the staminate plant taller. *Leaves.*—The lower wedge-shaped, obtuse, tapering into a petiole; the upper, linear, pointed. *Flowers.*—White. The pistillate and staminate growing on different plants, in a long wand-like, spiked raceme. *Perianth.*—Of six white segments; staminate flowers with six stamens, pistillate flowers with one pistil having three short styles.

From May to July the oft-times nodding staminate clusters, and the stiff erect pistillate spikes of the devil's-bit may be found in many of our wet meadows, from Massachusetts to Florida.

LADIES'-TRESSES.—*Spiranthes cernua.*

FRAGRANT WATER-LILY.

Nymphaea odorata. Water-lily Family.

Leaves.—Rounded; somewhat heart-shaped; floating on the surface of the water. *Flowers.*—Large; white or sometimes pink; fragrant. *Calyx.*—Of four sepals which are green without. *Corolla.*—Of many petals. *Stamens.*—Indefinite in number. *Pistil.*—With a many-celled ovary whose summit is tipped with a globular projection around which are the radiating stigmas.

This exquisite flower calls for little description. Many of us are so fortunate as to hold in our memories golden mornings devoted to its quest. We can hardly take the shortest railway journey in summer without passing some shadowy pool whose greatest adornment is this spotless and queenly blossom. The breath of the lily-pond is brought even into the heart of our cities, where children peddle clusters of the long-stemmed fragrant flowers about the streets.

In the water-lily may be seen an example of so-called *plant-metamorphosis.* The petals appear to pass gradually into stamens, it being difficult to decide where the petals end and the stamens begin. But whether stamens are transformed petals, or petals transformed stamens, seems to be a mooted question. In Gray we read, "Petals numerous, in many series, the innermost gradually passing into stamens;" while Mr. Grant Allen writes: "Petals are in all probability enlarged and flattened stamens, which have been set apart for the work of attracting insects," and goes on to say, "Flowers can and do exist without petals, . . . but no flower can possibly exist without stamens, which are one of the two essential reproductive organs in the plant." From this he argues that it is more rational to consider a petal a transformed stamen than *vice versa.* To go further into the subject here would be impossible, but a careful study of the water-lily is likely to excite one's curiosity in the matter.

ARROWHEAD.

Sagittaria latifolia. Water-plantain Family.

Scape.—A few inches to several feet high. *Leaves.*—Arrow-shaped. *Flowers.*—White; unisexual; in whorls of three on the leafless scape. *Calyx.*—Of three sepals. *Corolla.*—Of three white, rounded petals. *Stamens and Pistils.*—Indefinite in number; occurring in different flowers; the lower whorls of flowers usually being pistillate, the upper staminate.

Among our water-flowers none are more delicately lovely than those of the arrowhead. Fortunately the ugly and inconspicuous female flowers grow on the lower whorls, while the male ones, with their snowy petals and golden centres, are arranged about the upper part of the scape, where the eye first falls. It is a pleasure to chance upon a slow stream whose margins are bordered with these fragile blossoms and bright, arrow-shaped leaves.

WATER-PLANTAIN.

Alisma triviale. Water-plantain Family.

Scape.—One to three feet high; bearing the flowers in whorled, panicled branches. *Leaves.*—From the root; oblong, lance-shaped or linear, mostly rounded or heart-shaped at base. *Flowers.*—White or pale pink; small; in large, loose clusters which branch from the scape. *Calyx.*—Of three sepals. *Corolla.*—Of three petals. *Stamens.*—Usually six. *Pistils.*—Many, on a flattened receptacle.

The water-plantain is nearly related to the arrowhead, and is often found blossoming with it in marshy places or shallow water.

GROUNDSEL-TREE.

Baccharis halimifolia. Composite Family.

A shrub from six to twelve feet high. *Leaves.*—Somewhat ovate and wedge-shaped; coarsely toothed, or the upper entire. *Flower-heads.*—Whitish or yellowish; composed of unisexual tubular flowers; the stamens and pistils occurring on different plants.

Some October day, as we pick our way through the salt marshes which lie back of the beach, we may spy in the distance

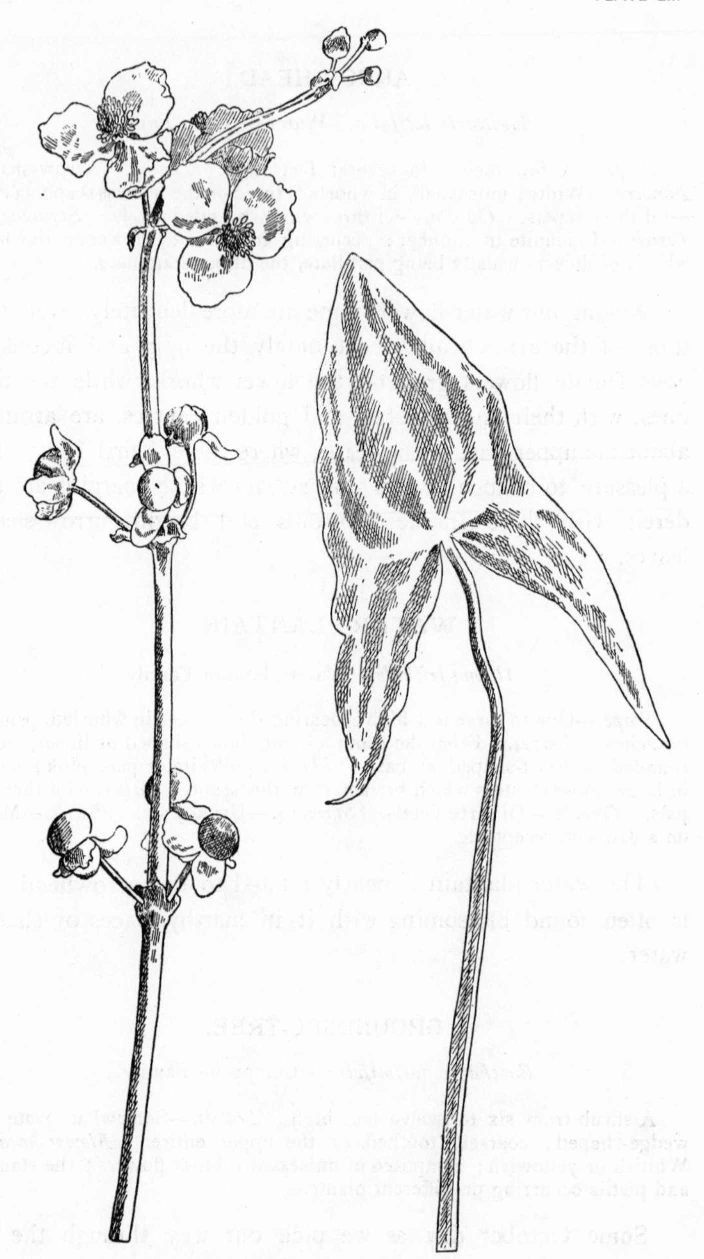

ARROWHEAD.—*Sagittaria latifolia.*

a thicket which looks as though composed of such white-flowered shrubs as belong to June. Hastening to the spot we discover that the silky-tufted seeds of the female groundsel-tree are responsible for our surprise. The shrub is much more noticeable and effective at this season than when—a few weeks previous—it was covered with its small white or yellowish flower-heads.

GRASS-OF-PARNASSUS.

Parnassia glauca. Saxifrage Family.

Stem.—Scape-like; nine inches to two feet high; with usually one small rounded leaf clasping it below; bearing at its summit a single flower. *Leaves.*—Thickish; rounded; often heart-shaped; from the root. *Flower.* -White or cream-color; veiny. *Calyx.*—Of five slightly united sepals. *Corolla.*—Of five veiny petals. *True Stamens.*—Five; alternate with the petals, and with clusters of sterile gland-tipped filaments. *Pistil.*—One, with four stigmas.

Gerarde indignantly declares that this plant has been described by blind men, not "such as are blinde in their eyes, but in their understandings, for if this plant be a kind of grasse then may the Butter-burre or Colte's-foote be reckoned for grasses—as also all other plants whatsoever." But if it covered Parnassus with its delicate veiny blossoms as abundantly as it does some moist New England meadows each autumn, the ancients may have reasoned that a plant almost as common as grass must somehow partake of its nature. The slender-stemmed creamy flowers are never seen to better advantage than when disputing with the fringed gentian the possession of some luxurious swamp.

PEARLY EVERLASTING.

Anaphalis margaritacea. Composite Family.

Stem.—Erect; one or two feet high. *Leaves.*—Broadly linear to lance-shaped. *Flower-heads.*—Composed entirely of tubular flowers with very numerous white involucral scales.

This species is common throughout our northern woods and pastures, blossoming in August. Thoreau writes of it in Sep-

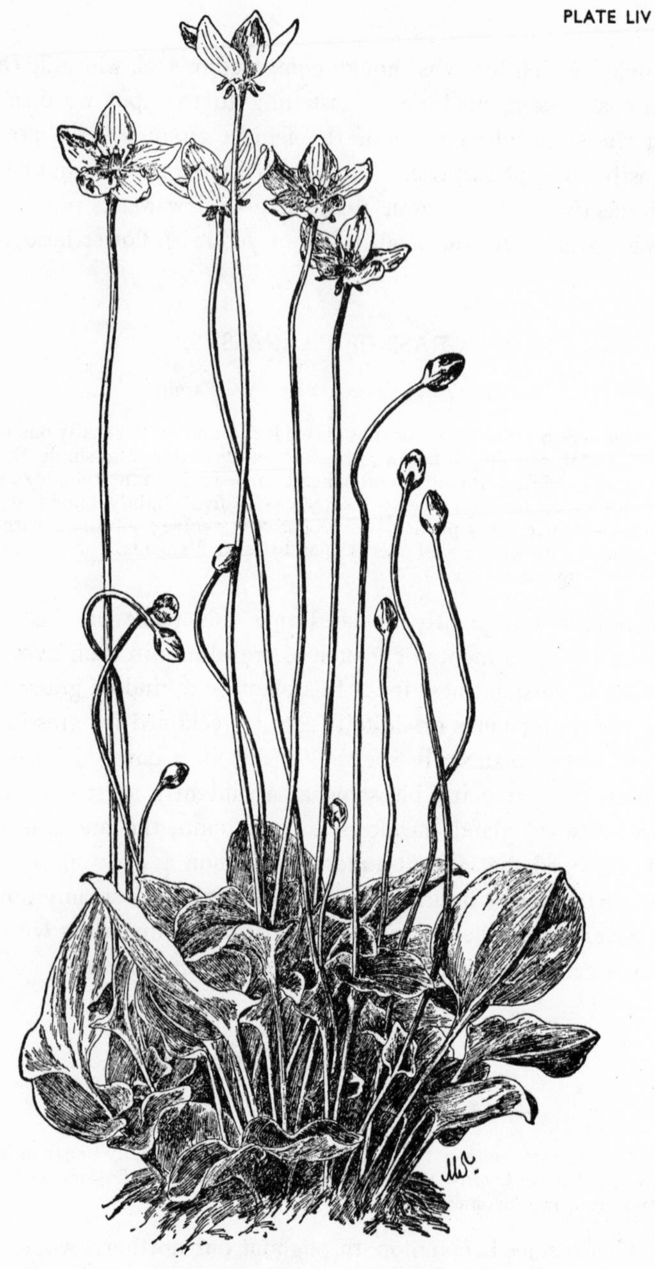

GRASS-OF-PARNASSUS.—*Parnassia glauca.*

tember: "The pearly everlasting is an interesting white at present. Though the stems and leaves are still green, it is dry and unwithering, like an artificial flower; its white, flexuous stem and branches, too, like wire wound with cotton. Neither is there any scent to betray it. Its amaranthine quality is instead of high color. Its very brown centre now affects me as a fresh and original color. It monopolizes small circles in the midst of sweet fern, perchance, on a dry hill-side."

EVERLASTING. CUDWEED.

Gnaphalium obtusifolium. Composite Family.

Stem.—Erect; one to three feet high; woolly. *Leaves.*—Lance-shaped. *Flower-heads.*—Yellowish-white; clustered at the summit of the branches, composed of many tubular flowers.

This is the "fragrant life-everlasting," as Thoreau calls it, of late summer. It abounds in rocky pastures and throughout the somewhat open woods.

II

GREEN

INDIAN POKE. FALSE HELLEBORE.

Veratrum viride. Lily Family.

Root.—Poisonous; coarse and fibrous. *Stem.*—Stout; two to seven feet high; very leafy to the top. *Leaves.*—Broadly oval; pointed; clasping. *Flowers.*—Dull greenish; clustered. *Perianth.*—Of six spreading sepals. *Stamens.*—Six. *Pistil.*—One, with three styles.

When we go to the swampy woods in March or April we notice an array of green, solid-looking spears which have just appeared above the ground. If we handle one of these we are impressed with its firmness and rigidity. When the increasing warmth and sunshine have tempted the veiny, many-plaited leaves of the false hellebore to unfold themselves it is difficult to realize that they composed that sturdy tool which so effectively tunnelled its way upward to the earth's surface. The tall stems and large bright leaves of this plant are very noticeable in the early year, forming conspicuous masses of foliage while the trees and shrubs are still almost leafless. The dingy flowers which appear in June rarely attract attention, unless by their lack of beauty.

CARRION-FLOWER. CATBRIER.

Smilax herbacea. Lily Family.

Stem.—Climbing, three to fifteen feet high. *Leaves.*—Ovate, or rounded heart-shaped, or abruptly cut off at base. *Flowers.*—Greenish or yellowish; small; clustered; unisexual. *Perianth.*—Six-parted. *Stamens.*—Six. *Pistil.*—One, with three spreading stigmas (Stamens and pistils occurring on different plants.) *Fruit.*—A bluish-black berry.

One whiff of the foul breath of the carrion-flower suffices for its identification. Thoreau likens its odor to that of "a dead

PLATE LV

CARRION-FLOWER.—*Smilax herbacea.*

rat in the wall." It seems unfortunate that this strikingly handsome plant, which clambers so ornamentally over the luxuriant thickets which border our lanes and streams, should be so handicapped each June. Happily with the disappearance of the blossoms, it takes its place as one of the most attractive of our climbers.

The common greenbrier, *S. rotundifolia*, is a near relation which is easily distinguished by its prickly stem.

The dark berries and deeply tinted leaves of this genus add greatly to the glorious autumnal display along our roadsides and in the woods and meadows.

POISON SUMAC.

Rhus Vernix. Cashew Family.

A shrub from six to eighteen feet high. *Leaves.*—Divided into seven to thirteen oblong leaflets. *Flowers.*—Greenish or yellowish-white ; in loose axillary clusters ; some perfect, others unisexual. *Fruit.*—Whitish or dun-colored ; small, globular.

The poison sumac infests swampy places and flowers in June. In early summer it can be distinguished from the harmless members of the family by the *slender flower-clusters* which grow from *the axils of the leaves*, those of the *innocent sumacs* being borne in *pyramidal, terminal clusters.* In the later year the fruits of the respective shrubs are, of course, similarly situated, but, to accentuate the distinction, they differ in color ; that of the poison sumac being *whitish* or *dun-colored*, while that of the other is *crimson.*

STAGHORN-SUMAC.

Rhus typhina. Cashew Family.

A shrub or tree from ten to thirty feet high. *Leaves.*—Divided into eleven to thirty-one somewhat lance-shaped, toothed leaflets. *Flowers.*—Greenish or yellowish-white ; in upright terminal clusters ; some perfect, others unisexual ; appearing in June. *Fruit.*—Crimson ; small ; globular ; hairy.

This is the common sumac which illuminates our hill-sides every autumn with masses of flame-like color. Many of us would

PLATE LVI

POISON IVY.—*Rhus radicans.*

like to decorate our homes with its brilliant sprays, but are deterred from handling them by the fear of being poisoned, not knowing that one glance at the crimson fruit-plumes should reassure us, as the poisonous sumacs are white-fruited. These tossing pyramidal fruit-clusters at first appear to explain the common title of staghorn-sumac. It is not till the foliage has disappeared, and the forked branches are displayed in all their nakedness, that we feel that these must be the feature in which the common name originated.

POISON IVY.

Rhus radicans. Cashew Family.

A shrub which usually climbs by means of rootlets over rocks, walls, and trees; sometimes low and erect. *Leaves.*—Divided into three somewhat four-sided pointed leaflets. *Flowers.*—Greenish or yellowish-white; small; some perfect, others unisexual; in loose clusters in the axils of the leaves in June. *Fruit.*—Small; globular; somewhat berry-like; dun-colored; clustered.

This much-dreaded plant is often confused with the beautiful Virginia creeper, occasionally to the ruthless destruction of the latter. Generally the two can be distinguished by the three-divided leaves of the poison ivy, the leaves of the Virginia creeper usually being five-divided. In the late year the whitish fruit of the ivy easily identifies it, the berries of the creeper being blackish. The poison ivy is reputed to be especially harmful during the night, or at any time in early summer when the sun is not shining upon it.

VIRGINIA CREEPER. WOODBINE.

Parthenocissus quinquefolia. Vine Family.

A woody vine, climbing by means of disk-bearing tendrils, and also by rootlets. *Leaves.*—Usually divided into five leaflets. *Flowers.*—Greenish; small; clustered; appearing in July. *Fruit.*—A small blackish berry in October.

Surely in autumn, if not always, this is the most beautiful of our native climbers. At that season its blood-like sprays are outlined against the dark evergreens about which they delight to twine, showing that marvellous discrimination in background which so constantly excites our admiration in nature. The Virginia creeper is extensively cultivated in Europe. Even in Venice, that sea-city where one so little anticipates any reminders of home woods and meadows, many a dim canal mirrors in October some crumbling wall or graceful trellis aglow with its vivid beauty.

GREEN ORCHIS.

Habenaria clavellata.

RAGGED ORCHIS.

Habenaria lacera. Orchis Family.

Leaves.—Oblong or lance-shaped. *Flowers.*—Greenish or yellowish-white; growing in a spike.

These two orchids are found in wet, boggy places during the earlier summer, the green antedating the ragged orchis by a week or more. The lip of the ragged is three-parted, the divisions being deeply fringed, giving what is called in Sweet's "British Flower-Garden" an "elegantly jagged appearance." The lip of the green orchis is furnished with a tooth on each side and a strong protuberance in the middle. So far as superficial beauty and conspicuousness are concerned these flowers do scant justice to the brilliant family to which they belong, and equally excite the scornful exclamation, "You call *that* an orchid!" when brought home for analysis or preservation.

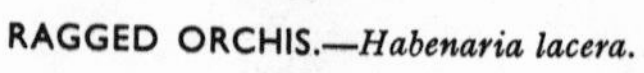

RAGGED ORCHIS.—*Habenaria lacera.*

GREEN-FLOWERED MILKWEED.

Asclepias verticillata. Milkweed Family.

Stem.—Slender; very leafy to the summit. *Leaves.*—Very narrow; from three to six in a whorl. *Flowers.*—Greenish-white; in small clusters at the summit and along the sides of the stem. *Fruit.*—Two erect pods, one often stunted.

This species is one commonly found on dry uplands, especially southward, with flowers resembling in structure those of the other milkweeds.

BLUE COHOSH.

Caulophyllum thalictroides. Barberry Family.

Stems.—One to two and a half feet high. *Leaf.*—Large; divided into many-lobed leaflets; often a smaller one at the base of the flower-cluster. *Flowers.*—Yellowish-green or purplish; clustered at the summit of the stem; appearing while the leaf is still small. *Calyx.*—Of six sepals; with three or four small bractlets at base. *Corolla.*—Of six thick, somewhat kidney-shaped or hooded petals, with short claws. *Stamens.*—Six. *Pistil.*—One. *Fruit.*—Bluish; berry-like.

In the deep rich woods of early spring, especially somewhat westward, may be found the smooth, purplish stem, divided leaves, and clustered green or purplish flowers of the blue cohosh. The generic name is from two Greek words signifying *stem* and *leaf*, "the stem seeming to form a stalk for the greatly expanded leaf." (Gray.)

EARLY MEADOW-RUE.

Thalictrum dioicum. Crowfoot Family.

One to two feet high. *Leaves.*—Divided into many smooth, lobed, pale drooping leaflets. *Flowers.*—Purplish and greenish; unisexual. *Calyx.*—Of four or five petal-like sepals. *Corolla.*—None. *Stamens.*—Indefinite in number; with linear yellowish anthers drooping on hair-like filaments (stamens and pistils occurring on different plants). *Pistils.*—Four to fourteen.

The graceful drooping foliage of this plant is perhaps more noticeable than the small flowers which appear in the rocky woods in April or May.

SWAMP-SAXIFRAGE.

Saxifraga pensylvanica. Saxifrage Family.

One to two feet high. *Leaves.*—Four to eight inches long; obscurely toothed; narrowed at base into a broad short stem. *Flowers.*—Small; greenish or reddish; in a large cluster. *Calyx.*—Five-parted. *Corolla.*—Of five petals. *Stamens.*—Ten. *Pistil.*—One, with two styles.

In boggy meadows and along water-courses this plant is conspicuous in spring. Oftentimes its leaf-stalks as well as its flowers are noticeably tinged with red.

BITTERSWEET.

Celastrus scandens. Staff-tree Family.

Stem.—Woody; twining. *Leaves.*—Alternate; oblong; finely toothed; pointed. *Flowers.*—Small; greenish or cream-color; in raceme-like clusters; appearing in June. *Pod.*—Orange-colored; globular and berry-like; curling back in three divisions when ripe so as to display the scarlet covering of the seeds within.

The small flowers of the bittersweet, which appear in June, rarely attract attention. But in October no lover of color can fail to admire the deep orange pods which at last curl back so as advantageously to display the brilliant scarlet covering of the seeds. Perhaps we have no fruit which illuminates more vividly the roadside thicket of late autumn; or touches with greater warmth those tumbled, overgrown walls which are so picturesque a feature in parts of the country, and do in a small way for our quiet landscapes what vine-covered ruins accomplish for the scenery of the Old World.

III

YELLOW

MARSH-MARIGOLD. COWSLIP.

Caltha palustris. Crowfoot Family.

Stem.—Hollow; furrowed. *Leaves.*—Rounded; somewhat kidney-shaped. *Flowers.*—Golden-yellow. *Calyx.*—Of five to nine petal-like sepals. *Corolla.*—None. *Stamens.*—Numerous. *Pistils.*—Five to ten; almost without styles.

> "Hark, hark! the lark at heaven's gate sings,
> And Phœbus 'gins arise,
> His steeds to water at those springs
> On chalic'd flowers that lies;
> And winking Mary-buds begin
> To ope their golden eyes;
> With everything that pretty is—
> My lady sweet, arise!
> Arise, arise."—*Cymbeline.*

We claim—and not without authority—that these "winking Mary-buds" are identical with the gay marsh-marigolds which border our springs and gladden our wet meadows every April. There are those who assert that the poet had in mind the garden marigold—*Calendula*—but surely no cultivated flower could harmonize with the spirit of the song as do these gleaming swamp blossoms. We will yield to the garden if necessary—

> "The marigold that goes to bed with the sun
> And with him rises weeping—"

MARSH-MARIGOLD.—*Caltha palustris.*

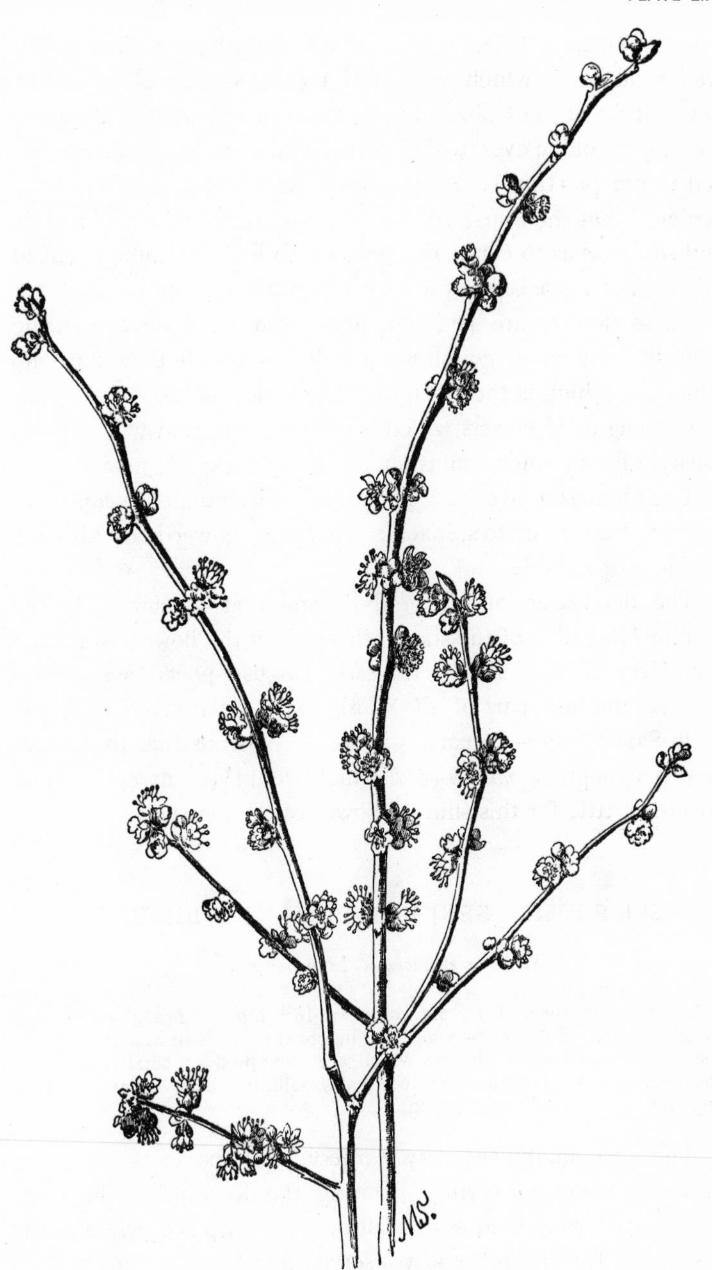

SPICEBUSH.—*Lindera Benzoin.*

of the "Winter's Tale," but insist on retaining for that larger, lovelier garden in which we all feel a certain sense of possession —even if we are not taxed on real estate in any part of the country—the "golden eyes" of the Mary-bud; and we feel strengthened in our position by the statement in Mr. Robinson's "Wild Garden" that the marsh-marigold is so abundant along certain English rivers as to cause the ground to look as though paved with gold at those seasons when they overflow their banks.

These flowers are peddled about our streets every spring under the name of cowslips—a title to which they have no claim, and which is the result of that reckless fashion of christening unrecognized flowers which is so prevalent, and which is responsible for so much confusion about their English names.

The plant is a favorite "pot-herb" with country people, far superior, I am told, to spinach; the young flower-buds also are considered palatable.

The derivation of marigold is somewhat obscure. In the "Grete Herball" of the sixteenth century the flower is spoken of as *Mary Gowles*, and by the early English poets as *gold* simply. As the first part of the word might be derived from the Anglo-Saxon *mere*—a marsh, it seems possible that the entire name may signify *marsh-gold*, which would be an appropriate and poetic title for this shining flower of the marshes.

SPICEBUSH. BENJAMIN-BUSH. FEVERBUSH.

Lindera Benzoin. Laurel Family.

An aromatic shrub from six to fifteen feet high. *Leaves.*—Oblong; pale underneath. *Flowers.*—Appearing before the leaves in March or April; honey-yellow; borne in clusters which are composed of smaller clusters, surrounded by an involucre of four early falling scales. *Fruit.*—Red; berry-like; somewhat pear-shaped.

These are among the very earliest blossoms to be found in the moist woods of spring. During the Revolution the powdered berries were used as a substitute for allspice; while at the time of the Rebellion the leaves served as a substitute for tea.

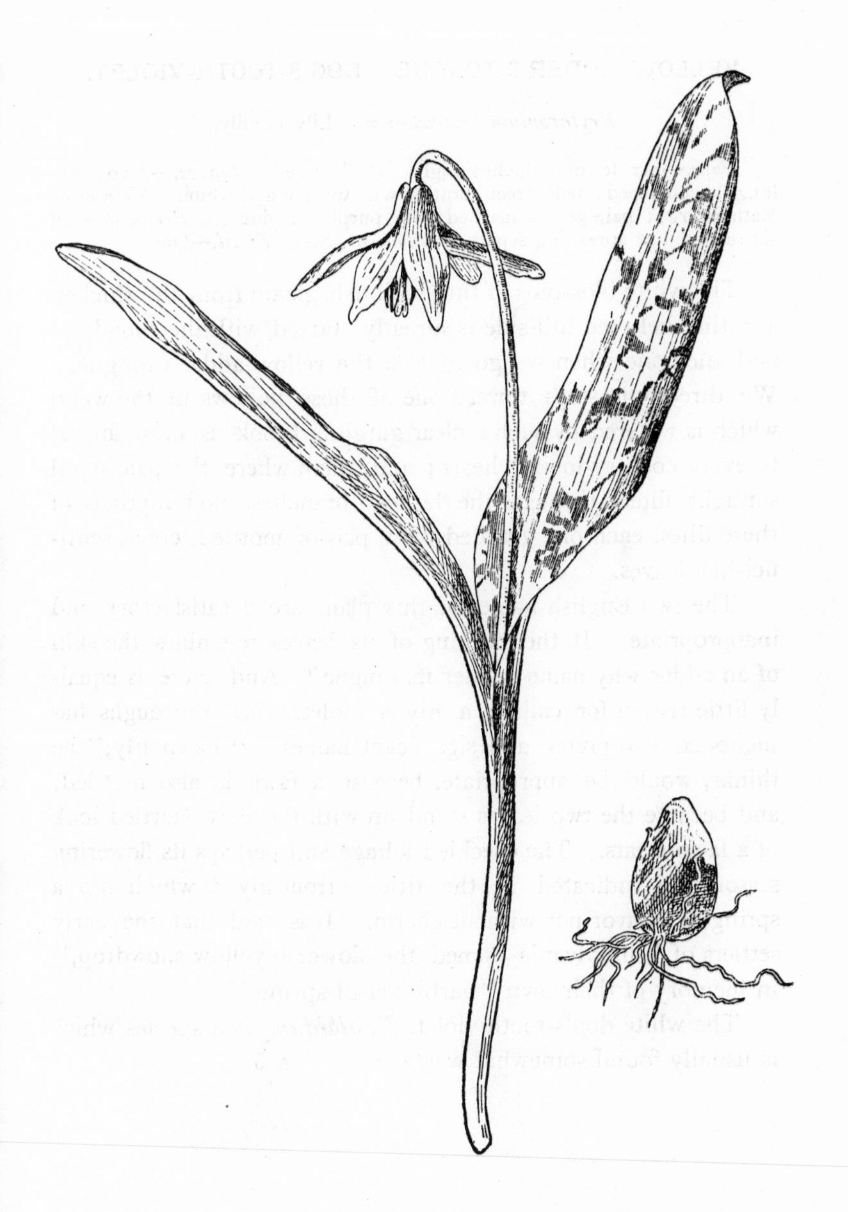

DOG'S-TOOTH-VIOLET.—*Erythronium americanum.*

YELLOW ADDER'S-TONGUE. DOG'S-TOOTH-VIOLET.

Erythronium americanum. Lily Family.

Scape.—Six to nine inches high; one-flowered. *Leaves.*—Two; oblong-lance-shaped; pale green mottled with purple and white. *Flowers.*—Rather large; pale yellow marked with purple; nodding. *Perianth.*—Of six recurved or spreading sepals. *Stamens.*—Six. *Pistil.*—One.

The white blossoms of the shadbush gleam from the thicket, and the sheltered hill-side is already starred with the bloodroot and anemone when we go to seek the yellow adder's-tongue. We direct our steps toward one of those hollows in the wood which is watered by such a clear gurgling brook as must appeal to every country-loving heart; and there where the pale April sunlight filters through the leafless branches, nod myriads of these lilies, each one guarded by a pair of mottled, erect, sentinel-like leaves.

The two English names of this plant are unsatisfactory and inappropriate. If the marking of its leaves resembles the skin of an adder why name it after its tongue? And there is equally little reason for calling a lily a violet. Mr. Burroughs has suggested two pretty and significant names. "Fawn lily," he thinks, would be appropriate, because a fawn is also mottled, and because the two leaves stand up with the alert, startled look of a fawn's ears. The speckled foliage and perhaps its flowering season are indicated in the title "trout-lily," which has a spring-like flavor not without charm. It is said that the early settlers of Pennsylvania named the flower "yellow snowdrop," in memory of their own "harbinger-of-spring."

The white dog's-tooth-violet, *E. albidum*, is a species which is usually found somewhat westward.

COLTSFOOT.

Tussilago Farfara. Composite Family.

Scape.—Slender, scaly, three to eighteen inches high, bearing a solitary large flower-head. *Leaves.*—Appearing later than the flowers, heart-shaped below, "angulately-lobed," woolly beneath. *Flower-head.*—Bright yellow, composed of both ray and disk-flowers, appearing in early spring before the leaves.

The coltsfoot is an immigrant from Europe which is now thoroughly wild in this country. For some years before I had succeeded in seeing the plant in flower I had noticed colonies of its lobed, heart-shaped leaves growing in moist ditches and along the banks or in the beds of streams. But my efforts to discover the name or blossom of the plant which sent up these conspicuous leaves were unsuccessful till one early May when, on the banks of a stream in Berkshire, I chanced upon a bright yellow flower-head, looking something like a dandelion with its heart plucked out, topping a leafless, scaly-bracted scape. I identified this as the coltsfoot, connecting it with the puzzling leaves only by means of the botanical descriptions.

This is a common plant in England, yielding what is supposed to be a remedy for coughs.

CELANDINE-POPPY.

Stylophorum diphyllum. Poppy Family.

Stem.—Low; two-leaved. *Stem-leaves.*—Opposite; deeply incised. *Root-leaves.*—Incised or divided. *Flowers.*—Deep-yellow; large; one or more at the summit of the stem. *Calyx.*—Of two hairy sepals. *Corolla.*—Of four petals. *Stamens.*—Many. *Pistil.*—One; with a two or four-lobed stigma.

In April or May, somewhat south and westward, the woods are brightened, and occasionally the hill-sides are painted yellow, by this handsome flower. In both flower and foliage the plant suggests the celandine.

WOOD-BETONY. LOUSEWORT.

Pedicularis canadensis. Figwort Family.

Stems.—Clustered; five to twelve inches high. *Leaves.*—The lower ones deeply incised; the upper less so. *Flowers.*—Yellow and red; growing in a short dense spike. *Calyx.*—Of one piece split in front. *Corolla.*—Two-lipped; the narrow upper lip arched, the lower three-lobed. *Stamens.*—Four. *Pistil.*—One.

The bright flowers of the wood betony are found in our May woods, often in the company of the columbine and yellow violet. Near Philadelphia they are said to be among the very earliest of the flowers, coming soon after the trailing arbutus. In the later year the plant attracts attention by its uncouth spikes of brown seed-pods.

Few wayside weeds have been accredited with greater virtue than the ancient betony, which a celebrated Roman physician claimed could cure forty-seven different disorders. The Roman proverb, "Sell your coat and buy betony," seems to imply that the plant did not flourish so abundantly along the Appian Way as it does by our American roadsides. Unfortunately we are reluctantly forced to believe once more that our native flower is not identical with the classic one, but that it has received its common name through some superficial resemblance to the original betony or *Betonica.*

SOLOMON'S-SEAL.

Polygonatum biflorum. Lily Family.

Stem.—Slender; curving; one to three feet long. *Leaves.*—Alternate; oval; set close to the stem. *Flowers.*—Yellowish; bell-shaped; nodding from the axils of the leaves. *Perianth.*—Six-lobed at the summit. *Stamens.*—Six. *Pistil.*—One. *Fruit.*—A dark blue berry.

The graceful leafy stems of the Solomon's-seal are among the most decorative features of our spring woods. The small blossoms which appear in May grow either singly or in clusters on a flower-stalk which is so fastened into the axil of each leaf that

WOOD-BETONY.—*Pedicularis canadensis.*

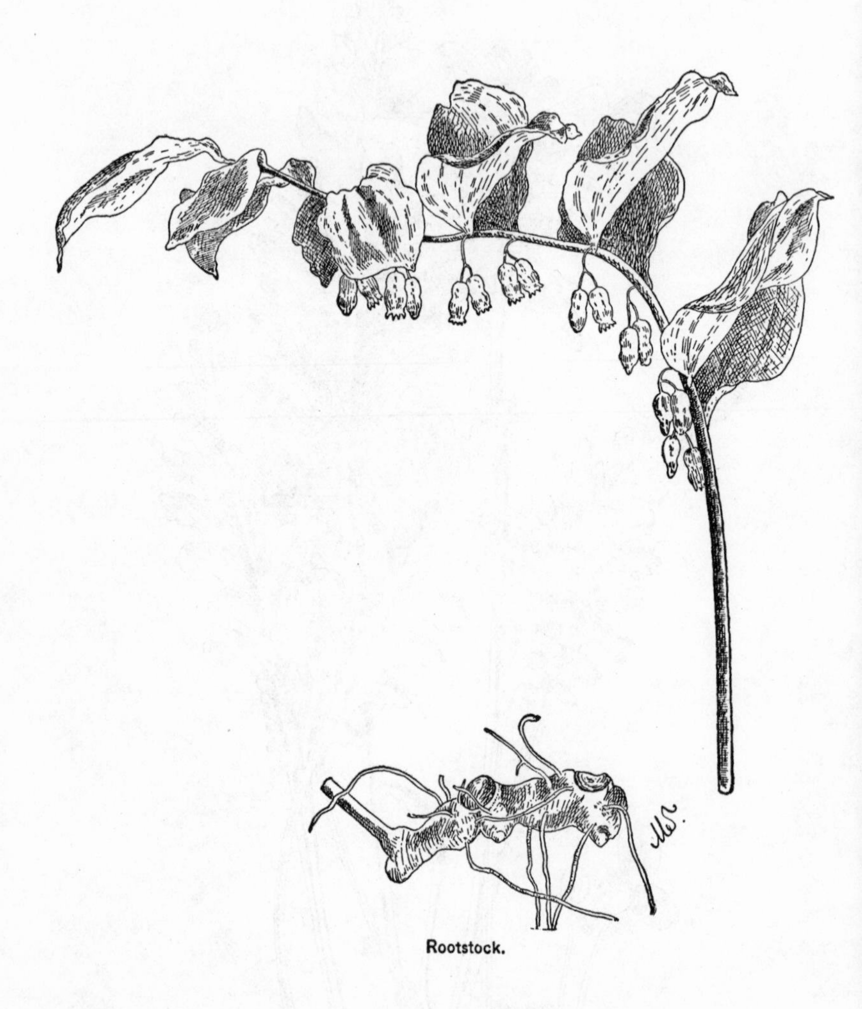

SOLOMON'S-SEAL.—*Polygonatum biflorum.*

they droop beneath, forming a curve of singular grace which is sustained in later summer by the dark blue berries.

The larger species, *P. canaliculatum*, grows to a height of from two to seven feet, blossoming in the meadows and along the streams in June.

The common name was suggested by the rootstocks, which are marked with large round scars left by the death and separation of the base of the stout stalks of the previous years. These scars somewhat resemble the impression of a seal upon wax.

The generic name is from two Greek words signifying *many* and *knee*, alluding to the numerous joints of the rootstock.

GOLDEN CORYDALIS.

Corydalis aurea. Fumitory Family.

Smooth, six to fourteen inches high, branching. *Leaves.*—Finely dissected. *Flowers.*—Bright yellow, about one-half inch long. *Calyx.*—Of two small sepals. *Corolla.*—Flattened, closed, with spur one-half or more as long as body of corolla, outer petals keeled. *Fruit.*—A many-seeded pod.

The golden corydalis is found flowering in the rocky woods from March till May.

EARLY CROWFOOT. SWAMP-BUTTERCUP.

Ranunculus septentrionalis. Crowfoot Family.

Stems.—Sometimes upright; again trailing along the ground and forming runners. *Leaves.*—Three-divided; the divisions often unequally cleft. *Flowers.*—Bright yellow; somewhat resembling buttercups. *Calyx.*—Of five sepals. *Corolla.*—Of five petals. *Stamens.*—Indefinite in number. *Pistils.*—Numerous, in a head.

Although it may be found in blossom until August, it is especially in spring that the wet woods and meadows are bright with the flowers of the early crowfoot. Until we look closely at the plant we are apt to confound it with its kinsmen the buttercups, but a look at its longish petals alone will show us our error.

Another and even earlier species of the crowfoot is *R. fascicularis*. This is especially plentiful along the hillsides. Its roots are a cluster of thick fleshy fibres.

WILD OATS.

Uvularia sessilifolia. Lily Family.

Stem.—Acutely angled; rather low. *Leaves.*—Set close to or clasping the stem; pale; lance-oblong. *Flower.*—Yellowish or straw-color. *Perianth.*—Narrowly bell-shaped; divided into six distinct sepals. *Stamens*—Six. *Pistil.*—One, with a deeply three-cleft style.

In spring this little plant is very abundant in the woods. It bears one or two small lily-like blossoms which droop modestly beneath the curving stems.

Bellwort, *Uvularia perfoliata*, is a related wild flower of similar appearance but with leaves which seem pierced by the stem.

LEATHERWOOD. MOOSEWOOD.

Dirca palustris. Mezereum Family.

A shrub two to six feet high. *Leaves.*—Oval or obovate. *Flowers.*—Light yellow, appearing before the leaves, small. *Calyx.*—Corolla-like, yellow, funnel-shaped, with wavy or obscurely four-toothed border. *Corolla.*—None. *Stamens.*—Eight, long and slender, protruding. *Pistil.*—One, with a long, thread-like style. *Fruit.*—Oval, reddish, about one-half inch long.

In April, while making our careful way through some wet thicket, we notice a leafless shrub with bunches of insignificant yellow blossoms and a bark so tough that we find it almost impossible to break off a branch. This is the "leatherwood" used for thongs by the Indians. It is known also as "moosewood." The leaves appear later and finally the reddish oval fruit.

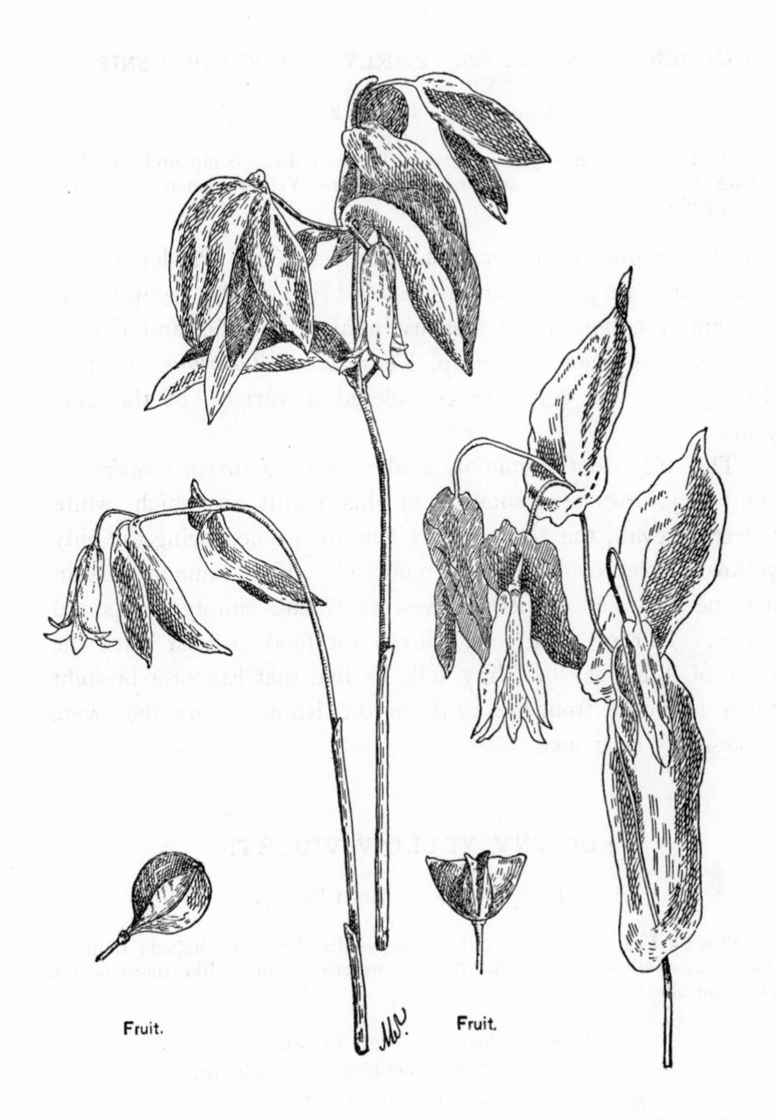

WILD OATS.—*Uvularia sessilifolia.* BELLWORT.—*Uvularia perfoliata.*

GOLDEN ALEXANDERS. EARLY MEADOW-PARSNIP.

Zizia aurea. Parsley Family.

One to three feet high. *Leaves.*—Twice or thrice-compound; leaflets oblong to lance-shaped; toothed. *Flowers.*—Yellow; small; in compound umbels.

This is one of the earliest members of the Parsley family to appear. Its golden flower-clusters brighten the damp meadows and the borders of streams in May or June, and closely resemble the meadow-parsnip, *Thaspium trifoliatum*, of which this species was formerly considered a variety, of the later year.

The tall, stout, common wild parsnip, *Pastinaca sativa*, is another yellow representative of this family in which white flowers prevail, the three plants here mentioned being the only yellow species commonly encountered. The common parsnip may be identified by its grooved stem and simply compound leaves. Its roots have been utilized for food at least since the reign of Tiberius, for Pliny tells us that that Emperor brought them to Rome from the banks of the Rhine, where they were successfully cultivated.

DOWNY YELLOW VIOLET.

Viola pubescens. Violet Family.

Stems.—Leafy above; erect. *Leaves.*—Broadly heart-shaped; toothed. *Flowers.*—Yellow, veined with purple; otherwise much like those of the common blue violet.

"When beechen buds begin to swell,
And woods the blue-bird's warble know,
The yellow violet's modest bell
Peeps from the last year's leaves below,"

sings Bryant, in his charming, but not strictly accurate poem, for the chances are that the "beechen buds" have almost burst into foliage, and that the "blue-bird's warble" has been heard

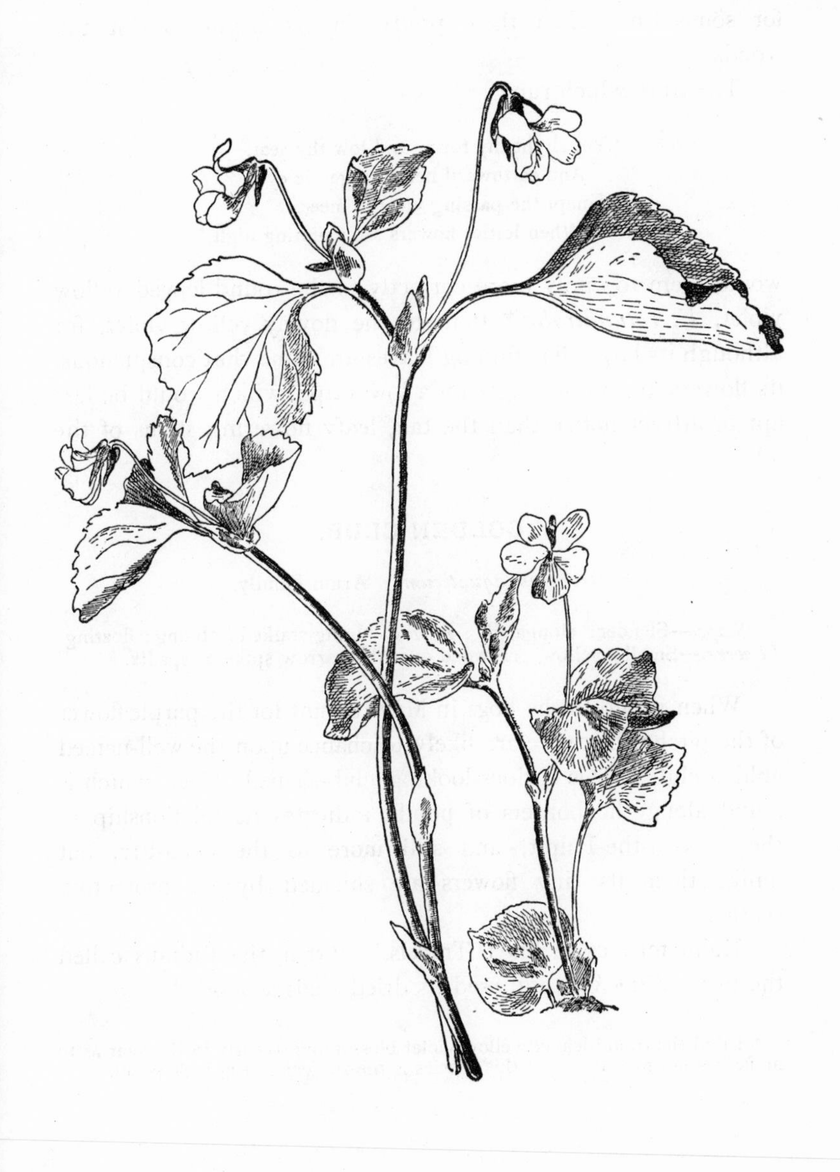

DOWNY YELLOW VIOLET.—*Viola pubescens.*

for some time when these pretty flowers begin to dot the woods.

The lines which run:

> "Yet slight thy form, and low thy seat,
> And earthward bent thy gentle eye,
> Unapt the passing view to meet,
> When loftier flowers are flaunting nigh,"

would seem to apply more correctly to the round-leaved yellow violet, *V. rotundifolia*,* than to the downy yellow violet, for although its large, flat shining leaves are somewhat conspicuous, its flowers are borne singly on a low scape, which would be less apt to attract notice than the tall, leafy flowering stems of the other.

GOLDEN CLUB.

Orontium aquaticum. Arum Family.

Scape.—Slender; elongated. *Leaves.*—Long-stalked; oblong; floating. *Flowers.*—Small; yellow; crowded over the narrow spike or spadix.

When we go to the bogs in May to hunt for the purple flower of the pitcher-plant we are likely to chance upon the well-named golden club. This curious-looking club-shaped object, which is found along the borders of ponds, indicates its relationship to the Jack-in-the-Pulpit, and still more to the calla-lily, but unlike them its tiny flowers are shielded by no protecting spathe.

Kalm tells us in his "Travels," "that the Indians called the plant *Taw-Kee*, and used its dried seeds as food."

* I find the round-leaved yellow violet blossoming so early in the year as to make it seem probable that this species is the subject of Bryant's poem.

CELANDINE.—*Chelidonium majus.*

FLY-HONEYSUCKLE.

Lonicera canadensis. Honeysuckle Family.

A bushy shrub three to five feet high, with straggling branches. *Leaves.*—Opposite, entire, oblong-ovate, often heart-shaped, thin, with thread-like leaf stems. *Flowers.*—Yellow, growing in pairs from the axils of the leaves. *Calyx.*—Slightly five-toothed, the teeth not persistent. *Corolla.*—Funnel-formed, almost spurred at base, with five lobes. *Stamens.*—Five. *Pistil.*—One. *Fruit.*—A red berry, growing close to, but distinct from the berry of sister flower.

In the moist, rocky woods of early May we find the yellow twin blossoms of the fly-honeysuckle.

CYNTHIA. DWARF DANDELION.

Krigia virginica. Composite Family.

Stems.—Usually becoming branched and leafy. (In *K. amplexicaulis*, a very similar species, there are from one to three stem-leaves only.) *Root-leaves.*—Usually somewhat lyre-shaped, or toothed. *Stem-leaves.*—Earlier ones roundish, not toothed; later ones narrower, and often deeply toothed or cleft. *Flower-heads.*—Deep orange-yellow; dandelion-like; composed entirely of strap-shaped flowers.

In some parts of the country the blossoms of the cynthia are among the earliest to appear, while in other localities they are especially abundant and conspicuous in June.

The smooth, pale-green stems of *K. biflora* bear but few leaves.

The cynthias are often confused with the hawkweeds.

CELANDINE.

Chelidonium majus. Poppy Family.

Stem.—Brittle; with saffron-colored, acrid juice. *Leaves.*—Compound or divided; toothed or cut. *Flowers.*—Yellow; clustered. *Calyx.*—Of two sepals falling early. *Corolla.*—Of four petals. *Stamens.*—Sixteen to twenty-four. *Pistil.*—One, with a two-lobed stigma. *Pod.*—Slender; linear.

The name of celandine must always suggest the poet who never seemed to weary of writing in its honor:

"Pansies, lilies, kingcups, daisies,
Let them live upon their praises;

PLATE LXVI

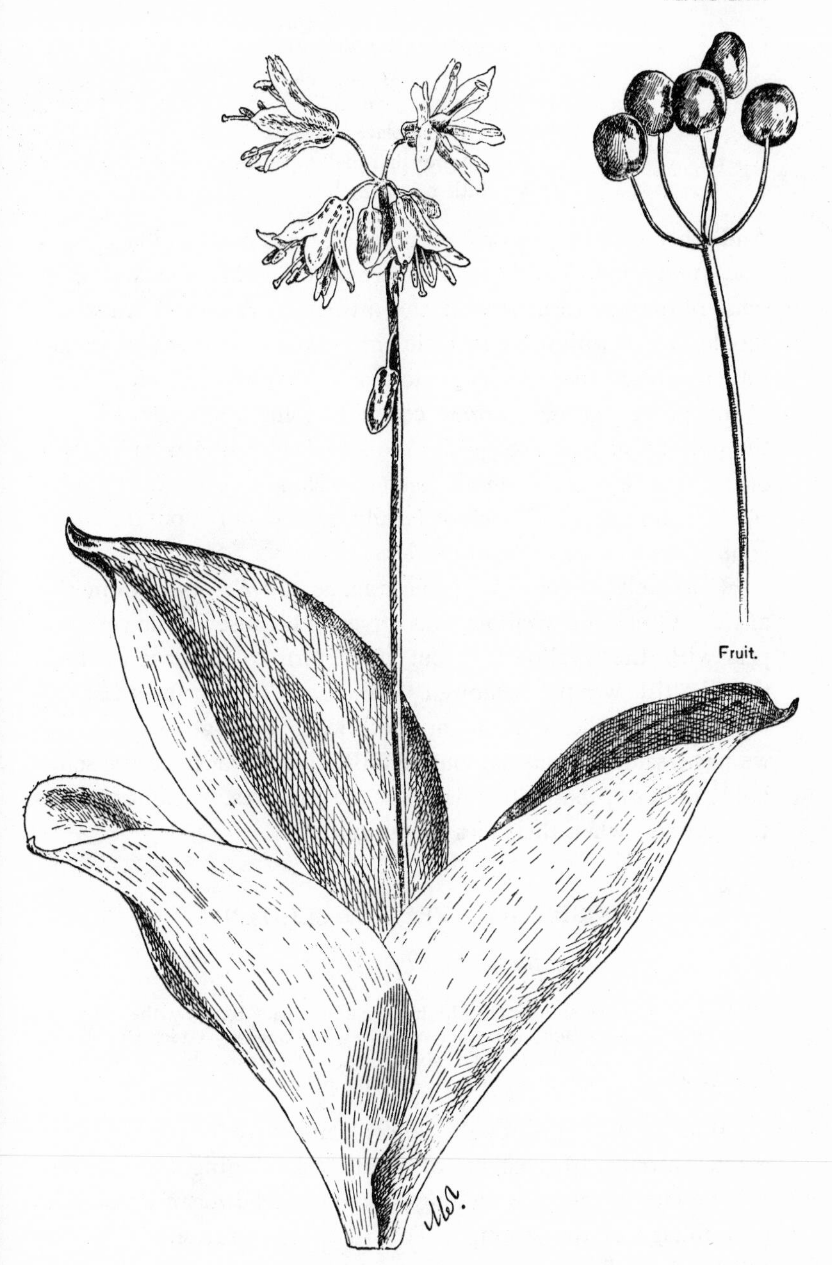

DOGBERRY.—*Clintonia borealis.*

Long as there's a sun that sets,
Primroses will have their glory;
Long as there are violets,
They will have a place in story;
There's a flower that shall be mine,
'Tis the little celandine."

And when certain yellow flowers which frequent the village roadside are pointed out to us as those of the celandine, we feel a sense of disappointment that the favorite theme of Wordsworth should arouse within us so little enthusiasm. So perhaps we are rather relieved than otherwise to realize that the botanical name of this plant signifies *greater* celandine; for we remember that the poet never failed to specify the *small* celandine as the object of his praise. The small [lesser] celandine is *Ranunculus Ficaria*, one of the Crowfoot family, and is only found in this country as an escape from gardens.

Gray tells us that the generic name, *Chelidonium*, from the ancient Greek for swallow, was given "because its flowers appear with the swallows;" but if we turn to Gerarde we read that the title was not bestowed "because it first springeth at the coming in of the swallows, or dieth when they go away, for as we have saide, it may be founde all the yeare, but because some holde opinion, that with this herbe the dams restore sight to their young ones, when their eies be put out."

DOGBERRY. YELLOW CLINTONIA.

Clintonia borealis. Lily Family.

Scape.—Five to eight inches high; sheathed at its base by the stalks of two to four large, oblong, conspicuous leaves. *Flowers.*—Greenish-yellow; rarely solitary. *Perianth.*—Of six sepals. *Stamens.*—Six; protruding. *Pistil.*—One; protruding. *Fruit.*—A blue berry.

When rambling through the cool, moist woods our attention is often attracted by patches of great dark, shining leaves; and if it be late in the year we long to know the flower of which this rich foliage is the setting. To satisfy our curiosity we must return the following May or June, when we shall probably find

GOLDEN RAGWORT.—*Senecio aureus.*

that a slender scape rises from its midst bearing at its summit several yellowish, bell-shaped flowers.

C. umbellulata is a more southern species, with smaller white flowers, which are speckled with green or purplish dots.

GOLDEN RAGWORT. SQUAW-WEED.

Senecio aureus. Composite Family.

Stem.—One to three feet high. *Root-leaves.*—Rounded; the larger ones mostly heart-shaped; toothed, and long-stalked. *Stem-leaves.*—The lower lyre-shaped; the upper lance-shaped; incised; set close to the stem. *Flower-heads.*—Yellow; clustered; composed of both ray and disk-flowers.

A child would perhaps liken the flower of the golden ragwort to a yellow daisy. Stain yellow the white rays of the daisy, diminish the size of the whole head somewhat, and you have a pretty good likeness of the ragwort. There need be little difficulty in the identification of this plant—although there are several marked varieties—for its flowers are abundant in the early year, at which season but few members of the Composite family are abroad.

The generic name is from *senex*—an old man—alluding to the silky down of the seeds, which is supposed to suggest the silvery hairs of age.

Closely allied to the golden ragwort is the common groundsel, *S. vulgaris*, which is given as food to caged birds. The flower-heads of this species are without rays.

YELLOW LADY'S-SLIPPER. WHIP-POOR-WILL SHOE.

Cypripedium Calceolus. Orchis Family.

Stem.—About two feet high; downy; leafy to the top; one to three-flowered. *Leaves.*—Alternate; broadly oval; many-nerved and plaited. *Flower.*—Large; the pale yellow lip an inflated pouch; the two lateral petals long and narrow; wavy-twisted; brownish.

The yellow lady's-slipper usually blossoms in May or June, a few days later than its pink sister, *C. acaule.* Regarding its

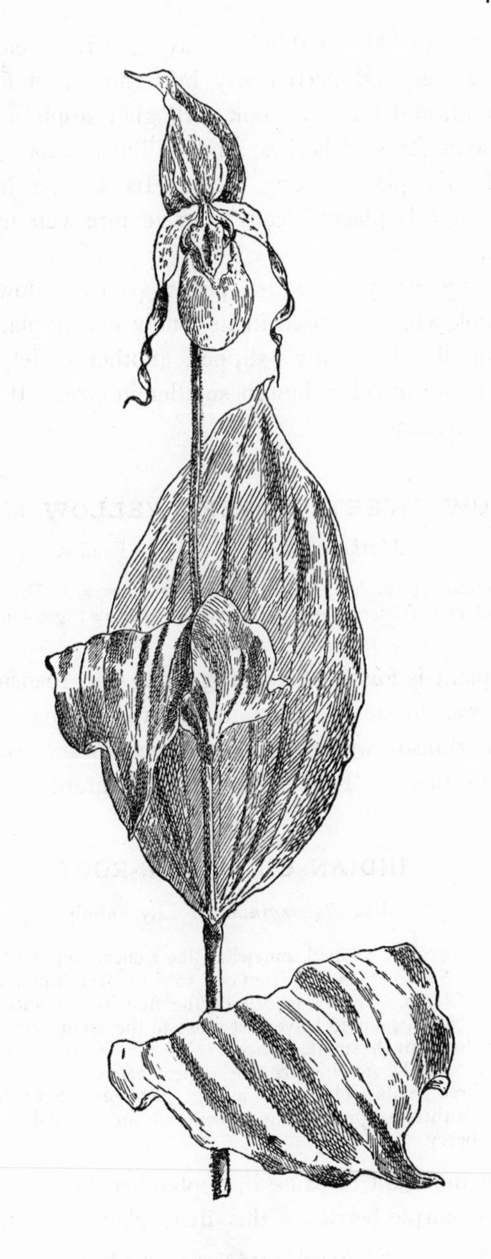

SMALL YELLOW LADY'S-SLIPPER.—*Cypripedium Calceolus.*

favorite haunts, Mr. Baldwin* says: "Its preference is for maples, beeches, and particularly butternuts, and for sloping or hilly ground, and I always look with glad suspicion at a knoll covered with ferns, cohoshes, and trilliums, expecting to see a clump of this plant among them. Its sentinel-like habit of choosing 'sightly places' leads it to venture well up on mountain sides."

The long, wavy, brownish petals give the flower an alert, startled look when surprised in its lonely hiding-places.

The small yellow lady's-slipper, another variety of *C. Calceolus*, is richer in color though smaller in size. It has also the charm of fragrance.

YELLOW SWEET CLOVER. YELLOW MELILOT.

Melilotus officinalis. Pulse Family.

Two to four feet high. *Stem.*—Upright. *Leaves.*—Divided into three toothed leaflets. *Flowers.*—Papilionaceous; yellow; growing in spike-like racemes.

This plant is found blossoming along the roadsides in summer. It was formerly called in England "king's-clover," because as Parkinson writes, "the yellowe flowers doe crown the top of the stalks." The leaves become fragrant in drying.

INDIAN CUCUMBER-ROOT.

Medeola virginiana. Lily Family.

Root.—Tuberous; shaped somewhat like a cucumber, with a suggestion of its flavor. *Stem.*—Slender; from one to three feet high; at first clothed with wool. *Leaves.*—In two whorls on the flowering plants; the lower of five to nine oblong, pointed leaves set close to the stem; the upper usually of three or four much smaller ones. *Flowers.*—Greenish-yellow; small; clustered; recurved; set close to the upper leaves. *Perianth.*—Of three sepals and three petals, oblong and alike. *Stamens.*—Six; reddish-brown. *Pistil.*—With three stigmas; long; recurved, and reddish-brown. *Fruit.*—A purple berry.

One is more apt to pause in September to note the brilliant foliage and purple berries of this little plant than to gather the

* Orchids of New England.

PLATE LXIX

INDIAN CUCUMBER-ROOT.—*Medeola virginiana.*

drooping inconspicuous blossoms for his bunch of wood-flowers in June. The generic name is after the sorceress Medea, on account of its supposed medicinal virtues, of which, however, there seems to be no record.

The tuberous rootstock has the flavor, and something the shape, of the cucumber, and was probably used as food by the Indians. It would not be an uninteresting study to discover which of our common wild plants are able to afford pleasant and nutritious food; in such a pursuit many of the otherwise unattractive popular names would prove suggestive.

WINTERCRESS. YELLOW ROCKET. HERB OF ST. BARBARA.

Barbarea vulgaris. Mustard Family.

Stem.—Smooth. *Leaves.*—The lower lyre-shaped; the upper ovate, toothed or deeply incised at their base. *Flowers.*—Yellow; growing in racemes. *Pod.*—Linear; erect or slightly spreading.

As early as May we find the bright flowers of the wintercress along the roadside. This is probably the first of the yellow mustards to appear.

BLACK MUSTARD.

Brassica nigra. Mustard Family.

Often several feet high. *Stem.*—Branching. *Leaves.*—The lower with a large terminal lobe and a few small lateral ones. *Flowers.*—Yellow; rather small; growing in a raceme. *Pods.*—Smooth; erect; appressed; about half an inch long.

Many are familiar with the appearance of this plant who are ignorant of its name. The pale yellow flowers spring from the waste places along the roadside and border the dry fields throughout the summer. The tall spreading branches recall the Biblical description: "It groweth up, and becometh greater than all herbs, and shooteth out great branches; so that the fowls of the air may lodge under the shadow of it."

WINTER-CRESS.—*Barbarea vulgaris.*

This plant is extensively cultivated in Europe, its ground seeds forming the well-known condiment. The ancients used it for medicinal purposes. It has come across the water to us, and is a troublesome weed in many parts of the country.

WILD RADISH.

Raphanus Raphanistrum. Mustard Family.

One to three feet high. *Leaves.*—Rough; lyre-shaped. *Flowers.*—Yellow; veiny; turning white or purplish; larger than those of the black mustard, otherwise resembling them. *Pod.*—Often necklace-form by constriction between the seeds.

This plant is a troublesome weed in many of our fields. It is the stock from which the garden radish has been raised.

YELLOW WATERCRESS.

Nasturtium officinale. Mustard Family.

Erect, branching, one to three feet high. *Leaves.*—Pinnately parted into oblong, toothed lobes. *Flowers.*—Yellow, small, growing in racemes. *Pod.*—Linear or oblong, spreading or curved.

The yellow watercress is common in wet places or in shallow water almost throughout North America. Its insignificant yellow flowers are found from May till September.

RATTLESNAKE-WEED. HAWKWEED.

Hieracium venosum. Composite Family.

Stem or Scape.—One to two feet high; naked or with a single leaf; slender; forking above. *Leaves.*—From the root; oblong; often making a sort of flat rosette; *usually conspicuously veined with purple.* *Flower-heads.*—Yellow; composed entirely of strap-shaped flowers.

The loosely clustered yellow flower-heads of the rattlesnake-weed somewhat resemble small dandelions. They abound in the pine-woods and dry, waste places of early summer. The purple-veined leaves, whose curious markings give to the plant its common name, grow close to the ground and are supposed to be

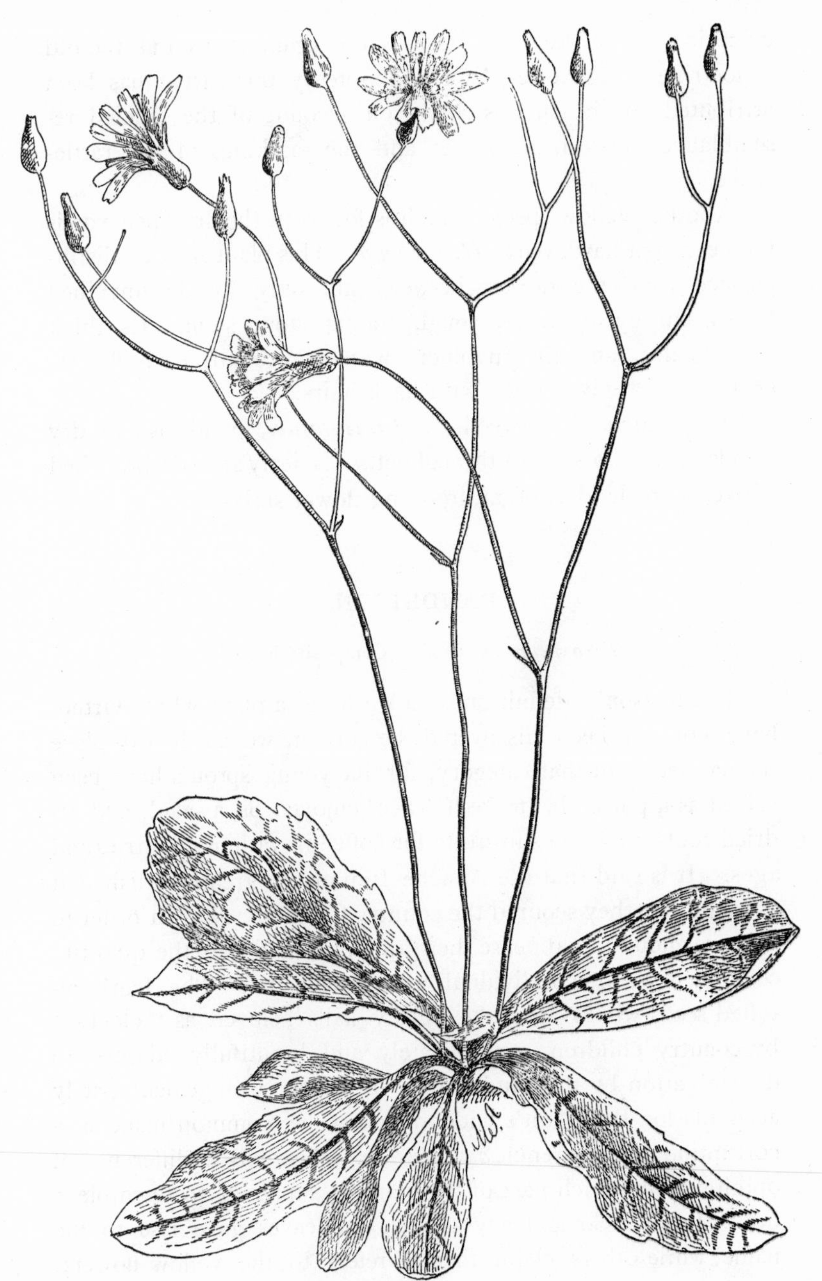

RATTLESNAKE-WEED.—*Hieracium venosum.*

efficacious in rattlesnake bites. Here again crops out the old "doctrine of signatures," for undoubtedly this virtue has been attributed to the species solely on account of the fancied resemblance between its leaves and the markings of the rattlesnake.

Another yellow species which is found in the dry open woods is the rough hawkweed, *H. scabrum*. This plant may be distinguished from the rattlesnake-weed not only by its unveined leaves, but by its *leafy*, rough, rather stout stem. Its thick flower-stalks, and the involucre which surrounds each flower-head, are densely clothed with dark hairs.

The panicled hawkweed, *H. paniculatum*, found also in dry woods, is usually smooth throughout. Its leafy stem is branched above, with slender, often drooping flower-stalks.

DANDELION.

Taraxacum officinale. Composite Family.

If Emerson's definition of a weed, as a plant whose virtues have not yet been discovered, be correct, we can hardly place the dandelion in that category, for its young sprouts have been valued as a pot-herb, its fresh leaves enjoyed as a salad, and its dried roots used as a substitute for coffee in various countries and ages. It is said that the Apache Indians so greatly relished it as food, that they scoured the country for many days in order to procure enough to appease their appetites, and that the quantity consumed by one individual exceeded belief. The feathery-tufted seeds which form the downy balls beloved as "clocks" by country children, are delicately and beautifully adapted to dissemination by the wind, which ingenious arrangement partly accounts for the plant's wide range. The common name is a corruption of the French *dent de lion*. There is a difference of opinion as to which part of the plant is supposed to resemble a lion's tooth. Some fancy the jagged leaves gave rise to the name, while others claim that it refers to the yellow flowers,

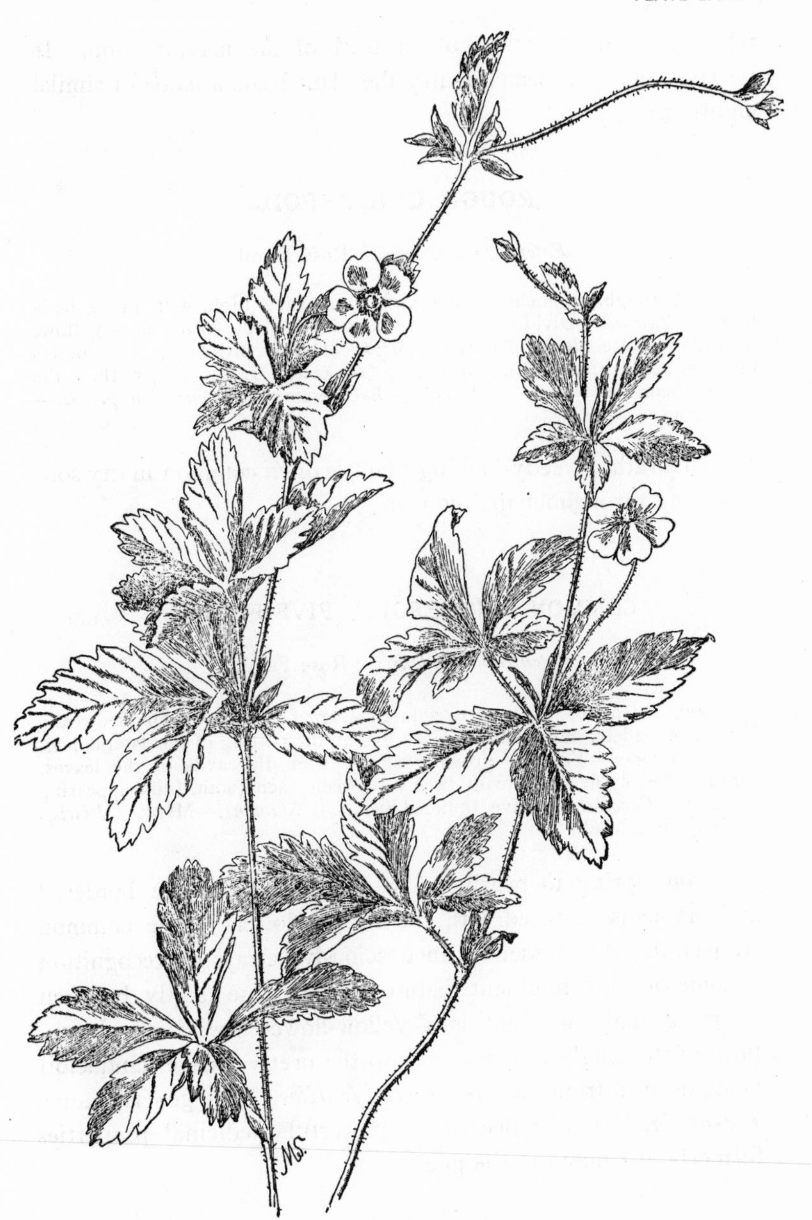

COMMON CINQUEFOIL.—*Potentilla canadensis.*

which they liken to the golden teeth of the heraldic lion. In nearly every European country the plant bears a name of similar significance.

ROUGH CINQUEFOIL.

Potentilla norvegica. Rose Family.

Stout, rough, six inches to two and one-half feet high, with many leafy bracts. *Leaves.*—Divided into three obovate leaflets. *Flowers.*—Yellow, in rather close, leafy clusters. *Calyx.*—Deeply five-cleft, with bracts between each tooth, thus appearing ten-cleft.—Lobes larger than the petals of corolla. *Corolla.*—Small, of five petals. *Stamens and pistils.*—Numerous.

This rather weedy-looking plant is often common in dry soil, flowering throughout the summer.

COMMON CINQUEFOIL. FIVE-FINGER.

Potentilla canadensis. Rose Family.

Stem.—Slender; prostrate, or sometimes erect. *Leaves.*—Divided really into three leaflets, but apparently into five by the parting of the lateral leaflets. *Flowers.*—Yellow; growing singly from the axils of the leaves. *Calyx.*—Deeply five-cleft, with bracts between each tooth, thus appearing ten-cleft. *Corolla.*—Of five rounded petals. *Stamens.*—Many. *Pistils.*—Many, in a head.

From spring to nearly midsummer the roads are bordered and the fields carpeted with the bright flowers of the common cinquefoil. The passer-by unconsciously betrays his recognition of some of the prominent features of the Rose family by often assuming that the plant is a yellow-flowered wild strawberry. Both of the English names refer to the pretty foliage, cinquefoil being derived from the French *cinq feuilles*. The generic name, *Potentilla*, has reference to the powerful medicinal properties formerly attributed to the genus.

PLATE LXXIII

Leaf.

SHRUBBY CINQUEFOIL.—*Potentilla fruticosa.*

SILVERWEED.

Potentilla anserina. Rose Family.

"Herbaceous, tufted, spreading by slender runners one to three feet long." *Leaves.*—Pinnately divided into seven to twenty-five oblong, sharply toothed leaflets which are silvery and silky below. *Flowers.*—Bright yellow, on slender, erect, solitary flower-stalks. *Calyx.*—Five-cleft, with bracts between each tooth, thus appearing ten-cleft. *Corolla.*—Of five broadly oval or obovate petals. *Stamens and pistils.*—Numerous.

These bright, pretty flowers, occasionally mistaken for buttercups by the unobservant passer-by, are found throughout the summer in wet marshes and along river banks from New Jersey northward. For these golden-flowered plants the name "goldenweed" would seem more appropriate than "silverweed." It is only when we turn over the leaves and note the downy undersides of the leaflets that we can reconcile ourselves to the established title.

SHRUBBY CINQUEFOIL. FIVE-FINGER.

Potentilla fruticosa. Rose Family.

Stem.—Erect; shrubby; one to four feet high. *Leaves.*—Divided into five to seven narrow leaflets. *Flowers.*—Yellow; resembling those of the common cinquefoil, but larger.

Of all the cinquefoils perhaps this one most truly merits the title five-finger. Certainly its slender leaflets are much more finger-like than those of the common cinquefoil. It is not a common plant in most localities, but is very abundant among the Berkshire Hills, where it takes entire possession of otherwise barren fields and roadsides; its peculiarly bluish-green foliage and bright yellow flowers (looking like buttercups growing on a shrub) arresting one's attention throughout the entire summer and occasionally late into the autumn.

YELLOW AVENS.—*Geum aleppicum.*

SILVERY CINQUEFOIL.

Potentilla argentea. Rose Family.

Stems.—Ascending ; branched at the summit ; white ; woolly. *Leaves.* —Divided into five wedge-oblong, deeply incised leaflets, which are green above, white with silvery wool, beneath. *Flowers.*—Much as in above.

The silvery cinquefoil has rather large yellow flowers, which are found in dry fields throughout the summer as far south as New Jersey.

YELLOW AVENS.

Geum aleppicum. Rose Family.

Somewhat hairy ; three to five feet high. *Stem-leaves.*—Divided into from three to five leaflets. *Flowers.*— Golden yellow. *Calyx.*—Five-cleft ; usually with a small bract between the divisions. *Corolla.*—Of five broad petals. *Stamens and Pistils.*—Numerous ; the latter enlarging finally into a round, burr-like head.

The bright flowers of the yellow avens are found in the moist meadows during the summer, finally giving way to the troublesome burrs which so often thrust upon us their unwelcome companionship

BUSH-HONEYSUCKLE.

Diervilla Lonicera. Honeysuckle Family.

An upright shrub from one to four feet high. *Leaves.*—Opposite ; oblong ; taper-pointed. *Flowers.*—Yellow, sometimes much tinged with red ; clustered usually in threes in the axils of the upper leaves and at the summit of the stem. *Calyx.*—With slender awl-shaped lobes. *Corolla.*—Funnel-form ; five-lobed ; the lower lobe larger than the others and of a deeper yellow, with a small nectar-bearing gland at its base. *Stamens.*—Five. *Pistil.*—One.

This pretty little shrub is found along our rocky hills and mountains. The blossoms appear in early summer, and form a good example of nectar-bearing flowers. The lower lobe of the corolla is crested and more deeply colored than the others, thus

BUSH-HONEYSUCKLE.—*Diervilla Lonicera.*

advising the bee of secreted treasure. The hairy filaments of the stamens are so placed as to protect the nectar from injury by rain. When the blossom has been despoiled and at the same time fertilized, for the nectar-seeking bee has probably deposited some pollen upon its pistil, the color of the corolla changes from a pale to a deep yellow, thus giving warning to the insect-world that further attentions would be useless to both parties.

POVERTY-GRASS.

Hudsonia tomentosa. Rock-rose Family.

"Bushy, heath-like little shrubs, seldom a foot high." (Gray.) *Leaves.*—Small; oval or narrowly oblong; pressed close to the stem. *Flowers.*—Bright yellow; small; numerous; crowded along the upper part of the branches. *Calyx.*—Of five sepals, the two outer much smaller. *Corolla.*—Of five petals. *Stamens.*—Nine to thirty. *Pistil.*—One, with a long and slender style.

In early summer many of the sand-hills along the New England coast are bright with the yellow flowers of this hoary little shrub. It is also found as far south as Maryland and near the Great Lakes. Each blossom endures for a single day only. The plant's popular name is due to its economical habit of utilizing sandy unproductive soil where little else will flourish.

ROCKROSE. FROSTWEED.

Helianthemum canadense. Rock-rose Family.

About one foot high. *Leaves.*—Set close to the stem; simple; lance-oblong. *Flowers.*—Of two kinds: the earlier, more noticeable ones, yellow, solitary, about one inch across; the latter ones small and clustered, usually without petals. *Calyx.*—(Of the petal-bearing flowers) of five sepals. *Corolla.*—Of five early falling petals which are crumpled in the bud. *Stamens.*—Numerous. *Pistil.*—One, with a three-lobed stigma.

These fragile, bright-yellow flowers are found in gravelly places in early summer. Under the influence of the sunshine they open once; by the next day their petals have fallen, and their brief beauty is a thing of the past. On June 17th Thoreau

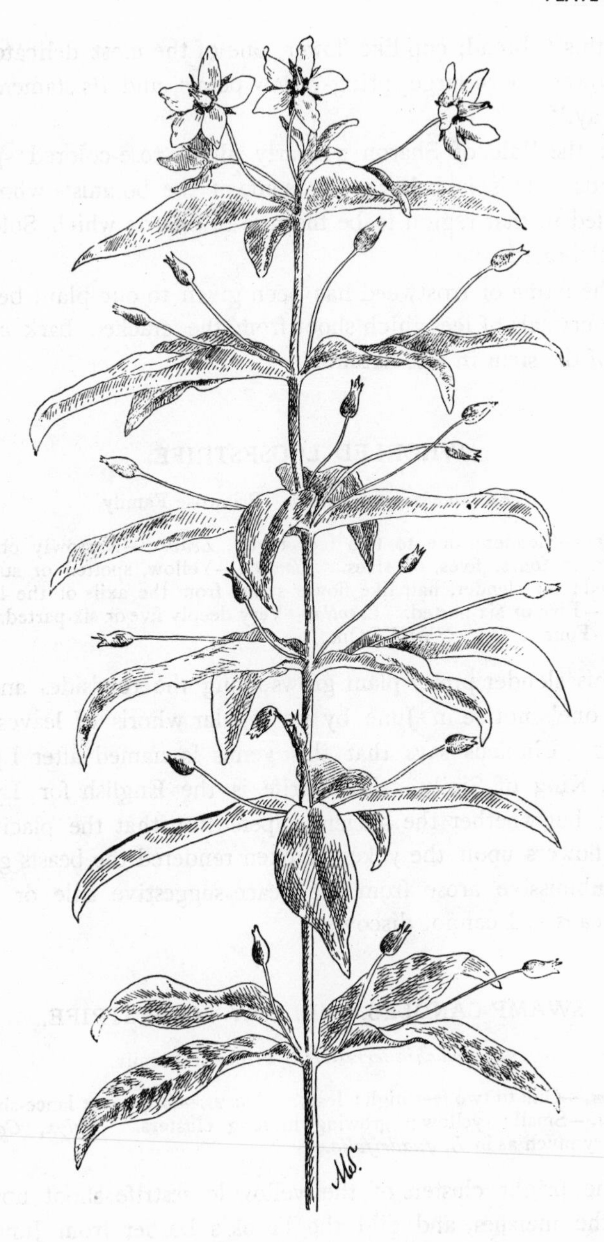

WHORLED LOOSESTRIFE.—*Lysimachia quadrifolia.*

finds this " broad, cup-like flower, one of the most delicate yellow flowers, with large spring-yellow petals, and its stamens laid one way."

In the Vale of Sharon a nearly allied rose-colored species abounds. This is believed by some of the botanists who have travelled in that region to be the rose of Sharon which Solomon has celebrated.

The name of frostweed has been given to our plant because of the crystals of ice which shoot from the cracked bark at the base of the stem in late autumn.

WHORLED LOOSESTRIFE.

Lysimachia quadrifolia. Primrose Family.

Stem.—Slender; one to two feet high. *Leaves.*—Narrowly oblong; whorled in fours, fives, or sixes. *Flowers.*—Yellow, spotted or streaked with red; on slender, hair-like flower-stalks from the axils of the leaves. *Calyx.*—Five or six-parted. *Corolla.*—Very deeply five or six-parted. *Stamens.*—Four or five. *Pistil.*—One.

This slender pretty plant grows along the roadsides and attracts one's notice in June by its regular whorls of leaves and flowers. Linnæus says that this genus is named after Lysimachus, King of Sicily. Loosestrife is the English for Lysimachus; but whether the ancient superstition that the placing of these flowers upon the yokes of oxen rendered the beasts gentle and submissive arose from the peace-suggestive title or from other causes, I cannot discover.

SWAMP-CANDLES. YELLOW LOOSESTRIFE.

Lysimachia terrestris. Primrose Family.

Stem.—One to two feet high; leafy. *Leaves.*—Opposite; lance-shaped. *Flowers.*—Small; yellow; growing in long clusters. *Calyx, Corolla, etc.*, very much as in *L. quadrifolia.*

The bright clusters of the yellow loosestrife shoot upward from the marshes, and gild the brook's border from June till August.

SWAMP-CANDLES.—*Lysimachia terrestris.*

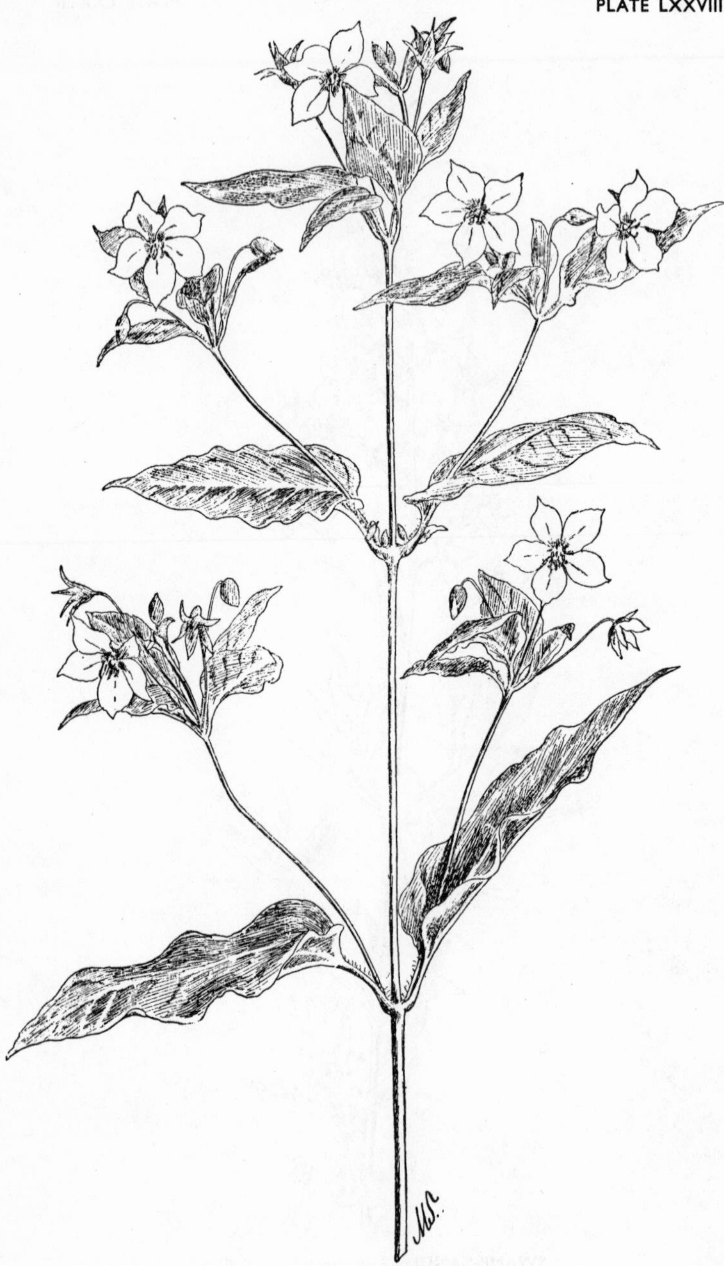

YELLOW LOOSESTRIFE.—*Lysimachia ciliata.*

COW-WHEAT.

Melampyrum lineare. Figwort Family.

Stem.—Low; erect; branching. *Leaves.*—Opposite; lance-shaped. *Flowers.*—Small; greenish-yellow; solitary in the axils of the upper leaves. *Calyx.*—Bell-shaped; four-cleft. *Corolla.*—Two-lipped; upper lip arched; lower three-lobed and spreading at the apex. *Stamens.*—Four. *Pistil.*—One.

In the open woods, from June until September, we encounter the pale-yellow flowers of this rather insignificant little plant. The cow-wheat was formerly cultivated by the Dutch as food for cattle. The Spanish name, *Trigo de Vaca,* would seem to indicate a similar custom in Spain. The generic name, *Melampyrum,* is from the Greek, and signifies *black wheat,* in reference to the appearance of the seeds of some species when mixed with grain. The flower would not be likely to attract one's attention were it not exceedingly common in some parts of the country, flourishing especially in our more eastern woodlands.

SPEARWORT.

Ranunculus ambigens. Crowfoot Family.

Stems.—One to two feet high. *Leaves.*—Oblong or lance-shaped; mostly toothed; contracted into a half-clasping leaf-stalk. *Flower.*—Bright yellow; solitary or clustered. *Calyx.*—Of five sepals. *Corolla.*—Of five to seven oblong petals. *Stamens.*—Indefinite in number, occasionally few. *Pistils.*—Numerous in a head.

Many weeks after the marsh-marigolds have passed away, just such marshy places as they affected are brightly flecked with gold. Wondering, perhaps, if they can be flowering for the second time in the season, we wade recklessly into the bog to rescue, not the marsh-marigold, but its near relation, the spearwort, which is still more closely related to the buttercup, as a little comparison of the two flowers will show. This plant is especially common at the North.

YELLOW LOOSESTRIFE.

Lysimachia ciliata. Primrose Family.

Stem.—Erect; two to four feet high. *Leaves.*—Opposite; narrowly oval; on fringed leaf-stalks. *Flowers.*—Yellow; on slender stalks from the axils of the leaves. *Calyx.*—Deeply five-parted. *Corolla.*—Deeply five-lobed; wheel-shaped; yellow, with a reddish centre. *Stamens.*—Five. *Pistil.*—One.

This plant is nearly akin to the swamp-candles. It abounds in low grounds and thickets, putting forth its bright wheel-shaped blossoms early in July.

YELLOW POND-LILY. SPATTER-DOCK.

Nuphar advena. Water-lily Family.

Leaves.—Floating or erect; roundish to oblong; with a deep cleft at their base. *Flowers.*—Yellow; sometimes purplish; large; somewhat globular. *Calyx.*—Of five or six sepals or more; yellow or green without. *Corolla.*—Of numerous small, thick, fleshy petals which are shorter than the stamens and resemble them. *Stamens.*—Very numerous. *Pistil.*—One, with a disk-like, many-rayed stigma.

Bordering the slow streams and stagnant ponds from May till August may be seen the yellow pond-lilies. These flowers lack the delicate beauty and fragrance of the white water-lilies; having, indeed, either from their odor, or appearance, or the form of their fruit, won for themselves in England the unpoetic title of "brandy-bottle." Owing to their love of mud they have also been called "frog-lilies." The Indians used their roots for food.

PRICKLY PEAR. INDIAN FIG.

Opuntia humifusa. Cactus Family.

Flowers.—Yellow; large; two and a half to three and a half inches across. *Calyx.*—Of numerous sepals. *Corolla.*—Of ten or twelve petals. *Stamens.*—Numerous. *Pistil.*—One, with numerous stigmas. *Fruit.*—Shaped liked a small pear; often with prickles over its surface.

This curious looking plant is the only representative of the Cactus family in the Northeastern States. It has deep green,

YELLOW STARGRASS.—*Hypoxis hirsuta.*

fleshy, prickly, rounded joints and large yellow flowers, which are often conspicuous in summer in dry, sandy places along the coast. Another form of *O. humifusa* has somewhat smaller flowers.

COMMON BARBERRY.

Berberis vulgaris. Barberry Family.

A shrub. *Leaves.*—Oblong; toothed; in clusters from the axil of a thorn. *Flower.*—Yellow; in drooping racemes. *Calyx.*—Of six sepals, with from two to six bractlets without. *Corolla.*—Of six petals. *Stamens.*—Six. *Pistil.*—One. *Fruit.*—An oblong scarlet berry.

This European shrub has now become thoroughly wild and very plentiful in parts of New England. The drooping yellow flowers of May and June are less noticeable than the oblong clustered berries of September, which light up so many overgrown lanes, and often decorate our lawns and gardens as well.

The ancients extracted a yellow hair-dye from the barberry; and to-day it is used to impart a yellow color to wool. Both its common and botanical names are of Arabic origin.

YELLOW STARGRASS.

Hypoxis hirsuta. Amaryllis Family.

Scapes.—Slender; few-flowered. *Leaves.*—Linear; grass-like; hairy. *Flowers.*—Yellow. *Perianth.*—Six-parted; spreading; the divisions hairy and greenish outside, yellow within. *Stamens.*—Six. *Pistil.*—One.

When our eyes fall upon what looks like a bit of evening sky set with golden stars, but which proves to be only a piece of shaded turf gleaming with these pretty flowers, we recall Longfellow's musical lines:

"Spake full well in language quaint and olden,
One who dwelleth on the castled Rhine,
When he called the flowers so blue and golden,
Stars, which in earth's firmament do shine."

The plant grows abundantly in open woods and meadows flowering in early summer.

YELLOW CLOVER.—*Trifolium agrarium.*

WILD INDIGO.

Baptisia tinctoria. Pulse Family.

Two or three feet high. *Stems.*—Smooth and slender. *Leaves.*—Divided into three rounded leaflets; somewhat pale with a whitish bloom; turning black in drying. *Flowers.*—Papilionaceous; yellow; clustered in many short, loose racemes.

This rather bushy-looking, bright-flowered plant is constantly encountered in midsummer in our rambles throughout the somewhat dry and sandy parts of the country. It is said that it is found in nearly every State in the Union, and that it has been used as a homœopathic remedy for typhoid fever. Its young shoots are eaten at times in place of asparagus. Both the botanical and common names refer to its having yielded an economical but unsuccessful substitute for indigo.

YELLOW CLOVER. HOP-CLOVER.

Trifolium agrarium. Pulse Family.

Six to twelve inches high. *Leaves.*—Divided into three oblong leaflets. *Flowers.*—Papilionaceous; yellow; small; in close heads.

Although this little plant is found in such abundance along our New England roadsides and in many other parts of the country as well, comparatively few people seem to recognize it as a member of the clover group, despite a marked likeness in the leaves and blossoms to others of the same family.

The name clover probably originated in the Latin *clava* (clubs), in reference to the fancied resemblance between the three-pronged club of Hercules and the clover leaf. The clubs of our playing-cards and the *trèfle* (trefoil) of the French are probably an imitation of the same leaf.

The nonesuch, *Medicago lupulina*, with downy, procumbent stems, and flowers which grow in short spikes, is nearly allied to

CANADA LILY.—*Lilium canadense.*

the hop-clover. In its reputed superiority as fodder its English name is said to have originated. Dr. Prior says that for many years this plant has been recognized in Ireland as the true shamrock.

SUNDROPS.

Oenothera fruticosa. Evening-Primrose Family.

Stem.—Erect; one to three feet high. *Leaves.*—Alternate; oblong to narrowly lance-shaped. *Flowers.*—Bright yellow; rather large; usually somewhat loosely clustered. *Calyx.*—With a long tube and four reflexed lobes. *Corolla.*—With four petals. *Stamens.*—Eight. *Pistil.*—One with a four-lobed stigma.

This is a day-blooming species of the evening primrose. Its pretty delicate flowers abound along the roadsides and in the meadows of early summer.

O. perennis is another day-bloomer belonging to this same genus. Its flowers are much smaller than the sundrops'.

CANADA LILY. WILD YELLOW LILY.

Lilium canadense. Lily Family.

Stem.—Two to five feet high. *Leaves.*—Whorled; lance-shaped. *Flowers.*—Yellow, spotted with reddish-brown; bell-shaped; two to three inches long. *Perianth.*—Of six recurved sepals, with a nectar-bearing furrow at their base. *Stamens.*—Six, with anthers loaded with brown pollen. *Pistil.*—One, with a three-lobed stigma.

What does the summer bring which is more enchanting than a sequestered wood-bordered meadow hung with a thousand of these delicate, nodding bells which look as though ready to tinkle at the least disturbance and sound an alarm among the flowers?

These too are true "lilies of the field," less gorgeous, less imposing than the Turk's-caps, but with an unsurpassed grace and charm of their own. "Fairy-caps" these pointed blossoms are sometimes called; "witch-caps" would be more appropriate still. Indeed they would make dainty headgear for any of the dim inhabitants of Wonder-land.

The growth of this plant is very striking when seen at its best. The erect stem is surrounded with regular whorls of leaves, from the upper one of which curves a circle of long-stemmed, nodding flowers. They suggest an exquisite design for church candelabra.

COMMON BLADDERWORT.

Utricularia vulgaris. Bladderwort Family.

Stems.—Immersed; one to three feet long. *Leaves.*—Many-parted; hair-like; bearing numerous bladders. *Scape.*—Six to twelve inches long. *Flowers.*—Yellow; five to twelve on each scape. *Calyx.*—Two-lipped. *Corolla.*—Two-lipped; spurred at the base. *Stamens.*—Two. *Pistil.*—One.

This curious water-plant may or may not have roots; in either case it is not fastened to the ground, but is floated by means of the many bladders which are borne on its finely dissected leaves. It is found commonly in ponds and slow streams, flowering throughout the summer. Thoreau calls it "a dirty conditioned flower, like a sluttish woman with a gaudy yellow bonnet."

The horned bladderwort, *U. cornuta*, roots in the peat-bogs and sandy swamps. Its large yellow helmet-shaped flowers are very fragrant, less than half a dozen being borne on each scape. There are a number of other species of yellow bladderwort, with smaller flowers, which are recognized easily as belonging to this group.

YELLOW-EYED GRASS.

Xyris flexuosa. Mayaca Family.

Scape.—Slender, ten to sixteen inches high, often from a bulbous base. *Leaves.*—Narrowly linear, sheathing the base of scape, commonly twisted with age, as is the scape. *Flowers.*—Yellow, small, growing in a head, usually about two opening at the same time. *Calyx.*—Of three sepals, one of which soon withers. *Corolla.*—Of three clawed petals. *Stamens.*—Three fertile, with anthers, and three sterile, without anthers. *Pistil.*—One, with three-cleft style.

In wet, boggy places, growing often in close companionship with the sundew and bladderwort, we notice during the summer the round heads of the yellow eyed grass.

BUTTER-AND-EGGS. TOADFLAX.

Linaria vulgaris. Figwort Family.

Stem.—Smooth; erect; one to three feet high. *Leaves.*—Alternate; linear or nearly so. *Flowers.*—Of two shades of yellow; growing in terminal racemes. *Calyx.*—Five-parted. *Corolla.*—Pale yellow tipped with orange; long-spurred; two-lipped; closed in the throat. *Stamens.*—Four. *Pistil.*—One.

The bright blossoms of butter-and-eggs grow in full, close clusters which enliven the waste places along the roadside so commonly that little attention is paid to these beautiful and conspicuous flowers. They would be considered a "pest" if they did not display great discrimination in their choice of locality, generally selecting otherwise useless pieces of ground. The common name of butter-and-eggs is unusually appropriate, for the two shades of yellow match perfectly their namesakes. Like nearly all our common weeds, this plant has been utilized in various ways by the country people. It yielded what was considered at one time a valuable skin lotion, while its juice mingled with milk constitutes a fly-poison. Its generic name, *Linaria*, and its English title, toadflax, arose from a fancied resemblance between its leaves and those of the flax.

DYER'S GREENWEED. WOAD-WAXEN. NEW ENGLAND WHIN.

Genista tinctoria. Pulse Family.

A shrubby plant from one to two feet high. *Leaves.*—Lance-shaped. *Flowers.*—Papilionaceous; yellow; growing in spiked racemes.

This is another foreigner which has established itself in Eastern New York and Massachusetts, where it covers the barren hill-sides with its yellow flowers in early summer. It is a common English plant, formerly valued for the yellow dye which it yielded. It is an undesirable intruder in pasture-lands, as it gives a bitter taste to the milk of cows which feed upon it.

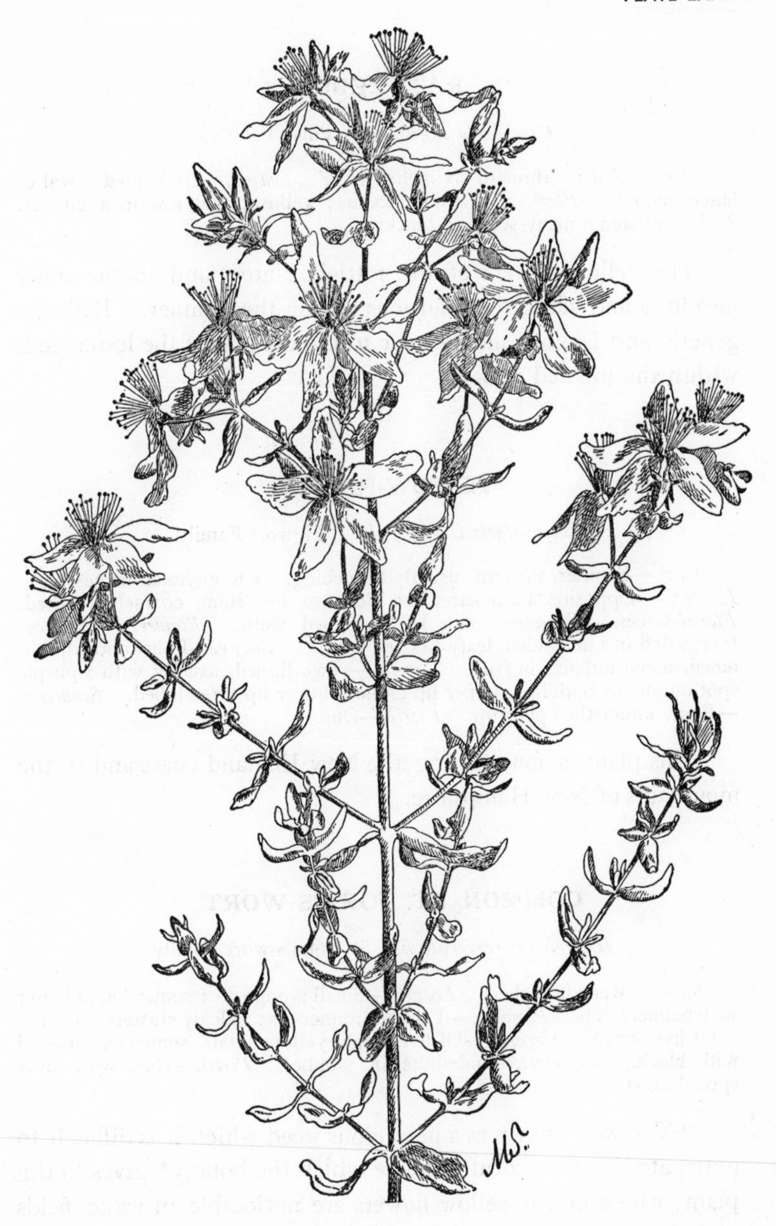

COMMON ST. JOHN'S-WORT.—*Hypericum perforatum.*

RATTLEBOX.

Crotalaria sagittalis. Pulse Family.

Stem.—Hairy; three to six inches high. *Leaves.*—Undivided; oval or lance-shaped. *Flowers.*—Papilionaceous; yellow; but few in a cluster. *Pod.*—Inflated; many-seeded; blackish.

The yellow flowers of the rattlebox are found in the sandy meadows and along the roadsides during the summer. Both the generic and English names refer to the rattling of the loose seeds within the inflated pod.

YELLOW-RATTLE.

Rhinanthus Crista-galli. Figwort Family.

Stem.—Slender, upright, usually branching, six to eighteen inches high. *Leaves.* — Opposite, lanceolate, set close to the stem, coarsely toothed. *Floral-leaves.* — Broader, with bristle-tipped teeth. *Flowers.* — Yellow, "crowded in a one-sided, leafy-bracted spike." *Calyx.*—Four-toothed, flattened, much inflated in fruit. *Corolla.*—Two-lipped, usually with a purple spot on one or both lips, upper lip arched, lower lip three-lobed. *Stamens.* —Four, under the upper lip. *Pistil.*—One.

This plant is found along the New England coast and in the mountains of New Hampshire.

COMMON ST. JOHN'S-WORT.

Hypericum perforatum. St. John's-wort Family.

Stem.—Much branched. *Leaves.*—Small; opposite; somewhat oblong; with pellucid dots. *Flowers.*—Yellow; numerous; in leafy clusters. *Calyx.* —Of five sepals. *Corolla.*—Of five bright yellow petals, somewhat spotted with black. *Stamens.*—Indefinite in number. *Pistil.*—One, with three spreading styles.

"Too well known as a pernicious weed which it is difficult to extirpate," is the scornful notice which the botany* gives to this plant, whose bright yellow flowers are noticeable in waste fields and along roadsides nearly all summer. Its rank, rapid growth proves very exhausting to the soil, and every New England

* Earlier than Eighth Edition.

farmer wishes it had remained where it rightfully belongs—on the other side of the water.

Perhaps more superstitions have clustered about the St. John's-wort than about any other plant on record. It was formerly gathered on St. John's eve, and was hung at the doors and windows as a safeguard against thunder and evil spirits. A belief prevailed that on this night the soul had power to leave the body and visit the spot where it would finally be summoned from its earthly habitation, hence the all-night vigils which were observed at that time.

> "The wonderful herb whose leaf will decide
> If the coming year shall make me a bride,"

is the St. John's-wort, and the maiden's fate is favorably forecast by the healthy growth and successful blossoming of the plant which she has accepted as typical of her future.

In early times poets and physicians alike extolled its properties. An ointment was made of its blossoms, and one of its early names was "balm-of-the-warrior's-wound." It was considered so efficacious a remedy for melancholia that it was termed "fuga dæmonum." Very possibly this name gave rise to the general idea that it was powerful in dispelling evil spirits.

The pale St. John's-wort, *H. ellipticum*, has thin, spreading, oval leaves which are set close to the stem, and pale yellow flowers, about half an inch broad.

The spotted St. John's-wort, *H. punctatum*, may be identified by its slender blossoms and copiously black-dotted, oblong leaves.

The Canadian St. John's-wort, *H. canadense*, has linear three-nerved leaves and small flowers with from five to twelve stamens only. It grows abundantly in wet, sandy places.

The dwarf St. John's-wort, *H. mutilum*, has even smaller blossoms, with from five to twelve stamens also, and narrowly oblong or ovate leaves, which are five-nerved and partly clasping. This is abundant in low grounds everywhere.

ORANGE-GRASS. PINEWEED.

Hypericum gentianoides. St. John's-wort Family.

Erect; bushy; four to twenty inches high, with wiry, thread-like branches. *Leaves.*—Opposite; minute; awl-shaped, pressed toward the stem. *Flowers.*—Yellow, very small, open in sunlight. *Calyx.*—Of five sepals. *Corolla.*—Of five petals. *Stamens.*—Five to twelve. *Pistil.*—One, with three separate styles. *Fruit.*—A red or purplish pod.

This little plant is common in sandy soil from Maine to Florida, and westward as well. Often it grows abundantly along the roadside.

ST. ANDREW'S CROSS.

Ascyrum Hypericoides. St. John's-wort Family.

Stems.—Low; branched. *Leaves.*—Opposite; narrowly oblong; black-dotted. *Flowers.*—Light yellow. *Calyx.*—Of four sepals; the two outer broad and leaflike; the inner much smaller. *Corolla.*—Of four narrowly oblong petals. *Stamens.*—Numerous. *Pistil.*—One, with two short styles.

From July till September these flowers may be found in the pine-barrens of New Jersey and farther south and westward, and on the island of Nantucket as well.

COMMON MULLEIN.

Verbascum Thapsus. Figwort Family.

Stems.—Tall and stout; from three to five feet high. *Leaves.*—Oblong; woolly. *Flowers.*—In a long dense spike. *Calyx.*—Five-parted. *Corolla.*—Yellow; with five slightly unequal rounded lobes. *Stamens.*—Ten, the three upper with white wool on their filaments. *Pistil.*—One.

The common mullein is a native of the island of Thapsos, from which it takes its specific name. It was probably brought to this country from Europe by the early colonists, notwithstanding the title of "American velvet plant," which it is rumored to bear in England. The Romans called it "candelaria," from their custom of dipping the long, dried stalk in suet and using it

COMMON MULLEIN.—*Verbascum Thapsus.*

as a funeral torch, and the Greeks utilized the leaves for lamp-wicks. In more modern times they have served as a remedy for the pulmonary complaints of men and beasts alike, "mullein tea" being greatly esteemed by country people. Its especial efficacy with cattle has earned the plant its name of "bullocks' lungwort."

A low rosette of woolly leaves is all that can be seen of the mullein during its first year, the yellow blossoms on their long spikes opening sluggishly about the middle of the second summer. It abounds throughout our dry, rolling meadows, and its tall spires are a familiar feature in the summer landscape.

MOTH-MULLEIN.

Verbascum Blattaria. Figwort Family.

Stem.—Tall and slender. *Leaves.*—Oblong; toothed; the lower sometimes lyre-shaped, the upper partly clasping. *Flowers.*—Yellow or white; tinged with red or purple; in a terminal raceme. *Calyx.*—Deeply five-parted. *Corolla.*—Butterfly shape; of five rounded, somewhat unequal lobes. *Stamens.*—Five, with filaments bearded with violet wool and anthers loaded with orange-colored pollen. *Pistil.*—One.

Along the highway from July till October one encounters a slender weed on whose erect stem it would seem as though a number of canary-yellow or purplish-white moths had alighted for a moment's rest. These are the fragile, pretty flowers of the moth-mullein, and they are worthy of a closer examination. The reddened or purplish centre of the corolla suggests the probability of hidden nectar, while the pretty tufts of violet wool borne by the stamens are well fitted to protect it from the rain. A little experience of the canny ways of these innocent-looking flowers leads one to ask the wherefore of every new feature.

MOTH-MULLEIN.—*Verbascum Blattaria.*

PARTRIDGE-PEA.

Cassia fasciculata. Pulse Family.

Stems.—Spreading; eight inches to a foot long. *Leaves.*—Divided into from ten to fifteen pairs of narrow delicate leaflets, which close at night and are somewhat sensitive to the touch. *Flowers.*—Yellow; rather large and showy; on slender stalks beneath the spreading leaves; not papilionaceous. *Calyx.*—Of five sepals. *Corolla.*—Of five rounded, spreading, somewhat unequal petals, two or three of which are usually spotted at the base with red or purple. *Stamens.*—Ten; unequal; dissimilar. *Pistil.*—One, with a slender style. *Pod.*—Flat.

The partridge-pea is closely related to the wild senna, and a pretty, delicate plant it is, with graceful foliage, and flowers in late summer which surprise us with their size, abounding in gravelly, sandy places where little else will flourish, brightening the railway embankments and the road's edge. It is at home all over the country south of Massachusetts and east of the Rocky Mountains, but it grows with a greater vigor and luxuriance in the South than elsewhere. The leaves can hardly be called sensitive to the touch, yet when a branch is snapped from the parent stem, or is much handled, the delicate leaflets will droop and fold, displaying their curious mechanism.

WILD SENNA.

Cassia marilandica. Pulse Family.

Stem.—Three or four feet high. *Leaves.*—Divided into from six to nine pairs of narrowly oblong leaflets. *Flowers.*—Yellow; in short clusters from the axils of the leaves. *Calyx.*—Of five sepals. *Corolla.*—Of five slightly unequal, spreading petals; usually somewhat spotted with reddish brown. *Stamens.*—Five to ten; unequal; some of them often imperfect. *Pistil.*—One. *Pod.*—Long and narrow, slightly curved, flat.

This tall, striking plant, with clusters of yellow flowers which appear in midsummer, grows abundantly along many of the New England roadsides, and also far south and west, thriving best in sandy soil. Although a member of the Pulse family its blossoms are not papilionaceous.

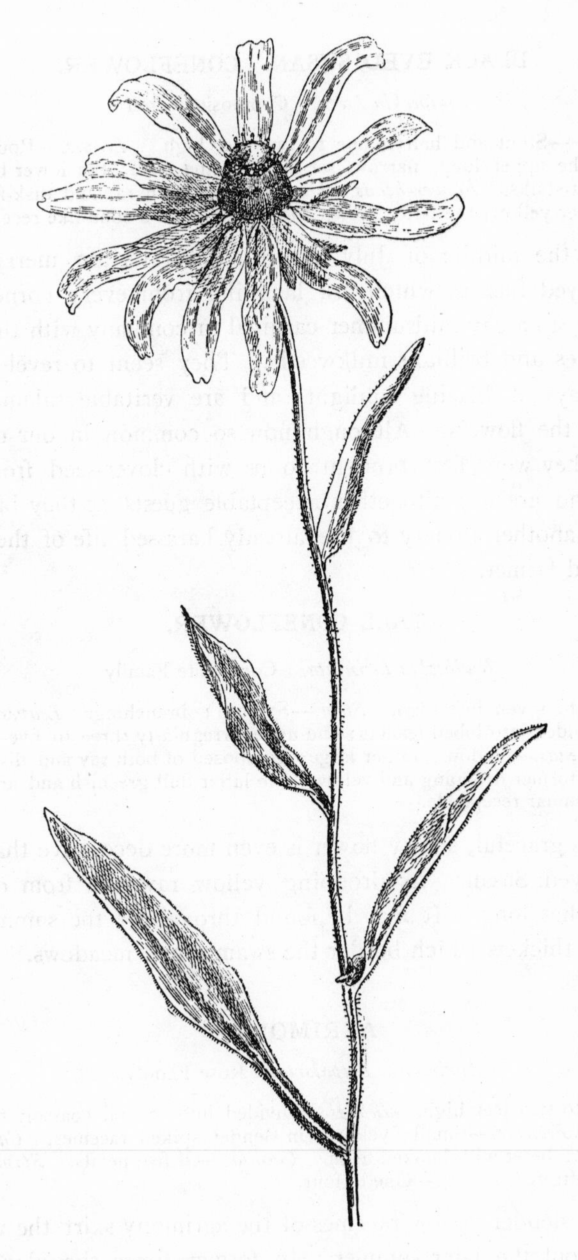

BLACK-EYED SUSAN.—*Rudbeckia hirta.*

BLACK-EYED SUSAN. CONEFLOWER.

Rudbeckia hirta. Composite Family.

Stem.—Stout and hairy; one to two feet high. *Leaves.*—Rough and hairy; the upper long, narrow, set close to the stem; the lower broader, with leaf-stalks. *Flower-heads.*—Composed of both ray and disk-flowers; the former yellow, the latter brown and arranged on a cone-like receptacle.

By the middle of July our dry meadows are merry with black-eyed Susans, which are laughing from every corner and keeping up a gay midsummer carnival in company with the yellow lilies and brilliant milkweeds. They seem to revel in the long days of blazing sunlight, and are veritable salamanders among the flowers. Although now so common in our eastern fields they were first brought to us with clover-seed from the west, and are not altogether acceptable guests, as they bid fair to add another anxiety to the already harassed life of the New England farmer.

TALL CONEFLOWER.

Rudbeckia laciniata. Composite Family.

Two to seven feet high. *Stem.*—Smooth; branching. *Leaves.*—The lower divided into lobed leaflets; the upper irregularly three to five-parted. *Flower-heads.*—Yellow; rather large; composed of both ray and disk-flowers; the former drooping and yellow; the latter dull greenish and arranged on a columnar receptacle.

This graceful, showy flower is even more decorative than the black-eyed Susan. Its drooping yellow rays are from one to two inches long. It may be found throughout the summer in the low thickets which border the swamps and meadows.

AGRIMONY.

Agrimonia Eupatoria. Rose Family.

One to two feet high. *Leaves.*—Divided into several coarsely toothed leaflets. *Flowers.*—Small; yellow; in slender spiked racemes. *Calyx.*—Five-cleft; beset with hooked teeth. *Corolla.*—Of five petals. *Stamens.*—Five to fifteen. *Pistils.*—One to four.

The slender yellow racemes of the agrimony skirt the woods throughout the later summer. In former times the plant was

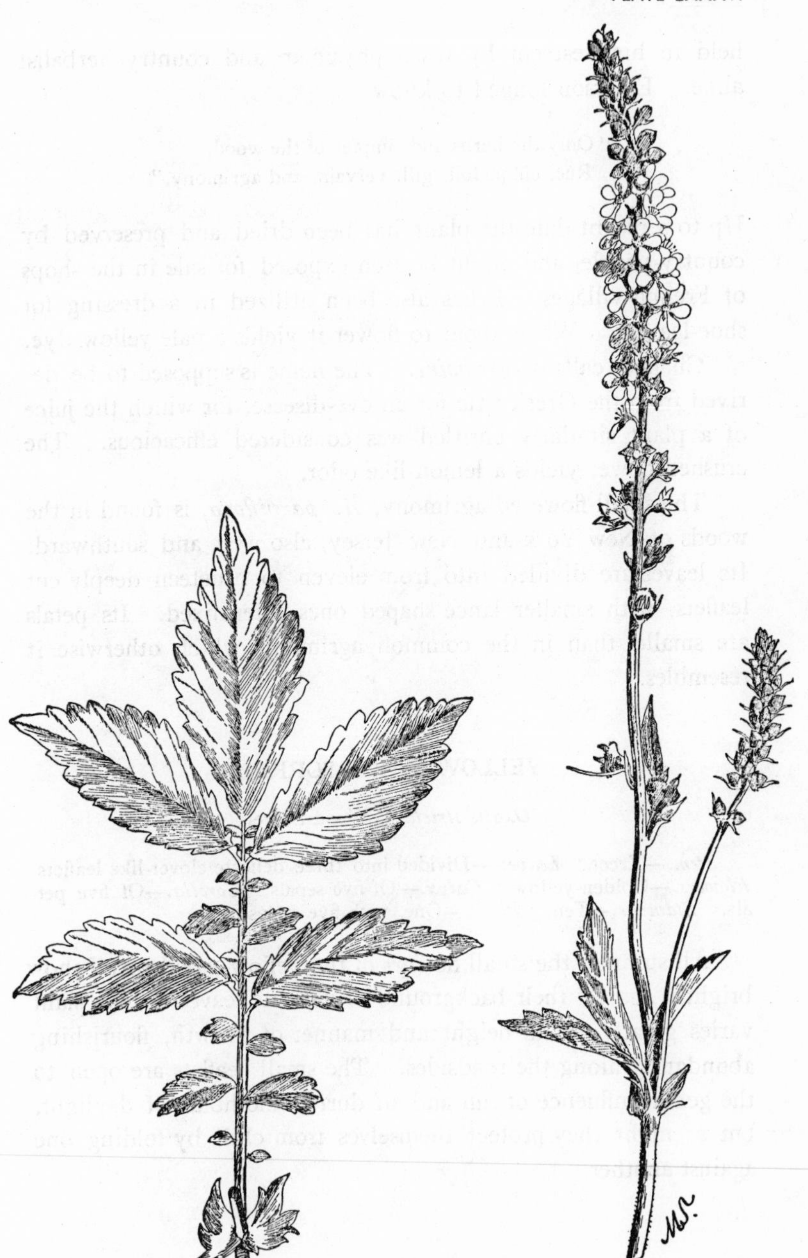

AGRIMONY.—*Agrimonia Eupatoria.*

held in high esteem by town physician and country herbalist alike. Emerson longed to know

> "Only the herbs and simples of the wood,
> Rue, cinquefoil, gill, vervain, and agrimony."

Up to a recent date the plant has been dried and preserved by country people, and might be seen exposed for sale in the shops of French villages. It has also been utilized in a dressing for shoe-leather. When about to flower it yields a pale yellow dye.

Chaucer calls it *egremoine*. The name is supposed to be derived from the Greek title for an eye-disease, for which the juice of a plant similarly entitled was considered efficacious. The crushed flower yields a lemon-like odor.

The small-flowered agrimony, *A. parviflora*, is found in the woods of New York and New Jersey, also west and southward. Its leaves are divided into from eleven to nineteen deeply cut leaflets, with smaller lance-shaped ones intermixed. Its petals are smaller than in the common agrimony, which otherwise it resembles.

YELLOW WOOD-SORREL.

Oxalis stricta. Wood-Sorrel

Stem.—Erect. *Leaves.*—Divided into three delicate clover-like leaflets *Flowers.*—Golden-yellow. *Calyx.*—Of five sepals. *Corolla.*—Of five petals. *Stamens.*—Ten. *Pistil.*—One, with five styles.

All summer the small flowers of the yellow wood-sorrel show brightly against their background of delicate leaves. The plant varies greatly in its height and manner of growth, flourishing abundantly along the roadsides. The small leaflets are open to the genial influence of sun and air during the hours of daylight, but at night they protect themselves from chill by folding one against another.

PALE JEWELWEED.—*Impatiens pallida.*

JEWELWEED. TOUCH-ME-NOT.

Geranium Family.

Impatiens pallida. Pale Jewelweed.

Flowers.—Pale yellow, somewhat spotted with reddish brown; common northward.

Impatiens capensis. Spotted Jewelweed.

Flowers.—Orange-yellow, spotted with reddish brown; common southward.

Two to six feet high. *Leaves.*—Alternate; coarsely toothed; oval. *Flowers.*—Nodding; loosely clustered, or growing from the axils of the leaves. *Calyx* and *Corolla.*—Colored alike, and difficult to distinguish; of six pieces, the largest one extended backward into a deep sac ending in a little spur, the two innermost unequally two-lobed. *Stamens.*—Five; very short; united over the pistil. *Pistil.*—One.

These beautiful plants are found along shaded streams and marshes, and are profusely hung with brilliant jewel-like flowers during the summer months. In the later year they bear those closed inconspicuous blossoms which fertilize in the bud and are called cleistogamous flowers. The jewelweed has begun to appear along the English rivers, and it is said that the ordinary showy blossoms are comparatively rare, while the cleistogamous ones abound. Does not this look almost like a determination on the part of the plant to secure a firm foothold in its new environment before expending its energy on flowers which, though radiant and attractive, are quite dependent on insect visitors for fertilization and perpetuation?

The name touch-me-not refers to the seed-pods, which burst open with such violence when touched, as to project their seeds to a comparatively great distance. This ingenious mechanism secures the dispersion of the seeds without the aid of the wind or animals. In parts of New York the plant is called "silver-leaf," from its silvery appearance when touched with rain or dew, or when held beneath the water.

YELLOW FRINGED ORCHIS—*Habenaria ciliaris.*

HORSE-BALM. RICHWEED. STONEROOT.

Collinsonia canadensis. Mint Family.

One to three feet high. *Leaves.*—Opposite; large; ovate; toothed; pointed. *Flowers.*—Yellowish; lemon-scented; clustered loosely. *Calyx.*—Two-lipped; the upper lip three-toothed; the lower two-cleft. *Corolla.*—Elongated; somewhat two-lipped; the four upper lobes nearly equal, the lower large and long, toothed or fringed. *Stamens.*—Two (sometimes four, the upper pair shorter), protruding, diverging. *Pistil.*—One, with a two-lobed style.

In the damp rich woods of midsummer these strong-scented herbs, with their loose terminal clusters of lemon-colored, lemon-scented flowers, are abundant. The plant was introduced into England by the amateur botanist and flower-lover, Collinson, after whom the species is named. The Indians formerly employed it as an application to wounds.

YELLOW FRINGED ORCHIS. ORANGE ORCHIS.

Habenaria ciliaris. Orchis Family.

Stem.—Leafy; one to two feet high. *Leaves.*—The lower oblong to lance-shaped; the upper passing into pointed bracts. *Flowers.*—Deep orange color, with a slender spur and deeply fringed lip; growing in an oblong spike.

Years may pass without our meeting this the most brilliant of our orchids. Suddenly one August day we chance upon just such a boggy meadow as we have searched in vain a hundred times, and behold myriads of its deep orange, dome-like spires erecting themselves in radiant beauty over whole acres of land. The separate flowers, with their long spurs and deeply fringed lips, will repay a close examination. They are well calculated, massed in such brilliant clusters, to arrest the attention of whatever insects may specially affect them. Although I have watched many of these plants I have never seen an insect visit one, and am inclined to think that they are fertilized by night-moths.

EVENING-PRIMROSE.—*Oenothera biennis.*

Mr. Baldwin declares: "If I ever write a romance of Indian life, my dusky heroine, Birch Tree or Trembling Fawn, shall meet her lover with a wreath of this orchis on her head."

EVENING-PRIMROSE.

Oenothera biennis. Evening-Primrose Family.

Stout; erect; one to five feet high. *Leaves.*—Alternate; lance-shaped to oblong. *Flowers.*—Pale yellow; in a leafy spike; opening at night. *Calyx.*—With a long tube; four-lobed. *Corolla.*—Of four somewhat heart-shaped petals. *Stamens.*—Eight, with long anthers. *Pistil.*—One, with a stigma divided into four linear lobes.

Along the roadsides in midsummer we notice a tall, rank-growing plant, which seems chiefly to bear buds and faded blossoms. And unless we are already familiar with the owl-like tendencies of the evening-primrose, we are surprised, some dim twilight, to find this same plant resplendent with a mass of fragile yellow flowers, which are exhaling their faint delicious fragrance on the evening air.

One brief summer night exhausts the vitality of these delicate blossoms. The faded petals of the following day might serve as a text for a homily against all-night dissipation, did we not know that by its strange habit the evening primrose guards against the depredations of those myriad insects abroad during the day, which are unfitted to transmit its pollen to the pistil of another flower.

We are impressed by the utilitarianism in vogue in this floral world, as we note that the pale yellow of these blossoms gleams so vividly through the darkness as to advertise effectively their whereabouts, while their fragrance serves as a mute invitation to the pink night-moth, which is their visitor and benefactor. That they change their habits in the late year and remain open during the day is due perhaps to the diminished power of the sun.

ELECAMPANE.—*Inula Helenium.*

ELECAMPANE.

Inula Helenium. Composite Family.

Stem.—Stout; three to five feet high. *Leaves.*—Alternate; large; woolly beneath; the upper partly clasping. *Flower-heads.*—Yellow; large; composed of both ray and disk-flowers.

When we see these great yellow disks peeping over the pasture walls or flanking the country lanes, we feel that midsummer is at its height. Flowers are often subservient courtiers, and make acknowledgment of whatever debt they owe by that subtlest of flatteries—imitation. Did not the blossoms of the dawning year frequently wear the livery of the snow which had thrown its protecting mantle over their first efforts? And these new-comers—whose gross, rotund countenances so clearly betray the results of high living—do not they pay their respects to their great benefactor after the same fashion?—with the result that a myriad miniature suns shine upward from meadow and roadside.

The stout, mucilaginous root of this plant is valued by farmers as a horse-medicine, especially in epidemics of epizootic, one of its common names in England being horse-heal.

In ancient times the elecampane was considered an important stimulant to the human brain and stomach, and it was mentioned as such over two thousand years ago in the writings of Hippocrates, the "Father of Medicine."

The common name is supposed to be a corruption of *ala Campania*, and refers to the frequent occurrence of the plant in that ancient province of Southern Italy.

GOLDEN ASTER.

Chrysopsis mariana. Composite Family.

Stem.—Silky with long weak hairs when young. *Leaves.*—Alternate; oblong. *Flower-heads.*—Golden yellow; rather large; composed of both ray and disk-flowers.

In dry places along the roadsides of Southern New York and farther south, one can hardly fail to notice in late summer and autumn the bright clusters of the golden aster.

TALL SUNFLOWER.—*Helianthus giganteus.*

C. falcata is a species which may be found in dry sandy soil as far north as Massachusetts, with very woolly stems, crowded linear leaves, and small, clustered flower-heads.

TALL SUNFLOWER.

Helianthus giganteus. Composite Family.

Stem.—Rough or hairy; from three to ten feet high; branched above.
Leaves.—Lance-shaped; pointed; rough to the touch, set close to the stem.
Flower-heads.—Yellow; composed of both ray and disk-flowers.

In late summer many of our lanes are hedged by this beautiful plant, which, like other members of its family, lifts its yellow flowers sunward in pale imitation of the great lifegiver itself.

We have over twenty different species of sunflower.

H. divaricatus is of a lower growth, with opposite, widely spreading leaves and larger flower-heads.

H. annuus is the garden species familiar to all; this is said to be a native of Peru. Mr. Ellwanger writes regarding it: "In the mythology of the ancient Peruvians it occupied an important place, and was employed as a mystic decoration in ancient Mexican sculpture. Like the lotus of the East, it is equally a sacred and an artistic emblem, figuring in the symbolism of Mexico and Peru, where the Spaniards found it rearing its aspiring stalk in the fields, and serving in the temple as a sign and a decoration, the sun-god's officiating handmaidens wearing upon their breasts representations of the sacred flower in beaten gold."

Gerarde describes it as follows: "The Indian Sun, or the golden floure of Peru, is a plant of such stature and talnesse that in one Sommer, being sowne of a seede in April, it hath risen up to the height of fourteen foot in my garden, where one floure was in weight three pound and two ounces, and crosse overthwart the floure by measure sixteen inches broad."

The generic name is from *helios*—the sun, and *anthos*—a flower.

STICK-TIGHT.—*Bidens frondosa.*

Barbed fruit.

SNEEZEWEED. SWAMP-SUNFLOWER.

Helenium autumnale. Composite Family.

One to six feet high. *Stem.*—Angled; erect; branching. *Leaves.*—Alternate; lance-shaped. *Flower-heads.*—Yellow; composed of both ray and disk-flowers, the rays three to five-cleft.

The general effect of this plant is similar to that of the tall sunflowers, but one is able to identify it easily on a close examination, by means of the stem, which is angled, and by the ray-flowers, which are pistillate and from three to five cleft.

During September it is abundant in Connecticut, and farther south and westward, its bright flower-heads bordering the rivers, gilding the meadows, and illuminating many of those dim woodland pools which flash upon us so constantly and enticingly as we travel through the country by rail.

FALL-DANDELION.

Leontodon autumnalis. Composite Family.

Scape.—Five to fifteen inches high; branching. *Leaves.*—From the root; toothed or deeply incised. *Flower-heads.*—Yellow; composed entirely of strap-shaped flowers; smaller than those of the common dandelion

From June till November we find the fall-dandelion along the New England roadsides, as well as farther south. While the yellow flower-heads somewhat suggest small dandelions the general habit of the plant recalls some of the hawkweeds.

STICK-TIGHT. BUR-MARIGOLD. BEGGAR-TICKS.

Bidens frondosa. Composite Family.

Two to six feet high. *Stem.*—Branching. *Leaves.*—Opposite; three to five-divided. *Flower-heads.*—Consisting of brownish-yellow tubular flowers; with a leaf-like involucre beneath.

If one were only describing the attractive wild flowers, the stick-tight would certainly be omitted, as its appearance is not

LARGER BUR-MARIGOLD.—[*Bidens chrysanthemoides.*]

prepossessing, and the small barbed seed-vessels so cleverly fulfil their destiny in making one's clothes a means of conveyance to "fresh woods and pastures new" as to cause all wayfarers heartily to detest them. "How surely the desmodium growing on some cliff-side, or the bidens on the edge of a pool, prophesy the coming of the traveller, brute or human, that will transport their seeds on his coat," writes Thoreau. But the plant is so constantly encountered in late summer, and yet so generally unknown, that it can hardly be overlooked.

The larger bur-marigold, *B. chrysanthemoides** (Pl. XCIII.), does its best to retrieve the family reputation for ugliness, and surrounds its dingy disk-flowers with a circle of showy golden rays which are strictly decorative, having neither pistils nor stamens, and leaving all the work of the household to the less attractive but more useful disk-flowers. Their effect is pleasing, and late into the autumn the moist ditches look as if sown with gold through their agency. The plant varies in height from six inches to two feet. Its leaves are opposite, lance-shaped, and regularly toothed.

B. cernua, the small bur-marigold, is found often without ray-flowers; when these are present they are shorter than the leaflike involucre which surrounds the flower-head. Its leaves are *irregularly toothed*, and lance-shaped. Its height varies, being anywhere from five inches to three feet.

WILD LETTUCE.

Lactuca canadensis. Composite Family.

Stems.—Noticeably tall, from four to nine feet high; leafy; smooth or nearly so. *Leaves.*—Usually six inches to a foot long; pale beneath; the upper lance-shaped and not toothed; the others usually wavy, lobed, or cut. *Flower-heads.*—Pale yellow; small; composed of strap-shaped flowers; numerous in usually long and narrow clusters.

The wild lettuce is common in the wet and somewhat open thickets of late summer. It is perhaps rendered more conspicuous by its unusual height and lobed leaves than by its insignifi-

* Obsolete scientific name.

PLATE XCIV

Disk and Ray-flowers.

LANCE-LEAVED GOLDENROD.—*Solidago graminifolia.*

cant flowers. For my own part I rarely notice this plant during its period of blossoming, although my eye is constantly arrested by its feathery seed-clusters during the fruiting season.

YELLOW THISTLE.

Carduus horridulum. Composite Family.

Stem.—Stout; one to three feet high. *Leaves.*—Partly clasping; deeply cut; the toothed and cut lobes spiny with yellowish prickles. *Flower-heads.*—Pale yellow or purple; composed entirely of tubular flowers; surrounded by leaf-like, prickly bracts.

In sandy fields near the coast the yellow thistle blossoms during the later summer.

GOLDENROD.

Solidago. Composite Family.

Flower-heads.—Golden-yellow; composed of both ray and disk-flowers.

About eighty species of goldenrod are native to the United States; of these over forty species can be found in our Northeastern States. Many of them are difficult of identification, and it would be useless to describe any but a few of the more conspicuous forms.

A common and noticeable species which flowers early in August is *S. canadensis*, with a tall, stout, rough stem from three to six feet high, lance-shaped leaves, which are usually sharply toothed and pointed, and small flower-heads clustered along the branches which spread from the upper part of the stem.

Another early flowering species is *S. rugosa*. This is a lower plant than *S. canadensis*, with broader leaves.

Still another is the dusty goldenrod, *S. nemoralis*, which has a hoary aspect and very bright yellow flowers which are common in dry fields.

S. juncea is also an early bloomer. Its lower leaves are lanceolate or oval, with sharp, spreading teeth and long, winged leaf-

Disk and ray-flowers.

SILVERROD.—*Solidago bicolor.*

stems. The upper ones are narrow and set close to the stem. Its flower-heads grow on the upper side of recurved branches, forming usually a full, spreading cluster.

S. graminifolia has lance-shaped or linear leaves, and flowers which grow in flat-topped clusters, unlike other members of the family; the information that this is a goldenrod often creates surprise, as for some strange reason it seems to be confused with the tansy.

The sweet goldenrod, *S. odora*, is recognized by its narrow, shining, dotted leaves, which when crushed yield a pleasant, permeating fragrance.

The seaside goldenrod, *S. sempervirens*, is a showy, beautiful plant of vigorous habit. Its large, orange-yellow flower-heads, and thick, bright green leaves make brilliant the salt-marshes, sand-hills, and rocky shores of the Atlantic coast every August.

S. caesia, or blue-stem goldenrod, is a wood-species and among the latest of the year, putting forth its bright clusters for nearly the whole length of its stem long after many of its brethren look like brown wraiths of their former selves.

S. flexicaulis usually has a simple, zigzag stem from one to three feet high, close to which, in the axils of the leaves, the flower-heads are bunched in short clusters. Toward the top of the stem these clusters may be prolonged into a narrow wand. Its leaves are thin, broadly ovate, sharply toothed and pointed at both ends. This plant loves somewhat moist, shaded localities.

The slender, wand-like silverrod, *S. bicolor* (Plate XCV.), whose partly whitish flower-heads are a departure from the family habit, also survives the early cold and holds its own in the dry woods.

The only species native to Great Britain is *S. Virgaurea*.

The generic name, from the Latin, signifies *to make whole*, and refers to the healing properties which have been attributed to the genus.

SMOOTH FALSE FOXGLOVE.—*Gerardia flava.*

SMOOTH FALSE FOXGLOVE.

Gerardia flava. Figwort Family.

Stem.—Smooth; three to six feet high; usually branching. *Leaves.*—The lower usually deeply incised; the upper narrowly oblong, incised, or entire. *Flowers.*—Yellow; large; in a raceme or spike. *Calyx.*—Five-cleft. *Corolla.*—Two inches long; somewhat tubular; swelling above; with five more or less unequal, spreading lobes; woolly within. *Stamens.*—Four; in pairs; woolly. *Pistil.*—One.

These large, pale yellow flowers are very beautiful and striking when seen in the dry woods of late summer. They are all the more appreciated because there are few flowers abroad at this season save the Composites, which are decorative and radiant enough, but usually somewhat lacking in the delicate charm we look for in a flower.

For me the plant is associated especially with two localities. One is a mountain-road whose borders, from early June, are brilliant with a show of lovely blossoms, but which, just before the appearance of the false foxglove, is threatened with a dismal break in the floral procession. Only the sharpest eyes are solaced by multitudes of round yellow buds, that burst suddenly into peculiarly fresh and pleasing flowers.

The other favored spot is a wooded island on the coast, surrounded by a salt marsh. In August, when the marsh itself is still brilliant with sea-pinks and milkwort, and beginning to wear its glowing mantle of asters and goldenrods, this island can scarcely boast a blossom save that of the false foxglove. But the plant succeeds in redeeming the lonely spot from any suspicion of dreariness by its lavish display of cheery flowers.

The members of this genus, which is named after Gerarde, the author of the famous "Herball," are supposed to be more or less parasitic in their habits, drawing their nourishment from the roots of other plants.

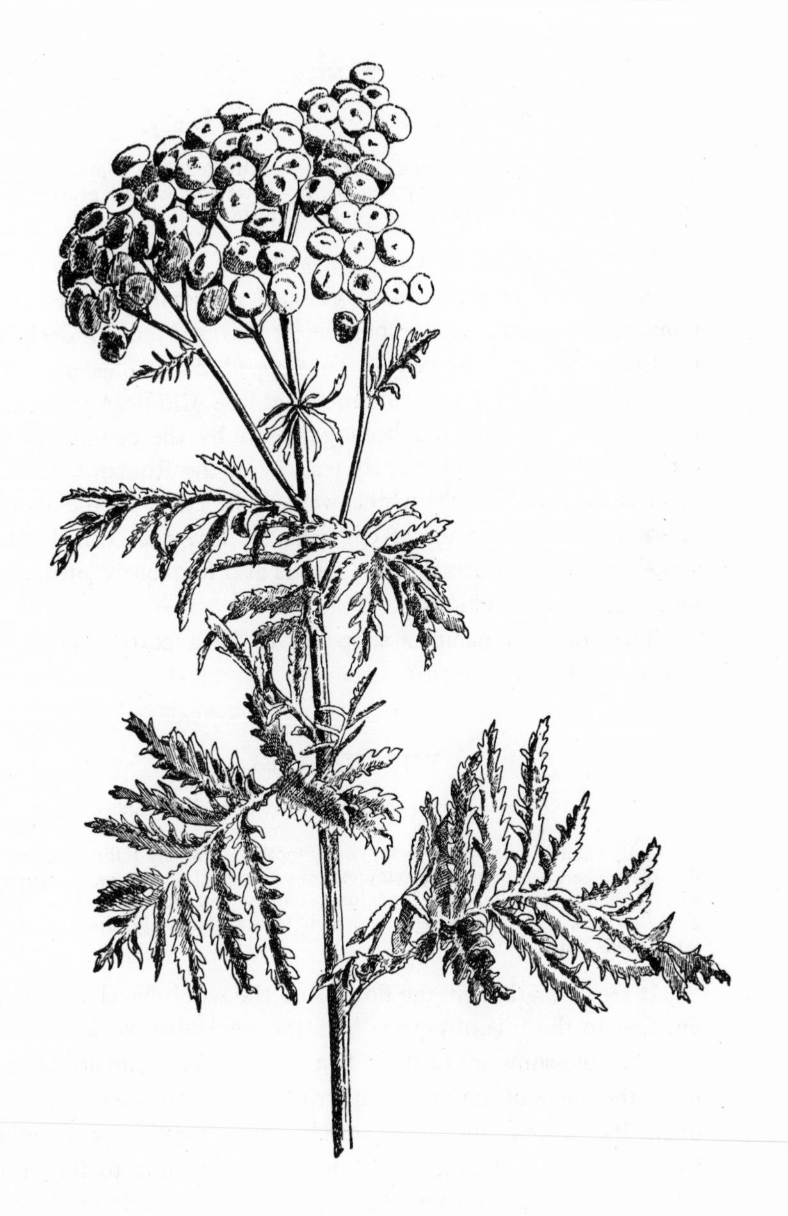

TANSY.—*Tanacetum vulgare.*

TANSY.

Tanacetum vulgare. Composite Family.

Stem.—Two to four feet high. *Leaves.*—Divided into toothed leaflets. *Flower-heads.*—Yellow; composed of tiny flowers which are nearly, if not all, tubular in shape; borne in flat-topped clusters.

With the name of tansy we seem to catch a whiff of its strong-scented breath and a glimpse of some New England homestead beyond whose borders it has strayed to deck the roadside with its deep yellow, flat topped flower-clusters. The plant has been used in medicine since the Middle Ages, and in more recent times it has been gathered by the country people for "tansy wine" and "tansy tea." In the Roman Church it typifies the bitter herbs which were to be eaten at the Paschal season; and cakes made of eggs and its leaves are called "tansies," and eaten during Lent. It is also frequently utilized in more secular concoctions.

The common name is supposed to be a corruption of the Greek word for *immortality*.

WITCH-HAZEL.

Hamamelis virginiana. Witch-hazel Family.

A tall shrub. *Leaves.*—Oval; wavy-toothed; mostly falling before the flowers appear. *Flowers.*—Honey-yellow; clustered; autumnal. *Calyx.*—Four-parted. *Corolla.*—Of four long, narrow petals. *Stamens.*—Eight. *Pistil.*—Two. *Fruit.*—A capsule which bursts elastically, discharging its large seeds with vigor.

It seems as though the flowers of the witch-hazel were fairly entitled to the "booby-prize" of the vegetable world. Surely no other blossoms make their first appearance so invariably late upon the scene of action. The fringed gentian often begins to open its "meek and quiet eye" quite early in September. Certain species of goldenrod and aster continue to flower till late in the year, but they began putting forth their bright clusters before the summer was fairly over; while the elusively fragrant, pale yellow blossoms of the witch-hazel need hardly be ex-

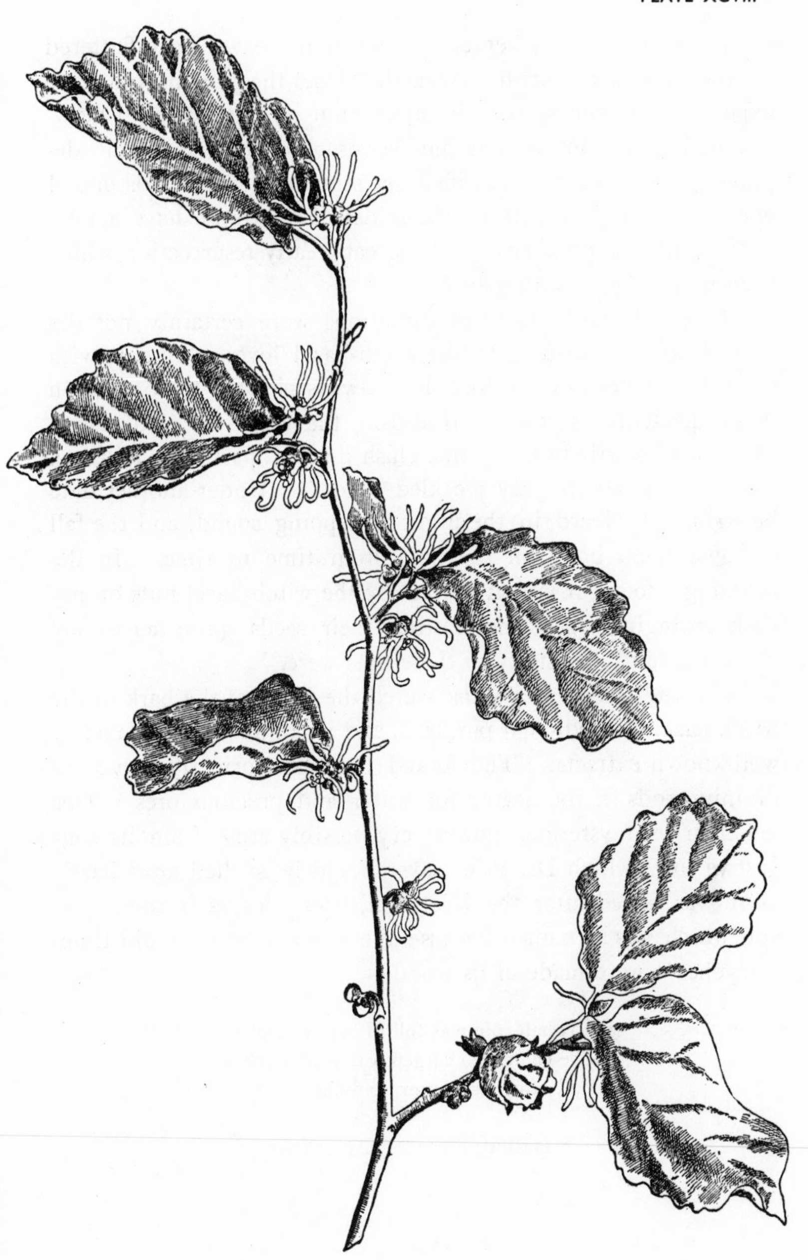

WITCH-HAZEL.—*Hamamelis virginiana.*

pected till well on in September, when its leaves have fluttered earthward and its fruit has ripened. Does the pleasure which we experience at the spring-like apparition of this leafless yellow-flowered shrub in the autumn woods arise from the same depraved taste which is gratified by strawberries at Christmas, I wonder? Or is it that in the midst of death we have a foretaste of life; a prophecy of the great yearly resurrection which even now we may anticipate?

Thoreau's tastes in such directions were certainly not depraved, and he writes: "The witch-hazel loves a hill-side with or without woods or shrubs. It is always pleasant to come upon it unexpectedly as you are threading the woods in such places. Methinks I attribute to it some elfish quality apart from its fame. I love to behold its gray speckled stems." Under another date he writes: "Heard in the night a snapping sound, and the fall of some small body on the floor from time to time. In the morning I found it was produced by the witch-hazel nuts on my desk springing open and casting their seeds quite across my chamber, hard and stony as these nuts were."

The Indians long ago discovered the value of the bark of the witch-hazel for medicinal purposes, and it is now utilized in many well-known extracts. The forked branches formerly served as divining-rods in the search for water and precious ores. This belief in its mysterious power very possibly arose from its suggestive title, which Dr. Prior says should be spelled *wych*-hazel, as it was called after the wych-elm, whose leaves it resembles, and which was so named because the chests termed in old times "wyches" were made of its wood—

"His hall rofe was full of bacon flytches,
The chambre charged was with wyches
Full of egges, butter, and chese." *

* Hazlitt's Early Popular Poetry

IV

PINK

[Pink or occasionally Pink Flowers not described in Pink Section.]

Wood-Anemone. *Anemone quinquefolia.* April and May. (White Section, p. 6.)

Rue-Anemone. *Anemonella thalictroides.* April and May. (White Section, p. 7.)

Pyxie. *Pyxidanthera barbulata.* March and April. (White Section, p. 11.)

Squirrel-corn. *Dicentra canadensis.* April and May. (White Section, p. 18.)

Trillium. *Trillium grandiflorum.* April and May. (White Section, p. 20.)

Mountain-Laurel. *Kalmia latifolia.* June. (White Section, p. 50.)

American Rhododendron. *Rhododendron maximum.* June. (White Section, p. 54.)

Arethusa. *Arethusa bulbosa.* June. (Blue and Purple Section, p. 344.)

Purple Fringed Orchises. *Habenaria fimbriata and psycodes.* June, July, and August. (Blue and Purple Section, p. 342.)

Daisy-Fleabane. *Erigeron annuus.* Summer. (White Section, p. 69.)

Dew-thread. *Drosera filiformis.* Summer. (White Section, p. 92.)

Turtlehead. *Chelone glabra.* Summer. (White Section, p. 111.)

TRAILING ARBUTUS. MAYFLOWER. GROUND-LAUREL.

Epigaea repens. Heath Family.

Stem.—With rusty hairs; prostrate or trailing. *Leaves.*—Rounded; heart-shaped at base; evergreen. *Flowers.*—Pink; clustered; fragrant. *Calyx.*—Of five sepals. *Corolla.*—Five-lobed; salver-shaped; with a slender tube which is hairy within. *Stamens.*—Ten. *Pistil.*—One, with a five-lobed stigma.

> "Pink, small and punctual,
> Aromatic, low,"

describes, but does scant justice to the trailing arbutus, whose waxy blossoms and delicious breath are among the earliest prophecies of perfume-laden summer. We look for these flowers in April—not beneath the snow, where tradition rashly locates them, but under the dead brown leaves of last year; and especially among the pines and in light sandy soil. Appearing as they do when we are eager for some tangible assurance that

> "——the Spring comes slowly up this way,"

they win from many of us the gladdest recognition of the year.

In New England they are called Mayflowers, being peddled about the streets of Boston every spring, under the suggestive and loudly emphasized title of "Ply-y-mouth Ma-ayflowers!" Whether they owe this name to the ship which is responsible for so much, or to their season of blooming, in certain localities, might remain an open question had we not the authority of Whittier for attributing it to both causes. In a note prefacing "The Mayflowers," the poet says: "The trailing arbutus or Mayflower grows abundantly in the vicinity of Plymouth, and was the first flower to greet the Pilgrims after their fearful winter." In the poem itself he wonders what the old ship had

> "Within her ice-rimmed bay
> In common with the wild-wood flowers,
> The first sweet smiles of May?"

TRAILING ARBUTUS.—*Epigaea repens.*

TWINFLOWER.—*Linnaea borealis.*

and continues—

> "Yet 'God be praised!' the Pilgrim said,
> Who saw the blossoms peer
> Above the brown leaves, dry and dead,
> 'Behold our Mayflower here!'
>
> "God wills it, here our rest shall be,
> Our years of wandering o'er,
> For us the Mayflower of the sea
> Shall spread her sails no more.
>
> "O sacred flowers of faith and hope,
> As sweetly now as then,
> Ye bloom on many a birchen slope,
> In many a pine-dark glen.
>
> . . . .
>
> "So live the fathers in their sons,
> Their sturdy faith be ours,
> And ours the love that overruns
> Its rocky strength with flowers."

If the poet's fancy was founded on fact, and if our lovely and widespread Mayflower was indeed the first blossom noted and christened by our forefathers, it seems as though the problem of a national flower must be solved by one so lovely and historic as to silence all dispute. And when we read the following prophetic stanzas which close the poem, showing that during another dark period in our nation's history these brave little blossoms, struggling through the withered leaves, brought a message of hope and courage to the heroic heart of the Quaker poet, our feeling that they are peculiarly identified with our country's perilous moments is intensified.

> "The Pilgrims wild and wintry day
> Its shadow round us draws;
> The Mayflower of his stormy bay
> Our Freedom's struggling cause.
>
> "But warmer suns erelong shall bring
> To life the frozen sod;
> And, through dead leaves of hope, shall spring
> Afresh the flowers of God!"

TWINFLOWER.

Linnæa borealis. Honeysuckle Family.

Stem.—Slender; creeping and trailing. *Leaves.*—Rounded; evergreen. *Flowers.*—Growing in pairs; delicate pink; fragrant; nodding on thread-like, upright flower-stalks. *Calyx.*—Five-toothed. *Corolla*—Narrowly bell-shaped; five-lobed; hairy within. *Stamens.*—Four; two shorter than the others. *Pistil.*—One.

Whoever has seen

> "——beneath dim aisles, in odorous beds,
> The slight Linnæa hang its twin-born heads,"

will not soon forget the exquisite carpeting made by its nodding pink flowers, or the delicious perfume which actually filled the air and drew one's attention to the spot from which it was exhaled, tempting one to exclaim, with Richard Jefferies, "Sweetest of all things is wild-flower air!" That this little plant should have been selected as "the monument of the man of flowers" by the great Linnæus himself bears testimony to his possession of that appreciation of the beautiful which is supposed to be lacking in men of long scientific training. I believe that there is extant at least one contemporary portrait of Linnæus in which he wears the tiny flowers in his buttonhole. The rosy twin-blossoms are borne on thread-like, forking flower-stalks, and appear in June in the deep, cool, mossy woods of the North.*

SPRING-BEAUTY.

Claytonia virginica. Purslane Family.

Stem.—From a small tuber; often somewhat reclining. *Leaves.*—Two; opposite; long and narrow; *Flowers.*—White, with pink veins, or pink with deeper-colored veins; growing in a loose cluster. *Calyx.*—Of two sepals. *Corolla.*—Of five petals. *Stamens.*—Five. *Pistil.*—One, with style three-cleft at apex.

* They are also found occasionally until the fall. Late one September I received a cluster which had just been gathered on the shores of Saranac Lake in the Adirondacks.

SPRING-BEAUTY.—*Claytonia virginica.*

"So bashful when I spied her
So pretty, so ashamed!
So hidden in her leaflets
Lest anybody find:

So breathless till I passed her,
So helpless when I turned
And bore her struggling, blushing,
Her simple haunts beyond!

For whom I robbed the dingle,
For whom betrayed the dell,
Many will doubtless ask me,
But I shall never tell!"

Yet we are all free to guess—and what flower—at least in the early year, before it has gained that touch of confidence which it acquires later—is so bashful, so pretty, so flushed with rosy shame, so eager to defend its modesty by closing its blushing petals when carried off by the despoiler—as the spring-beauty? To be sure, she is not "hidden in her leaflets," although often seeking concealment beneath the leaves of other plants—but why not assume that Miss Dickinson has availed herself of something of the license so freely granted to poets—especially, it seems to me—to poets of nature? Perhaps of this class few are more accurate than she, and although we wonder at the sudden blindness which leads her to claim that

"Nature rarer uses yellow
Than another hue—"

when it seems as though it needed but little knowledge of flowers to recognize that yellow, probably, occurs more frequently among them than any other color, and also at the representation of this same nature as

"Spending scarlet like a woman—"

when in reality she is so chary of this splendid hue, still we cannot but appreciate that this poet was in close and peculiar sympathy with flowers, and was wont to paint them with more than customary fidelity.

We look for the spring-beauty in April and May, and often find it in the same moist places—on a brook's edge or skirting the wet woods—as the yellow adder's-tongue. It is sometimes mistaken for an anemone, but its rose-veined corolla and linear leaves easily identify it. One is always glad to discover these children of the country within our city limits, where they can be known and loved by those other children who are so unfortunate as to be denied the knowledge of them in their usual haunts. If the day chances to be cloudy these flowers close and are only induced to open again by an abundance of sunlight. This habit of closing in the shade is common to many flowers, and should be remembered by those who bring home their treasures from the woods and fields, only to discard the majority as hopelessly wilted. If any such exhausted blossoms are placed in the sunlight, with their stems in fresh water, they will probably regain their vigor. Should this treatment fail, an application of very hot—almost boiling—water should be tried. This heroic measure often meets with success.

SHOWY ORCHIS.

Orchis spectabilis. Orchis Family.

Stem.—Four-angled; with leaf-like bracts; rising from fleshy, fibrous roots. *Leaves.*—Two; oblong; shining; three to six inches long. *Flowers.*—In a loose spike; purple-pink, the lower lip white.

This flower not only charms us with its beauty when its clusters begin to dot the rich May woods, but interests us as being usually the first member of the Orchis family to appear upon the scene; although it is claimed in certain localities that the beautiful Calypso always, and the Indian moccasin occasionally, precedes it.

A certain fascination attends the very name of orchid. Botanist and unscientific flower-lover alike pause with unwonted interest when the discovery of one is announced. With the former there is always the possibility of finding some rare species, while the excitement of the latter is apt to be whetted with the hope of beholding a marvellous imitation of bee or butterfly fluttering

SHOWY ORCHIS.—*Orchis spectabilis.*

from a mossy branch with roots that draw their nourishment from the air! While this little plant is sure to fail of satisfying the hopes of either, it is far prettier if less rare than many of its brethren, and its interesting mechanism will repay our patient study. It is said closely to resemble the "long purples," *O. mascula*, which grew near the scene of Ophelia's tragic death.

TWISTED-STALK.

Streptopus roseus. Lily Family.

Stems.—Rather stout and zigzag; forking and diverging. *Leaves.*—Taper-pointed; slightly clasping. *Flowers.*—Dull purplish-pink; hanging on thread-like flower stalks from the axils of the leaves. *Perianth.*—Somewhat bell-shaped; of six distinct sepals. *Stamens.*—Six. *Pistil.*—One, with a three-cleft stigma. *Fruit.*—Red; roundish; late summer.

This plant presents a graceful group of forking branches and pointed leaves. No blossom is seen from above, but on picking a branch one finds beneath each of its outspread leaves one or two slender, bent stalks from which hang the pink, bell-like flowers. In general aspect the plant somewhat resembles its relation, the Solomon's-seal, with which it is found blossoming in the woods of May or June. The English title is a translation of the generic name, *Streptopus*.

In August one finds the curved leafy stems hung with bright red berries.

S. amplexifolius usually is a somewhat larger plant than the above. Its strongly clasping leaves are very smooth, their under sides covered with a whitish bloom. Its small flowers (with entire, not three-cleft stigmas) are greenish white, drooping on a long, abruptly bent flower-stalk. In August, when its forking branches, hung with bright red berries, are reflected in the clear water of some mountain stream, the plant is singularly striking and decorative.

Fruit.

TWISTED-STALK.—*Streptopus roseus.*

RHODORA.

Rhododendron canadense. Heath Family.

A shrub from one to two feet high. *Leaves.*—Oblong; pale. *Flowers.*—Purplish pink. *Calyx.*—Small. *Corolla.*—Two-lipped; almost without any tube. *Stamens.*—Ten, not protruding. *Pistil.*—One, not protruding.

> " In May, when sea-winds pierced our solitudes,
> I found the fresh Rhodora in the woods,
> Spreading its leafless blooms in a damp nook,
> To please the desert and the sluggish brook.
> The purple petals, fallen in the pool,
> Made the black water with their beauty gay;
> Here might the red-bird come his plumes to cool,
> And court the flower that cheapens his array.
> Rhodora! If the sages ask thee why
> This charm is wasted on the earth and sky,
> Tell them, dear, that if eyes were made for seeing,
> Then Beauty is its own excuse for being;
> Why thou wert there, O rival of the rose!
> I never thought to ask, I never knew;
> But in my simple ignorance, suppose
> The self-same Power that brought me there, brought you. '

WILD PINK.†

Silene caroliniana. Pink Family.

Stems.—Four to eight inches high. *Leaves.*—Those from the root narrowly wedge-shaped; those on the stem lance-shaped, opposite. *Flowers.*—Bright pink; clustered. *Calyx.*—Five-toothed. *Corolla.*—Of five petals. *Stamens.*—Ten. *Pistil.*—One, with three styles.

When a vivid cluster of wild pinks gleams from some rocky opening in the May woods, it is difficult to restrain one's eagerness, for there is something peculiarly enticing in these fresh, vigorous-looking flowers. They are quite unlike most of their fragile contemporaries, for already they seem imbued with the

* Emerson.

† Although from their English names the Wild Pink and the Moss Pink would seem to be allied, a reference to their generic and family titles shows them to belong to quite different groups of plants.

WILD PINK.—*Silene caroliniana.*

glowing warmth of summer, and to have no memory of that snowy past which appears to leave its imprint on so many blossoms of the early year.

In waste places, from June until September or later, we find the small clustered pink flowers, which open transiently in the sunshine, of the sleepy catchfly, *S. antirrhina.*

MOSS-PINK.* GROUND-PINK.*

Phlox subulata. Polemonium Family.

Stems.—Creeping; tufted. *Leaves.*—Evergreen; awl-shaped; crowded; small. *Flowers.*—Bright purple-pink; with a darker, or sometimes with a white centre. *Calyx.*—With five awl-shaped teeth. *Corolla.*—Five-lobed. *Stamens.*—Five; unequally inserted in the tube of the corolla. *Pistil.*—One; with a three-lobed style.

Every spring this little evergreen plant clothes the dry hillsides with a glowing mantle of purple-pink. Southern New York is probably its most northerly range in our Eastern States.

PINK LADY'S-SLIPPER. MOCCASIN-FLOWER.

Cypripedium acaule. Orchis Family.

Scape.—Eight to twelve inches high; two-leaved at base; downy; one-flowered. *Leaves.*—Two; large; many-nerved and plaited; sheathing at the base. *Flowers.*—Solitary; the pink,.veiny lip, an inflated pouch; sepals and petals greenish and spreading.

> 'Graceful and tall the slender, drooping stem,
> With two broad leaves below,
> Shapely the flower so lightly poised between,
> And warm her rosy glow,"

writes Elaine Goodale of the moccasin-flower. This is a blossom whose charm never wanes. It seems to be touched with the spirit of the deep woods, and there is a certain fitness in its Indian name, for it looks as though it came direct from the home of

* See note, p. 238.

PINK LADY'S-SLIPPER.—*Cypripedium acaule.*

the red man. All who have found it in its secluded haunts will sympathize with Mr. Higginson's feeling that each specimen is a rarity, even though he should find a hundred to an acre. Gray assigned it to "dry or moist woods," while Mr. Baldwin writes: "The finest specimens I ever saw sprang out of cushions of crisp reindeer moss high up among the rocks of an exposed hill-side, and again I have found it growing vigorously in almost open swamps, but nearly colorless from excessive moisture." The same writer quotes a lady who is familiar with it in the Adirondacks. She says: "It seems to have a great fondness for decaying wood, and I often see a whole row perched like birds along a crumbling log;" while I recall a mountain lake where the steep cliffs rise from the water's edge; here and there, on a tiny shelf strewn with pine-needles, can be seen a pair of large veiny leaves, above which, in early June, the pink balloon-like blossom floats from its slender scape.

PALE CORYDALIS.

Corydalis sempervirens. Fumitory Family.

Stem.—Six inches to two feet high. *Leaves.*—Pale; divided into delicate leaflets. *Flowers.*—Pink and yellow; in loose clusters. *Calyx.*—Of two small, scale-like sepals. *Corolla.*—Pink, tipped with yellow; closed and flattened, of four petals, with a short spur at the base of the upper petal. *Stamens.*—Six; maturing before the pistil, thus avoiding self-fertilization. *Pistil.*—One.

From rocky clefts in the early summer woods springs the pale corydalis, its graceful foliage dim with a whitish bloom, and its delicate, rosy, yellow-tipped flowers betraying, by their odd, flat corollas, their kinship with the Dutchman's-breeches and squirrel-corn of the early year, as well as with the bleeding-hearts of the garden. Thoreau assigns them to the middle of May, and says they are "rarely met with," which statement does not coincide with the experience of those who find the rocky woodlands each summer abundantly decorated with their fragile clusters.

The generic name, *Corydalis*, is the ancient Greek title for

PALE CORYDALIS.—*Corydalis sempervirens.*

the crested lark, and is said to refer to the crested seeds of this genus.

CALYPSO.

Calypso bulbosa. Orchis Family.

Leaf.—Single; thin; ovate or slightly heart-shaped; from a solid bulb. *Flower.*—Variegated pink and yellow; lip sac-shaped and inflated; woolly, hairy inside.

Gray called this "a little bog-herb, . . . a very local and beautiful plant." I have seen the Calypso but once,* and that once in the city, where it was brought to me by one who had been so fortunate as to know it in all the beauty of its home environment. But we need never regret that some of the loveliest flowers are still to be discovered for the first time. The anticipation of such discoveries only lends a keener zest to the approach of spring, the season that brings so much of delight and actual excitement to the flower-lover.

Mr. Baldwin, it seems to me, is the prophet of the Calypso. He celebrates her beauty in eloquent pages. He says it is abundant in Oregon and the Northwest, but so rare in New England that we can be well acquainted with its flora and yet never have seen it. Yet he tells us that Professor Scribner came on a place in Maine, "not a foot square, containing over fifty plants in bloom."

And here is Mr. Baldwin's own description of the flower's home:

"Even when her sanctuary is discovered Calypso does not always reveal herself. The ground and the fallen tree-trunks are thickly padded with moss and embroidered with trailing vines of snowberry and Linnæa; painted trilliums dot with their white stars the shadows lying under the tangled fragrant branches, the silence of the forest, disturbed only by the chirr of a squirrel or

* Since writing the above I have found the Calypso growing abundantly on the beautiful slopes of the Canadian Rockies.

PLATE CVI

PINK AZALEA.—*Rhododendron nudiflorum.*

the sudden jubilance of the oven-bird, envelops you and seems the proper accompaniment of such an expedition. You follow, perhaps, a winding path made by the wild animals among the underbrush, moving slowly, and you easily overlook the dainty blossom, nestling in some soft, damp nook, and poised lightly on its stem as if ready to flutter away between your covetous fingers."

PINK AZALEA. WILD HONEYSUCKLE. PINXTER-FLOWER. SWAMP-PINK.

Rhododendron nudiflorum. Heath Family.

A shrub from two to six feet high. *Leaves.*—Narrowly oblong; downy underneath; usually appearing somewhat later than the flowers. *Flowers.*—Pink; clustered. *Calyx.*—Minute. *Corolla.*—Funnel-shaped; with five long recurved lobes. *Stamens.*—Five or ten; long, protruding noticeably. *Pistil.*—One; long; protruding.

Our May swamps and moist woods are made rosy by masses of the pink azalea, which is often known as the wild honeysuckle, although not even a member of the Honeysuckle family. It is in the height of its beauty before the blooming of the laurel, and heralds the still lovelier pageant which is even then in rapid course of preparation.

In the last century the name of Mayflower was given to the shrub by the Swedes in the neighborhood of Philadelphia. Peter Kalm, the pupil of Linnæus, after whom our laurel, *Kalmia*, is named, writes the following description of the shrub in his "Travels," which were published in English in 1771, and which explains the origin of one of its titles: "Some of the Swedes and Dutch call them Pinxter-bloom (Whitsunday-flower), as they really are in bloom about Whitsuntide; and at a distance they have some similarity to the Honeysuckle or 'Lonicera.' . . . Its flowers were now open and added a new ornament to the woods. . . . They sit in a circle round the stem's extremity and have either a dark red or a lively red color; but by standing for some time the sun bleaches them, and at last they

PLATE CVII

RACEMED MILKWORT.

Polygala polygama.

FRINGED POLYGALA.

Polygala paucifolia.

PURPLE MILKWORT.

Polygala sanguinea.

get to a whitish hue. . . . They have some smell, but I cannot say it is very pleasant. However, the beauty of the flowers entitles them to a place in every flower-garden." While our pink azalea could hardly be called "dark red" under any circumstances, it varies greatly in the color of its flowers.

The azalea is the national flower of Flanders.

FRINGED POLYGALA.

Polygala paucifolia. Milkwort Family.

Flowering-stems.—Three or four inches high, from long, prostrate or underground shoots which also bear cleistogamous flowers. *Leaves.*—The lower, small and scale-like, scattered; the upper, ovate, and crowded at the summit. *Flowers.*—Purple-pink, rarely white; rather large. *Keel of Corolla.*—Conspicuously fringed and crested. *Stamens.*—Six. *Pistil.*—One.

"I must not forget to mention that delicate and lovely flower of May, the fringed polygala. You gather it when you go for the fragrant showy orchis—that is, if you are lucky enough to find it. It is rather a shy flower, and is not found in every wood. One day we went up and down through the woods looking for it—woods of mingled oak, chestnut, pine, and hemlock —and were about giving it up when suddenly we came upon a gay company of them beside an old wood-road. It was as if a flock of small rose-purple butterflies had alighted there on the ground before us. The whole plant has a singularly fresh and tender aspect. Its foliage is of a slightly purple tinge and of very delicate texture. Not the least interesting feature about the plant is the concealed fertile flower which it bears on a subterranean stem, keeping, as it were, one flower for beauty and one for use."

It seems unnecessary to tempt "odorous comparisons" by endeavoring to supplement the above description of Mr. Burroughs.

SHEEP-LAUREL.—*Kalmia angustifolia.*

RACEMED MILKWORT.

Polygala polygama. Milkwort Family.

Stems.—Very leafy; six to nine inches high; with cleistogamous flowers on underground runners. *Leaves.*—Lance-shaped or oblong. *Flowers.*—Purple-pink; loosely clustered in a terminal raceme. *Keel of Corolla.*—Crested. *Stamens.*—Eight. *Pistil.*—One.

Like its more attractive sister, the fringed polygala, this little plant hides its most useful, albeit unattractive, blossoms in the ground, where they can fulfil their destiny of perpetuating the species without danger of molestation by thievish insects or any of the distractions incidental to a more worldly career. Exactly what purpose the little above-ground flowers, which appear so plentifully in sandy soil in July, are intended to serve, it is difficult to understand.

SHEEP-LAUREL. LAMBKILL.

Kalmia angustifolia. Heath Family.

A shrub from one to three feet high. *Leaves.*—Narrowly oblong; light green. *Flowers.*—Deep pink; in lateral clusters. *Calyx.*—Five-parted. *Corolla.*—Five-lobed; between wheel and bell-shaped; with stamens caught in its depressions as in the mountain laurel. *Stamens.*—Ten. *Pistil.*—One.

This low shrub grows abundantly with the mountain-laurel, bearing smaller deep pink flowers at the same season, and narrower, paler leaves. It is said to be the most poisonous of the genus, and to be especially deadly to sheep, while deer are supposed to feed upon its leaves with impunity.

The flower is one of Thoreau's favorites. In his journal, June 13, 1852, he writes: "Lambkill is out. I remember with what delight I used to discover this flower in dewy mornings. All things in this world must be seen with the morning dew on them, must be seen with youthful, early opened, hopeful eyes."

And two years later, oddly enough on the same day of the

SHOWY LADY'S-SLIPPER.—*Cypripedium reginae.*

month, he finds them equally admirable at the approach of "dewy eve." "How beautiful the solid cylinders of the lamb-kill now just before sunset; small ten-sided rosy-crimson basins, about two inches above the recurved, drooping, dry capsules of last year, and sometimes those of the year before, two inches lower."

PALE LAUREL.

Kalmia polifolia. Heath Family.

A rather straggling shrub about one foot high. *Leaves.*—Evergreen; opposite; oblong; with *revolute* margins and a white bloom beneath. *Flowers.*—Pink, one inch broad, in terminal, few-flowered clusters. *Calyx.* Five-parted. *Corolla.*—Five-lobed. *Stamens.*—Ten. *Pistil.*—One.

The pale laurel is easily identified by its leaves, which are noticeable for their revolute margins and for the white bloom on their under sides. The pretty pink flowers which are due in May or June may be found occasionally much later in cool northern localities. The shrub is most at home in peat bogs and in the mountains from Newfoundland to Pennsylvania.

SHOWY LADY'S-SLIPPER.

Cypripedium reginae. Orchis Family.

Stems.—Downy; two feet high. *Leaves.*—Large; ovate; pointed; plaited. *Flowers.*—Large; the three sepals and two lateral petals, white; the lip white, pink in front, much inflated.

My eager hunts for this, the most beautiful of our orchids, have never been crowned with success.* But once I saw a fresh cluster of these lovely flowers in a friend's house, and regaled myself with their rich, stately beauty and delicious fragrance. Strangely enough I find no mention of this latter quality either in Gray or in Mr. Baldwin's work on orchids.

Mr. Baldwin describes the lip of this flower as "crimped, shell-shaped, varying from a rich pink-purple blotched with

* Since writing the above I have tracked it to its home.

white to pure white." He says that in southern Connecticut it may be found by the 20th of June, but that the White Mountains rarely afford it before July. It is due in the Berkshires, Mass., late in June.

It grows in peat-bogs, and its height and foliage strongly suggest the false hellebore.

This flower is one of a species whose life is threatened owing to the oft-lamented ruthlessness of the "flower-picker."

Near Lenox, Mass., there is one locality where the showy lady's-slipper can be found. Fortunately, one would suppose, this spot is known only to a few; but as one of the few who possess the secret is a country boy who *uproots these plants and sells them by the dozen* in Lenox and Pittsfield, the time is not distant when the flower will no longer be found in the shadowy silences of her native haunts, but only, robbed of half her charm, languishing in stiff rows along the garden-path.

AMERICAN CRANBERRY.

Vaccinium macrocarpon. Heath Family.

Stems.—Slender; trailing; one to four feet long. *Leaves.*—Oblong; obtuse; whitened beneath. *Flowers.*—Pale pink; nodding. *Calyx.*—With short teeth. *Corolla.*—Four-parted. *Stamens.*—Eight or ten; protruding. *Fruit.*—A large, acid, red berry.

In the peat-bogs of our Northeastern States we may look in June for the pink nodding flowers, and in late summer for the large red berries of this well-known and useful plant.

The small cranberry, *V. Oxycoccos*, bears a much smaller fruit. Its ovate, acute leaves have strongly revolute margins and are whitish beneath. The acid berries are edible when cooked.

The mountain-cranberry, *V. Vitis-Idaea*, is found along the coast and mountains of New England, inland to Lake Superior and far northward. Its smooth, shining, obovate leaves also have revolute margins. Below they are dotted with. black, bristly points. The blossoms grow in short terminal clusters. These berries also are smaller than those of the common cranberry.

ADDER'S-MOUTH. ROSE POGONIA.

Pogonia ophioglossoides. Orchis Family.

Stem.—Six to nine inches high; from a fibrous root. *Leaves.*—An oval or lance-oblong one near the middle of the stem, and a smaller or bract-like one near the terminal flower, occasionally one or two others, with a flower in their axils. *Flower.*—Pale pink, sometimes white; sweet-scented; one inch long; lip bearded and fringed.

Mr. Baldwin maintains that there is no wild flower of as pure a pink as this unless it be the *Sabbatia.* Its color has also been described as a "peach-blossom red." As already mentioned, the plant is found blossoming in bogs during the early summer in company with the *Calopogons* and sundews. Its violet-like fragrance greatly enhances its charm.

The botanists have great difficulty at times in describing the colors of certain flowers, and when the blossoms look to one eye pink, to another purple, they compromise and give the color as "pink-purple." It has been no easy matter to settle satisfactorily the positions in this book of many of the flowers, more especially as the individuals vary constantly in depth of color, and even in actual color.

July 7, 1852, Thoreau devotes a page in his journal to some of these doubtful-colored flowers, whose heathenish titles excite his ire. "Pogonias are still abundant in the meadows, but arethusas I have not lately seen. . . . The very handsome 'pink-purple' * flowers of the *Calopogon pulchellus* enrich the grass all around the edge of Hubbard's blueberry swamp, and are now in their prime. The *Arethusa bulbosa*, 'crystalline purple,' *Pogonia ophioglossoides*, snake-mouthed (tongued) arethusa, 'pale purple,' and the *Calopogon pulchellus*, grass pink, 'pink-purple,'

* As the Calopogon and Pogonia seem to me far more pink than purple, they are placed in the Pink Section. The Arethusa and the Purple Fringed Orchis will be found in the Purple Section.

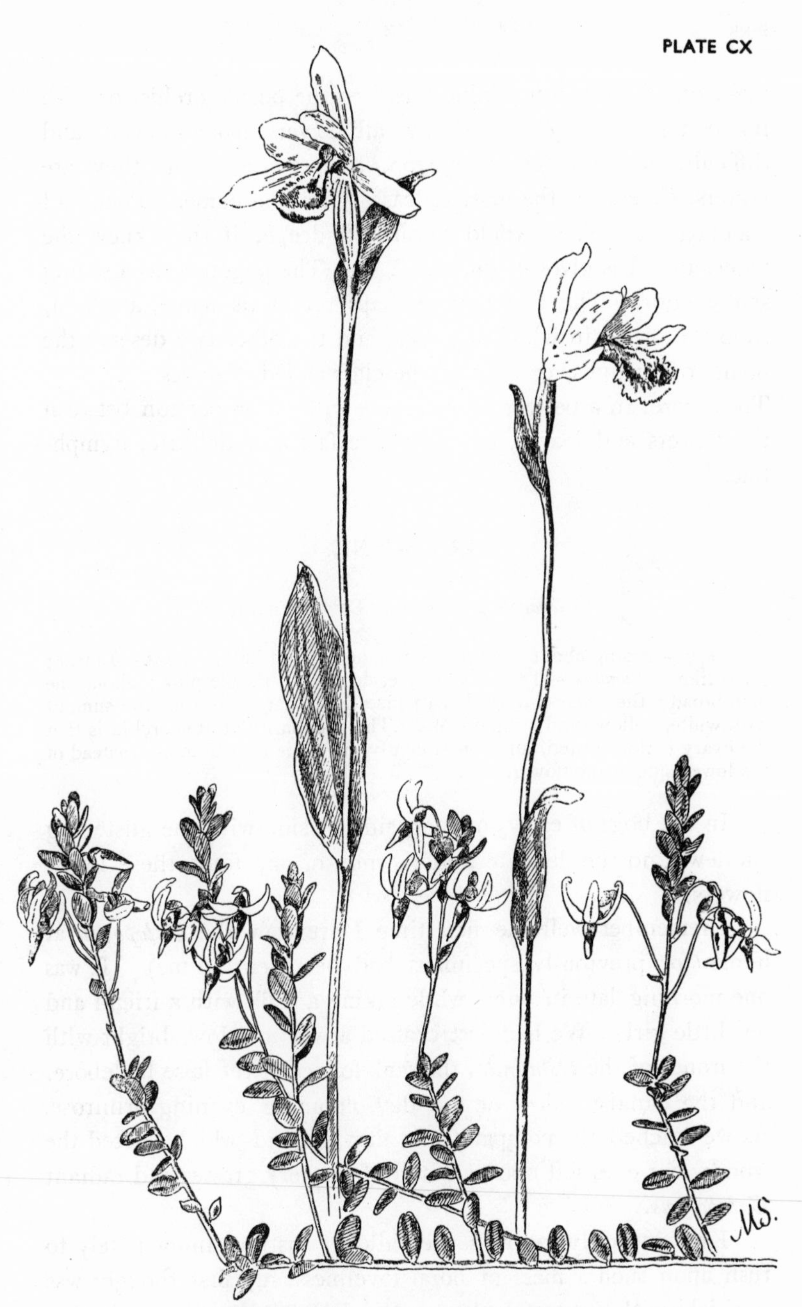

ROSE POGONIA.—*Pogonia ophioglossoides.*
AMERICAN CRANBERRY.—*Vaccinium macrocarpon.*

make one family in my mind (next to the purple orchis, or with it), being flowers *par excellence,* all flowers, naked flowers, and difficult, at least the calopogon, to preserve. But they are flowers, excepting the first, at least, without a name. Pogonia! Calopogon! They would blush still deeper if they knew the names man has given them. . . . The pogonia has a strong snaky odor. The first may perhaps retain its name, arethusa, from the places in which it grows, and the other two deserve the names of nymphs, perhaps of the class called Naiades. . . . To be sure, in a perfect flower there will be proportion between the flowers and leaves, but these are fair and delicate, nymph-like."

GRASS-PINK.

Calopogon pulchellus. Orchis Family.

Scape.—Rising about one foot from a small solid bulb. *Leaf.*—Linear; grass-like. *Flowers.*—Two to six on each scape; purple-pink; about one inch broad; the lip as if hinged at its insertion, bearded toward the summit with white, yellow, and purple hairs. The peculiarity of this orchid is that the ovary is not twisted, and consequently the lip is on the upper instead of the lower side of the flower.

In the bogs of early summer, side by side with the glistening sundew, and the delicate adder's-mouth, one finds these lovely flowers.

I remember well the first time I ever saw the *Calopogon* at home (for previously specimens had been sent to me). It was one morning late in June, while taking a walk with a friend and her little girl. We had just crossed a wet meadow, bright with the fronds of the *Osmunda,* the rank foliage of the false hellebore, and the canary-yellow of the day-blooming evening-primrose. As we reached the comparatively firm ground which skirted the woods, our eyes fell upon a patch of feathery grasses and radiant *Calopogons.*

Knowing only too well the childish instinct immediately to rush upon such a mass of floral loveliness, my first thought was to shield with outstretched arms the delicate beauties, hesitating

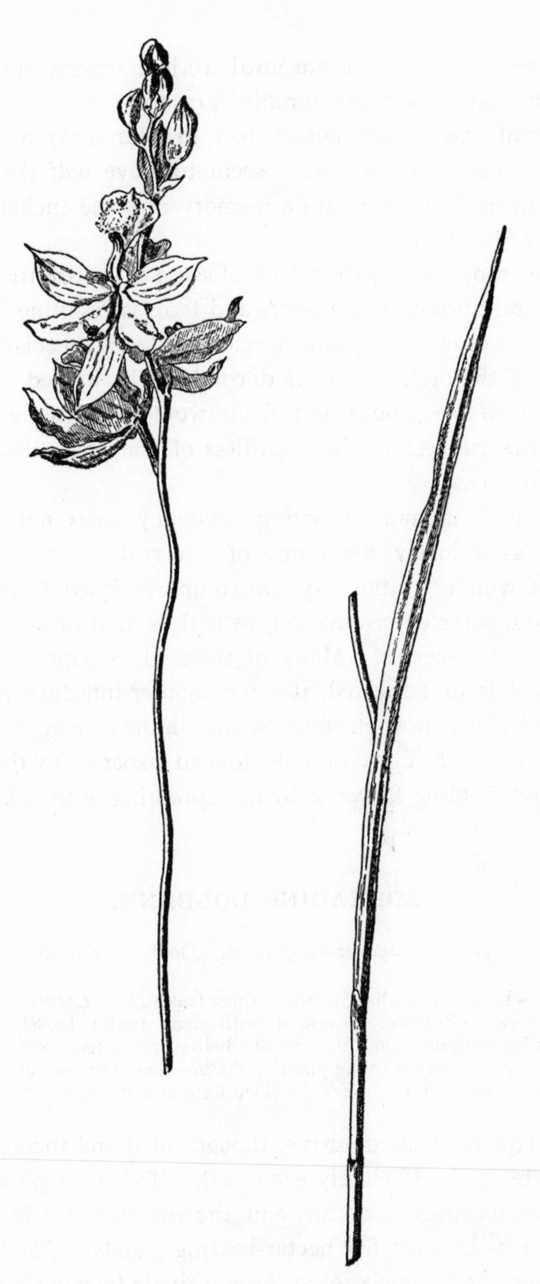

GRASS-PINK.—*Calopogon pulchellus*.

to pick even a single blossom until we had feasted our eyes, for a time at least, upon their unruffled grace.

After all, how much better than to bear away a burden of blossoms, which nearly always seem to leave half their beauty behind them, is it to retain a memory of some enchanted spot unrifled of its charm.

Then, too, the prevalent lack of sense of self-restraint in the picking and uprooting of flowers and ferns is resulting in the extermination of many valuable species. This is especially true in the case of the orchids. It is devoutly to be wished that every true lover of our woods and fields would set his face sternly against the ruthless habit, regardless of the pleas that may be offered in excuse.

This picking and uprooting tendency does not begin to threaten as seriously the future of our really common flowers (some of which, by the way, are so unprincipled themselves as almost to deserve extermination) as it does that of our rarer and more beautiful species. Many of these will disappear from the country, it is to be feared, if some counter-influence is not exerted, and if it is not remembered that in the case of annuals and biennials as much injury may be done to a species by the picking of the seed-yielding flower as by the uprooting of the plant itself.

SPREADING DOGBANE.

Apocynum androsaemifolium. Dogbane Family.

Stems.—Erect; branching; two or three feet high. *Leaves.*—Opposite; oval. *Flowers.*—Rose-color, veined with deep pink; loosely clustered. *Calyx.*—Five-parted. *Corolla.*—Small; bell-shaped; five-cleft. *Stamens.*—Five, slightly adherent to the pistil. *Pistil.*—Two ovaries surmounted by a large, two-lobed stigma. *Fruit.*—Two long and slender pods.

The flowers of the dogbane, though small and inconspicuous, are very beautiful if closely examined. The deep pink veining of the corolla suggests nectar, and the insect-visitor is not misled, for at its base are five nectar-bearing glands. The two long, slender seed-pods which result from a single blossom seem inap-

SPREADING DOGBANE.—*Apocynum androsaemifolium.*

propriately large, often appearing while the plant is still in flower. Rafinesque states that from the stems may be obtained a thread similar to hemp which can be woven into cloth, from the pods, cotton, and from the blossoms, sugar. Its generic and one of its English titles arose from the belief, which formerly prevailed, that it was poisonous to dogs. The plant is constantly found growing in roadside thickets, with bright, pretty foliage, and blossoms that appear in early summer.

PURPLE-FLOWERING RASPBERRY.

Rubus odoratus. Rose Family.

Stem.—Shrubby, three to five feet high; branching; branches bristly and glandular. *Leaves.*—Three to five-lobed, the middle lobe prolonged. *Flowers.*—Purplish-pink; large and showy; two inches broad. *Calyx.*—Five-parted. *Corolla.*—Of five rounded petals. *Stamens and Pistils.*—Numerous. *Fruit.*—Reddish, resembling the garden raspberry.

This flower betrays its relationship to the wild rose, and might easily be mistaken for it, although a glance at the undivided leaves would at once correct such an error. The plant is a decorative one when covered with its showy blossoms, constantly arresting our attention along the wooded roadsides in June and July.

BASIL.

Satureja vulgaris. Mint Family.

Hairy; erect; one to two feet high. *Leaves.*—Opposite; oval; scarcely toothed. *Flower.*—Small; pink or purplish; in close globular clusters with noticeably long, hairy bracts. *Calyx.*—Two-lipped; upper lip three, the lower two-cleft. *Corolla.*—Two-lipped; upper lip erect, sometimes notched; the lower spreading; three-parted. *Stamens.*—Four. *Pistil.*—One, with two-lobed style. *Ovary.*—Deeply four-lobed.

Bordering the woods and fields in midsummer we notice the rounded, silky-bracted flower-clusters of the basil.

PURPLE-FLOWERING RASPBERRY.—*Rubus odoratus.*

DEPTFORD PINK.

Dianthus Armeria. Pink Family.

One to two feet high. *Leaves.*—Opposite; long and narrow; hairy. *Flowers.*—Pink, with white dots; clustered. *Calyx.*—Five-toothed, cylindrical; with awl-shaped bracts beneath. *Corolla.*—Of five small petals. *Stamens.*—Ten. *Pistil.*—One, with two styles.

In July and August we find these little flowers in our Eastern fields. The generic name, which signifies *Jove's own flower*, hardly applies to these inconspicuous blossoms. Perhaps it was originally bestowed upon *D. caryophyllus*, a large and fragrant English member of the genus, which was the origin of our garden carnation.

PHILADELPHIA FLEABANE.

Erigeron philadelphicus. Composite Family.

Stem.—Hairy, leafy. *Leaves.*—Oblong, the upper rather smooth, clasping by a heart-shaped base, almost entire; the lowest wedge-shaped, toothed. *Flower-heads.*—Small, clustered, with numerous very narrow, pinkish ray-flowers and a centre of yellow disk flowers.

This often attractive member of the fleabane group is commonly found in moist ground from June to August.

WILD MORNING-GLORY. HEDGE-BINDWEED.

Convolvulus sepium. Convolvulus Family.

Stem.—Twining or trailing. *Leaves.*—Somewhat arrow-shaped. *Flowers.*—Pink. *Calyx.*—Of five sepals enclosed in two broad leafy bracts. *Corolla.*—Five-lobed; bell-shaped. *Stamens.*—Five. *Pistil.*—One, with two stigmas.

Many an unsightly heap of rubbish left by the roadside is hidden by the delicate pink bells of the hedge-bindweed, which again will clamber over the thickets that line the streams and about the tumbled stone-wall that marks the limit of the pasture.

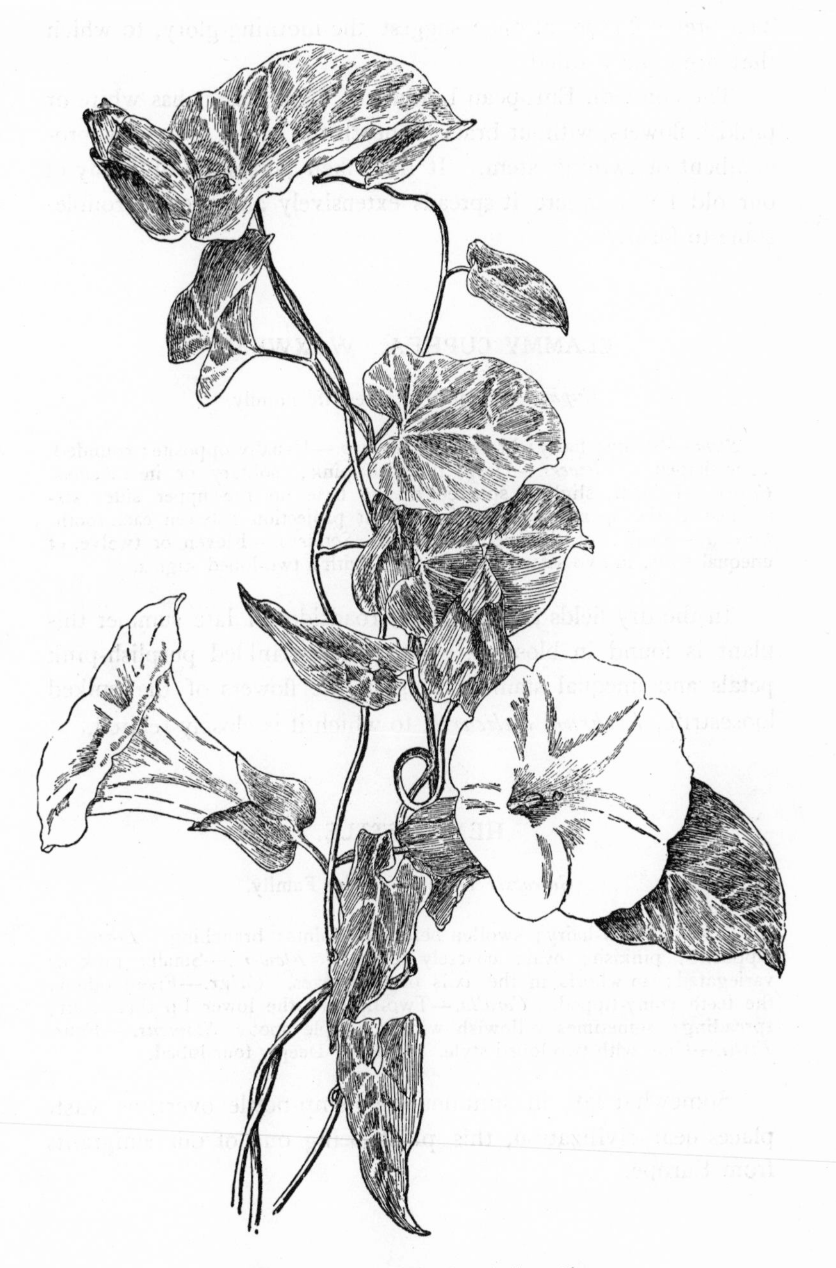

WILD MORNING-GLORY.—*Convolvulus sepium.*

The pretty flowers at once suggest the morning-glory, to which they are closely allied.

The common European bindweed, *C. arvensis*, has white or pinkish flowers, without bracts beneath the calyx, and a low procumbent or twining stem. It has taken possession of many of our old fields, where it spreads extensively and proves troublesome to farmers.

CLAMMY CUPHEA. WAXWEED.

Cuphea petiolata. Loosestrife Family.

Stem.—Sticky; hairy; branching. *Leaves.*—Usually opposite; rounded, lance-shaped. *Flowers.*—Deep purplish pink; solitary or in racemes. *Calyx.*—Tubular, slightly spurred at the base on the upper side, six-toothed at the apex, usually with a slight projection between each tooth. *Corolla.*—Small; of six unequal petals. *Stamens.*—Eleven or twelve, of unequal sizes, in two sets. *Pistil.*—One, with a two-lobed stigma.

In the dry fields and along the roadsides of late summer this plant is found in blossom. Its rather wrinkled purplish-pink petals and unequal stamens suggest the flowers of the spiked loosestrife, *Lythrum Salicaria*, to which it is closely related.

HEMP-NETTLE.

Galeopsis Tetrahit. Mint Family.

Stem.—Bristly-hairy; swollen below the joints; branching. *Leaves.*—Opposite; pinkish; oval; coarsely toothed. *Flowers.*—Small; pink or variegated; in whorls in the axils of the leaves. *Calyx.*—Five-toothed; the teeth spiny-tipped. *Corolla.*—Two-lipped; the lower lip three-cleft; spreading; sometimes yellowish with a purple spot. *Stamens.*—Four. *Pistil.*—One, with two-lobed style. *Ovary.*—Deeply four-lobed.

Somewhat late in summer the hemp-nettle overruns waste places near civilization, this plant being one of our emigrants from Europe.

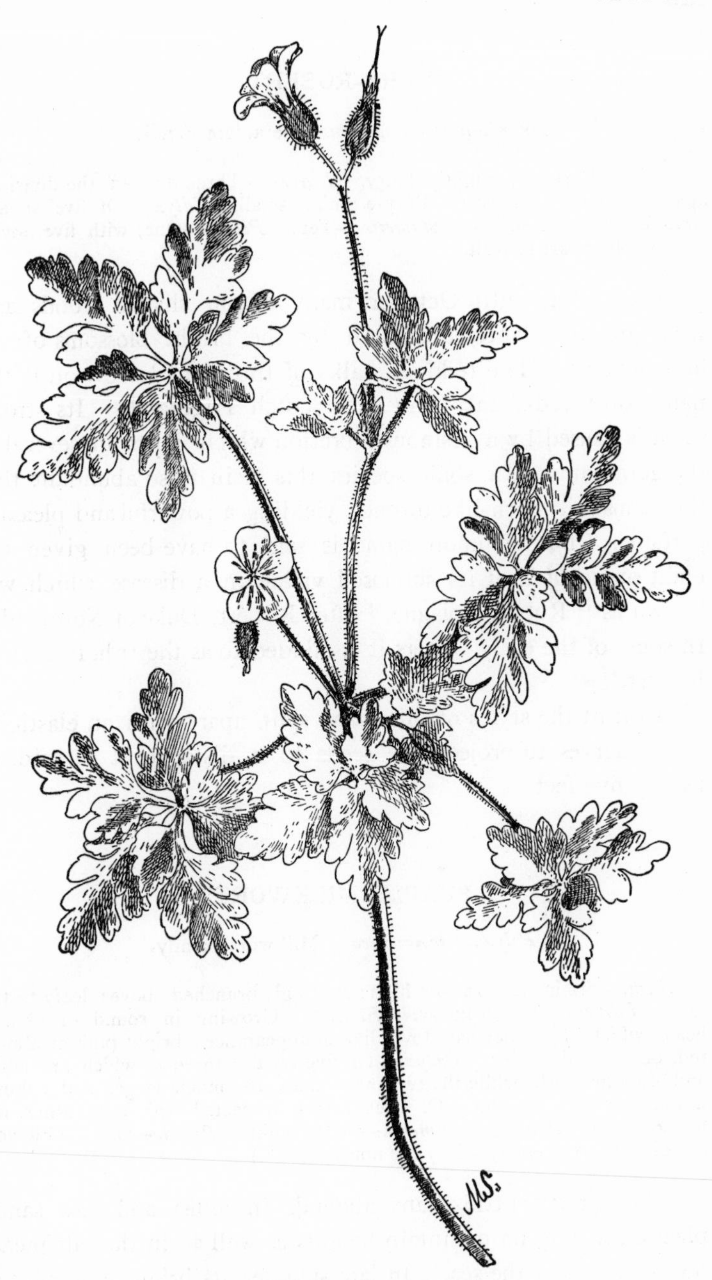

HERB-ROBERT.—*Geranium Robertianum.*

HERB-ROBERT.

Geranium Robertianum. Geranium Family.

Stem.—Forking; slightly hairy. *Leaves.*—Three-divided, the divisions again dissected. *Flowers.*—Purple-pink; small. *Calyx.*—Of five sepals. *Corolla.*—Of five petals. *Stamens.*—Ten. *Pistil.*—One, with five styles which split apart in fruit.

From June until October many of our shaded woods and glens are abundantly decorated by the bright blossoms of the herb-Robert. The reddish stalks of the plant have won it the name of "red-shanks" in the Scotch Highlands. Its strong scent is caused by a resinous secretion which exists in several of the geraniums. In some species this resin is so abundant that the stems will burn like torches, yielding a powerful and pleasant perfume. The common name is said to have been given the plant on account of its supposed virtue in a disease which was known as "Robert's plague," after Robert, Duke of Normandy. In some of the early writers it is alluded to as the "holy herb of Robert."

In fruit the styles of this plant split apart with an elasticity which serves to project the seeds to a distance, it is said, of twenty-five feet.

PURPLE MILKWORT.

Polygala sanguinea. Milkwort Family.

Stem.—Six inches to a foot high; sparingly branched above; leafy to the top. *Leaves.*—Oblong-linear. *Flowers.*—Growing in round or oblong heads which are somewhat clover-like in appearance; bright pink or almost red, occasionally paler. *Calyx.*—Of five sepals, three of which are small and often greenish, while the two inner ones are much larger and colored like the petals. *Corolla.*—Of three petals connected with each other, the lower one keel-shaped. *Stamens.*—Six or eight. *Pistil.*—One. (Flowers too difficult to be analyzed by the non-botanist.)

This pretty little plant abounds in moist and also sandy places, growing on mountain heights as well as in the salt meadows which skirt the sea. In late summer its bright flower-heads

MOUNTAIN-FRINGE.—*Adlumia fungosa.*

gleam vividly through the grasses, and from their form and color might almost be mistaken for pink clover. Occasionally they are comparatively pale and inconspicuous.

MARSH POLYGALA.

Polygala cruciata. Milkwort Family.

Stems.—Three to ten inches high; almost winged at the angles, with spreading, opposite leaves and branches. *Leaves.* — Linear; nearly all whorled in fours. *Flowers.*—Greenish or purplish-pink; growing in short, thick spikes which terminate the branches.

There is something very moss-like in the appearance of this little plant which blossoms in late summer. It is found near moist places and salt marshes along the coast, being very common in parts of New England.

MOUNTAIN-FRINGE. CLIMBING FUMITORY.

Adlumia fungosa. Fumitory Family.

Leaves.—Thrice-pinnate, with cut-lobed leaflets. *Flowers.* — Pinkish, drooping in full clusters. *Calyx.*—Of two small sepals. *Corolla.*—Flattened, closed. *Stamens.*—In two sets of three each. *Pistil.*—One.

The root-leaves of this plant remind one of the meadow-rue, or remotely of maidenhair-fern. From among these root-leaves rises the vine which climbs by means of slender leaf-stalks over the bushes and tall goldenrod or aster stalks. The foliage is extremely delicate, and the clustered pinkish flowers recall the blossoms of their kinsfolk the pale corydalis and the Dutchman's-breeches. This dainty little plant festooning the undergrowth is always a delight when found growing in the woods, and it is so charming that one is not surprised to learn from Gray that it is "often cultivated."

COMMON MILKWEED—*Asclepias syriaca.*

COMMON MILKWEED.

Asclepias syriaca. Milkweed Family.

Stem.—Tall; stout; downy; with a milky juice. *Leaves.*—Generally opposite or whorled; the upper sometimes scattered; large; oblong; pale; minutely downy underneath. *Flowers.*—Dull purplish-pink; clustered at the summit and along the sides of the stem. (These flowers are too difficult to be successfully analyzed by the non-botanist.) *Calyx.*—Five-parted; the divisions small and reflexed. *Corolla.*—Deeply five-parted; the divisions reflexed; above them a crown of five hooded nectaries, each containing an incurved horn. *Stamens.*—Five; inserted on the base of the corolla; united with each other and enclosing the pistils. *Pistils.*—Properly two; enclosed by the stamens, surmounted by a large five-angled disk. *Fruit.*—Two pods, one of which is large and full of silky-tufted seeds, the other often stunted.

This is probably the commonest representative of this striking and beautiful native family. The tall, stout stems, large, pale leaves, dull pink clustered flowers which appear in July, and later the puffy pods filled with the silky-tufted seeds beloved of imaginative children, are familiar to nearly everyone who spends a portion of the year in the country. The young sprouts are said to make an excellent pot-herb; the silky hairs of the seed-pods have been used for the stuffing of pillows and mattresses, and can be mixed with flax or wool and woven to advantage; while paper has been manufactured from the stout stalks.

The four-leaved milkweed, *A. quadrifolia*, is the most delicate member of the family, with fragrant rose-tinged flowers which appear on the dry wooded hill-sides quite early in June, and slender stems which are usually leafless below, and with one or two whorls and one or two pairs of oval, taper-pointed leaves above.

The swamp-milkweed, *A. incarnata*, grows commonly in moist places. Its very leafy stems are two or three feet high, with narrowly oblong, pointed leaves. Its intense purple-pink flowers gleam from the wet meadows nearly all summer. They are smaller than those of the purple milkweed, *A. purpurascens*, which abounds in dry ground, and which may be classed among the deep pink or purple flowers according to the eye of the beholder.

PLATE CXVIII

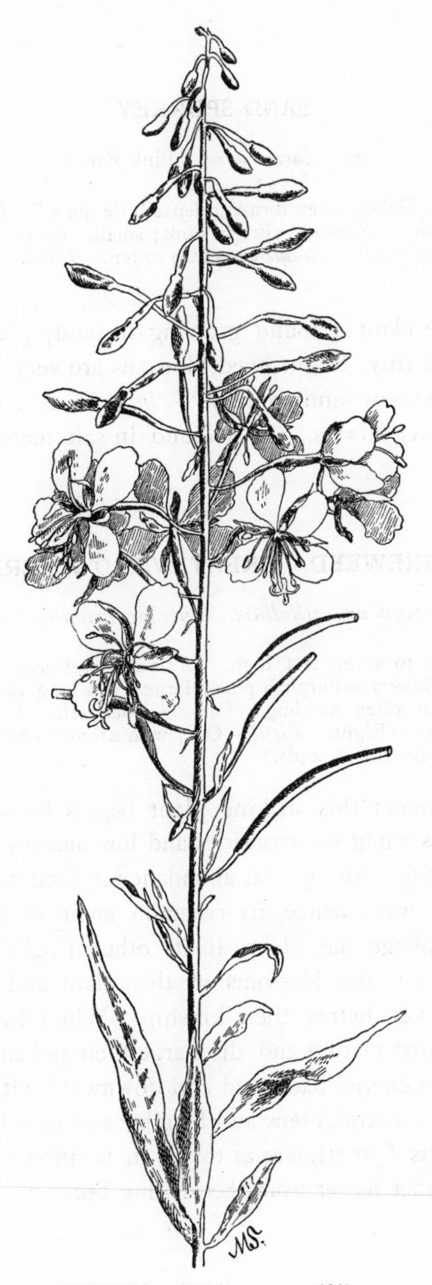

FIREWEED.—*Epilobium angustifolium.*

SAND-SPURREY.

Spergularia rubra. Pink Family.

"Two to six inches, often forming dense little mats." *Leaves.*—Linear, flat, scarcely fleshy. *Flowers.*—Bright pink; small. *Calyx.*—Of five sepals. *Corolla.*—Of five petals. *Stamens.*—Two to ten. *Pistil.*—One, with three styles.

This little plant is found growing in sandy places along the roadside. Its tiny, bright-hued blossoms are very dainty.

The salt-marsh sand-spurrey, *S. marina*, is a much fleshier plant with paler flowers. It is found in salt marshes along the coast.

FIREWEED. GREAT WILLOW-HERB.

Epilobium angustifolium. Evening-Primrose Family.

Stem.—Four to seven feet high. *Leaves.*—Scattered; lance-shaped; willow-like. *Flowers.*—Purplish-pink; large; in a long raceme the upper part of which is often nodding. *Calyx.*—Four-cleft. *Corolla.*—Of four petals. *Stamens.*—Eight. *Pistil.*—One, with a four-lobed stigma. *Fruit.*—A pod with silky-tufted seeds.

In midsummer this striking plant begins to mass its deep-hued blossoms along the roadsides and low meadows. It is supposed to flourish with especial abundance in land that has newly been burned over; hence, its common name of fireweed. Its willow-like foliage has given it its other English title. The likeness between the blossoms of this plant and those of the evening-primrose betray their kinship. When the stamens of the fireweed first mature and discharge their pollen the still immature style is curved backward and downward with its stigmas closed. Later it straightens and lengthens to its full dimensions, so spreading its four stigmas as to be in position to receive the pollen of another flower from the visiting bee.

STEEPLE-BUSH.—*Spiraea tomentosa.*

SMALL WILLOW-HERB.

Epilobium coloratum. Evening-Primrose Family.

One to three feet high. *Leaves.*—Rather large; lance-shaped; sharply toothed. *Flowers.*—Pale pink; small; more or less nodding, resembling in structure those of the hairy willow-herb. *Pistil.*—One, with a club-shaped stigma.

The small willow-herb is abundant in wet places in summer.

HAIRY WILLOW-HERB.

Epilobium hirsutum.—Evening-Primrose Family.

Three to five feet high. *Stem.*—Densely hairy; stout; branching. *Leaves.*—Mostly opposite; lance-oblong; finely toothed. *Flowers.*—Pink, in the axils of the upper leaves, or in a leafy, short raceme. *Calyx.*—Four or five-parted. *Corolla.*—Of four petals. *Stamens.*—Eight. *Pistil.*—One, with a four-parted stigma.

The hairy willow-herb is found in waste places, blossoming in midsummer. It is an emigrant from Europe.

STEEPLE-BUSH. HARDHACK.

Spiraea tomentosa. Rose Family.

Stems.—Very woolly. *Leaves.*—Alternate; oval; toothed. *Flowers.*—Small; pink; in pyramidal clusters. *Calyx.*—Five-cleft. *Corolla.*—Of five rounded petals. *Stamens.*—Numerous. *Pistils.*—Five to eight.

The pink spires of this shrub justify its rather unpoetic name of steeple-bush. It is closely allied to the meadow-sweet, blossoming with it in low ground during the summer. It differs from that plant in the color of its flowers and in the woolliness of its stems and the lower surface of its leaves.

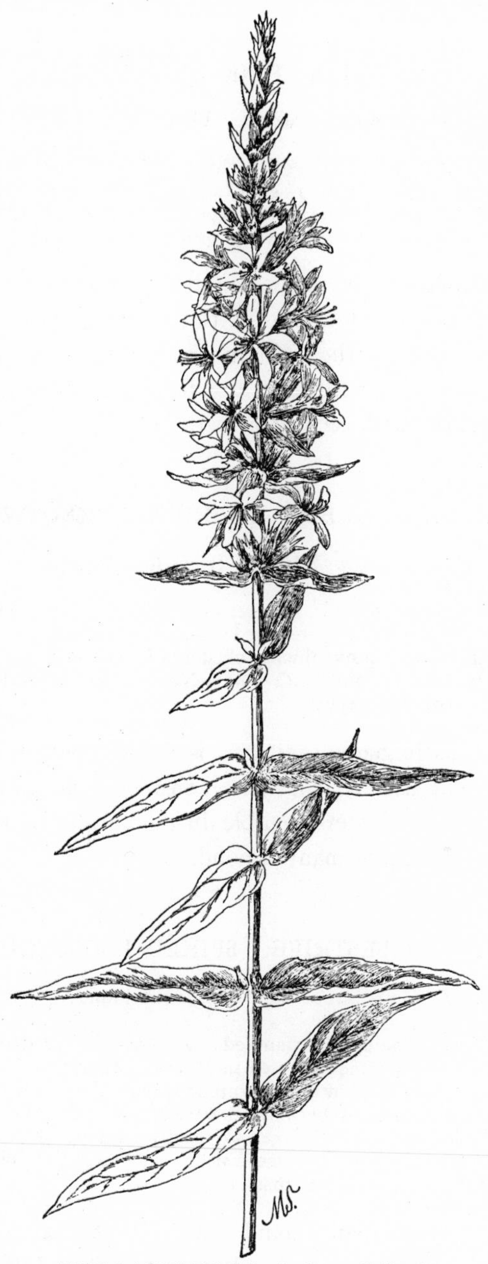

PURPLE LOOSESTRIFE.—*Lythrum Salicaria.*

PINKWEED. PINK KNOTWEED.

Polygonum pensylvanicum. Buckwheat Family.

One to four feet high. *Stem.*—Branching. *Leaves.*—Alternate; lance-shaped. *Flowers.*—Bright pink; growing in thick, short, erect spikes. *Calyx.*—Mostly five-parted; the divisions petal-like, pink. *Corolla.*—None. *Stamens.*—Usually eight. *Pistil.*—One, with a two-cleft style.

In late summer this plant can hardly escape notice. Its erect pink spikes direct attention to some neglected corner in the garden or brighten the field and roadside. The rosy divisions of the calyx persist till after the fruit has formed, pressing closely against the dark seed-vessel within.

WATER-SMARTWEED. AMPHIBIOUS KNOTWEED.

Polygonum amphibium. Buckwheat Family.

Growing in water or in mud. *Leaves.*—Usually floating; thick; smooth and shining above; mostly long-stemmed; somewhat oblong or lance-shaped. *Flowers.*—Small; bright pink, thickly clustered in a close spike. *Calyx.*—Five-parted; petal-like; pink. *Corolla.*—None. *Stamens.*—Five. *Pistil.*—One, with a two-cleft style.

This plant, as its name indicates, is found both on land and in the water, but usually it may be considered an aquatic. Its rose-colored flower-clusters tremble in the current of the stream and flush the borders of many a pond.

PURPLE LOOSESTRIFE. SPIKED LOOSESTRIFE.

Lythrum Salicaria. Loosestrife Family.

Stem.—Tall and slender; four-angled. *Leaves.*—Lance-shaped, with a heart-shaped base; sometimes whorled in threes. *Flowers.*—Deep purple-pink; crowded and whorled in an interrupted spike. *Calyx.*—Five to seven-toothed; with little processes between the teeth. *Corolla.*—Of five or six somewhat wrinkled petals. *Stamens.*—Usually twelve; in two sets, six longer and six shorter. *Pistil.*—One, varying in size in the different blossoms, being of three different lengths.

One who has seen an inland marsh in August aglow with this beautiful plant is almost ready to forgive the Old Country

MEADOW-BEAUTY.—*Rhexia virginica.*

some of the many pests she has shipped to our shores in view of this radiant acquisition. The botany locates it anywhere between Nova Scotia and Delaware. It may be seen in the perfection of its beauty along the marshy shores of the Hudson and in the swamps of the Wallkill Valley.

When we learn that these flowers are called "long purples" by the English country people, the scene of Ophelia's tragic death rises before us:

> "There is a willow grows aslant a brook,
> That shows his hoar leaves in the glassy stream,
> There with fantastic garlands did she come,
> Of crow-flowers, nettles, daisies, and long purples
> That liberal shepherds give a grosser name,
> But our cold maids do dead men's fingers call them."

Dr. Prior, however, says that it is supposed that Shakespeare intended to designate the purple flowering orchis, *O. mascula*, which is said closely to resemble the showy orchis of our spring woods.

The flowers of the purple loosestrife are especially interesting to botanists on account of their *trimorphism*, which word signifies *occurring in three forms*, and refers to the stamens and pistils, which vary in size in the different blossoms, being of three different lengths, the pollen from any given set of stamens being especially fitted to fertilize a pistil of corresponding length.

MEADOW-BEAUTY. DEERGRASS.

Rhexia virginica. Melastoma Family.

Stem.—Square; with wing-like angles. *Leaves.*—Opposite; narrowly oval. *Flowers.*—Purplish-pink; clustered. *Calyx-tube.*—Urn-shaped; four-cleft at the apex. *Corolla.*—Of four large, rounded petals. *Stamens.*—Eight, with long, curved anthers. *Pistil.*—One.

It is always a pleasant surprise to happen upon a bright patch of these delicate deep-hued flowers along the marshes or in the sandy fields of midsummer. Their fragile beauty is of that order which causes it to seem natural that they should belong to a genus which is the sole northern representative of a tropical family. In parts of New England they grow in profusion, while in Arkansas the plant is said to be a great favorite with the deer, hence one of its common names. The flower has been likened to a scarlet evening-primrose, and there is certainly a suggestion of the evening-primrose in the four rounded, slightly heart-shaped petals. The protruding stamens, with their long yellow anthers, are conspicuous.

Of the plant in the late year Thoreau writes: "The scarlet leaves and stems of the rhexia, sometime out of flower, make almost as bright a patch in the meadows now as the flowers did. Its seed-vessels are perfect little cream-pitchers of graceful form."

LOPSEED.

Phryma Leptostachya. Vervain Family.

Two to three feet high; with slender, branching stems. *Leaves.*—Opposite; oval; coarsely toothed; the lower long-stemmed. *Flowers.*—Pinkish; small, in long, slender terminal spikes. *Calyx.*—Two-lipped; the upper lip of three sharp teeth; the lower shorter, twice toothed. *Corolla.*—Two-lipped; upper lip small, notched; the lower much larger; three-lobed. *Stamens.*—Four; in two pairs of unequal length; within corolla. *Pistil.*—One; with a slender style and two-lobed stigma.

Very noticeable in summer in somewhat open woods are the slender, branching clusters made up of the small pink flowers of the lopseed.

Later the hooked, slender teeth of the ribbed calyx close about the one-seeded fruit. The branching fruit-clusters then make this plant almost as conspicuous as during its flowering season.

SEA-PINK. MARSH-PINK.

Sabatia stellaris. Gentian Family.

Stem.—Slender; loosely branched. *Leaves.*—Opposite; oblong to lance-shaped; the upper narrowly linear. *Flowers.*—Large; deep pure pink to almost white. *Calyx.*—Usually five-parted; the lobes long and slender. *Corolla.*—Usually five-parted; conspicuously marked with red and yellow in the centre. *Stamens.*—Usually five. *Pistil.*—One, with two-cleft style.

The advancing year has few fairer sights to show us than a salt meadow flushed with these radiant blossoms. They are so

MARSH-PINK.—*Sabatia stellaris.*

abundant, so deep-hued, so delicate! One feels tempted to lie down among the pale grasses and rosy stars in the sunshine of the August morning and drink his fill of their beauty. How often nature tries to the utmost our capacity of appreciation and leaves us still insatiate! At such times it is almost a relief to turn from the mere contemplation of beauty to the study of its structure; it rests our overstrained faculties.

The vivid coloring and conspicuous marking of these flowers indicate that they aim to attract certain members of the insect world. As in the fireweed the pistil of the freshly opened blossom is curved sideways, with its lobes so closed and twisted as to be inaccessible on their stigmatic surfaces to the pollen which the already mature stamens are discharging. When the effete anthers give evidence that they are *hors de combat* by their withered appearance, the style erects itself and spreads its stigmas.

*S. angularis** is a species which may be found in rich soil inland. Its somewhat heart-shaped, clasping, five-nerved leaves and angled stem serve to identify it.

S. Kennedyana is a larger and peculiarly beautiful species which borders brackish ponds along the coast. Its corolla is about two inches broad and eight- to twelve-parted.

Many of our readers will be interested in the following information, copied from "Garden and Forest," as to the tradition in Plymouth concerning the scientific name of this genus:

"No more beautiful flower grows in New England than the *Sabbatia*, and at Plymouth, where it is especially profuse and luxuriant on the borders of the ponds so characteristic of that part of eastern Massachusetts, it is held in peculiar affection and, one may almost say, reverence. It is locally called 'the rose of Plymouth,' and during its brief season of bloom is sold in quantities in the streets of the town and used in the adornment of houses and churches. Its name comes from that of an early botanist, Liberatus Sabbatia; but this well-established truth is totally disregarded by local tradition. Almost every one in Plymouth firmly believes that the title is due to the fact that the Pilgrims of 1620 first saw

* Common name Rose-pink or Bitter-bloom.

the flower on a Sabbath day, and, entranced by its masses of pinkish lilac-color, named it for the holy day. Indeed, this belief is so deeply ingrained in the Plymouth mind that, we are told, strong objections are made if any other flowers are irreverently mingled with it in church decoration. Yet the legend was invented not more than twenty-five years ago by a man whose identity is still well remembered ; and thus it is of even more recent origin than the one, still more universally credited, which says that the Pilgrim Fathers landed upon Plymouth Rock."

BUSH-CLOVER.

Lespedeza procumbens. Pulse Family.

Stems.—Slender ; trailing, and prostrate. *Leaves.*—Divided into three clover-like leaflets. *Flowers.*—Papilionaceous ; purplish-pink ; veiny. *Pod.*—Small ; rounded ; flat ; one-seeded.

The flowers of this plant often have the appearance of springing directly from the earth amid a mass of clover leaves. They are common in dry soil in the late summer and autumn, as are the other members of the same genus.

*L. reticulata** is an erect, very leafy species with similar blossoms, which are chiefly clustered near the upper part of the stem. The bush-clovers betray at once their kinship with the tick-trefoils, but usually are found in more sandy, open places.

*L. polystachya** has upright wand-like stems from two to four feet high. Its yellowish flowers, usually with a pink or purple spot on the standard, grow in oblong spikes on elongated stalks. Those of *L. capitata* are also yellowish with a purple spot, and are clustered in globular heads.

* Obsolete scientific names.

ROSE-MALLOW.—*Hibiscus Moscheutos.*

ROSE-MALLOW. SWAMP-ROSE-MALLOW.

Hibiscus Moscheutos. Mallow Family.

Stem.—Stout and tall; four to eight feet high. *Leaves.*—The lower three-lobed; the upper oblong, whitish and downy beneath. *Flowers.*—Large and showy; pink. *Calyx.*—Five-cleft, with a row of narrow bractlets beneath. *Corolla.*—Of five large petals. *Stamens.*—Many; on a tube which encloses the lower part of the style. *Pistils.*—Five; united into one, with five stigmas which are like pin-heads.

When the beautiful rose-mallow slowly unfolds her pink banner-like petals and admits the eager bee to her stores of golden pollen, then we feel that the summer is far advanced. As truly as the wood-anemone and the bloodroot seem filled with the essence of spring and the promise of the opening year, so does this stately flower glow with the maturity and fulfilment of late summer. Here is none of the timorousness of the early blossoms which peep shyly out, as if ready to beat a hasty retreat should a late frost overtake them, but rather a calm assurance that the time is ripe, and that the salt marshes and brackish ponds are only awaiting their rosy lining.

The marshmallow, whose roots yield the mucilaginous substance utilized in the well-known confection, is *Althaea officinalis*, an emigrant from Europe. It is a much less common plant than the *Hibiscus*, its pale pink flowers being found in some of the salt marshes of New England and New York.

The common mallow, *Malva rotundifolia*, which overruns the country dooryards and village waysides, is a little plant with rounded, heart-shaped leaves and small purplish flowers. It is used by the country people for various medicinal purposes and is cultivated and commonly boiled with meat in Egypt. Job pictures himself as being despised by those who had been themselves so destitute as to "cut up mallows by the bushes . . . for their meat." *

* Job xxx. 4.

MARSH ST. JOHN'S-WORT.—*Hypericum virginicum.*

MUSK-MALLOW.

Malva moschata. Mallow Family.

Erect, branching, one to two feet high. *Stem-leaves.*—Five-parted, the divisions cleft into linear lobes. *Flowers.*—Pink or white, clustered at the summit of the stem. *Calyx.*—Five-cleft, with three bracts at the base. *Corolla.*—Of five obcordate petals. *Stamens.*—Numerous, united in a column. *Pistils.*—Several, their ovaries united in a ring.

The musk-mallow is an attractive foreign adventurer which has wandered from the garden to the roadside. Its faintly musk-like odor is responsible for its name.

MARSH ST. JOHN'S-WORT.

Hypericum virginicum. St. John's-wort Family.

Stem.—One to two feet high; often pinkish; later bright red. *Leaves.*—Opposite; set close to the stem or clasping by a broad base. *Flowers.*—Pinkish or flesh-color; small; closely clustered at the summit of the stem and in the axils of the leaves. *Calyx.*—Of five sepals; often pinkish. *Corolla.*—Of five petals. *Stamens.*—Nine, in three sets; the sets separated by orange-colored glands. *Pistil.*—One, with three styles.

If one has been so unlucky, from the usual point of view, or so fortunate, looking at the matter with the eyes of the flower-lover, as to find himself in a rich marsh early in August, his eye is likely to fall upon the small, pretty pinkish flowers and pale clasping leaves of the marsh St. John's-wort. A closer inspection will discover that the foliage is dotted with the pellucid glands, and that the stamens are clustered in groups after the family fashion. Should the same marsh be visited a few weeks later, dashes of vivid color will guide one to the spot where the little pink flowers were found. In their place glow the conspicuous ovaries and bright leaves which make the plant very noticeable in late August.

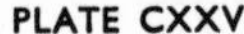
PLATE CXXV

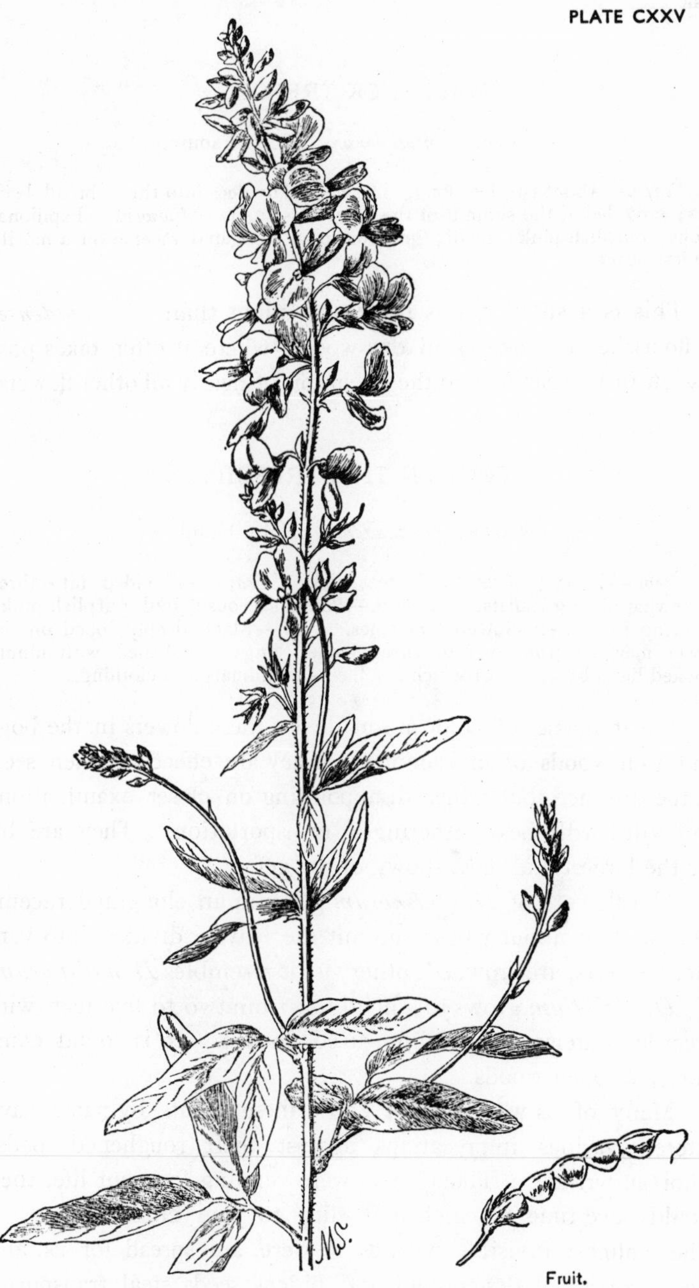

COMMON TICK-TREFOIL.—*Desmodium canadense.*

SMALL TICK-TREFOIL.

Desmodium nudiflorum. Pulse Family.

Scape.—About two feet long. *Leaves.*—Divided into three broad leaflets; crowded at the summit of the flowerless stems. *Flowers.*—Papilionaceous; purplish-pink; small; growing in an elongated raceme on a mostly leafless scape.

This is a smaller, less noticeable plant than *D. canadense.* It flourishes abundantly in dry woods, where it often takes possession in late summer to the exclusion of nearly all other flowers.

COMMON TICK-TREFOIL.

Desmodium canadense. Pulse Family.

Stem.—Hairy; three to six feet high. *Leaves.*—Divided into three somewhat oblong leaflets. *Flowers.*—Papilionaceous; dull purplish-pink; growing in densely flowered racemes. *Pod.*—Flat; deeply lobed on the lower margin; from one to three inches long; roughened with minute hooked hairs by means of which it adheres to animals and clothing.

Great masses of color are made by these flowers in the bogs and rich woods of midsummer. They are effective when seen in the distance, but rather disappointing on closer examination, and will hardly bear gathering or transportation. They are by far the largest and most showy of the genus.

The flowers of *D. glutinosum* grow in an elongated raceme from a stem about whose summit the leaves, divided into very large leaflets, are crowded; otherwise it resembles *D. nudiflorum.*

D. glabellum grows to a height of from two to five feet, with erect leafy stems and medium-sized flowers. It is found commonly in open woods.

Many of us who do not know these plants by name have uttered various imprecations against their roughened pods. Thoreau writes: "Though you were running for your life, they would have time to catch and cling to your clothes. . . . These almost invisible nets, as it were, are spread for us, and whole coveys of desmodium and bidens seeds steal transporta-

BOUNCING-BET.—*Saponaria officinalis.*

tion out of us. I have found myself often covered, as it were, with an imbricated coat of the brown desmodium seeds or a bristling *chevaux-de-frise* of beggar-ticks, and had to spend a quarter of an hour or more picking them off in some convenient spot; and so they get just what they wanted—deposited in another place."

BOUNCING-BET. SOAPWORT.

Saponaria officinalis. Pink Family.

Stem.—Rather stout; swollen at the joints. *Leaves.*—Oval; opposite. *Flowers.*—Pink or white; clustered. *Calyx.*—Of five united sepals. *Corolla.*—Of five pinkish, long-clawed petals (frequently the flowers are double). *Stamens.*—Ten. *Pistil.*—One, with two styles.

A cheery pretty plant is this with large, rose-tinged flowers which are especially effective when double.

Bouncing-Bet is of a sociable turn and is seldom found far from civilization, delighting in the proximity of farm-houses and their belongings, in the shape of children, chickens, and cattle. She comes to us from England, and her "feminine comeliness and bounce" suggest to Mr. Burroughs a Yorkshire housemaid. The generic name is from *sapo*—soap—and refers to the lather which the juice forms with water, and which is said to have been used as a substitute for soap.

PURPLE GERARDIA.

Gerardia purpurea. Figwort Family.

Stem.—One to four feet high; widely branching. *Leaves.*—Linear; sharply pointed. *Flowers.*—Bright purplish-pink; rather large. *Calyx.*—Five-toothed. *Corolla.*—One inch long; somewhat tubular; swelling above; with five more or less unequal, spreading lobes; often downy and spotted within. *Stamens.*—Four; in pairs; hairy. *Pistil.*—One.

In late summer and early autumn these pretty, noticeable flowers brighten the low-lying ground along the coast and in the neighborhood of the Great Lakes. The sandy fields of New

PURPLE GERARDIA.—*Gerardia purpurea.*

England and Long Island are oftentimes a vivid mass of color owing to their delicate blossoms. The plant varies somewhat in the size of its flowers and in the manner of its growth.

The little seaside gerardia, *G. maritima,* is from four inches to a foot high. Its smaller blossoms are also found in salt marshes.

The slender gerardia, *G. tenuifolia,* is common in mountainous regions. The leaves of this species are exceedingly narrow. Like the false foxglove (Pl. XCVI.) and other members of this genus, these plants are supposed to be parasitic in their habits.

SALT-MARSH-FLEABANE.

Pluchea camphorata. Composite Family.

Stem.—Two to five feet high. *Leaves.*—Pale; thickish; oblong or lance-shaped; toothed. *Flower-heads.*—Pink; small; in flat-topped clusters; composed entirely of tubular flowers.

In the salt marshes where we find the starry sea-pinks and the feathery sea-lavender, we notice a pallid-looking plant whose pink flower-buds are long in opening. It is late summer or autumn before the salt-marsh-fleabane is fairly in blossom. There is a strong fragrance to the plant which hardly suggests camphor, despite its specific title.

FALSE DRAGONHEAD.

Physostegia virginiana. Mint Family.

Stems.—Square; upright; wand-like. *Leaves.*—Opposite; sessile; narrow; usually toothed. *Flowers.*—Showy; rose-pink; purple-veined; crowded in terminal leafless spikes. *Calyx.*—Five-toothed. *Corolla.*—One inch long; funnel-form, with an inflated throat; two-lipped. Upper lip erect; lower lip small, spreading, three-parted, its middle lobe the largest, broad and notched. *Stamens.*—Four. *Pistil.*—One, with two-lobed style. *Ovary.*—Deeply four-lobed.

By the roadside, and in wet meadows, during the late summer or even early in the fall, we find the pink clusters of the false dragonhead.

These blossoms are likely to arouse the suspicion that the

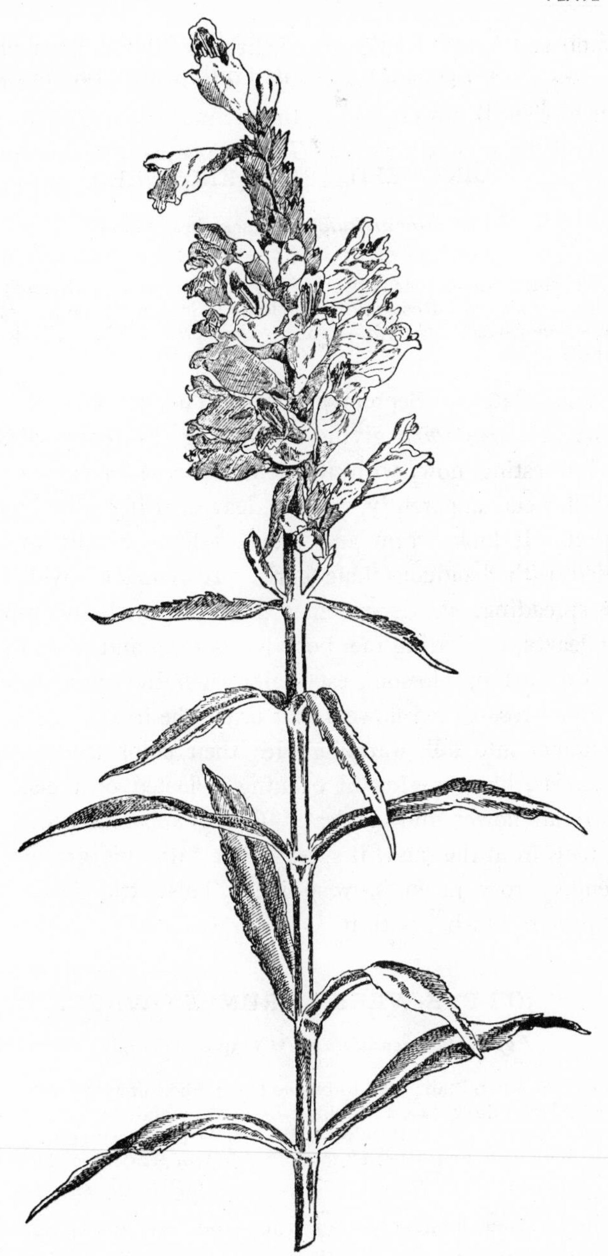

FALSE DRAGONHEAD.—*Physostegia virginiana.*

plant is related to the turtlehead, but the square stem and four-lobed ovary soon persuade us of its kinship with the members of the Mint Family.

JOINTWEED. SAND KNOTWEED.

Polygonella articulata. Buckwheat Family.

Erect; branching; four to twelve inches high. *Leaves.*—Linear; inconspicuous. *Flowers.*—Rose-color; nodding; in very slender racemes. *Calyx.*—Five-parted. *Corolla.*—None. *Stamens.*—Eight. *Pistil.*—One, with three styles.

Under date of September 26th, Thoreau writes: "The *Polygonum articulatum*, giving a rosy tinge to Jenny's desert, is very interesting now, with its slender dense racemes of rose-tinted flowers, apparently without leaves, rising cleanly out of the sand. It looks warm and brave, a foot or more high, and mingled with deciduous blue curls. It is much divided, with many spreading, slender-racemed branches, with inconspicuous linear leaves, reminding me, both by its form and its colors, of a peach-orchard in blossom, especially when the sunlight falls on it; minute rose-tinted flowers that brave the frosts, and advance the summer into fall, warming with their color sandy hill-sides and deserts, like the glow of evening reflected on the sand, apparently all flower and no leaf. Rising apparently with clean bare stems from the sand, it spreads out into this graceful head of slender, rosy racemes, wisp-like. This little desert of less than an acre blushes with it."

JOE-PYE-WEED. TRUMPET-WEED.

Eupatorium maculatum. Composite Family.

Stem.—Stout and tall; two to twelve feet high; often dotted. *Leaves.*—In whorls of three to six; oblong or oval; pointed; rough; veiny; toothed. *Flower-heads.*—Purplish-pink; small; composed entirely of tubular blossoms, with long protruding styles; growing in large clusters at or near the summit of the stem.

The summer is nearly over when the tall, conspicuous Joe-Pye-weeds begin to tinge with "crushed raspberry" the low-

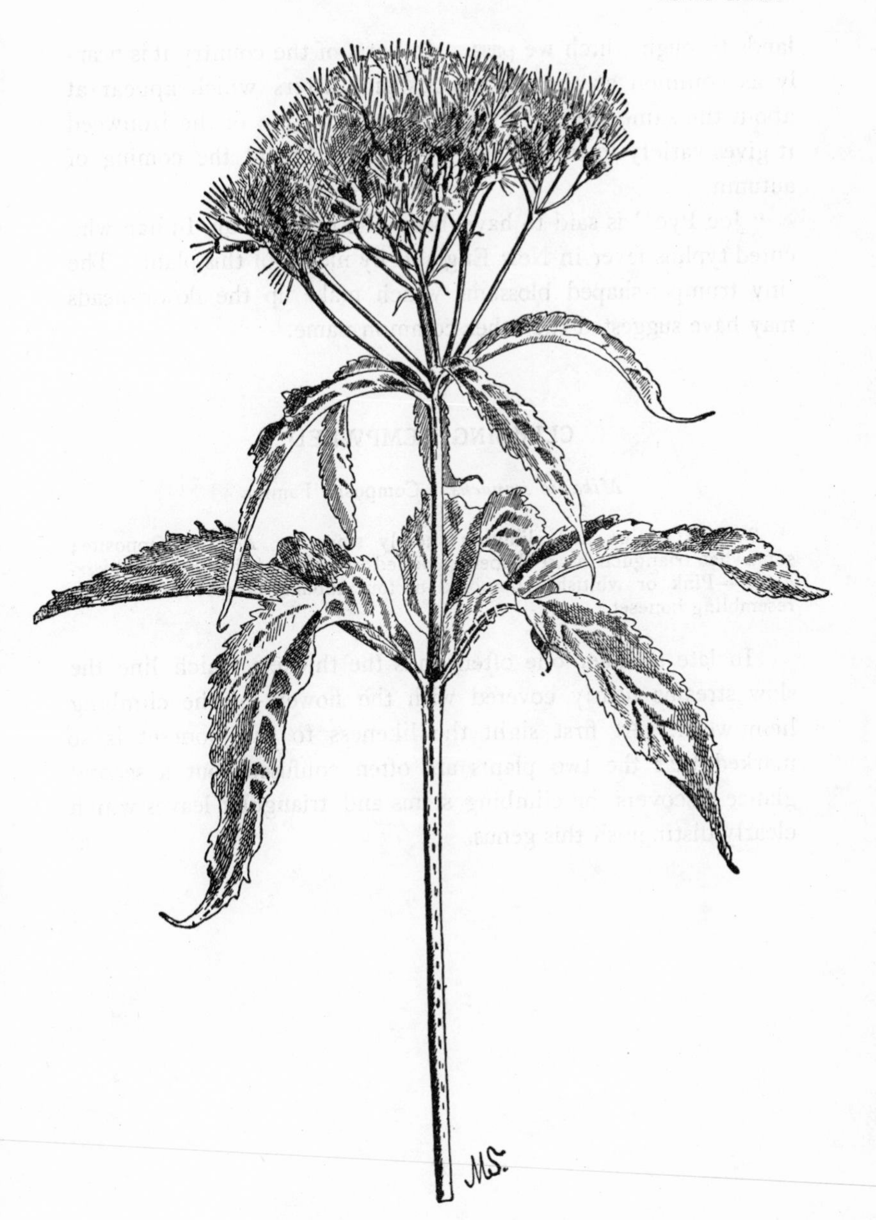

JOE-PYE-WEED.—*Eupatorium maculatum.*

lands through which we pass. In parts of the country it is nearly as common as the goldenrods and asters which appear at about the same season. With the deep purple of the ironweed it gives variety to the intense hues which herald the coming of autumn.

"Joe Pye" is said to have been the name of an Indian who cured typhus fever in New England by means of this plant. The tiny trumpet-shaped blossoms which make up the flower-heads may have suggested the other common name.

CLIMBING HEMPWEED.

Mikania scandens. Composite Family.

Stem.—Twining and climbing; nearly smooth. *Leaves.*—Opposite; somewhat triangular-heart-shaped; pointed; toothed at the base. *Flower-heads.*—Pink or whitish; composed of four tubular flowers; clustered; resembling boneset.

In late summer one often finds the thickets which line the slow streams nearly covered with the flowers of the climbing hempweed. At first sight the likeness to the boneset is so marked that the two plants are often confused, but a second glance discovers the climbing stems and triangular leaves which clearly distinguish this genus.

V

RED

[Red or occasionally Red Flowers not found in Red Section.]

Wood-betony. *Pedicularis canadensis.* April or May. (Yellow Section, p. 146.)

Huckleberries, etc.———. May and June. (White Section, pp. 59–62.)

Herb-Robert. *Geranium Robertianum.* Summer. (Pink Section, p. 266.)

WILD COLUMBINE.

Aquilegia canadensis. Crowfoot Family.

Twelve to eighteen inches high. *Stems.*—Branching. *Leaves.*—Much-divided; the leaflets lobed. *Flowers.*—Large; bright red; yellow within; nodding. *Calyx.*—Of five red petal-like sepals. *Corolla.*—Of five petals in the form of large hollow spurs, which are red without and yellow within. *Stamens.*—Numerous. *Pistils.*—Five, with slender styles.

"——A woodland walk,
A quest of river-grapes, a mocking thrush,
A wild-rose or rock-loving columbine,
Salve my worst wounds,"

declares Emerson; and while perhaps few among us are able to make so light-hearted and sweeping a claim for ourselves, yet many will admit the soothing power of which the woods and fields know the secret, and will own that the ordinary annoyances of life may be held more or less in abeyance by one who lives in close sympathy with nature.

About the columbine there is a daring loveliness which stamps

WILD COLUMBINE.—*Aquilegia canadensis.*

it on the memories of even those who are not ordinarily minute observers. It contrives to secure a foothold in the most precipitous and uncertain of nooks, its jewel-like flowers gleaming from their lofty perches with a graceful *insouciance* which awakens our sportsmanlike instincts and fires us with the ambition to equal it in daring and make its loveliness our own. Perhaps it is as well if our greediness be foiled and we get a tumble for our pains, for no flower loses more with its surroundings than the columbine. Indeed, these destructive tendencies, which are strong within most of us, generally defeat themselves by decreasing our pleasure in a blossom the moment we have ruthlessly and without purpose snatched it from its environment. If we honestly wish to study its structure, or to bring into our homes for preservation a bit of the woods' loveliness, its interest and beauty are sure to repay us. But how many pluck every striking flower they see only to toss it carelessly aside when they reach their destination, if they have not already dropped it by the way. Surely if in such small matters sense and self-control were inculcated in children, more would grow up to the poet's standard of worthiness:

> "Hast thou named all the birds without a gun?
> Loved the wood-rose and left it on its stalk?
> At rich men's tables eaten bread and pulse?
> Unarmed, faced danger with a heart of trust?
> And loved so well a high behavior,
> In man or maid, that thou from speech refrained,
> Nobility more nobly to repay?
> O, be my friend, and teach me to be thine!" *

The name of columbine is derived from *columba*—a dove, but its significance is disputed. Some believe that it was associated with the bird-like claws of the blossom; while Dr. Prior maintains that it refers to the "resemblance of its nectaries to the heads of pigeons in a ring around a dish, a favorite device of ancient artists."

* Emerson.

The meaning of the generic title is also doubtful. Gray derived it from *aquilegus*—water-drawing, but gave no further explanation,* while other writers claim that it is from *aquila*, an eagle, seeing a likeness to the talons of an eagle in the curved nectaries.

WAKEROBIN. BIRTHROOT.

Trillium erectum. Lily Family.

Stem.—Stout; from a tuber-like rootstock. *Leaves.*—Broadly ovate; three in a whorl a short distance below the flower. *Flower.*—Single; terminal; usually purplish red, occasionally whitish, pinkish, or greenish; on an erect or somewhat inclined flower-stalk. *Calyx.*—Of three green spreading sepals. *Corolla.*—Of three large lance-shaped petals. *Stamens.*—Six. *Pistil.*—One, with three large spreading stigmas. *Fruit.*—A large, ovate, six-angled reddish berry.

This wakerobin is one of the few self-assertive flowers of the early year. Its contemporaries act as if somewhat uncertain as to whether the spring had really come to stay, but no such lack of confidence possesses our brilliant young friend, who almost flaunts her lurid petals in our faces, as if to force upon us the welcome news that the time of birds and flowers is at hand. Pretty and suggestive as is the common name, it is hardly appropriate, as the robins have been on the alert for many days before our flower unfurls its crimson signal. Its odor is most unpleasant. Its reddish fruit is noticeable in the woods of late summer.

The sessile trillium [toadshade], *T. sessile*, has no separate flower-stalk, its red or greenish blossom being set close to the stem leaves. Its petals are narrower, and its leaves are often blotched or spotted. Its berry is globular, six-angled, and red or purplish.

The wakerobins are native to North America, only one species being found just beyond the boundaries in the Russian territory.

* But see Eighth Edition of Gray, 1950.

WAKEROBIN.—*Trillium erectum.*

PAINTED-CUP.

Castilleja coccinea. Figwort Family.

Stem.—Hairy; six inches to a foot high. *Root-leaves.*—Clustered; oblong. *Stem-leaves.*—Incised; those among the flowers three to five-cleft, bright scarlet toward the summit; showy. *Flowers.*—Pale yellow; spiked. *Calyx.*—Tubular; flattened. *Corolla.*—Two-lipped; its upper lip long and narrow; its lower short and three-lobed. *Stamens.*—Four; unequal. *Pistil.*—One.

> "——Scarlet tufts
> Are glowing in the green like flakes of fire;
> The wanderers of the prairie know them well,
> And call that brilliant flower the painted cup."*

But we need not go to the prairie in order to see this plant, for it is equally abundant in certain low sandy New England meadows as well as in the near vicinity of New York City. Under date of June 3d, Thoreau graphically describes its appearance near Concord, Mass.: "The painted cup is in its prime. It reddens the meadow, painted-cup meadow. It is a splendid show of brilliant scarlet, the color of the cardinal flower, and surpassing it in mass and profusion. . . . I do not like the name. It does not remind me of a cup, rather of a flame when it first appears. It might be called flame-flower, or scarlet tip. Here is a large meadow full of it, and yet very few in the town have ever seen it. It is startling to see a leaf thus brilliantly painted, as if its tip were dipped into some scarlet tincture, surpassing most flowers in intensity of color."

PITCHER-PLANT. SIDESADDLE-FLOWER. HUNTSMAN'S-CUP.

Sarracenia purpurea. Pitcher-plant Family.

Scape.—Naked; one-flowered; about one foot high. *Leaves.*—Pitcher-shaped; broadly winged; hooded. *Flower.*—Red, pink, or greenish; large; nodding. *Calyx.*—Of five colored sepals, with three bractlets at the base. *Corolla.*—Of five fiddle-shaped petals which are arched over the greenish-yellow style. *Stamens.*—Numerous. *Pistil.*—One, with a short style which expands at the summit into a petal-like umbrella-shaped body, with five small hooked stigmas.

* Bryant.

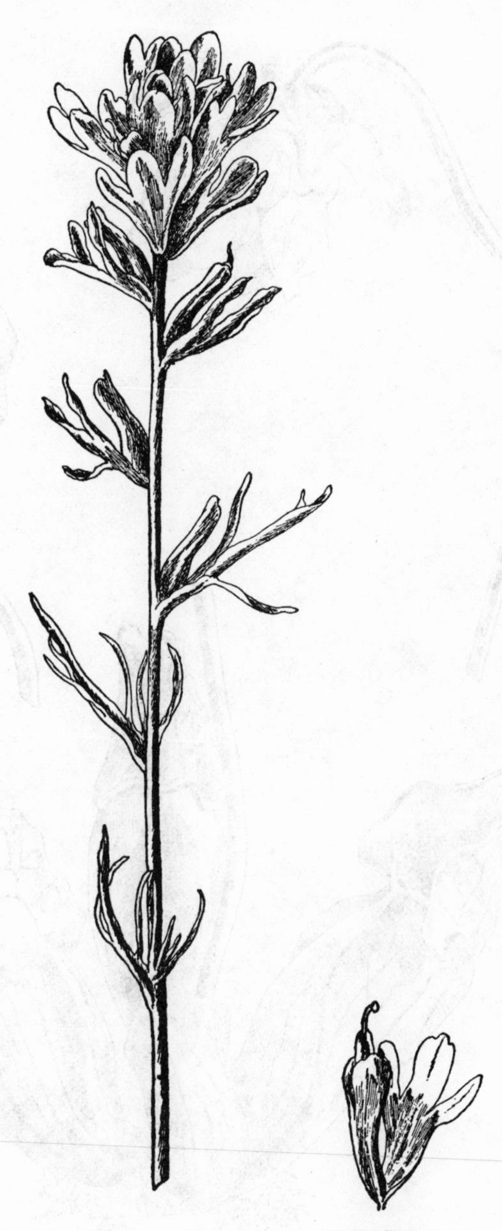

PAINTED-CUP.—*Castilleja coccinea.*

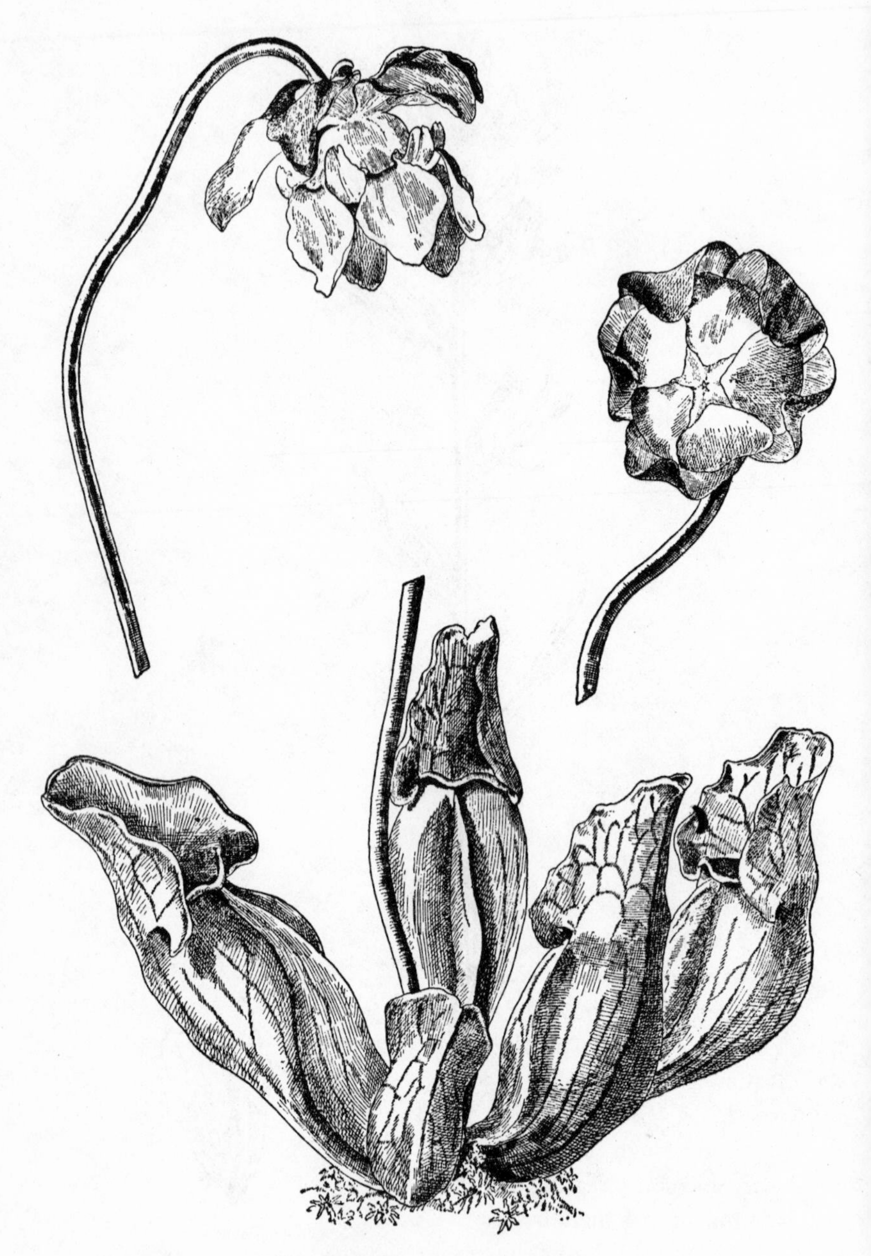

PITCHER-PLANT.—*Sarracenia purpurea.*

The first finding of even the leaves of the pitcher-plant is not to be forgotten. For the leaves not only attract attention by their occasional rich markings, and by their odd pitcher-like shape, but they arouse curiosity by the trap which they set for unwary insects. They are partly lined with a sugary exudation, below which, for a space, they are highly polished, while still lower grow stiff, down-pointing bristles. Insects attracted by the sweet secretion soon find themselves prisoners, as they can seldom fight their way upward through the opposing bristles, or escape by a flight so perpendicular as would be necessary from the form of the cavity. It is rarely that one finds a plant whose leaves are not partially filled with water and drowned insects, and these latter are believed to contribute to its nourishment. In an entry in his journal one September, Thoreau writes of a certain swamp:

"Though the moss is comparatively dry, I cannot walk without upsetting the numerous pitchers, which are now full of water, and so wetting my feet;" and continues: "I once accidentally sat down on such a bed of pitcher plants, and found an uncommonly wet seat where I expected a dry one. These leaves are of various colors, from plain green to a rich striped yellow or deep red. Old Josselyn called this 'hollow-leaved lavender.' I think we have no other plant so singular and remarkable." And November 15th he finds "the water frozen solid in the leaves of the pitcher plant." But singular and interesting though these leaves are, the greatest charm of the plant, it seems to me, lies in its beautiful and unusual flower. This flower we find, if we have the luck, during the early part of June. Although I believe its most frequent color is red (Thoreau likens it to "a great dull red rose," but Gray accuses it of being "deep purple"), I have usually found it either pink or green — fresh delicate shades of both colors—and with a fragrance suggesting sandalwood.

And though (unlike some fortunate friends) I have never found these blossoms rearing themselves by the hundred in an open swamp, baring their beauty to the sunlight, it will be long before I forget the throb of delight which followed my first sight of the plant in a shaded bog, where its delicately tinted flowers nodded almost undetected under bending ferns and masses of false hellebore.

WOOD-LILY. WILD RED LILY.

Lilium philadelphicum. Lily Family.

Stem.—Two to three feet high. *Leaves.*—Whorled or scattered; narrowly lance-shaped. *Flower.*—Erect; orange-red or scarlet, spotted with purple. *Perianth.*—Of six erect narrowly clawed sepals, with nectar-bearing furrows at their base. *Stamens.*—Six. *Pistil.*—One, with three-lobed stigma.

Here and there in the shadowy woods is a vivid dash of color made by some wild red lily which has caught a stray sunbeam in its glowing cup. The purple spots on its sepals guide the greedy bee to the nectar at their base; we too can take the hint and reap a sweet reward if we will, after which we are more in sympathy with those eager, humming bees.

This erect, deep-hued flower is so different from its nodding sister of the meadows, that we wonder that the two should be so often confused. When seen away from its surroundings it has less charms perhaps than either the yellow or the Turk's-cap-lily; but when it rears itself in the cool depths of its woodland home we feel the uniqueness of its beauty.

TURK'S-CAP-LILY.

Lilium superbum. Lily Family.

Stem.—Three to seven feet high. *Leaves.*—Lance-shaped; the lower whorled. *Flowers.*—Orange or scarlet, with purple spots within; three inches long; from three to forty growing in pyramidal clusters. *Perianth.*—Of six strongly recurved sepals. *Stamens.*—Six, with long anthers. *Pistil.*—One, with a three-lobed stigma.

> "Consider the lilies of the field, how they grow;
> They toil not, neither do they spin;
> And yet I say unto you, that even Solomon in all his glory
> Was not arrayed like one of these."

How they come back to us, the beautiful hackneyed lines, and flash into our memories with new significance of meaning

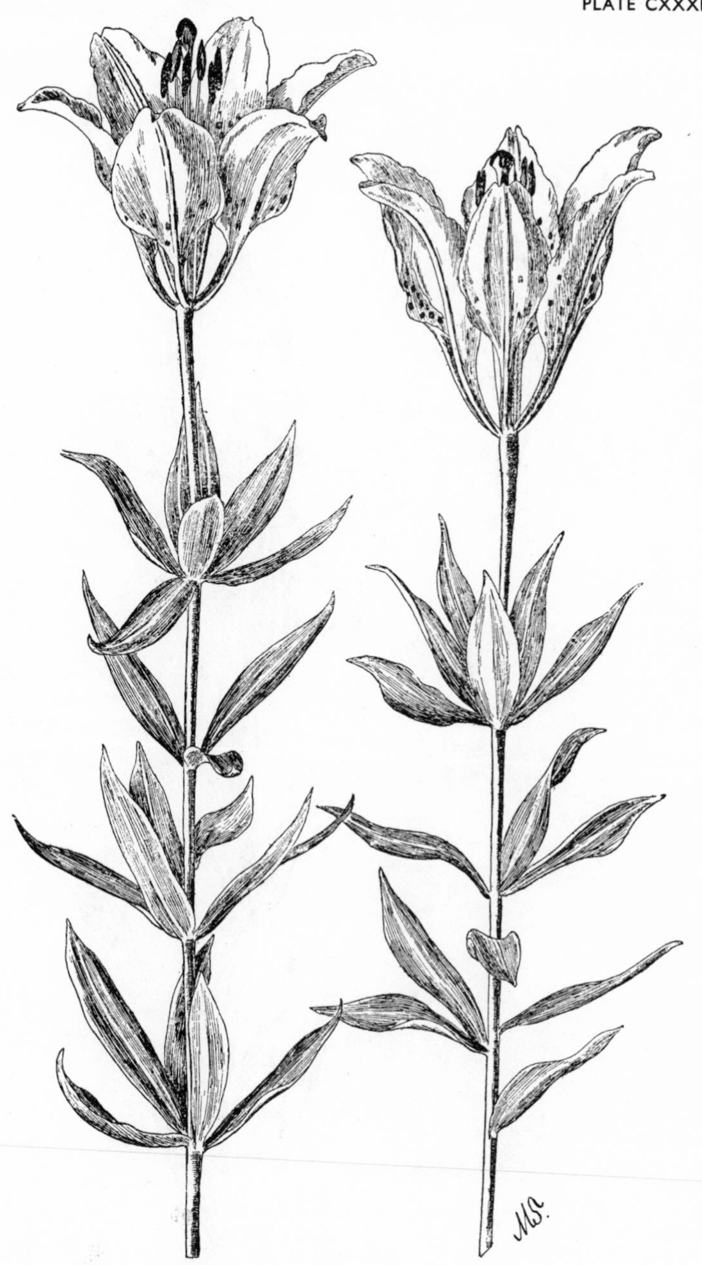

WOOD-LILY.—*Lilium philadelphicum.*

TURK'S-CAP-LILY.—*Lilium superbum.*

when we chance suddenly upon a meadow bordered with these the most gorgeous of our wild flowers.

We might doubt whether our native lilies at all resembled those alluded to in the scriptural passage, if we did not know that a nearly allied species grew abundantly in Palestine; for we have reason to believe that *lily* was a title freely applied by many Oriental poets to any beautiful flower.

Perhaps this plant never attains far inland the same luxuriance of growth which is common to it in some of the New England lowlands near the coast. Its radiant, nodding blossoms are seen in great profusion as we travel by rail from New York to Boston.

BUTTERFLY-WEED. PLEURISY-ROOT.

Asclepias tuberosa. Milkweed Family.

Stem.—Rough and hairy; one to two feet high; erect; very leafy, branching at the summit; without milky juice. *Leaves.*—Linear to narrowly lance-shaped. *Flowers.*—Bright orange-red; in flat-topped, terminal clusters, otherwise closely resembling those of the common milkweed. *Fruit.*—Two hoary erect pods, one of them often stunted.

Few if any of our native plants add more to the beauty of the midsummer landscape than the milkweeds, and of this family no member is more satisfying to the color-craving eye than the gorgeous butterfly-weed, whose vivid flower clusters flame from the dry sandy meadows with such luxuriance of growth as to seem almost tropical. Even in the tropics one hardly sees anything more brilliant than the great masses of color made by these flowers along some of our New England railways in July, while farther south they are said to grow even more profusely. Its gay coloring has given the plant its name of butterfly-weed,* while that of pleurisy-root arose from the belief that the thick, deep root was a remedy for pleurisy. The Indians used it as food and prepared a crude sugar from the flowers; the young seed-pods they boiled and ate with buffalo-meat. The

* It is believed by some that the name springs from the fact that butterflies visit the plant.

BUTTERFLY-WEED.—*Asclepias tuberosa.*

plant is worthy of cultivation and is easily transplanted, as the fleshy roots when broken in pieces form new plants. Oddly enough, at the Centennial Exhibition much attention was attracted by a bed of these beautiful plants which were brought from Holland. Truly, flowers, like prophets, are not without honor save in their own country.

OSWEGO-TEA. BEE-BALM.

Monarda didyma. Mint Family.

Stem.—Square; erect; about two feet high. *Leaves.*—Opposite; ovate, pointed; aromatic; those near the flowers tinged with red. *Flowers.*—Bright red; clustered in a close round head. *Calyx.*—Reddish; five-toothed. *Corolla.*—Elongated; tubular; two-lipped. *Stamens.*—Two; elongated; protruding. *Pistil.*—One, with a two-lobed style; protruding.

We have so few red flowers that when one flashes suddenly upon us it gives us a pleasant thrill of wonder and surprise. The red flowers know so well how to enhance their beauty by seeking an appropriate setting. They select the rich green backgrounds only found in moist, shady places, and are peculiarly charming when associated with a lonely marsh or a mountain-brook. The bee-balm especially haunts these cool nooks, and its rounded flower-clusters touch with warmth the shadows of the damp woods of midsummer. The Indians named the flower *O-gee-chee*—flaming flower, and are said to have made a tea-like decoction from the blossoms.

HOUND'S-TONGUE.

Cynoglossum officinale. Borage Family.

Stem.—Clothed with soft hairs. *Leaves.*—Alternate; hairy; the upper ones lance-shaped; clasping somewhat by a rounded or heart-shaped base. *Flowers.*—Purplish-red; growing in a curved raceme-like cluster which straightens as the blossoms expand. *Calyx.*—Five-parted. *Corolla.*—Funnel-form; five-lobed. *Stamens.*—Five. *Pistil.*—One. *Fruit.*—A large nutlet roughened with barbed or hooked prickles.

This coarse plant, whose disagreeable odor strongly suggests mice, is not only a troublesome weed in pasture-land but a

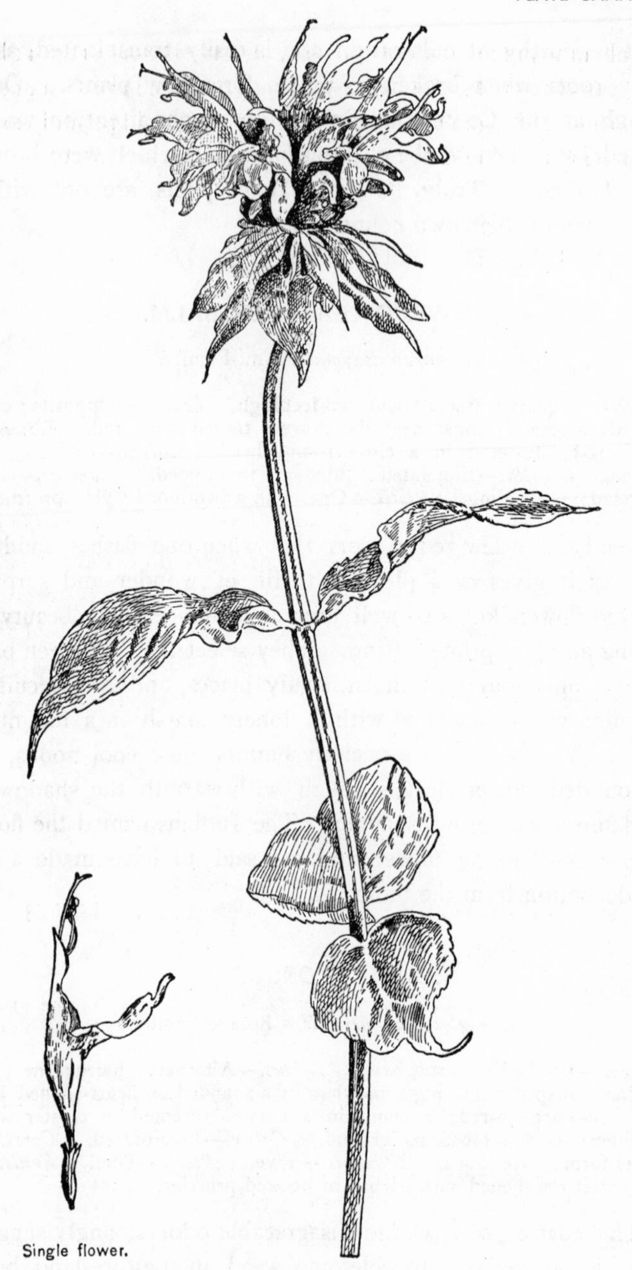

OSWEGO-TEA.—*Monarda didyma.*

special annoyance to wool-growers, as its prickly fruit adheres with pertinacity to the fleece of sheep. Its common name is a translation of its generic title and refers to the shape and texture of the leaves. The dull red flowers appear in summer.

PIMPERNEL. POOR MAN'S WEATHERGLASS.

Anagallis arvensis. Primrose Family.

Stems.—Low; spreading. *Leaves.*—Opposite; ovate; set close to the stem; usually with dark spots. *Flowers.*—Bright red, occasionally blue or white; growing singly from the axils of the leaves. *Calyx.*—Five-parted. *Corolla.*—Five-parted; wheel-shaped. *Stamens.*—Five, with bearded filaments. *Pistil.*—One.

This flower is found in clefts of rocks or in sandy fields, and is noted for its sensitiveness to the weather. It folds its petals at the approach of rain and fails to open at all on a wet or cloudy day. Even in fine weather it closes in the early afternoon and "sleeps" till the next morning. Its ripened seeds are of value as food for many song-birds. It was thought at one time to be serviceable in liver complaints, which reputed virtue may have given rise to the old couplet:

> "No ear hath heard, no tongue can tell
> The virtues of the pimpernell."

ORANGE HAWKWEED. DEVIL'S PAINT-BRUSH.

Hieracium aurantiacum. Composite Family.

Stem.—Hairy; erect. *Leaves.*—Hairy; oblong; close to the ground. *Flower-heads.*—Orange-red; composed entirely of strap-shaped flowers, clustered.

In parts of New York and of New England the midsummer meadows are ablaze with the brilliant orange-red flowers of this striking European weed. It is among the most recent emigrants to this country and bids fair to become an annoyance to the farmer, hence its not altogether inappropriate title of devil's paint-brush. In England it was called "Grimm the Collier,"

POOR MAN'S WEATHERGLASS.—*Anagallis arvensis*.

CARDINAL-FLOWER.—*Lobelia Cardinalis.*

on account of its black hairs and after a comedy of the same title which was popular during the reign of Queen Elizabeth. Both its common and generic names refer to an ancient superstition to the effect that birds of prey used the juices of this genus to strengthen their eyesight.

CARDINAL-FLOWER.

Lobelia Cardinalis. Lobelia Family.

Stem.—From two to four feet high. *Leaves.*—Alternate; narrowly oblong; slightly toothed. *Flowers.*—Bright red; growing in a raceme. *Calyx.*—Five-cleft. *Corolla.*—Somewhat two-lipped; the upper lip of two rather erect lobes, the lower spreading and three-cleft. *Stamens.*—Five, united into a tube. *Pistil.*—One, with a fringed stigma.

We have no flower which can vie with this in vivid coloring. In late summer its brilliant red gleams from the marshes or is reflected from the shadowy water's edge with unequalled intensity—

"As if some wounded eagle's breast
Slow throbbing o'er the plain,
Had left its airy path impressed
In drops of scarlet rain." *

The early French Canadians were so struck with its beauty that they sent the plant to France as a specimen of what the wilds of the New World could yield. Perhaps at that time it received its English name which likens it to the gorgeously attired dignitaries of the Roman Church.

TRUMPET-HONEYSUCKLE.

Lonicera sempervirens. Honeysuckle Family.

A twining shrub. *Leaves.*—Entire; opposite; oblong; the upper pairs united around the stem. *Flowers.*—Deep red without, yellowish within; in close clusters from the axils of the upper leaves. *Calyx.*—With very short teeth. *Corolla.*—Trumpet-shaped; five-lobed. *Stamens.*—Five. *Pistil.*—One. *Fruit.*—A red or orange berry.

Many of us are so familiar with these flowers in our gardens that we have, perhaps, considered them "escapes" when we

* Holmes.

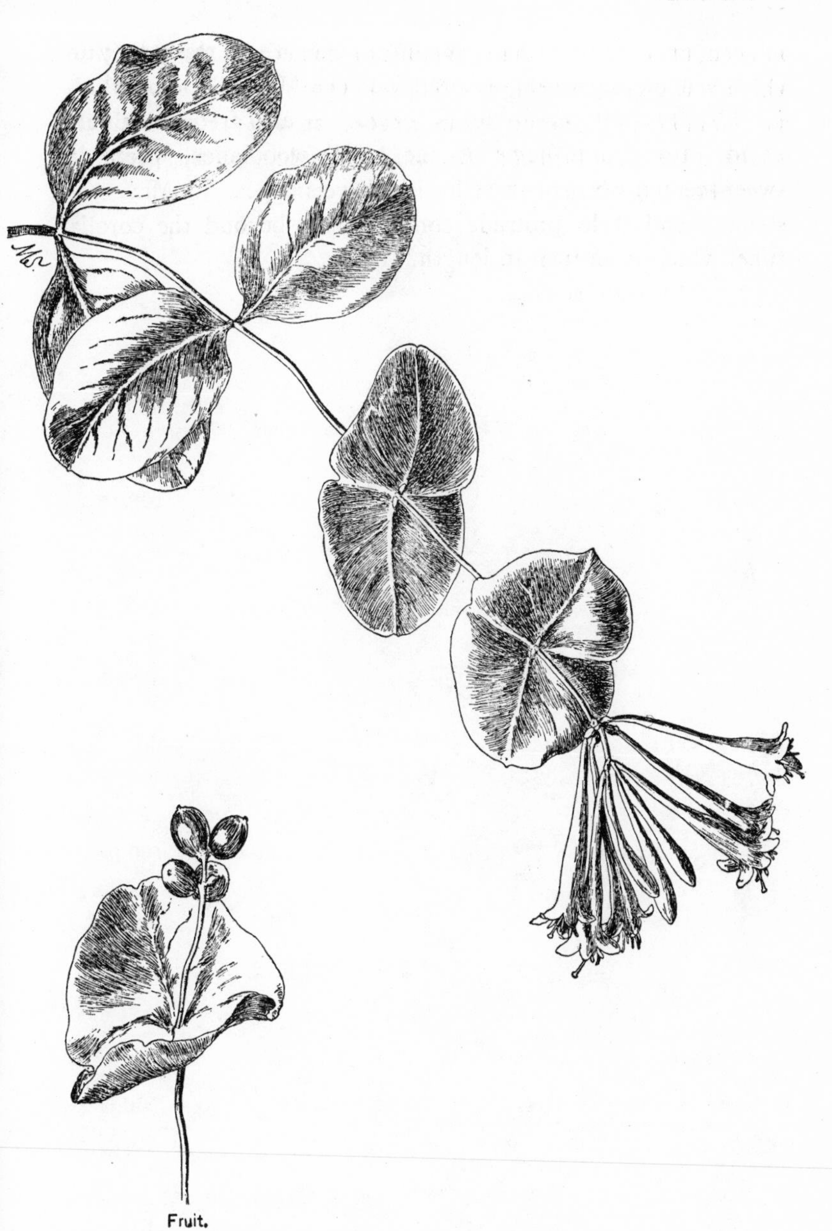

TRUMPET-HONEYSUCKLE.—*Lonicera sempervirens.*

found them brightening the pasture thicket where really they are most at home, appearing at any time from May till October.

The fragrant woodbine, *L. grata*,* is also frequently cultivated. Its natural home is the rocky woodlands, where its sweet-scented whitish or yellowish flowers appear in May. Its stamens and style protrude conspicuously beyond the corolla-tube, which is an inch in length.

* Obsolete scientific name.

VI

BLUE AND PURPLE

[Blue or Purple or occasionally Blue or Purple flowers not found in Blue and Purple Section.]

Wood-Anemone. *Anemone quinquefolia.* April and May. (White Section, p. 6.)

Rue-Anemone. *Anemonella thalictroides.* April and May. (White Section, p. 7.)

Fringed Polygala. *Polygala paucifolia.* May. (Pink Section, p. 248.)

Showy Orchis. *Orchis spectabilis.* May. (Pink Section, p. 234.)

Grass-pink. *Calopogon pulchellus.* June and July. (Pink Section, p. 256.)

Rose Pogonia. *Pogonia ophioglossoides.* June and July. (Pink Section, p. 254.)

Daisy-Fleabane. *Erigeron annuus.* Summer. (White Section, p. 69.)

Purple-flowering Raspberry. *Rubus odoratus.* Early summer. (Pink Section, p. 260.)

Purple Milkweed. *Asclepias purpurascens.* Early summer. (Pink Section, p. 270.)

Purple Loosestrife. *Lythrum Salicaria.* Late summer. (Pink Section, p. 276.)

Thorn-apple. *Datura Stramonium.* Late summer. (White Section, p. 113.)

HEPATICA. LIVERLEAF.

Hepatica americana. Crowfoot Family.

Scape.—Fuzzy; one-flowered. *Leaves.*—Rounded; three-lobed; from the root. *Flowers.*—Blue, white, or pinkish. *Calyx.*—Of six to twelve petal-like sepals; easily taken for a corolla, because directly underneath are three little leaves which resemble a calyx. *Corolla.*—None. *Stamens.*—Usually numerous. *Pistils.*—Several.

"The liver-leaf puts forth her sister blooms
Of faintest blue——"

soon after the late snows have melted. Indeed these fragile-looking, enamel-like flowers are sometimes found actually be-

HEPATICA.—*Hepatica americana.*

neath the snow, and form one of the many instances which we encounter among flowers, as among their human contemporaries, where the frail and delicate-looking withstand storm and stress far better than their more robust-appearing brethren. We welcome these tiny newcomers with especial joy, not alone for their delicate beauty, but because they are usually the first of all the flowers upon the scene of action, if we rule out the never-tardy skunk-cabbage. The rusty leaves of last summer are obliged to suffice for the plant's foliage until some little time after the blossoms have appeared, when the young fresh leaves begin to uncurl themselves. Someone has suggested that the fuzzy little buds look as though they were still wearing their furs as a protection against the wintry weather which so often stretches late into our spring. The flowers vary in color from a lovely blue to pink or white. They are found chiefly in the woods, but occasionally on the sunny hill-sides as well.

The generic name, *Hepatica*, is from the Greek for liver, and was probably given to the plant on account of the shape of its leaf. Dr. Prior says that " in consequence of this fancied likeness it was used as a remedy for liver-complaints, the common people having long labored under the belief that Nature indicated in some such fashion the uses to which her creations might be applied."

COMMON BLUE VIOLET.

Viola cucullata. Violet Family.

Scape.—Slender; one-flowered. *Leaves.*—Heart-shaped, all from the root. *Flowers.*—Varying from a pale blue to deep purple, borne singly on a scape. *Calyx.*—Of five sepals extended into ears at the base. *Corolla.*—Of five somewhat unequal petals, the lower one spurred at the base. *Stamens.*—Short and broad, somewhat united around the pistil. *Pistil.*—One, with a club-shaped style and bent stigma.

Perhaps this is the best-beloved as well as the best-known of the early wild flowers. Whose heart has not been gladdened at one time or another by a glimpse of some fresh green nook in early May where

'——purple violets lurk,
With all the lovely children of the shade?"

It seems as if no other flower were so suggestive of the dawning year, so associated with the days when life was full of promise. Although I believe that more than a hundred species of violets have been recorded, only about thirty are found in our country; of these perhaps twenty are native to the Northeastern States. Unfortunately we have no strongly sweet-scented species, none

> "——sweeter than the lids of Juno's eyes
> Or Cytherea's breath,—"

as Shakespeare found the English blossom. Prophets and warriors as well as poets have favored the violet; Mahomet preferred it to all other flowers, and it was chosen by the Bonapartes as their emblem.

Perhaps its frequent mention by ancient writers is explained by the discovery that the name was once applied somewhat indiscriminately to sweet-scented blossoms.

The birdfoot-violet, *V. pedata*, unlike other members of the family, has leaves which are divided into linear lobes. Its flower is peculiarly lovely, being large and velvety. The variety *bicolor* is especially striking and pansy-like, its two upper petals being of a deeper hue than the others. It is found in the neighborhood of Washington in abundance, and on the shaly soil of New Jersey.

An interesting feature of many of these plants is their cleistogamous flowers. These are small and inconspicuous blossoms, which never open (thus guarding their pollen against all depredations), but which are self-fertilized, ripening their seeds in the dark. They are usually found near or beneath the ground, and are often taken for immature buds.

PLATE CXLII

BLUETS.—*Houstonia caerulea.*

BLUETS. QUAKER-LADIES.

Houstonia caerulea. Madder Family.

Stem.—Erect; three to five inches high. *Leaves.*—Very small; opposite. *Flowers.*—Small; delicate blue, lilac, or nearly white, with a yellowish eye. *Calyx.*—Four-lobed. *Corolla.*—Salver-shaped; four-lobed; corolla-tube long and slender. *Stamens.*—Four. *Pistil.*—One, with two stigmas.

No one who has been in New England during the month of May can forget the loveliness of the bluets. The roadsides, meadows, and even the lawns are thickly carpeted with the dainty enamel-like blossoms, which are always pretty, but which seems to flourish with especial vigor and in great profusion in this lovely region. Less plentiful, perhaps, but still common is the little plant in grassy places far south and west, blossoming in early spring.

The flowers are among those which botanists term "dimorphous." This word signifies *occurring in two forms*, and refers to the stamens and pistils, which vary in size, some flowers having a tall pistil and short stamens, others tall stamens and a short pistil. Darwin has proved, not only that one of these flowers can seldom fully fertilize itself, but that usually the blossoms with tall pistils must be fertilized with pollen from the tall stamens, and that the short pistils are only acted upon by the short stamens. With a good magnifier and a needle these two forms can easily be studied. This is one of the many interesting safeguards against close fertilization.

GILL-OVER-THE-GROUND. GROUND-IVY.

Glechoma hederacea. Mint Family.

Stems.—Creeping and trailing. *Leaves.*—Small and kidney-shaped. *Flowers.*—Bluish-purple; loosely clustered in the axils of the leaves. *Calyx.*—Five-toothed. *Corolla.*—Two-lipped; the upper lip erect and two-cleft, the lower spreading and three-cleft. *Stamens.*—Four. *Pistil.*—One, two-lobed at the apex.

As the pleasant aroma of its leaves suggests, this little plant is closely allied to the catnip. Its common title of Gill-over-the-

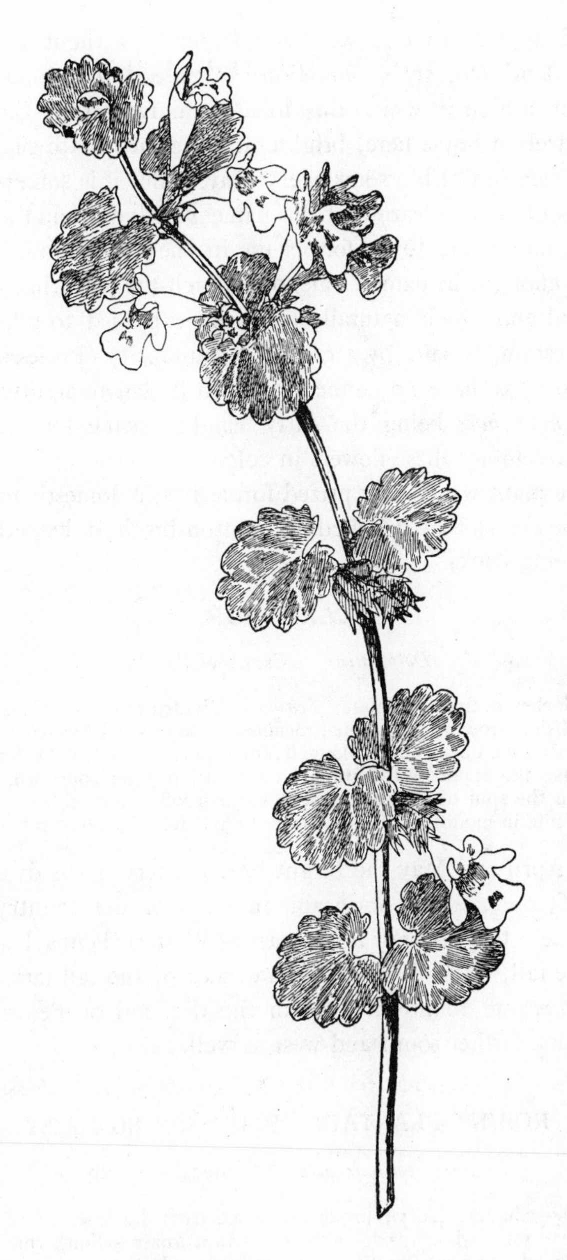

GROUND-IVY.—*Glechoma hederacea.*

ground appeals to one who is sufficiently without interest in pasture-land (for it is obnoxious to cattle) to appreciate the pleasant fashion in which this little immigrant from Europe has made itself at home here, brightening the earth with such a generous profusion of blossoms every May. But it is somewhat of a disappointment to learn that this name is derived from the French *guiller*, and refers to its former use in the fermentation of beer. Oddly enough the name of alehoof, which the plant has borne in England and which naturally has been supposed to refer to this same custom, is said by a competent authority (Professor Earle, of Oxford) to have no connection with it, but to signify *another sort of hofe*, *hofe* being the early English name for the violet, which resembles these flowers in color.

The plant was highly prized formerly as a domestic medicine. Gerarde claims that "boiled in mutton-broth it helpeth weake and akeing backs."

LARKSPUR.

Delphinium. Crowfoot Family.

Six inches to five feet high. *Leaves.*—Divided or cut. *Flowers.*—Blue or purplish; growing in terminal racemes. *Calyx.*—Of five irregular petal-like sepals; the upper one prolonged into a spur. *Corolla.*—Of four irregular petals; the upper pair continued backward in long spurs which are enclosed in the spur of the calyx, the lower pair with short claws. *Stamens.*—Indefinite in number. *Pistils.*—One to five, forming pods in fruit.

In April and May the bright blue clusters of the dwarf larkspur, *D. tricorne*, are noticeable in parts of the country. Unfortunately they are not found east of Western Pennsylvania.

The tall, wand-like purplish racemes of the tall larkspur, *D. exaltatum*, are found in July in the rich soil of Pennsylvania, and much farther south and west as well.

ROBIN'S-PLANTAIN. BLUE SPRING-DAISY.

Erigeron pulchellus. Composite Family.

Stem.—Simple; hairy; producing offsets from the base. *Root-leaves.*—Somewhat rounded or wedge-shaped. *Stem-leaves.*—Somewhat oblong; lance-shaped; partly clasping. *Flower-heads.*—Rather large; on slender

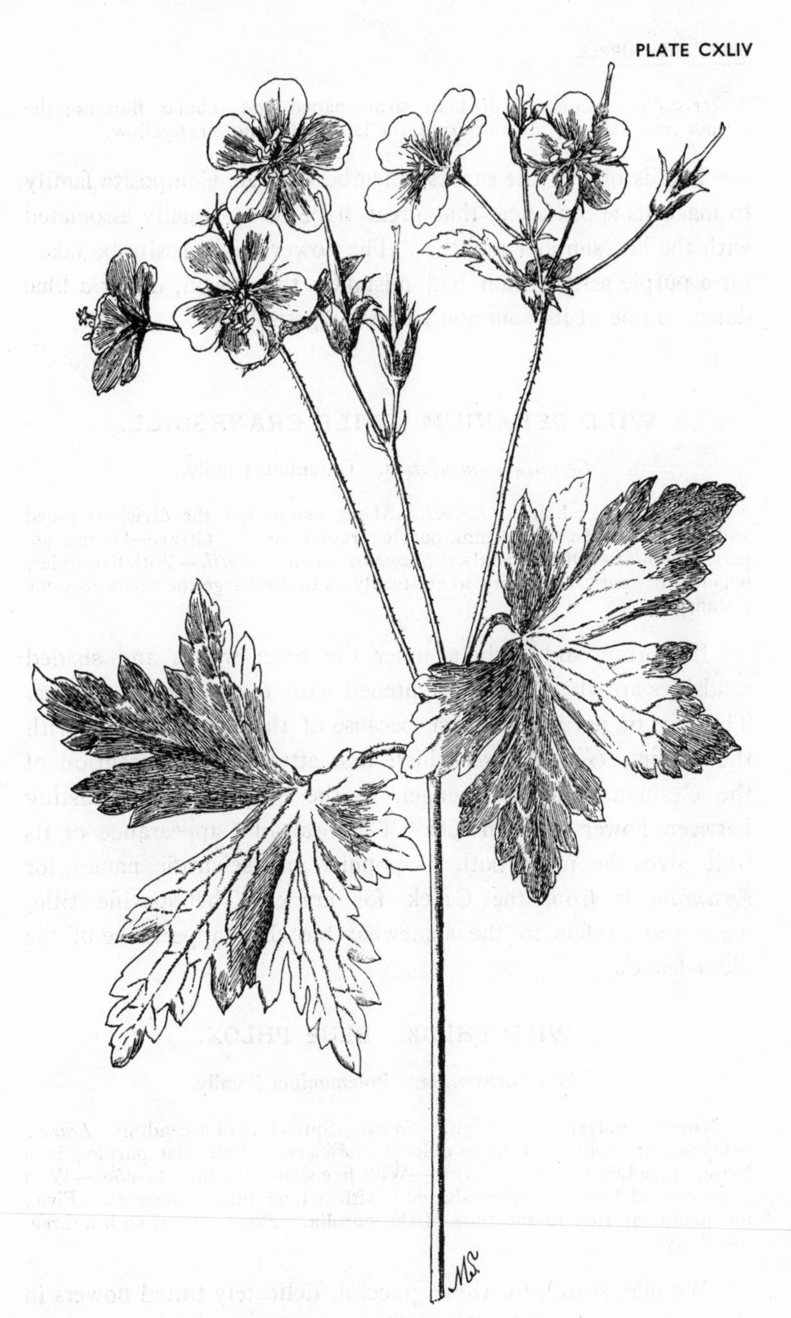

WILD GERANIUM.—*Geranium maculatum.*

flower-stalks; composed of both strap-shaped and tubular flowers; the former (ray-flowers) bluish-purple, the latter (disk-flowers) yellow.

This is one of the earliest members of the Composite family to make its appearance, that great tribe being usually associated with the late summer months. The flower might easily be taken for a purple aster which had mistaken the season, or for a blue daisy, as one of its common names suggests.

WILD GERANIUM. WILD CRANESBILL.

Geranium maculatum. Geranium Family.

Stem.—Erect; hairy. *Leaves.*—About five-parted, the divisions lobed and cut. *Flowers.*—Pale pink-purple; rather large. *Calyx.*—Of five sepals. *Corolla.*—Of five petals. *Stamens.*—Ten. *Pistil.*—With five styles, which split apart at maturity so elastically as to discharge the seeds to some distance.

In spring and early summer the open woods and shaded roadsides are abundantly brightened with these graceful flowers. They are of peculiar interest because of their close kinship with the species, *G. pratense*, which first attracted the attention of the German scholar, Sprengel, to the close relations existing between flowers and insects. The beak-like appearance of its fruit gives the plant both its popular and scientific names, for *geranium* is from the Greek for crane. The specific title, *maculatum*, refers to the somewhat blotched appearance of the older leaves.

WILD PHLOX. BLUE PHLOX.

Phlox divaricata. Polemonium Family.

Nine to eighteen inches high. *Stems.*—Spreading or ascending. *Leaves.*—Opposite; oblong or lance-oblong. *Flowers.*—Pale lilac-purple; in a loose, spreading cluster. *Calyx.*—With five slender teeth. *Corolla.*—With a five-parted border; salver-shaped; with a long tube. *Stamens.*—Five; unequally inserted in the tube of the corolla. *Pistil.*—One, with a three-lobed style.

We may search for these graceful, delicately tinted flowers in the rocky woods of April and May.

Nearly allied to them is the wild Sweet William, *P. maculata*, the pink-purple blossoms of which are found along the streams and in the rich woods of somewhat southern localities.

The beautiful moss-pink, *P. subulata* (p. 240), is also a member of this genus.

BLUE-EYED MARY. INNOCENCE.

Collinsia verna. Figwort Family.

Six to twenty inches high. *Stems.*—Branching; slender. *Leaves.*—Opposite; the lower oval, the upper ovate-lance-shaped; clasping by the heart-shaped base. *Flowers.*—Blue and white, long-stalked; appearing whorled in the axils of the upper leaves. *Calyx.*—Deeply five-cleft. *Corolla.*—Deeply two-lipped; the upper lip two-cleft, the lower three-cleft. *Stamens.*—Four. *Pistil.*—One.

Unfortunately these dainty flowers are not found farther east than Western New York. From there they spread south and westward, abounding so plentifully in the vicinity of Cincinnati that the moist meadows are blue with their blossoms in spring or early summer.

BLUEBELLS. VIRGINIAN COWSLIP. LUNGWORT.

Mertensia virginica. Borage Family.

One to two feet high. *Stem.*—Smooth; pale, erect. *Leaves.*—Oblong; veiny. *Flowers.*—Blue, pinkish in bud; in raceme-like clusters which are rolled up from the end and straighten as the flowers expand. *Calyx.*—Five-cleft. *Corolla.*—Trumpet-shaped; one inch long; spreading. *Stamens.*—Five. *Pistil.*—One.

These very lovely blossoms are found in moist places during April and May in parts of New York as well as south and westward. The English naturalist, Mr. Alfred Wallace, seeing them, for the first time, in the vicinity of Cincinnati, writes in the *Fortnightly Review*: "In a damp river bottom the exquisite blue *Mertensia Virginica* was found. It is called here the 'Virginian cowslip,' its drooping porcelain-blue bells being somewhat of the size and form of those of the true cowslip.

SEA-LUNGWORT.

Mertensia maritima. Borage Family.

Smooth, fleshy, spreading. *Leaves.*—Ovate or wedge-shaped, with a bloom. *Flowers.*—Blue; occasionally white; pink in bud; clustered. *Calyx.*—Five-parted. *Corolla.*—Bell-shaped; five-lobed. *Stamens.*—Five. *Pistil.*—One, with a deeply four-parted ovary.

On the sandy beaches along the coast from Massachusetts northward, or perhaps on the pebbly rocks, the sea-lungwort spreads its mats of pale, bluish-green leaves. These leaves blend harmoniously with their background of gray sand, or of rounded, wave-washed, bluish stones, forming oftentimes great beds of foliage so symmetrical in their star-like or horseshoe-shaped outlines as to suggest the gardener's art rather than the wayward whims of an undomesticated plant. The pink flower-buds are noticeable late in June. They open into small, somewhat bell-shaped blue or occasionally white blossoms. As the flowers open one by one, the result is an attractive combination of delicate pinks and blues, a combination which recalls the kinship of these blossoms with the blueweed and the forget-me-not.

BLUE-EYED GRASS.

Sisyrinchium angustifolium. Iris Family.

Four to twelve inches high. *Leaves.*—Narrow and grass-like. *Flowers.*—Blue or purple, with a yellow centre. *Perianth.*—Six-parted; the divisions bristle-pointed. *Stamens.*—Three, united. *Pistil.*—One, with three thread-like stigmas.

> "For the sun is no sooner risen with a burning heat,
> But it withereth the grass,
> And the flower thereof falleth,
> And the grace of the fashion of it perisheth."

So reads the passage in the Epistle of St. James, which seems so graphically to describe the brief life of this little flower that we might almost believe the Apostle had had it in mind, were it to be found in the East.

BLUE-EYED GRASS.—*Sisyrinchium angustifolium.*

The blue-eyed grass belongs to the same family as the showy fleur-de-lis, and blossoms during the summer, being especially plentiful in moist meadows. It is sometimes called "eyebright," which name belongs by rights to *Euphrasia americana*.

EYEBRIGHT.

Euphrasia americana. Figwort Family.

Low; branching. *Leaves.*—Ovate or oval; mottled. *Flowers.*—Lavender or nearly white; veined; lower lip patched with deep orange-yellow; small; spiked. *Calyx.*—Four-cleft. *Corolla.*—Two-lipped; upper lip erect; two-lobed; lower lip spreading; three-cleft. *Stamens.*—Four, under upper lip. *Pistil.*—One.

In places along the coast of Maine this cheery little plant, which is said to owe its generic name to its reported healing properties, but which might well be called "cheerfulness" on account of its unfailing sturdy brightness, carpets thickly the grassy roadsides.

ONE-FLOWERED CANCER-ROOT.

Orobanche uniflora. Broom-rape Family.

Scape.—Slender; fleshy; three to five inches high; one-flowered. *Leaves.*—None. *Flower.*—Pale purple; solitary; one inch long; with a delicate fragrance. *Calyx.*—Five-cleft. *Corolla.*—Somewhat two-lipped; with two yellow bearded folds in the throat. *Stamens.*—Four. *Pistil.*—One.

In April and May the odd pretty flower of the parasitic one-flowered cancer-root is found in the damp woodlands.

VIOLET WOOD-SORREL.

Oxalis violacea. Geranium Family.

Scape.—Five to nine inches high; several-flowered. *Leaves.*—Divided into three clover-like leaflets. *Flowers.*—Violet-colored; clustered on the scape. *Calyx.*—Of five sepals. *Corolla.*—Of five petals. *Stamens.*—Ten. *Pistil.*—One, with five styles.

This little plant is found in somewhat open or rocky woods, its lovely, delicate flower-clusters appearing in May or June.

This species is more common southward, while the pink-veined wood sorrel abounds in the cool woods of the North.

LARGER BLUE FLAG. FLEUR-DE-LIS.

Iris versicolor. Iris Family.

Stem.—Stout; angled on one side; leafy; one to three feet high. *Leaves.*—Flat and sword-shaped, with their inner surfaces coherent for about half of their length. *Flowers.*—Large and showy; violet-blue, variegated with green, yellow, or white; purple-veined. *Perianth.*—Six-cleft; the three outer divisions recurved, the three inner smaller and erect. *Stamens.*—Three, covered by the three overarching, petal-like divisions of the style. *Pistil.*—One, with its style cleft into three petal-like divisions, each of which bears its stigma on its inner surface.

"Born in the purple, born to joy and pleasance,
Thou dost not toil nor spin,
But makest glad and radiant with thy presence
The meadow and the lin." *

In both form and color this is one of the most regal of our wild flowers, and it is easy to understand why the fleur-de-lis was chosen as the emblem of a royal house, although the especial flower which Louis VII. of France selected as his badge was probably white.

It will surprise most of us to learn that the common name which we have borrowed from the French does not signify "flower-of-the-lily," as it would if literally translated, but "flower of Louis," *lis* being a corruption of the name of the king who first adopted it as his badge.

For the botanist the blue flag possesses special interest. It is a conspicuous example of a flower which has guarded itself against self-fertilization, and which is beautifully calculated to secure the opposite result. The position of the stamens is such that their pollen could not easily reach the stigmas of the same flower, for these are borne on the inner surface of the petal-like, overarching styles. There is no prospect here of any seed being set unless the pollen of another flower is secured. Now what are

* Longfellow.

PLATE CXLVI

LARGER BLUE FLAG.—*Iris versicolor.*

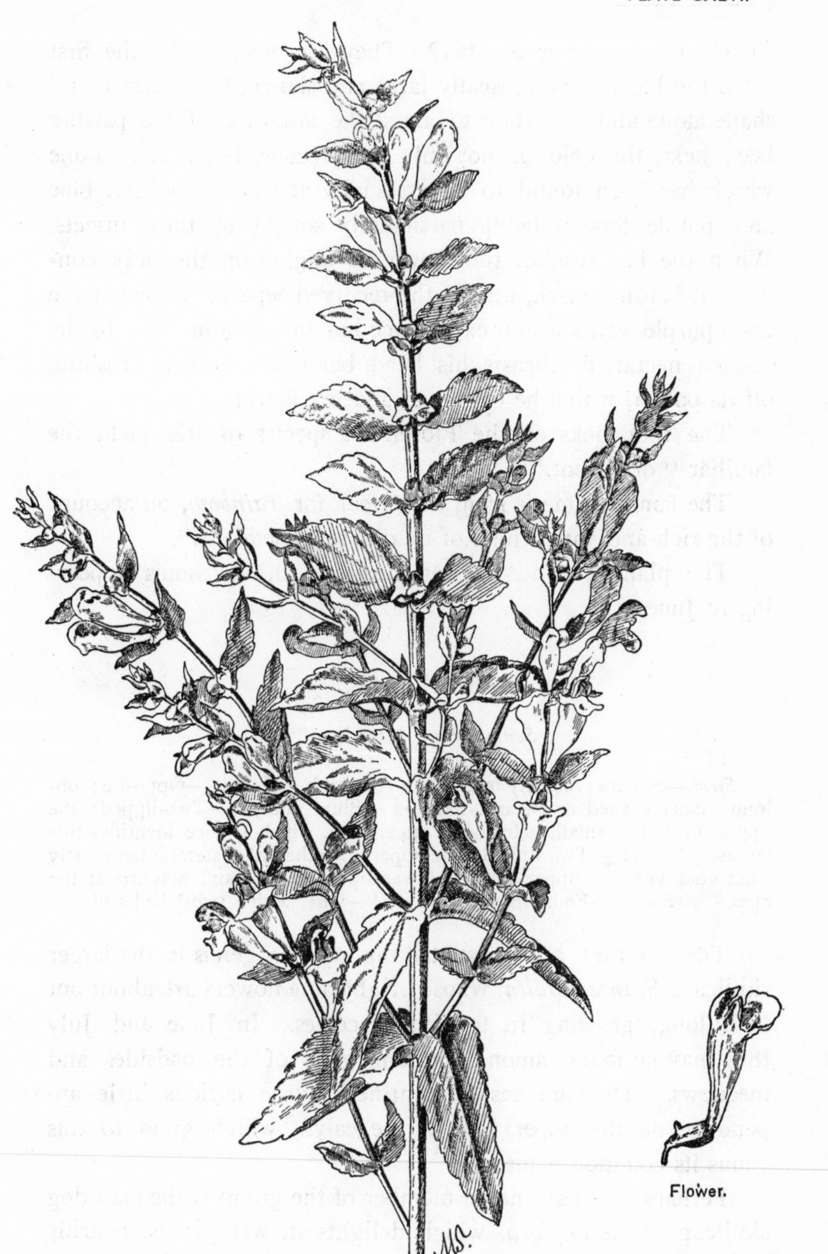

HOODED SKULLCAP.—*Scutellaria epilobiifolia.*

the chances in favor of this? They are many: In the first place the blossom is unusually large and showy, from its size and shape alone almost certain to arrest the attention of the passing bee; next, the color is not only conspicuous, but it is also one which has been found to be especially attractive to bees, blue and purple flowers being particularly sought by these insects. When the bee reaches the flower he alights on the only convenient landing-place, one of the recurved sepals; following the deep purple veins which experience has taught him lead to the hidden nectar, he thrusts his head below the anther, brushing off its pollen, which he carries to another flower.

The rootstocks of the Florentine species of iris yield the familiar "orris-root."

The family name is from the Greek for *rainbow*, on account of the rich and varied hues of its different members.

The plant abounds in wet meadows, the blossoms appearing in June.

SKULLCAP.

Scutellaria. Mint Family.

Stem.—Square; usually one to two feet high. *Leaves.*—Opposite; oblong; lance-shaped or linear. *Flowers.*—Blue. *Calyx.*—Two-lipped; the upper lip with a small, helmet-like appendage, which at once identifies this genus. *Corolla.*—Two-lipped; the upper lip arched, the lateral lobes mostly connected with the upper lip, the lower lip spreading and notched at the apex. *Stamens.*—Four, in pairs. *Pistil.*—One, with a two-lobed style.

The prettiest and most striking of this genus is the larger skullcap, *S. integrifolia*, whose bright blue flowers are about one inch long, growing in terminal racemes. In June and July they may be found among the long grass of the roadsides and meadows. They are easily identified by the curious little appendage on the upper part of the calyx, which gives to this genus its common name.

Perhaps the best-known member of the group is the mad-dog skullcap, *S. lateriflora*, which delights in wet places, bearing small, inconspicuous flowers in one-sided racemes. This plant

PLATE CXLVIII

AMERICAN BROOKLIME.—*Veronica americana.*

is quite smooth, while that of *S. integrifolia* is rather downy. It was formerly believed to be a sure cure for hydrophobia.

*S. epilobiifolia** is usually found somewhat northward. Its flowers are much larger than those of *S. lateriflora*, but smaller than those of *S. integrifolia.* They grow singly from the axils of the upper leaves.

AMERICAN BROOKLIME.

Veronica americana. Figwort Family.

Stem.—Smooth; reclining at base, then erect; eight to fifteen inches high. *Leaves.*—Mostly opposite; oblong; toothed. *Flowers.*—Blue; clustered in the axils of the leaves. *Calyx.*—Four-parted. *Corolla.*—Wheel-shaped; four-parted. *Stamens.*—Two. *Pistil.*—One.

Perhaps the prettiest of the blue *Veronicas* is the American brooklime. Its clustered flowers make bright patches in moist ground which might, at a little distance, be mistaken for beds of forget-me-nots. It blossoms from June till August, and is almost as common in wet ditches and meadows as its sister, the common speedwell, is in dry and open places. Some of the members of this genus were once believed to possess great medicinal virtues, and won for themselves in Europe the laudatory names of Honor and Praise.

COMMON SPEEDWELL.

Veronica officinalis. Figwort Family.

Stem.—Prostrate; rooting. *Leaves.*—Short-stemmed; downy; toothed. *Flowers.*—Pale blue; small; in thick clusters which grow from an axil of the leaves. *Calyx.*—Usually four-parted. *Corolla.*—Usually four-parted. *Stamens.*—Two. *Pistil.*—One.

"The little speedwell's darling blue" is noticeable during June and July, when clusters of these tiny flowers brighten the roadside banks.

* Common or Hooded Skullcap.

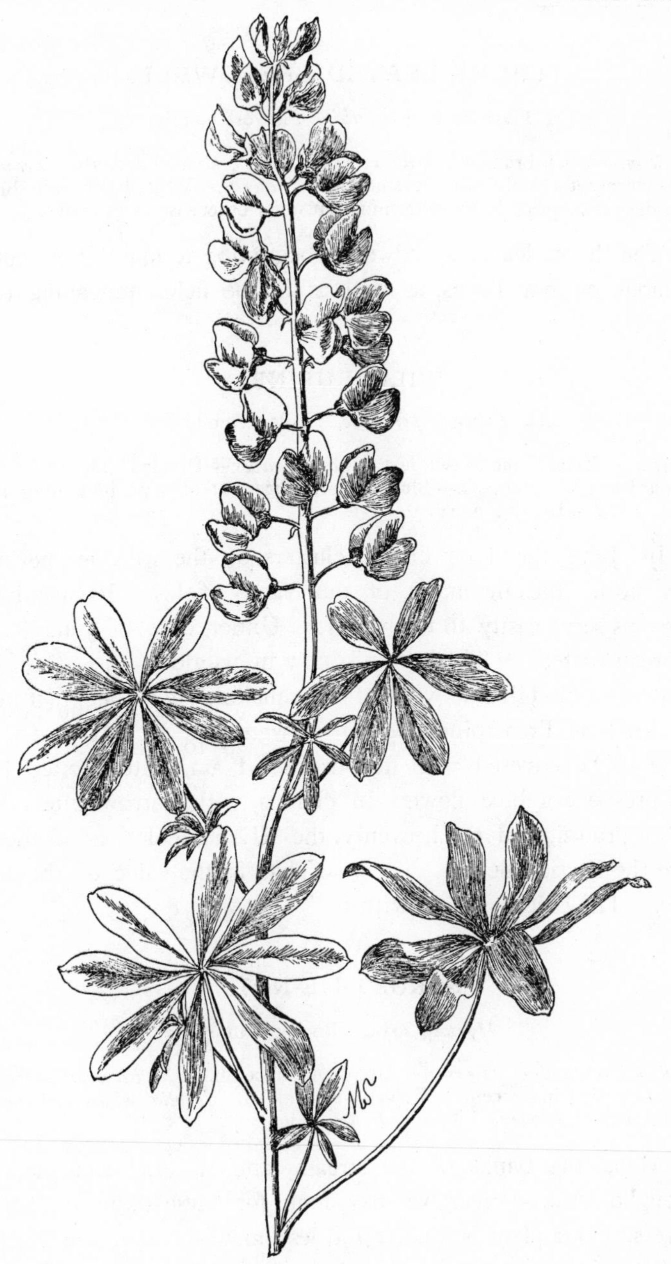

WILD LUPINE.—*Lupinus perennis.*

THYME-LEAVED SPEEDWELL.

Veronica serpyllifolia. Figwort Family.

Stem.—Much branched at the creeping base; almost smooth. *Leaves.*—Obscurely toothed; almost smooth. *Flowers.*—Whitish or pale blue with deeper stripes; in loose terminal clusters, otherwise as in above.

The thyme-leaved speedwell is beginning to make itself conspicuous on our lawns, as well as in the fields and along the roadsides.

WILD LUPINE.

Lupinus perennis. Pulse Family.

Stem.—Erect; one to two feet high. *Leaves.*—Divided into seven to eleven leaflets. *Flowers.*—Blue; papilionaceous; showy; in a long raceme. *Pod.*—Broad; hairy.

In June the long bright clusters of the wild lupine are very noticeable in many of our sandy fields. Its pea-like blossoms serve easily to identify it. Under date of June 8th, Thoreau writes: "The lupine is now in its glory. . . . It paints a whole hill-side with its blue, making such a field (if not meadow) as Proserpine might have wandered in. Its leaf was made to be covered with dew-drops. I am quite excited by this prospect of blue flowers in clumps, with narrow intervals, such a profusion of the heavenly, the Elysian color, as if these were the Elysian fields. . . . That is the value of the lupine. The earth is blued with it."

FORGET-ME-NOT.

Myosotis laxa. Borage Family.

Stems.—Slender. *Leaves.*—Alternate, lance-oblong. *Flowers.*—Blue; small, growing in a raceme. *Calyx.*—Five-lobed. *Corolla.*—Salver-shaped, five-toothed. *Stamens.*—Five. *Pistil.*—One.

Along the banks of the stream, and in low, wet places, throughout the summer, we may look for these exquisite little flowers. Our plant is smaller and less luxuriant than the European species.

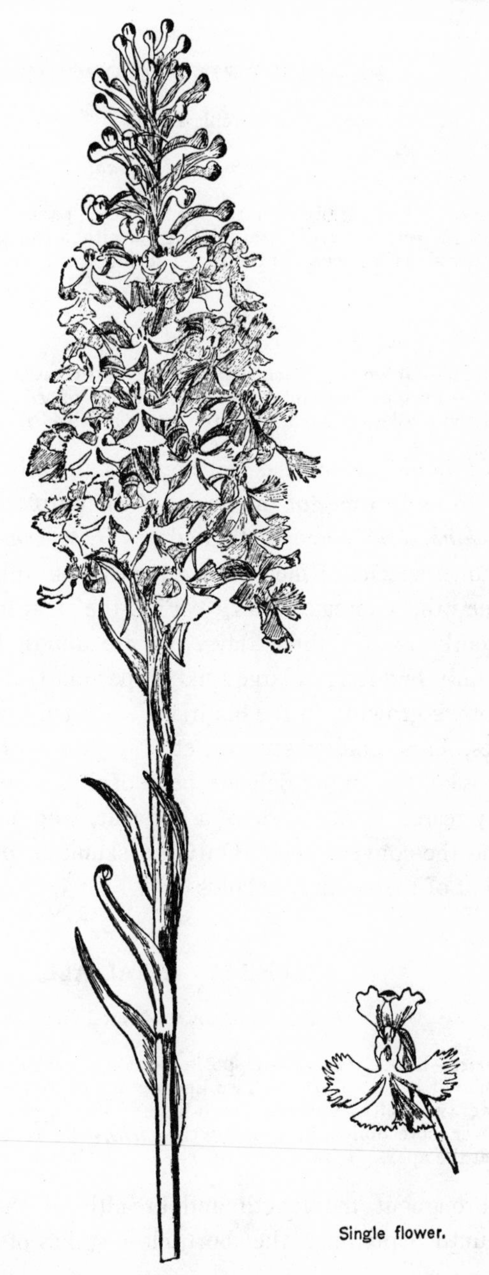

SMALL PURPLE FRINGED ORCHIS.—*Habenaria psycodes.*

PURPLE FRINGED ORCHISES.

Orchis Family.

Habenaria fimbriata.

Leaves.—Oval or oblong; the upper, few, passing into lance-shaped bracts. *Flowers*.—Purple; rather large; with a fan-shaped, three-parted lip, its divisions fringed; with a long curving spur; growing in a spike.

Habenaria psycodes.

Leaves.—Oblong or lance-shaped; the upper passing into linear bracts. *Flowers*.—Purple; fragrant; resembling those of *H. fimbriata*, but much smaller, with a less fringed lip; growing in a spike.

We should search the wet meadows in early June if we wish surely to be in time for the larger of the purple fringed orchises, for *H. fimbriata** somewhat antedates *H. psycodes*,† which is the commoner species of the two and appears in July. Under date of June 9th, Thoreau writes: "Find the great fringed-orchis out apparently two or three days, two are almost fully out, two or three only budded; a large spike of peculiarly delicate, pale-purple flowers growing in the luxuriant and shady swamp, amid hellebores, ferns, golden senecio, etc. . . . The village belle never sees this more delicate belle of the swamp. . . . A beauty reared in the shade of a convent, who has never strayed beyond the convent-bell. Only the skunk or owl, or other inhabitant of the swamp, beholds it."

SELFHEAL. HEAL-ALL.

Prunella vulgaris. Mint Family.

Stems.—Low. *Leaves*.—Opposite; oblong. *Flowers*.—Bluish-purple; in a spike or head. *Calyx*.—Two-lipped; upper lip with three short teeth, the lower two-cleft. *Corolla*.—Two-lipped; the upper lip arched, entire, the lower spreading, three-cleft. *Stamens*.—Four. *Pistil*.—One, two-lobed at the apex.

Throughout the length and breadth of the country, from June until September, the short, close spikes of the selfheal can

* Large Purple Fringed Orchis. † Small Purple Fringed Orchis.

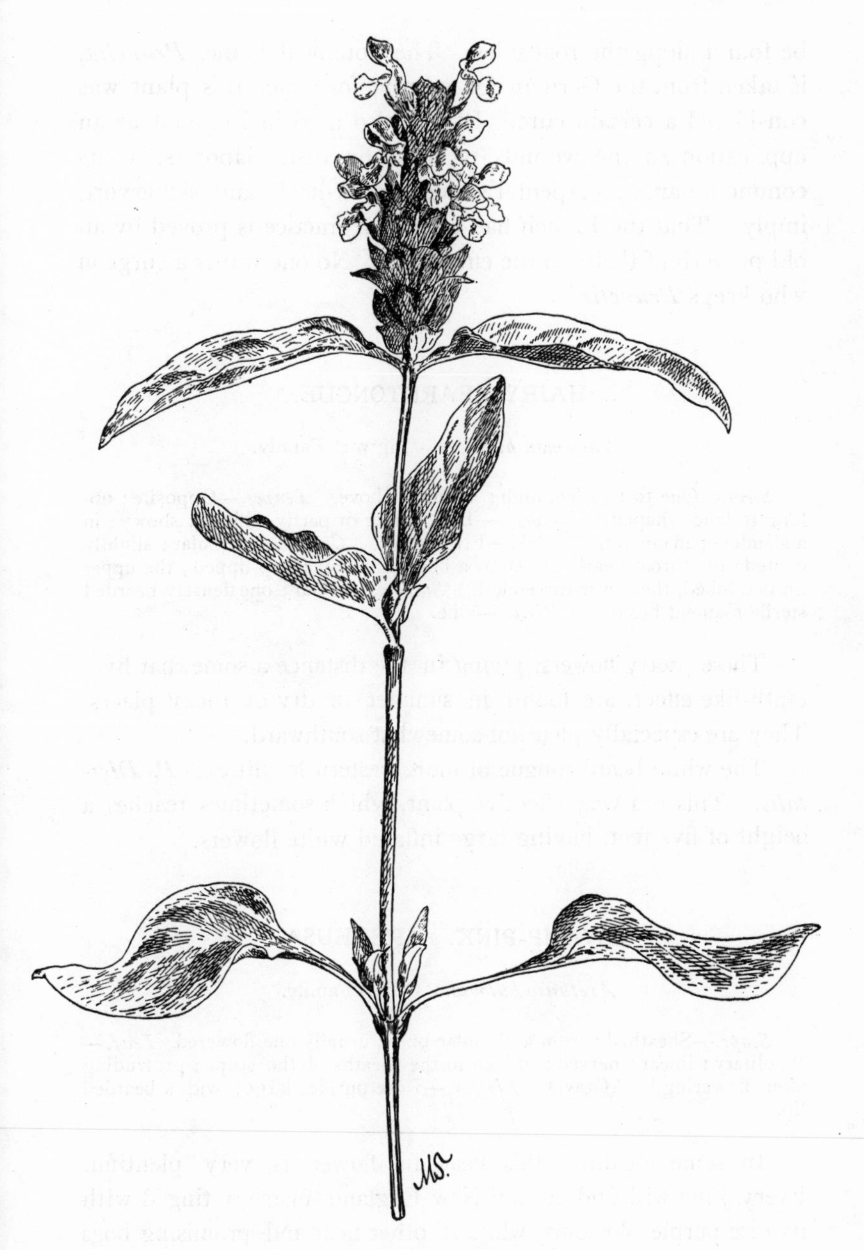

HEAL-ALL.—*Prunella vulgaris.*

be found along the roadsides. The botanical name, *Prunella*, is taken from the German for quinsy, for which this plant was considered a certain cure. It was also used in England as an application to the wounds received by rustic laborers, as its common names, carpenter's herb, hook-heal, and sicklewort, imply. That the French had a similar practice is proved by an old proverb of theirs to the effect that "No one wants a surgeon who keeps *Prunelle*."

HAIRY BEARDTONGUE.

Penstemon hirsutus. Figwort Family.

Stem.—One to two feet high; clammy above. *Leaves.*—Opposite; oblong to lance-shaped. *Flowers.*—Dull purple or partly whitish; showy; in a slender open cluster. *Calyx.*—Five-parted. *Corolla.*—Tubular; slightly dilated; the throat nearly closed by a bearded palate; two-lipped; the upper lip two-lobed, the lower three-cleft. *Stamens.*—Four; one densely bearded sterile filament besides. *Pistil.*—One.

These pretty flowers, giving in the distance a somewhat hyacinth-like effect, are found in summer in dry or rocky places. They are especially plentiful somewhat southward.

The white beard-tongue of more western localities is *P. Digitalis.* This is a very effective plant, which sometimes reaches a height of five feet, having large inflated white flowers.

SWAMP-PINK. ARETHUSA.

Arethusa bulbosa. Orchis Family.

Scape.—Sheathed; from a globular bulb; usually one-flowered. *Leaf.*—"Solitary; linear; nerved; hidden in the sheaths of the scape; protruding after flowering." (Gray.) *Flower.*—Rose-purple; large; with a bearded lip.

In some localities this beautiful flower is very plentiful. Every June will find certain New England marshes tinged with its rose-purple blossoms, while in other near and promising bogs it may be sought vainly for years. At least it may be hoped for

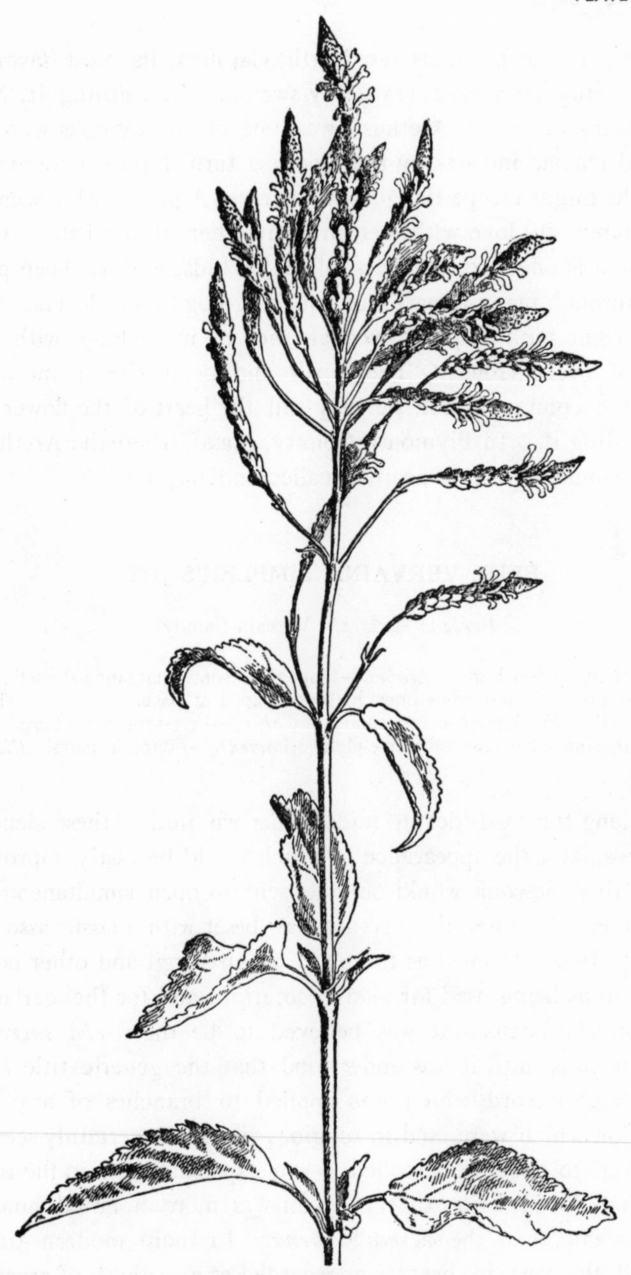

BLUE VERVAIN.—*Verbena hastata.*

in wet places as far south as North Carolina, its most favorite haunt being perhaps a cranberry-swamp. Concerning it, Mr. Burroughs writes: "Arethusa was one of the nymphs who attended Diana, and was by that goddess turned into a fountain, that she might escape the god of the river Alpheus, who became desperately in love with her on seeing her at her bath. Our Arethusa is one of the prettiest of the orchids, and has been pursued through many a marsh and quaking-bog by her lovers. She is a bright pink-purple flower, an inch or more long, with the odor of sweet violets. The sepals and petals rise up and arch over the column, which we may call the heart of the flower, as if shielding it. In Plymouth County, Mass., where the Arethusa seems common, I have heard it called Indian pink."

BLUE VERVAIN. SIMPLER'S-JOY.

Verbena hastata. Vervain Family.

Four to six feet high. *Leaves.*—Opposite; somewhat lance-shaped; the lower often lobed and sometimes halberd-shaped at base. *Flowers.*—Purple; small; in slender erect spikes. *Calyx.*—Five-toothed. *Corolla.*—Tubular, somewhat unequally five-cleft. *Stamens.*—Four; in pairs. *Pistil.*—One.

Along the roadsides in midsummer we notice these slender purple spikes, the appearance of which would be vastly improved if the tiny blossoms would only consent to open simultaneously.

In earlier times the vervain was beset with classic associations. It was claimed as the plant which Virgil and other poets mention as being used for altar-decorations and for the garlands of sacrificial beasts. It was believed to be the *herba sacra* of the ancients, until it was understood that the generic title *Verbena* was a word which was applied to branches of any description which were used in religious rites. It certainly seems, however, to have been applied to some special plant in the time of Pliny, for he writes that no plant was more honored among the Romans than the sacred *Verbena*. In more modern times as well the vervain has been regarded as an "herb of grace,"

MONKEY-FLOWER.—*Mimulus ringens.*

and has been gathered with various ceremonies and with the invocation of a blessing, which began as follows:

> ' Hallowed be thou, Vervain,
> As thou growest on the ground,
> For in the Mount of Calvary
> There thou wast first found."

It was then supposed to be endued with especial virtue, and was worn on the person to avert disaster.

The time-honored title of simpler's-joy arose from the remuneration which this popular plant brought to the "simplers"—as the gatherers of medicinal herbs were entitled.

MONKEY-FLOWER.

Mimulus ringens. Figwort Family.

Stem.—Square; one to two feet high. *Leaves.*—Opposite; oblong or lance-shaped. *Flowers.*—Pale violet-purple, rarely white; growing singly from the axils of the leaves. *Calyx.*—Five-angled; five-toothed; the upper tooth largest. *Corolla.*—Tubular; two-lipped; the upper lip erect or spreading, two-lobed, the lower spreading and three-lobed; the throat closed. *Stamens.*—Four. *Pistil.*—One, with a two-lobed stigma.

From July onward the monkey-flowers tinge the wet fields and border the streams and ponds; not growing in the water like the pickerelweed, but seeking a hummock in the swamp, or a safe foothold on the brook's edge, where they can absorb the moisture requisite to their vigorous growth.

The name is a diminutive of *mimus*—a buffoon, and refers to the somewhat grinning blossom. The plant is a common one throughout the eastern part of the country.

WATER-SHIELD.

Brasenia Schreberi. Water-lily Family.

Leaves.—Floating; shield-shaped; long-stemmed. *Flowers.*—Dull purple; small; growing from the axils of the leaves. *Calyx.*—Of three or four sepals. *Corolla.*—Of three or four linear petals. *Stamens.*—Twelve to eighteen. *Pistils.*—Four to eighteen, forming little club-shaped pods.

This plant is found growing in many of our ponds and slow streams. Its inconspicuous flowers appear in summer. Perhaps

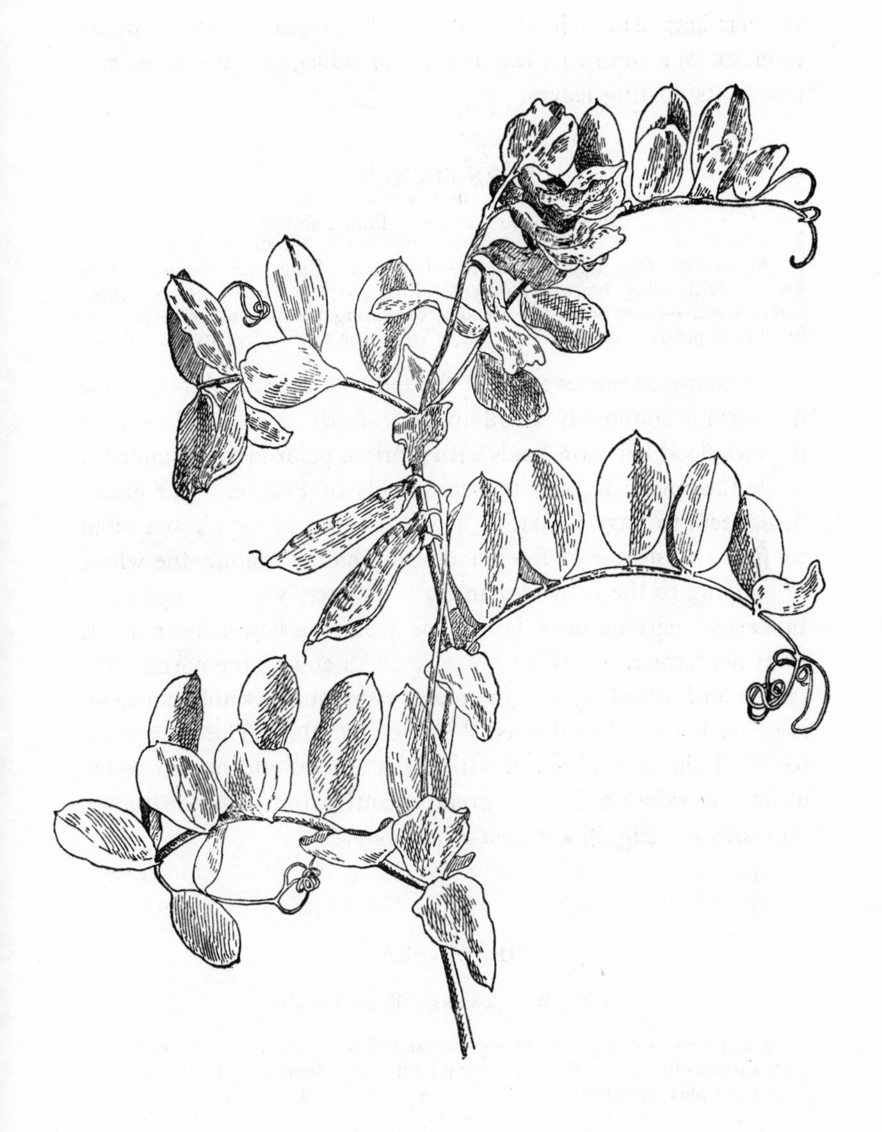

BEACH-PEA.—*Lathyrus japonicus.*

its most noticeable characteristic is the gelatinous matter which coats its long stems, its leaf and flower stalks, and the lower surface of its floating leaves.

CORN-COCKLE.

Agrostemma Githago. Pink Family.

About two feet high. *Leaves.*—Opposite; long and narrow; pale green; with silky hairs. *Flowers.*—Rose-purple; large; long-stalked. *Calyx-lobes.*—Five; long and slender, exceeding the petals. *Corolla.*—Of five broad petals. *Stamens.*—Ten. *Pistil.*—One, with five styles.

In many countries some of the most beautiful and noticeable flowers are commonly found in grain-fields. England's scarlet poppies flood her farm-lands with glorious color in early summer; while the bluets lighten the corn-fields of France. Our grain-fields seem to have no native flower peculiar to them; but often we find a trespasser of foreign descent hiding among the wheat or straying to the roadsides in early summer, whose deep-tinted blossoms secure an instant welcome from the flower-lover if not from the farmer. "What hurte it doeth among the corne! the spoyle unto bread, as well in colour, taste, and unwholesomeness, is better known than desired," wrote Gerarde. The large dark seeds fill the ground wheat with black specks, and might be injurious if existing in any great quantity. Its generic name, *Agrostemma*, signifies *crown of the fields.*

BEACH-PEA.

Lathyrus japonicus. Pulse Family.

About one foot high, or more. *Stem.*—Stout. *Leaves.*—Divided into from three to five pairs of thick oblong leaflets. *Flowers.*—Papilionaceous; large; purple; clustered.

The deep-hued flowers of this stout plant are commonly found along the sand-hills of the seashore, and also on the shores of the Great Lakes, blooming in early summer. Both flowers and leaves are at once recognized as belonging to the Pulse family.

PLATE CLV

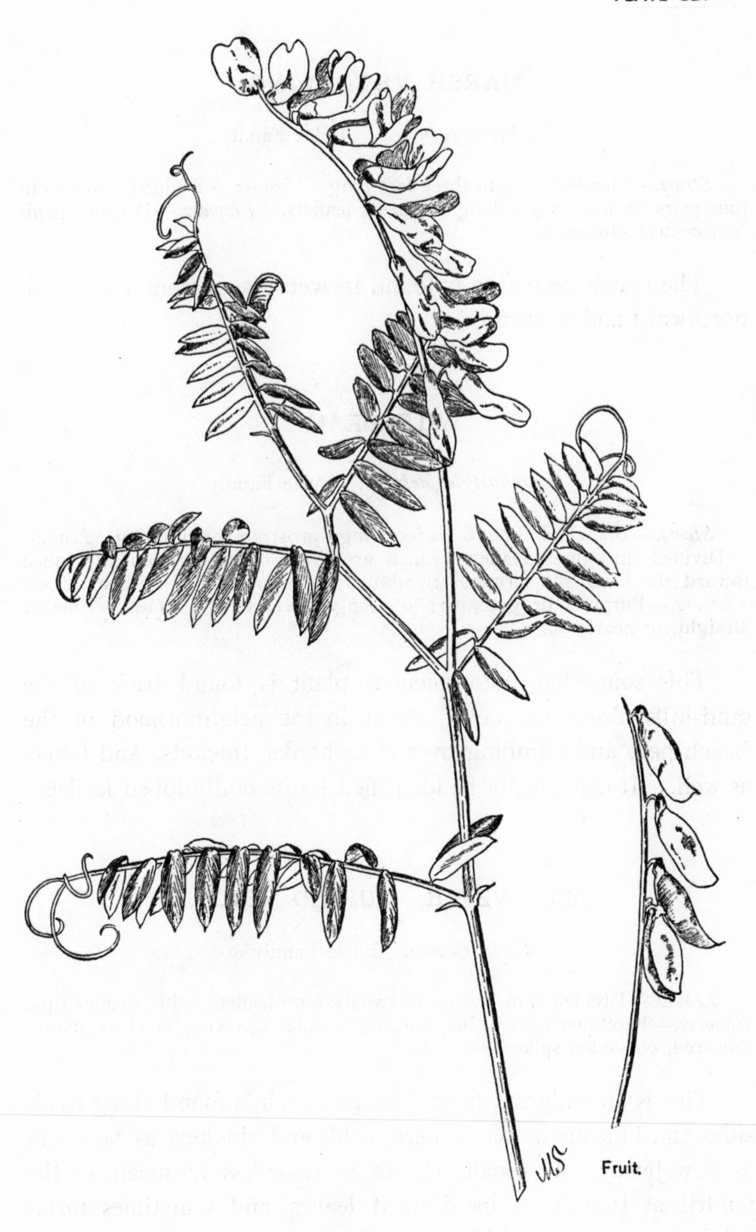

BLUE VETCH.—*Vicia Cracca.*

MARSH VETCHLING.

Lathyrus palustris. Pulse Family.

Stems.—Slender; one to three feet long. *Leaves.*—Divided into two to four pairs of narrowly oblong to linear leaflets. *Flowers.*—Purple; papilionaceous; clustered.

The marsh vetchling is found in wet places from New York northward and westward.

WILD BEAN.

Strophostyles helvola. Pulse Family.

Stems.—Branched; one to six feet long; prostrate, or climbing. *Leaves.*—Divided into three leaflets, which are more or less prominently lobed toward the base, the terminal two-lobed; or some or all without lobes. *Flowers.*—Purplish or greenish; on long flower-stalks. *Pods.*—Linear; straight, or nearly so.

This somewhat inconspicuous plant is found back of the sand-hills along the coast, often in the neighborhood of the beach-pea, and climbing over river-banks, thickets, and fences as well. It can usually be identified by its oddly lobed leaflets.

BLUE VETCH. TUFTED VETCH.

Vicia Cracca. Pulse Family.

Leaves.—Divided into twenty to twenty-four leaflets, with slender tips. *Flowers.*—Papilionaceous; blue, turning purple; growing in close, many-flowered, one-sided spikes.

This is an emigrant from Europe which is found along roadsides and in some of our eastern fields and thickets as far south as New Jersey. It usually climbs more or less by means of the tendril at the tip of its divided leaves, and sometimes forms bright patches of vivid blue over the meadows.

Another member of this genus is *V. sativa*, the common

vetch or tare,* with purplish or pinkish flowers, growing singly or in pairs from the axils of the leaves, which leaves are divided into fewer leaflets than those of the blue vetch. This species also takes possession of cultivated fields, as well as of waste places along the roadside.

WILD MINT.

Mentha arvensis. Mint Family.

Leaves.—Opposite; aromatic; oval to lance-shaped; toothed; tapering to both ends. *Flowers.*—Small; purplish or whitish; in globular clusters in the axils of the leaves. *Calyx.*—Five-toothed *Corolla.*—Four-cleft; the upper lobe broadest and sometimes notched. *Stamens.*—Four. *Pistil.*—One, with a two-lobed style. *Ovary.*—Deeply four-lobed.

In wet places, throughout the Northern States, we find our native wild mint.

SPEARMINT.

Mentha spicata. Mint Family.

Leaves.—Opposite; aromatic; unequally toothed; narrowly oblong; sessile, or nearly so. *Flowers.*—Small; purple or whitish; in narrow, leafless, densely crowded *spikes;* otherwise as in above.

In wet places, in all cultivated districts, we find the spearmint, this plant being an escape from gardens.

PEPPERMINT.

Mentha piperita. Mint Family.

Leaves.—Opposite; aromatic; with leaf-stems; sharply toothed; pungent-tasting. *Flowers.*—Small; purple or whitish; in loose, narrow, interrupted leafless spikes; otherwise as in above.

The peppermint is another European emigrant, and an escape from gardens, which has made itself thoroughly at home along our brooks.

* Also known as Spring-Vetch.

BLUEWEED. VIPER'S BUGLOSS.

Echium vulgare. Borage Family.

Stem.—Rough; bristly; erect; about two feet high. *Leaves.*—Alternate; lance-shaped; set close to the stem. *Flowers.*—Bright blue; spiked on one side of the branches, which are at first rolled up from the end, straightening as the blossoms expand. *Calyx.*—Five-parted. *Corolla.*—Of five somewhat unequal, spreading lobes. *Stamens.*—Five; protruding; red. *Pistil.*—One.

When the blueweed first came to us from across the sea it secured a foothold in Virginia. Since then it has gradually worked its way northward, lining the Hudson's shores, overrunning many of the dry fields in its vicinity, and making itself at home in parts of New England. We should be obliged to rank it among the "pestiferous" weeds were it not that, as a rule, it only seeks to monopolize land which is not good for very much else. The pinkish buds and bright blue blossoms, with their red protruding stamens, make a valuable addition, from the æsthetic point of view, to the bunch of midsummer field-flowers in which hitherto the various shades of red and yellow have predominated.

VENUS'S LOOKING-GLASS.

Specularia perfoliata. Campanula Family.

Stem.—Somewhat hairy; three to twenty inches high. *Leaves.*—Toothed; rounded; clasping by the heart-shaped base. *Flowers.*—Blue. *Calyx.*—Three, four, or five-lobed. *Corolla.*—Wheel-shaped; five-lobed. *Stamens.*—Five. *Pistil.*—One, with three stigmas.

We borrow from Mr. Burrough's "Bunch of Herbs" a description of this little plant, which blossoms from May till August. "A pretty and curious little weed, sometimes found growing in the edge of the garden, is the clasping specularia, a relative of the harebell and of the European Venus's looking-glass. Its leaves are shell-shaped, and clasp the stalk so as to form little shallow cups. In the bottom of each cup three buds

BLUEWEED.—*Echium vulgare.*

appear that never expand into flowers, but when the top of the stalk is reached, one and sometimes two buds open a large, delicate purple-blue corolla. All the first-born of this plant are still-born as it were; only the latest, which spring from its summit, attain to perfect bloom."

PICKERELWEED.

Pontederia cordata. Pickerelweed Family.

Stem.—Stout; usually one-leaved. *Leaves.*—Arrow or heart-shaped. *Flowers.*—Blue; fading quickly; with an unpleasant odor; growing in a dense spike. *Perianth.*—Two-lipped; the upper lip three-lobed and marked with a double greenish-yellow spot, the lower of three spreading divisions. *Stamens.*—Six; three long and protruding, the three others, which are often imperfect, very short and inserted lower down. *Pistil.*—One.

The pickerelweed grows in such shallow water as the pickerel seek, or else in moist, wet places along the shores of streams and rivers. We can look for the blue, closely spiked flowers from late July until some time in September. They are often found near the delicate arrowhead.

HAREBELL.

Campanula rotundifolia. Campanula Family.

Stem.—Slender; branching; from five to twelve inches high. *Root-leaves.*—Heart-shaped or ovate; early withering. *Stem-leaves.*—Numerous; long and narrow. *Flowers.*—Bright blue; nodding from hair-like stalks. *Calyx.*—Five-cleft; the lobes awl-shaped. *Corolla.*—Bell-shaped; five-lobed. *Stamens.*—Five. *Pistil.*—One, with three stigmas.

This slender, pretty plant, hung with its tremulous flowers, springs from the rocky cliffs which buttress the river as well as from those which crown the mountain. I have seen the west shore of the Hudson bright with its delicate bloom in June, and the summits of the Catskills tinged with its azure in September. The drooping posture of these flowers protects their pollen from rain or dew. They have come to us from Europe, and are identical, I believe, with the celebrated Scotch bluebells.

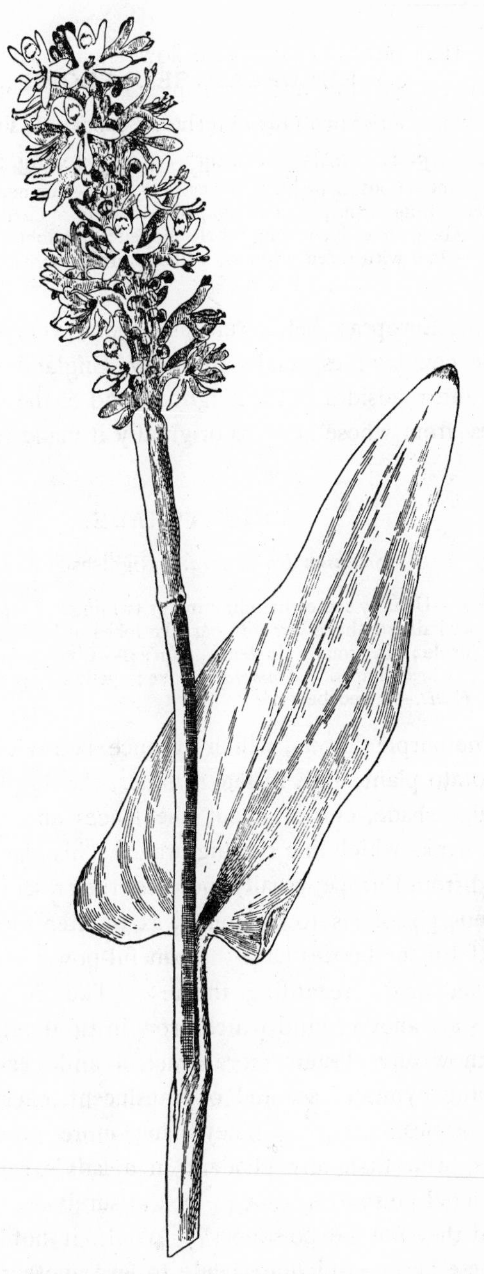

PICKERELWEED.—*Pontederia cordata.*

EUROPEAN BELLFLOWER.

Campanula rapunculoides. Campanula Family.

Stem.—Erect; slender; usually rather tall. *Stem-leaves.*—Narrowly oval; pointed; alternate; the lower ones long-stemmed and heart-shaped. *Flowers.*—Blue or purple; bell-shaped; nodding. *Calyx.*—Five-cleft. *Corolla.*—About one inch long; bell-shaped; five-lobed. *Stamens.*—Five. *Pistil.*—One, with three stigmas, which unfold rather late in the flower's life.

This European bellflower has become very common in parts of the country; especially in New England it brightens the fields and roadsides in the neighborhood of the villages and farmhouses from whose gardens originally it made its escape.

NIGHTSHADE.

Solanum Dulcamara. Nightshade Family.

Stem.—Usually somewhat climbing or twining. *Leaves.*—Heart-shaped; the upper halberd-shaped or with ear-like lobes or leaflets at the base. *Flowers.*—Purple; in small clusters. *Calyx.*—Five-parted. *Corolla.*—Five-parted; wheel-shaped. *Stamens.*—Five; yellow; protruding. *Pistil.*—One. *Fruit.*—A red berry.

The purple flowers, which at once betray their kinship with the potato plant, and, in late summer, the bright red berries of the nightshade, cluster about the fences and clamber over the moist banks which line the highway. This plant, which was imported from Europe, usually indicates the presence of civilization. It is not poisonous to the touch, as is often supposed, and it is doubtful if the berries have the baneful power attributed to them. Thoreau writes regarding them: "The Solanum Dulcamara berries are another kind which grow in drooping clusters. I do not know any clusters more graceful and beautiful than these drooping cymes of scented or translucent, cherry-colored elliptical berries. . . . They hang more gracefully over the river's brim than any pendant in a lady's ear. Yet they are considered poisonous; not to look at surely. . . . But why should they not be poisonous? Would it not be bad taste to eat these berries which are ready to feed another sense?"

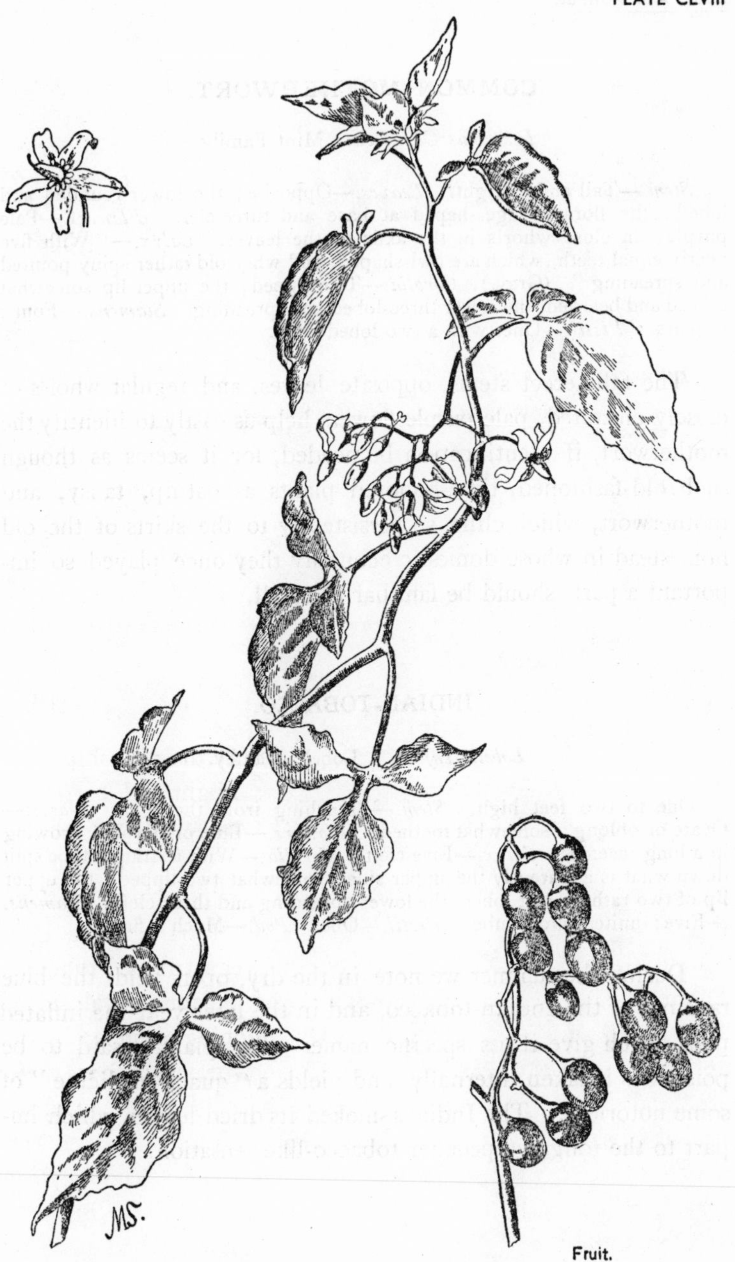

NIGHTSHADE.— *Solanum Dulcamara.*

COMMON MOTHERWORT.

Leonurus Cardiaca. Mint Family.

Stem.—Tall and upright. *Leaves.*—Opposite; the lower rounded and lobed; the floral wedge-shaped at base and three-cleft. *Flowers.*—Pale purple; in close whorls in the axils of the leaves. *Calyx.*—"With five nearly equal teeth, which are awl-shaped, and when old rather spiny-pointed and spreading." (Gray.) *Corolla.*—Two-lipped; the upper lip somewhat arched and bearded, the lower three-lobed and spreading. *Stamens.*—Four; in pairs. *Pistil.*—One, with a two-lobed style.

The tall, erect stems, opposite leaves, and regular whorls of closely clustered, pale purple flowers help us easily to identify the motherwort, if identification be needed, for it seems as though such old-fashioned, time-honored plants as catnip, tansy, and motherwort, which cling so persistently to the skirts of the old homestead in whose domestic economy they once played so important a part, should be familiar to us all.

INDIAN-TOBACCO.

Lobelia inflata. Lobelia Family.

One to two feet high. *Stem.*—Branching from the root. *Leaves.*—Ovate or oblong; somewhat toothed. *Flowers.*—Blue or purple; growing in a long raceme. *Calyx.*—Five-cleft. *Corolla.*—With a straight tube split down what is apparently the upper side; somewhat two-lipped; the upper lip of two rather erect lobes, the lower spreading and three-cleft. *Stamens.*—Five; united into a tube. *Pistil.*—One. *Pod.*—Much inflated.

During the summer we note in the dry, open fields the blue racemes of the Indian-tobacco, and in the later year the inflated pods which give it its specific name. The plant is said to be poisonous if taken internally, and yields a "quack-medicine" of some notoriety. The Indians smoked its dried leaves, which impart to the tongue a peculiar tobacco-like sensation.

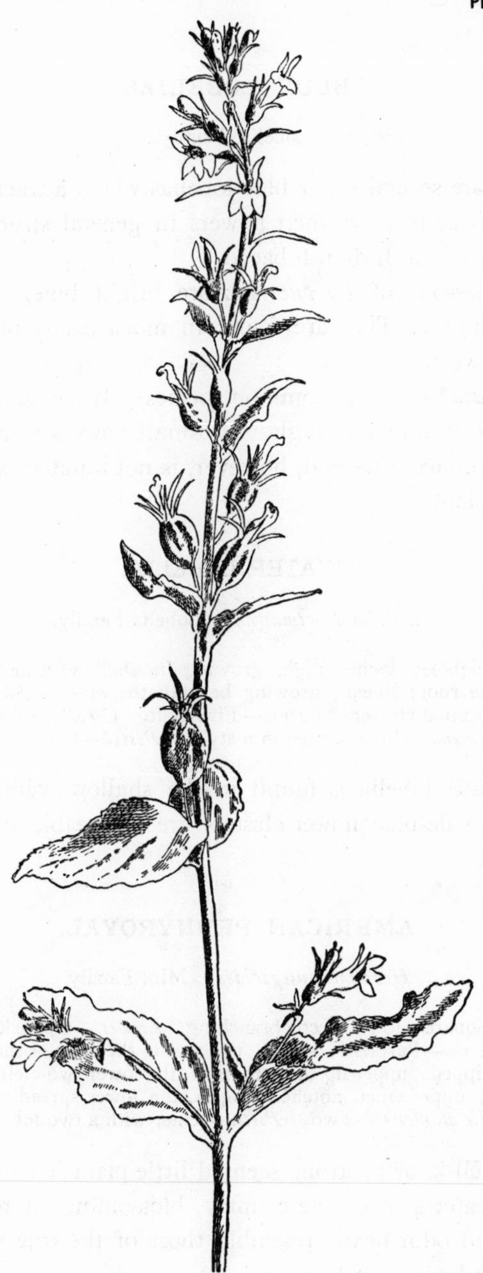

INDIAN-TOBACCO.—*Lobelia inflata.*

BLUE LOBELIAS.

Lobelia Family.

There are several other blue lobelias which attract our attention from time to time, their flowers in general structure resembling those of the Indian tobacco.

The blossoms of *L. puberula* are bright blue, and half an inch in length. They are found in moist sandy places to the south and west.

*L. spicata** is a very common species. Its slender leafy stem is from one to four feet high. Its small flowers resemble those of Indian-tobacco; its pod, however, is not inflated, as is that of the latter plant.

WATER-LOBELIA.

Lobelia Dortmanna. Lobelia Family.

Six to eighteen inches high, growing in shallow water. *Leaves.*—Tufted at the root; linear; growing beneath the water. *Flowers.*—Blue, in a loose terminal cluster. *Calyx.*—Five-cleft. *Corolla.*—Somewhat two-lipped. *Stamens.*—Five, united in a style. *Pistil.*—One.

The water-lobelia is found in the shallow water of ponds. Its pretty, pale-blue flower clusters are noticeable from July to September.

AMERICAN PENNYROYAL.

Hedeoma pulegioides. Mint Family.

Stem.—Square; low; erect; branching. *Leaves.*—Opposite; aromatic; small. *Flowers.*—Purplish; small; whorled in the axils of the leaves. *Calyx.*—Two-lipped; upper lip three-toothed, the lower two-cleft. *Corolla.*—Two-lipped; upper erect, notched at apex, the lower spreading and three-cleft. *Fertile stamens.*—Two. *Pistil.*—One, with a two-lobed style.

This well-known, strong-scented little plant is found throughout the greater part of the country, blossoming in midsummer. Its taste and odor nearly resemble those of the true pennyroyal, *Mentha Pulegium*, of Europe.

* Pale-spike-Lobelia.

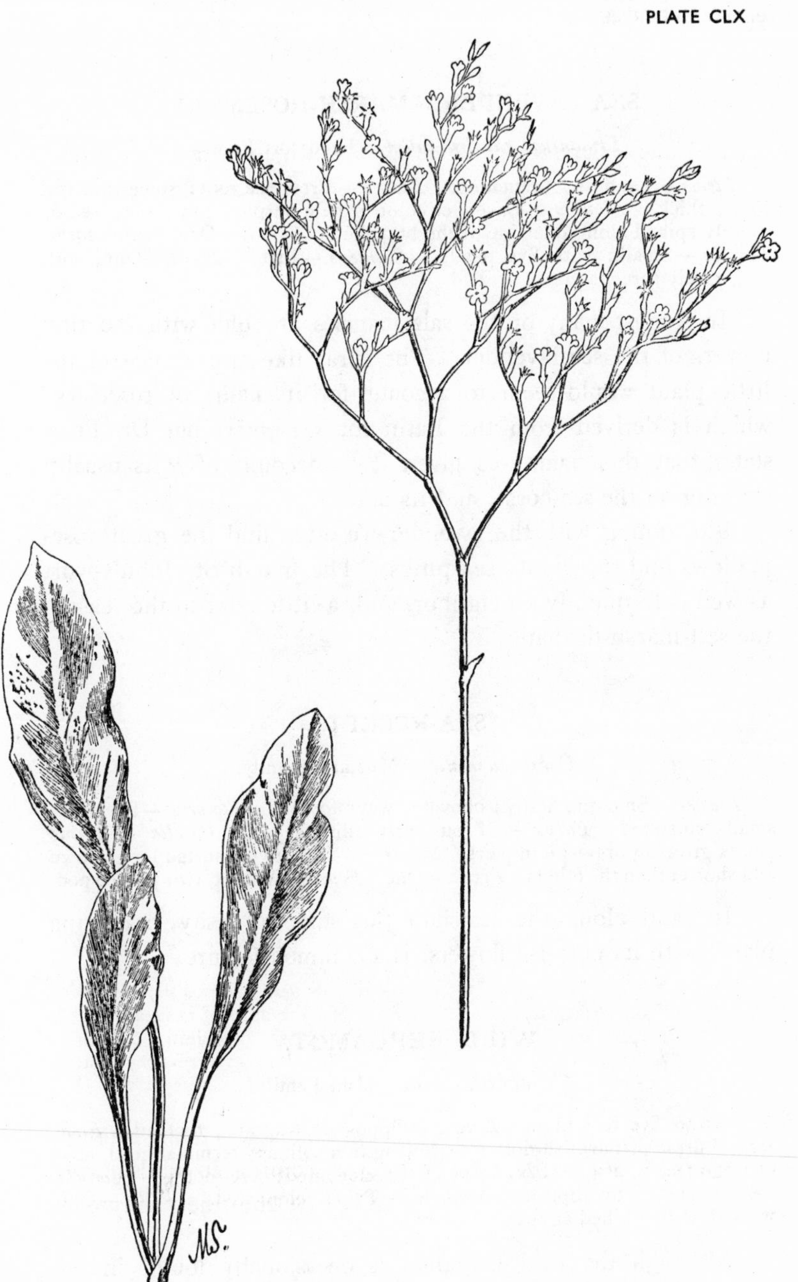

SEA-LAVENDER.—*Limonium carolinianum.*

SEA-LAVENDER. MARSH-ROSEMARY.

Limonium carolinianum. Leadwort Family.

Stems.—Leafless; branching. *Leaves.*—From the root; somewhat oblong; thick. *Flowers.*—Lavender color or pale purple; tiny; scattered or loosely spiked along one side of the branches. *Calyx.*—Dry; funnel-form. *Corolla.*—Small; with five petals. *Stamens.*—Five. *Pistil.*—One, with five, rarely three, styles.

In August many of the salt marshes are blue with the tiny flowers of the sea-lavender. The spray-like appearance of the little plant would seem to account for its name of rosemary, which is derived from the Latin for *sea-spray*, but Dr. Prior states that this name was given it on account of "its usually growing on the sea-coast, and its odor."

Blossoming with the lavender we often find the great rose-mallows and the dainty sea-pinks. The marsh St. John's-wort as well is frequently a neighbor, and, a little later in the season, the salt-marsh-fleabane.

SEA-ROCKET.

Cakile edentula. Mustard Family.

Leaves.—Smooth; fleshy; obovate; wavy-toothed. *Flowers.*—Purplish; small; clustered. *Calyx.*—Of four early falling sepals. *Corolla.*—Of four petals growing opposite in pairs. *Stamens.*—Six; two inserted lower down and shorter than the others. *Pistil.*—One. *Fruit.*—A short, two-jointed pod.

In sand along the sea-shore this smooth, fleshy, branching plant, with its purplish flowers, is a common feature.

WILD BERGAMOT.

Monarda fistulosa. Mint Family.

Two to five feet high. *Leaves.*—Opposite; fragrant; toothed. *Flowers.*—Purple or purplish-dotted; growing in a solitary, terminal head, as in Oswego tea, p. 264. *Calyx.*—Tubular; elongated; five-toothed. *Corolla.*—Elongated; two-lipped. *Stamens.*—Two; elongated. *Pistil.*—One, with style two-lobed at apex.

Although the wild bergamot is occasionally found in our eastern woods, it is far more abundant westward, where it is found in rocky places in summer. This is a near relative of the Oswego-tea, which it closely resembles in its manner of growth.

DAYFLOWER.

Commelina virginica. Spiderwort Family.

Stem.—Slender; branching. *Leaves.*—Lance-shaped to linear; the floral ones heart-shaped and clasping, folding so as to enclose the flowers. *Flowers.*—Blue. *Calyx.*—Of three unequal somewhat colored sepals; the two lateral ones partly united. *Corolla.*—Of three petals; two large, rounded, pale blue; one small, whitish, and inconspicuous. *Stamens.*—Six; unequal in size; three small and sterile, with yellow cross-shaped anthers; three fertile, one of which is bent inward. *Pistil.*—One.

The odd dayflower is so named because its delicate blossoms expand only for a single morning. At the first glance there seem to be but two petals which are large, rounded, and of a delicate shade of blue. A closer examination, however, discovers still another, so inconspicuous in form and color as to escape the notice of the casual observer. This inequality recalls the quaint tradition as to the origin of the plant's generic name. There were three brothers Commelin, natives of Holland. Two of them were botanists of repute, while the tastes of the third had a less marked botanical tendency. The genus was dedicated to the trio: the two large bright petals commemorating the brother botanists, while the small and unpretentious one perpetuates the memory of him who was so unwise as to take little or no interest in so noble a science. These flowers appear throughout the summer in cool woods and on moist banks.

HIGH MALLOW.

Malva sylvestris. Mallow Family.

Stem.—Two to three feet high; erect; branched. *Leaves.*—Five to seven-lobed. *Flowers.*—Purple or pink; rather large. *Calyx.*—Of five sepals, with three bracts below. *Corolla.*—Of five somewhat heart-shaped petals. *Stamens.*—United in a column. *Pistils.*—Several.

The high mallow is an emigrant from Europe, which we encounter frequently along our roadsides in summer.

PLATE CLXI

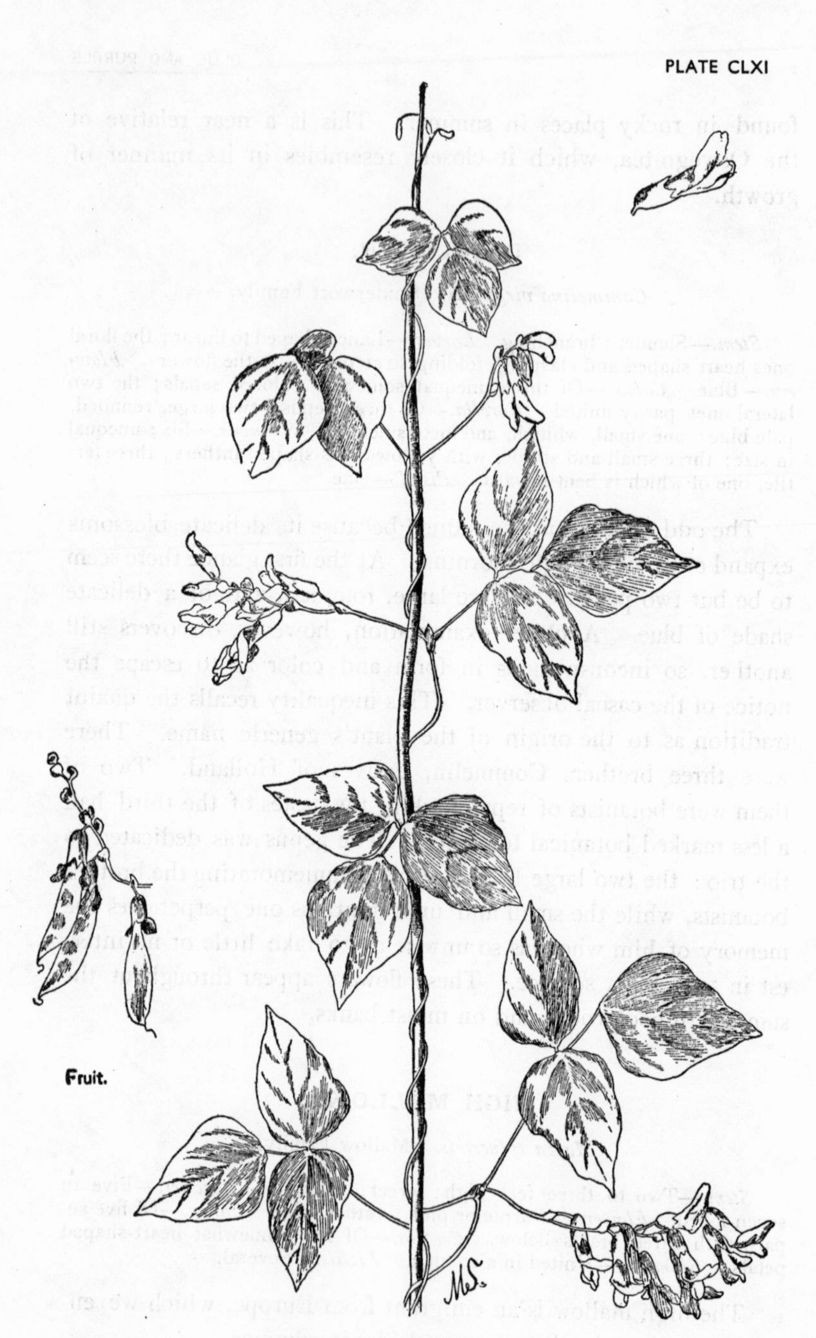

HOG-PEANUT.—*Amphicarpa bracteata.*

HOG-PEANUT.

Amphicarpa bracteata. Pulse Family.

Stem.—Climbing and twining over plants and shrubs. *Leaves.*—Divided into three somewhat four-sided leaflets. *Flowers.*—Papilionaceous; pale lilac or purplish; in nodding racemes. *Pod.*—One inch long.

Along the shadowy lanes which wind through the woods the climbing members of the Pulse family are very abundant. During the late summer and autumn the lonely wayside is skirted by

> "Vines, with clust'ring bunches growing;
> Plants, with goodly burden bowing."

And in and out among this luxuriant growth twist the slender stems of the ill-named hog-peanut, its delicate lilac blossoms nodding from the coarse stalks of the goldenrods and ironweeds, or blending with the purple asters.

This plant bears flowers of two kinds: the upper ones are perfect, but apparently useless, as they seldom ripen fruit; while the lower or subterranean ones are without petals or attractiveness of appearance, but yield eventually at least one large ripe seed.

CHICORY. SUCCORY.

Cichorium Intybus. Composite Family.

Stems.—Branching. *Leaves.*—The lower oblong or lance-shaped, partly clasping, sometimes sharply incised; the floral ones minute. *Flower-heads.*—Blue; set close to the stem; composed entirely of strap-shaped flowers; opening at different times.

> "Oh, not in Ladies' gardens,
> My peasant posy!
> Smile thy dear blue eyes,
> Nor only—nearer to the skies—
> In upland pastures, dim and sweet,—
> But by the dusty road
> Where tired feet
> Toil to and fro;

CHICORY.—*Cichorium Intybus.*

> Where flaunting Sin
> May see thy heavenly hue,
> Or weary Sorrow look from thee
> Toward a more tender blue." *

This roadside weed blossoms in late summer. It is extensively cultivated in France, where the leaves are blanched and used in a salad which is called "Barbe des Capucins." The roots are roasted and mixed with coffee, both there and in England.

Horace mentions its leaves as part of his frugal fare, and Pliny remarks upon the importance of the plant to the Egyptians, who formerly used it in great quantities, and of whose diet it is still a staple article.

PURPLE AVENS. WATER-AVENS.

Geum rivale. Rose Family.

Stems.—About two feet high; several-flowered. *Root-leaves.*—Deeply parted. *Stem-leaves.*—Few; three-parted (into three leaflets) or three-lobed. *Flowers.*—Large; purplish. *Calyx.*—Brown-purple; deeply five-cleft. *Corolla.*—Of five petals, these contracted into claws. *Stamens.*—Many. *Pistils.*—Numerous.

During the summer, in wet meadows, we notice the nodding flowers of the water-avens.

BLUE LINARIA. BLUE TOADFLAX. OLD-FIELD-TOADFLAX.

Linaria canadensis. Figwort Family.

Stems.—Slender; six to thirty inches high. *Leaves.*—Linear. *Flowers.*—Pale blue or purple; small; in a long terminal raceme. *Calyx.*—Five-parted. *Corolla.*—Two-lipped, with a slender spur; closed in the throat. *Stamens.*—Four. *Pistil.*—One.

The slender spikes of the blue linaria flank the sandy roadsides nearly all summer, and even in November we find a few

* Margaret Deland.

delicate blossoms still left upon the elongated stems. These flowers have a certain spirituality which is lacking in their handsome, self-assertive relation, butter-and-eggs.

GREAT LOBELIA.

Lobelia siphilitica. Lobelia Family.

Stem.—Leafy; somewhat hairy; one to three feet high. *Leaves.*—Alternate; ovate to lance-shaped; thin; irregularly toothed. *Flowers.*—Rather large; light blue; spiked. *Calyx.*—Five-cleft; with a short tube. *Corolla.*—Somewhat two-lipped; the upper lip of two rather erect lobes, the lower spreading and three-cleft. *Pistil.*—One, with a fringed stigma.

The great lobelia is a striking plant which grows in low ground, flowering from midsummer into the fall. In some places it is called "High-Belia," a pun which is supposed to reflect upon the less tall and conspicuous species, such as the Indian-tobacco, *L. inflata*, which are found flowering at the same season.

If one of its blossoms is examined, the pistil is seen to be enclosed by the united stamens in such a fashion as to secure self-fertilization, one would suppose. But it is hardly probable that a flower so noticeable as this, and wearing a color as popular as blue, should have adorned itself so lavishly to no purpose. Consequently we are led to inquire more closely into its domestic arrangements. Our curiosity is rewarded by the discovery that the lobes of the stigma are so tightly pressed together that they can at first receive no pollen upon their sensitive surfaces. We also find that the anthers open only by a pore at their tips, and when irritated by the jar of a visiting bee, discharge their pollen upon its body through these outlets. This being accomplished the fringed stigma pushes forward, brushing aside whatever pollen may have fallen within the tube. Finally, when it projects beyond the anthers, it opens, and is ready to receive its pollen from the next insect-visitor.

The genus is named after an early Flemish herbalist, de l'Obel.

GREAT LOBELIA.—*Lobelia siphilitica.*

BLUE AND PURPLE ASTERS.

Aster. Composite Family.

Flower-heads.—Composed of blue or purple ray-flowers, with a centre of yellow disk-flowers.

As about one hundred and twenty different species of aster are native to the United States, and as fifty-four of these are found in Northeastern America, all but a dozen being purple or blue (*i.e.*, with purple or blue ray-flowers), and as even botanists find that it requires patient application to distinguish these many species, only a brief description of the more conspicuous and common ones is here attempted.

The broad-leaved aster, *A. macrophyllus*, is best known, perhaps, by the great colonies of large, rounded, somewhat heart-shaped, long-stemmed leaves with which it carpets the woods long before the flowers appear. Finally it sends up a stout, rigid stalk two to three feet high, bearing smaller oblong leaves and clusters of lavender or violet-colored flower-heads.

Along the dry roadsides in early August we may look for the bright blue-purple flowers of *A. patens*.* This is a low-growing species, with rough, narrowly oblong, clasping leaves, and widely spreading branches, whose slender branchlets are usually terminated by a solitary flower-head.

Probably no member of the group is more striking than the New England aster, *A. novae-angliae* (Plate CLXIV.), whose stout hairy stem (sometimes eight feet high), numerous lance-shaped leaves, and large violet-purple or sometimes pinkish flower-heads, are conspicuous in the swamps of late summer.

A. puniceus† is another tall swamp species, with long showy pale lavender ray-flowers.

One of the most commonly encountered asters is *A. cordifolius*,‡ which is far from being the only heart-leaved species, despite its title. Its many small, pale blue or almost white flower-heads mass themselves abundantly along the wood-borders and shaded roadsides.

* Late Purple Aster. † Purple-stemmed Aster. ‡ Heart-leaved Aster.

PLATE CLXIV

NEW ENGLAND ASTER.—*Aster novae-angliae.*

The New York aster, *A. novi-belgii*, is a slender-stemmed, branching plant, usually from one to three feet high, with lance-shaped leaves and violet flower-heads. It is found in swampy places near the coast from August to October. Gray calls it "the commonest late-flowered aster of the Atlantic border, and variable."

Perhaps the loveliest of all the tribe is the seaside purple aster, *A. spectabilis*, a low plant with narrowly oblong leaves and large bright heads, the violet-purple ray-flowers of which are nearly an inch long. This grows in sandy soil near the coast and may be found putting forth its royal, daisy-like blossoms into November.

Great Britain can claim but one native aster, *A. tripolium*, or sea-starwort, as it is called. Many American species are cultivated in English gardens under the general title of Michaelmas daisies. The starwort of Italy is *A. amellus*. The Swiss species is *A. alpinum*.

This beautiful genus, like that of the goldenrod, is one of the peculiar glories of our country. Every autumn these two kinds of flowers clothe our roadsides and meadows with so regal a mantle of purple and gold that we cannot but wonder if the flowers of any other region combine in such a radiant display.

IRONWEED.

Vernonia noveboracensis. Composite Family.

Stem.—Leafy; usually tall. *Leaves.*—Alternate; somewhat lance-oblong. *Flower-heads.*—An intense red-purple; loosely clustered; composed entirely of tubular flowers.

Along the roadsides and low meadows near the coast the ironweed adds its deep purple hues to the color-pageant of late August. By the uninitiated the plant is often mistaken for an aster, but a moment's inspection will discover that the minute flowers which compose each flower-head are all tubular in shape, and that the ray or strap-shaped blossoms which an aster must

Flower.

IRONWEED.—*Vernonia noveboracensis.*

have are wanting. These flower-heads are surrounded by an involucre composed of small scales which are tipped with a tiny point and are usually of a purplish color also.

SPIDERWORT.

Tradescantia virginiana. Spiderwort Family.

Stems.—Mucilaginous; leafy; mostly upright. *Leaves.*—Linear; keeled. *Flowers.*—Blue; clustered; with floral leaves as in the day-flower. *Calyx.*—Of three sepals. *Corolla.*—Of three petals. *Stamens.*—Six; with bearded filaments. *Pistil.*—One.

The flowers of the spiderwort, like those of the dayflower, to which they are nearly allied, are very perishable, lasting only a few hours. They are found throughout the summer, somewhat south and westward. The genus is named in honor of Tradescant, gardener to Charles I. of England.

BLAZING-STAR.

Liatris scariosa. Composite Family.

Stem.—Simple; stout; hoary; two to five feet high. *Leaves.*—Alternate, narrowly lance-shaped. *Flower-heads.*—Racemed along the upper part of the stem; composed entirely of tubular flowers of a beautiful shade of rose-purple.

These showy and beautiful flowers lend still another tint to the many-hued salt marshes and glowing inland meadows of the falling year. Gray [earlier editions] assigns them to dry localities from New England to Minnesota and southward, while my own experience of them is limited to the New England coast, where their stout leafy stems and bright-hued blossoms are noticeable among the goldenrods and asters of September. The hasty observer sometimes confuses the plant with the ironweed, but the two flowers are very different in color and in their manner of growth.

BLAZING-STAR.—*Liatris scariosa.*

CREEPING THYME.

Thymus Serpyllum. Mint Family.

Stems.—Prostrate. *Leaves.*—Small; ovate; strongly-veined; not toothed. *Flowers.*—Small; purplish; crowded at the ends of the branches. *Calyx.*—Two-lipped. *Corolla.*—Slightly two-lipped. *Stamens.*—Two. *Pistil.*—One, with a two-lobed style.

This classic little plant is an emigrant from Europe, which is not as yet extensively naturalized with us. The only

"bank whereon the wild thyme blows"

for me is somewhat too exposed a spot to be chosen as sleeping-place by any fairy-queen. Neither is it

"Over-canopied with luscious woodbine,
With sweet musk-roses and with eglantine."

Instead it borders the beautiful but open highway leading from Lenox into Stockbridge, filling the air with its pungent fragrance.

BLUE CURLS. BASTARD PENNYROYAL.

Trichostema dichotomum. Mint Family.

Stem.—Rather low; branching; clammy. *Leaves.*—Opposite; narrowly oblong or lance-shaped; glutinous; with a balsamic odor. *Flowers.*—Purple, occasionally pinkish; not usually clustered. *Calyx.*—Five-cleft; two-lipped. *Corolla.*—Five-lobed; the three lower lobes more or less united. *Stamens.*—Four; very long and curved; protruding. *Pistil.*—One, with a two-lobed style.

In the sandy fields of late summer this little plant attracts notice by its many purple flowers. Its corolla soon falls and exposes to view the four little nutlets of the ovary lying within the enlarged calyx like tiny eggs in their nest. Its aromatic odor is very perceptible, and the little glands with which it is covered may be seen with the aid of a magnifier. The generic name, *Trichostema*, signifies *hairy stamens*, and alludes to the curved hair-like filaments.

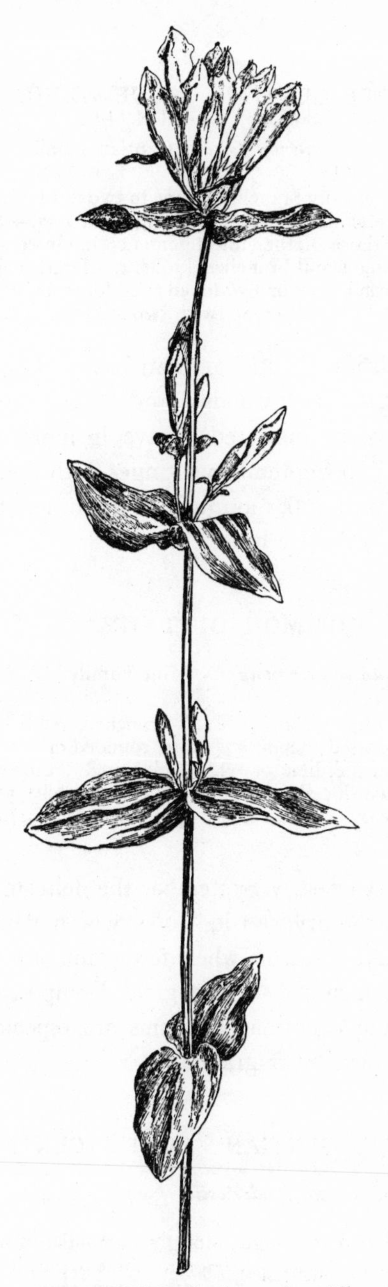

STIFF GENTIAN.—*Gentiana quinquefolia.*

STIFF GENTIAN. AGUE-WEED.

Gentiana quinquefolia. Gentian Family.

Stem.—Slender; usually branching; one to two feet high. *Leaves.*—Opposite; ovate; lance-shaped; partly clasping. *Flowers.*—Pale blue or purplish; smaller than those of the closed gentian; in clusters of five or more at the summit of stems and branches. *Calyx.*—Four or five-cleft; small. *Corolla.*—Funnel-form; four or five-lobed; its lobes bristle-pointed. *Stamens.*—Four or five. *Pistil.*—One, with two stigmas.

In some localities the stiff gentian is very abundant. Gray assigns the plant to "rich woods" and "damp fields;" I never remember to have encountered it save in more or less mountainous regions. In September it tinges with delicate color the slopes of the Shawangunk mountains and borders the woods and roadsides of the Berkshire hills.

COMMON DITTANY.

Cunila origanoides. Mint Family.

About one foot high. *Stem.*—Much branched, reddish. *Leaves.*—Opposite; aromatic; dotted; smooth; ovate, rounded or heart-shaped at base. *Flowers.*—Small, purple, lilac or white; clustered. *Calyx.*—Five-toothed. *Corolla.*—Small; two-lipped; the upper lip erect, usually notched, the lower three-cleft. *Stamens.*—Two; erect; protruding. *Pistil.*—One, with a two-lobed style.

In late August or early September the delicate flowers of the dittany brighten the dry, sterile banks which flank so many of our roadsides. At a season when few plants are flowering save the omnipresent members of the great Composite family these dainty though unpretentious blossoms are especially attractive. The plant has a pleasant fragrance.

CLOSED GENTIAN. BOTTLE-GENTIAN.

Gentiana Andrewsii. Gentian Family.

Stem.—One to two feet high; upright; smooth. *Leaves.*—Opposite; narrowly oval or lance-shaped. *Flowers.*—Blue to purple; clustered at the summit of the stem and often in the axils of the leaves. *Calyx.*—Four or

CLOSED GENTIAN.—*Gentiana Andrewsii.*

five cleft. *Corolla.*—Closed at the mouth; large; oblong. *Stamens.*—Four or five. *Pistil.*—One, with two stigmas.

Few flowers adapt themselves better to the season than the closed gentian. We look for it in September when the early waning days and frost-suggestive nights prove so discouraging to the greater part of the floral world. Then in somewhat moist, shaded places along the roadside we find this vigorous, autumnal-looking plant, with stout stems, leaves that bronze as the days advance, and deep-tinted flowers firmly closed as though to protect the delicate reproductive organs within from the sharp touches of the late year.

To me the closed gentian usually shows a deep blue or even purple countenance, although, like the fringed gentian and so many other flowers, its color is lighter in the shade than in the sunlight. But Thoreau claims for it a "transcendent blue," "a splendid blue, light in the shade, turning to purple with age." "Bluer than the bluest sky, they lurk in the moist and shady recesses of the banks," he writes. Mr. Burroughs also finds it "intensely blue."

FRINGED GENTIAN.

Gentiana crinita. Gentian Family.

Stem.—One to two feet high. *Leaves.*—Opposite, lance-shaped or narrowly oval. *Flowers.*—Blue; large. *Calyx.*—Four-cleft; the lobes unequal. *Corolla.*—Funnel-form, with four fringed, spreading lobes. *Stamens.*—Four. *Pistil.*—One, with two stigmas.

In late September, when we have almost ceased to hope for new flowers, we are in luck if we chance upon this

"—blossom bright with autumn dew,"

whose

"—sweet and quiet eye
Looks through its fringes to the sky,
Blue—blue—as if that sky let fall,
A flower from its cerulean wall;"

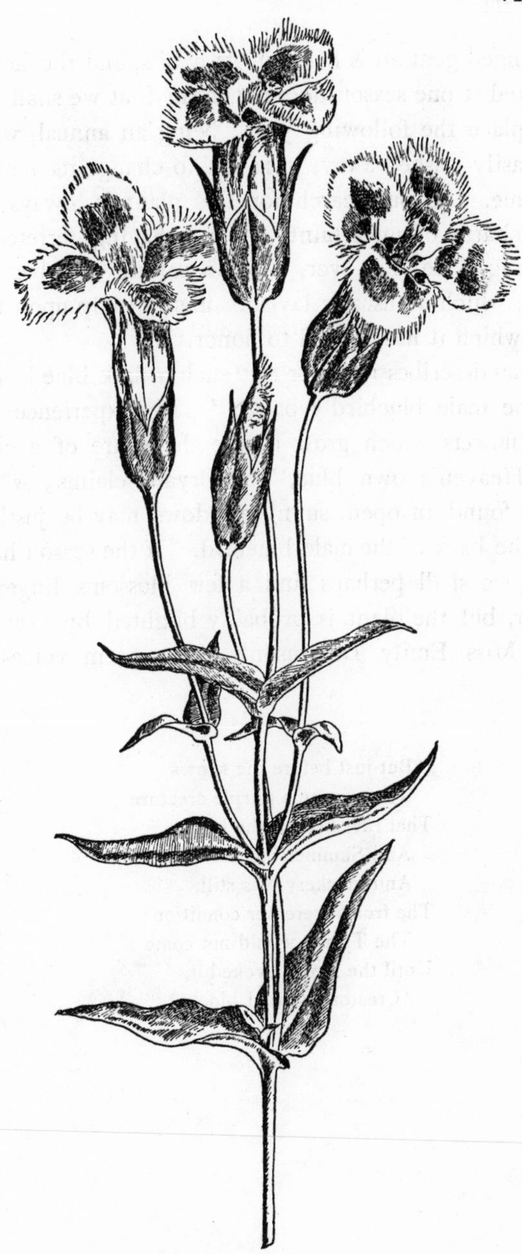

FRINGED GENTIAN.—*Gentiana crinita.*

for the fringed gentian is fickle in its habits, and the fact that we have located it one season does not mean that we shall find it in the same place the following year; being an annual, with seeds that are easily washed away, it is apt to change its haunts from time to time. So our search for this plant is always attended with the charm of uncertainty. Once having ferreted out its new abiding-place, however, we can satiate ourselves with its loveliness, which it usually lavishes unstintingly upon the moist meadows which it has elected to honor.

Thoreau describes its color as "such a dark blue! surpassing that of the male bluebird's back!" My experience has been that the flowers which grow in the shade are of a clear pure azure, "Heaven's own blue," as Bryant claims; while those which are found in open, sunny meadows may be justly said to vie with the back of the male bluebird. If the season has been a mild one we shall perhaps find a few blossoms lingering into November, but the plant is probably blighted by a severe frost, although Miss Emily Dickinson's little poem voices another opinion:

. . . . . .

"But just before the snows
  There came a purple creature
That ravished all the hill:
  And Summer hid her forehead,
  And mockery was still.
The frosts were her condition:
  The Tyrian would not come
Until the North evoked it,
  'Creator! shall I bloom!'"

VII

MISCELLANEOUS

SKUNK-CABBAGE. SWAMP-CABBAGE.

Symplocarpus foetidus. Arum Family.

Leaves.—Large; becoming one or two feet long; heart-shaped, appearing later than the purple-mottled spathe and hidden flowers. *Flowers.*—Small and inconspicuous; packed on the fleshy spike which is hidden within the spathe.

If we are bold enough to venture into certain swampy places in the leafless woods and brown cheerless meadows of March, we notice that the sharply pointed spathes of the skunk-cabbage have already pierced the surface of the earth. Until I chanced upon a passage in Thoreau's Journal under date of October 31st, I had supposed that these "hermits of the bog" were only encouraged to make their appearance by the advent of those first balmy, spring-suggestive days which occasionally occur as early as February. But it seems that many of these young buds had pushed their way upward before the winter set in, for Thoreau counsels those who are afflicted with the melancholy of autumn to go to the swamps, "and see the brave spears of skunk-cabbage buds already advanced toward a new year." "Mortal and human creatures must take a little respite in this fall of the year," he writes. "Their spirits do flag a little. There is a little questioning of destiny, and thinking to go like cowards to where the weary shall be at rest. But not so with the skunk-cabbage. Its withered leaves fall and are transfixed by a rising bud. Winter and death are ignored. The circle of life is complete.

Are these false prophets? Is it a lie or a vain boast underneath the skunk-cabbage bud pushing it upward and lifting the dead leaves with it?"

The purplish shell-like leaf, which curls about the tiny flowers which are thus hidden from view, is a rather grewsome-looking object, suggestive of a great snail when it lifts itself fairly above its muddy bed. When one sees it grouped with brother-cabbages it is easy to understand why a nearly allied species, which abounds along the Italian Riviera, should be entitled "Cappucini" by the neighboring peasants, for the bowed, hooded appearance of these plants might easily suggest the cowled Capuchins.

It seems unfortunate that our earliest spring flower (for such it undoubtedly is) should possess so unpleasant an odor as to win for itself the unpoetic title of skunk-cabbage. There is also some incongruity in the heading of the great floral procession of the year by the minute hidden blossoms of this plant. That they are enabled to survive the raw March winds which are rampant when they first appear is probably due to the protection afforded them by the leathery leaf or spathe. When the true leaves unfold they mark the wet woods and meadows with bright patches of rich foliage, which with that of the hellebore, flash constantly into sight as we travel through the country in April.

It is interesting to remember that the skunk-cabbage is nearly akin to the spotless calla-lily, the purple-mottled spathe of the one answering to the snowy petal-like leaf of the other. Meehan tells us that the name bear-weed was given to the plant by the early Swedish settlers in the neighborhood of Philadelphia. It seems that the bears greatly relished this early green, which Meehan remarks "must have been a hot morsel, as the juice is acrid, and is said to possess some narcotic power, while that of the root, when chewed, causes the eyesight to grow dim."

SKUNK-CABBAGE.—*Symplocarpus foetidus.*

WILD GINGER.

Asarum canadense. Birthwort Family.

Leaves.—One or two on each plant; kidney or heart-shaped; fuzzy; long-stalked. *Flowers.*—Dull purplish-brown; solitary; close to the ground on a short flower-stalk from the fork of the leaves. *Calyx.*—Three-cleft; bell-shaped. *Corolla.*—None. *Stamens.*—Twelve. *Pistil.*—One, with a thick style and six thick, radiating stigmas.

Certain flowers might be grouped under the head of "vegetable cranks." Here would be classed the evening-primrose, which only opens at night, the closed gentian, which never opens at all, and the wild ginger, whose odd, unlovely flower seeks protection beneath its long-stemmed fuzzy leaves, and hides its head upon the ground as if unwilling to challenge comparison with its more brilliant brethren. Unless already familiar with this plant there is nothing to tell one when it has reached its flowering season; and many a wanderer through the rocky woods in early May quite overlooks its shy, shamefaced blossom.

The ginger-like flavor of the rootstock is responsible for its common name. It grows wild in many parts of Europe and is cultivated in England, where at one time it was considered a remedy for headache and deafness.

JACK-IN-THE-PULPIT. INDIAN-TURNIP.

Arisaema triphyllum. Arum Family.

Scape.—Terminated by a hood-like leaf or spathe. *Leaves.*—Generally two; each divided into three leaflets. *Flowers.*—Small and inconspicuous; packed about the lower part of the fleshy spike or spadix which is shielded by the spathe. *Fruit.*—A bright scarlet berry which is packed upon the spadix with many others.

These quaint little preachers, ensconced in their delicate pulpits, are well known to all who love the woods in early spring Sometimes these "pulpits" are of a light green, veined with a deeper tint; again they are stained with purple. This differ-

WILD GINGER.—*Asarum canadense.*

ence in color has been thought to indicate the sex of the flowers within—the males are said to be shielded by the green, the females by the purple, hoods. In the nearly allied cuckoo-pints of England, matters appear to be reversed: these plants are called "Lords and Ladies" by the children, the purple-tinged ones being the "Lords," the light green ones the "Ladies." The generic name, *Arisæma*, signifies *bloody arum*, and refers to the dark purple stains of the spathe. An old legend claims that these were received at the Crucifixion:

> 'Beneath the cross it grew;
> And in the vase-like hollow of the leaf,
> Catching from that dread shower of agony
> A few mysterious drops, transmitted thus
> Unto the groves and hills their healing stains,
> A heritage, for storm or vernal shower
> Never to blow away."

The Indians were in the habit of boiling the bright scarlet berries which are so conspicuous in our autumn woods and devouring them with great relish; they also discovered that the bulb-like base, or *corm*, as it is called, lost its acridity on cooking, and made nutritious food, winning for the plant its name of Indian-turnip. One of its more local titles is memory-root, which it owes to a favorite school-boy trick of tempting others to bite into the blistering corm with results likely to create a memorable impression.

The English cuckoo-pint yielded a starch which was greatly valued in the time of Elizabethan ruffs, although it proved too blistering to the hands of the washerwomen to remain long in use. Owing to the profusion with which the plant grows in Ireland efforts have been made to utilize it as food in periods of scarcity. By grating the corm into water, and then pouring off the liquid and drying the sediment, it is said that a tasteless, but nutritious, powder can be procured.

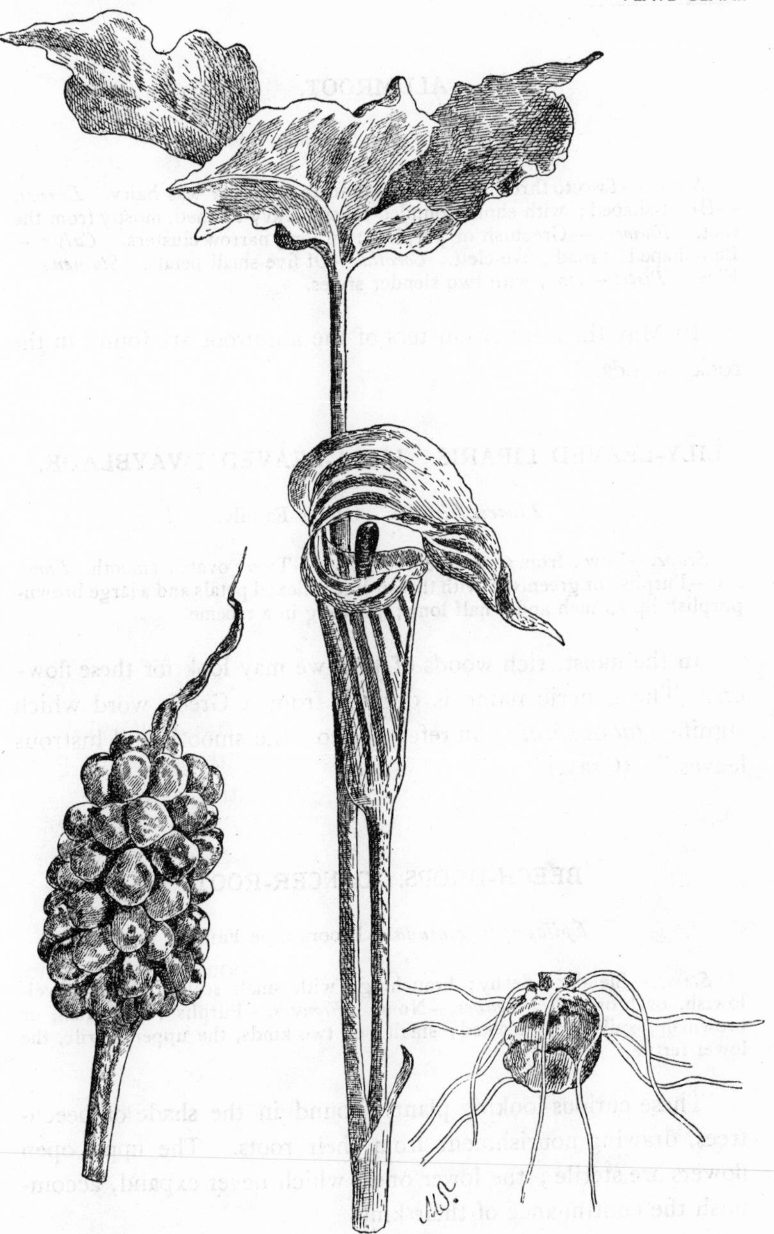

JACK-IN-THE-PULPIT.—*Arisaema triphyllum.*

ALUMROOT.

Heuchera americana. Saxifrage Family.

Stems.—Two to three feet high; glandular; more or less hairy. *Leaves.*—Heart-shaped; with short, rounded lobes; wavy-toothed, mostly from the root. *Flowers.*—Greenish or purplish; in long narrow clusters. *Calyx.*—Bell-shaped; broad; five-cleft. *Corolla.*—Of five small petals. *Stamens.*—Five. *Pistil.*—One, with two slender styles.

In May the slender clusters of the alumroot are found in the rocky woods.

LILY-LEAVED LIPARIS. LILIA-LEAVED TWAYBLADE.

Liparis lilifolia. Orchis Family.

Scape.—Low; from a solid bulb. *Leaves.*—Two; ovate; smooth. *Flowers.*—Purplish or greenish; with thread-like reflexed petals and a large brown-purplish lip an inch and a half long; growing in a raceme.

In the moist, rich woods of June we may look for these flowers. The generic name is derived from a Greek word which signifies *fat* or *shining*, in reference to "the smooth and lustrous leaves." (Gray.)

BEECH-DROPS. CANCER-ROOT.

Epifagus virginiana. Broom-rape Family.

Stems.—Slender; fleshy; branching; with small scales; purplish, yellowish, or brownish. *Leaves.*—None. *Flowers.*—Purplish, yellowish, or brownish; spiked or racemed; small; of two kinds, the upper sterile, the lower fertile.

These curious-looking plants abound in the shade of beech-trees, drawing nourishment from their roots. The upper open flowers are sterile; the lower ones, which never expand, accomplish the continuance of their kind.

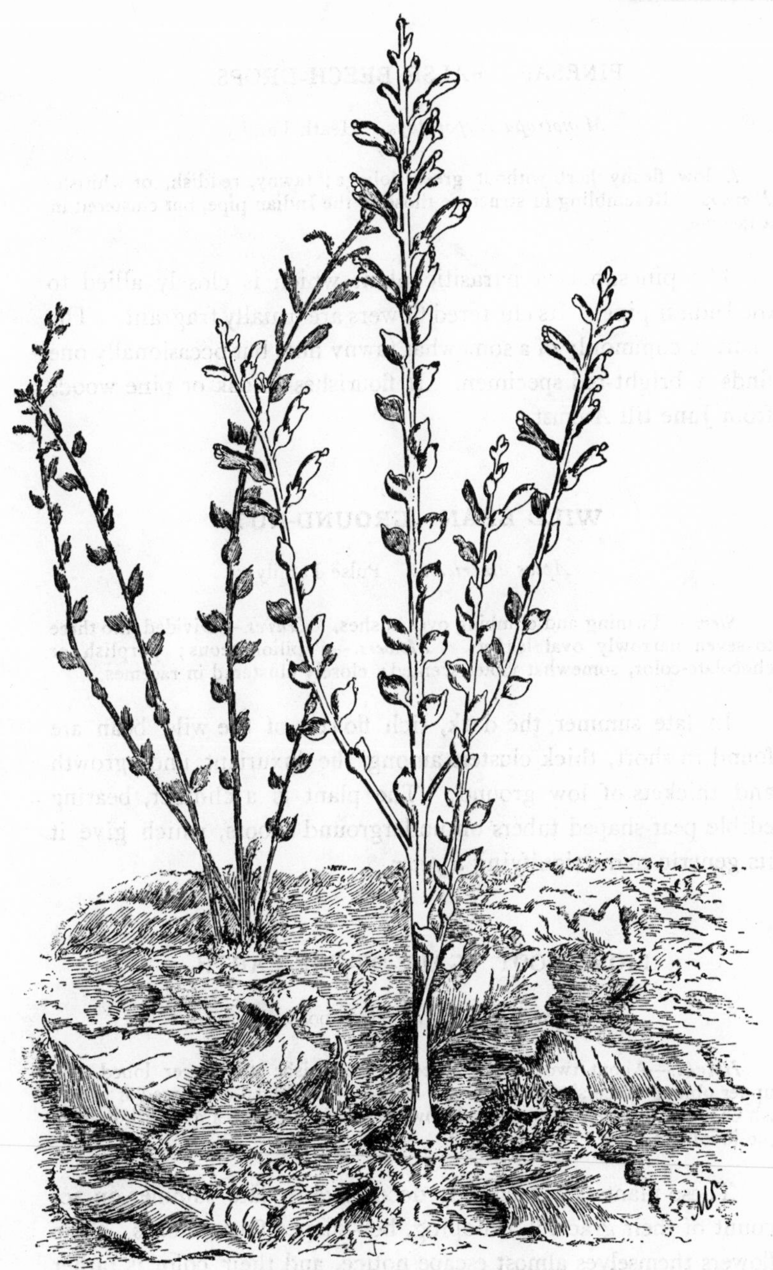

BEECH-DROPS.—*Epifagus virginiana.*

PINESAP. FALSE BEECH-DROPS.

Monotropa Hypopithys. Heath Family.

A low fleshy herb without green foliage; tawny, reddish, or whitish. *Flowers.*--Resembling in structure those of the Indian pipe, but clustered in a raceme.

The pinesap is a parasitic plant which is closely allied to the Indian-pipe. Its clustered flowers are usually fragrant. The plant is commonly of a somewhat tawny hue, but occasionally one finds a bright-red specimen. It flourishes in oak or pine woods from June till August.

WILD BEAN. GROUND-NUT.

Apios americana. Pulse Family.

Stem.—Twining and climbing over bushes. *Leaves.*—Divided into three to seven narrowly oval leaflets. *Flowers.*—Papilionaceous; purplish or chocolate-color, somewhat violet-scented; closely clustered in racemes.

In late summer the dark, rich flowers of the wild bean are found in short, thick clusters among the luxuriant undergrowth and thickets of low ground. The plant is a climber, bearing edible pear-shaped tubers on underground shoots, which give it its generic name signifying *a pear.*

LION'S-FOOT. GALL-OF-THE-EARTH.

Prenanthes Serpentaria. Composite Family.

Height.—About two feet. *Leaves.*—Roughish; the lower lobed, the upper oblong lance-shaped. *Flower-heads.*—Nodding; composed of greenish or cream-colored strap-shaped flowers surrounded by a greenish or purple involucre.

These plants are peculiarly decorative in late summer on account of their graceful, drooping, bell-shaped flower-heads. The flowers themselves almost escape notice, and their color is rather

WILD BEAN.—*Apios americana.*

difficult to determine, the purplish or greenish involucre being the plant's conspicuous feature.

The generic name is from the Greek, and signifies *drooping blossom.*

RATTLESNAKE-ROOT.

Prenanthes alba.

Height.—Two to four feet. *Leaves.*—The lower cleft or toothed; the uppermost oblong and undivided. *Flower-heads.*—Nodding; composed of white or greenish strap-shaped flowers surrounded by a purplish involucre.

This plant is almost similar to the above.

CORAL-ROOT.

Corallorhiza maculata. Orchis Family.

Rootstock.—Much branched; coral-like; toothed. *Stem.*—Nine to eighteen inches high, without green foliage. *Flowers.*—Rather small; dull brownish-purple or yellowish, sometimes mottled with red; growing in a raceme.

In the dry summer woods one frequently encounters the dull racemes of this rather inconspicuous little plant. It is often found in the immediate neighborhood of the Indian-pipe and pinesap. Being, like them, without green foliage, it might be taken for an allied species by the casual observer. This is one of those orchids which are popularly considered unworthy to bear the name, giving rise to so much incredulity or disappointment in the unbotanical.

INDEX TO LATIN NAMES

INDEX TO LATIN NAMES

INDEX TO ENGLISH NAMES

INDEX TO ENGLISH NAMES

INDEX TO ENGLISH NAMES

INDEX OF TECHNICAL TERMS

A CATALOGUE OF SELECTED DOVER BOOKS IN ALL FIELDS OF INTEREST

A CATALOGUE OF SELECTED DOVER BOOKS IN ALL FIELDS OF INTEREST

RACKHAM'S COLOR ILLUSTRATIONS FOR WAGNER'S RING. Rackham's finest mature work—all 64 full-color watercolors in a faithful and lush interpretation of the *Ring*. Full-sized plates on coated stock of the paintings used by opera companies for authentic staging of Wagner. Captions aid in following complete Ring cycle. Introduction. 64 illustrations plus vignettes. 72pp. 8⅝ x 11¼. 23779-6 Pa. $6.00

CONTEMPORARY POLISH POSTERS IN FULL COLOR, edited by Joseph Czestochowski. 46 full-color examples of brilliant school of Polish graphic design, selected from world's first museum (near Warsaw) dedicated to poster art. Posters on circuses, films, plays, concerts all show cosmopolitan influences, free imagination. Introduction. 48pp. 9⅜ x 12¼. 23780-X Pa. $6.00

GRAPHIC WORKS OF EDVARD MUNCH, Edvard Munch. 90 haunting, evocative prints by first major Expressionist artist and one of the greatest graphic artists of his time: *The Scream, Anxiety, Death Chamber, The Kiss, Madonna,* etc. Introduction by Alfred Werner. 90pp. 9 x 12. 23765-6 Pa. $5.00

THE GOLDEN AGE OF THE POSTER, Hayward and Blanche Cirker. 70 extraordinary posters in full colors, from Maitres de l'Affiche, Mucha, Lautrec, Bradley, Cheret, Beardsley, many others. Total of 78pp. 9⅜ x 12¼. 22753-7 Pa. $5.95

THE NOTEBOOKS OF LEONARDO DA VINCI, edited by J. P. Richter. Extracts from manuscripts reveal great genius; on painting, sculpture, anatomy, sciences, geography, etc. Both Italian and English. 186 ms. pages reproduced, plus 500 additional drawings, including studies for *Last Supper,* Sforza monument, etc. 860pp. 7⅞ x 10¾. (Available in U.S. only) 22572-0, 22573-9 Pa., Two-vol. set $15.90

THE CODEX NUTTALL, as first edited by Zelia Nuttall. Only inexpensive edition, in full color, of a pre-Columbian Mexican (Mixtec) book. 88 color plates show kings, gods, heroes, temples, sacrifices. New explanatory, historical introduction by Arthur G. Miller. 96pp. 11⅜ x 8½. (Available in U.S. only) 23168-2 Pa. $7.95

UNE SEMAINE DE BONTÉ, A SURREALISTIC NOVEL IN COLLAGE, Max Ernst. Masterpiece created out of 19th-century periodical illustrations, explores worlds of terror and surprise. Some consider this Ernst's greatest work. 208pp. 8⅛ x 11. 23252-2 Pa. $6.00

CATALOGUE OF DOVER BOOKS

ART FORMS IN NATURE, Ernst Haeckel. Multitude of strangely beautiful natural forms: Radiolaria, Foraminifera, jellyfishes, fungi, turtles, bats, etc. All 100 plates of the 19th-century evolutionist's *Kunstformen der Natur* (1904). 100pp. 9⅜ x 12¼. 22987-4 Pa. $5.00

CHILDREN: A PICTORIAL ARCHIVE FROM NINETEENTH-CENTURY SOURCES, edited by Carol Belanger Grafton. 242 rare, copyright-free wood engravings for artists and designers. Widest such selection available. All illustrations in line. 119pp. 8⅜ x 11¼. 23694-3 Pa. $4.00

WOMEN: A PICTORIAL ARCHIVE FROM NINETEENTH-CENTURY SOURCES, edited by Jim Harter. 391 copyright-free wood engravings for artists and designers selected from rare periodicals. Most extensive such collection available. All illustrations in line. 128pp. 9 x 12. 23703-6 Pa. $4.50

ARABIC ART IN COLOR, Prisse d'Avennes. From the greatest ornamentalists of all time—50 plates in color, rarely seen outside the Near East, rich in suggestion and stimulus. Includes 4 plates on covers. 46pp. 9⅜ x 12¼. 23658-7 Pa. $6.00

AUTHENTIC ALGERIAN CARPET DESIGNS AND MOTIFS, edited by June Beveridge. Algerian carpets are world famous. Dozens of geometrical motifs are charted on grids, color-coded, for weavers, needleworkers, craftsmen, designers. 53 illustrations plus 4 in color. 48pp. 8¼ x 11. (Available in U.S. only) 23650-1 Pa. $1.75

DICTIONARY OF AMERICAN PORTRAITS, edited by Hayward and Blanche Cirker. 4000 important Americans, earliest times to 1905, mostly in clear line. Politicians, writers, soldiers, scientists, inventors, industrialists, Indians, Blacks, women, outlaws, etc. Identificatory information. 756pp. 9¼ x 12¾. 21823-6 Clothbd. $40.00

HOW THE OTHER HALF LIVES, Jacob A. Riis. Journalistic record of filth, degradation, upward drive in New York immigrant slums, shops, around 1900. New edition includes 100 original Riis photos, monuments of early photography. 233pp. 10 x 7⅞. 22012-5 Pa. $7.00

NEW YORK IN THE THIRTIES, Berenice Abbott. Noted photographer's fascinating study of city shows new buildings that have become famous and old sights that have disappeared forever. Insightful commentary. 97 photographs. 97pp. 11⅜ x 10. 22967-X Pa. $5.00

MEN AT WORK, Lewis W. Hine. Famous photographic studies of construction workers, railroad men, factory workers and coal miners. New supplement of 18 photos on Empire State building construction. New introduction by Jonathan L. Doherty. Total of 69 photos. 63pp. 8 x 10¾. 23475-4 Pa. $3.00

AMERICAN BIRD ENGRAVINGS, Alexander Wilson et al. All 76 plates. from Wilson's *American Ornithology* (1808-14), most important ornithological work before Audubon, plus 27 plates from the supplement (1825-33) by Charles Bonaparte. Over 250 birds portrayed. 8 plates also reproduced in full color. 111pp. 9⅜ x 12½. **23195-X Pa. $6.00**

CRUICKSHANK'S PHOTOGRAPHS OF BIRDS OF AMERICA, Allan D. Cruickshank. Great ornithologist, photographer presents 177 closeups, groupings, panoramas, flightings, etc., of about 150 different birds. Expanded *Wings in the Wilderness.* Introduction by Helen G. Cruickshank. 191pp. 8¼ x 11. **23497-5 Pa. $6.00**

AMERICAN WILDLIFE AND PLANTS, A. C. Martin, et al. Describes food habits of more than 1000 species of mammals, birds, fish. Special treatment of important food plants. Over 300 illustrations. 500pp. 5⅜ x 8½. **20793-5 Pa. $4.95**

THE PEOPLE CALLED SHAKERS, Edward D. Andrews. Lifetime of research, definitive study of Shakers: origins, beliefs, practices, dances, social organization, furniture and crafts, impact on 19th-century USA, present heritage. Indispensable to student of American history, collector. 33 illustrations. 351pp. 5⅜ x 8½. **21081-2 Pa. $4.50**

OLD NEW YORK IN EARLY PHOTOGRAPHS, Mary Black. New York City as it was in 1853-1901, through 196 wonderful photographs from N.-Y. Historical Society. Great Blizzard, Lincoln's funeral procession, great buildings. 228pp. 9 x 12. **22907-6 Pa. $8.95**

MR. LINCOLN'S CAMERA MAN: MATHEW BRADY, Roy Meredith. Over 300 Brady photos reproduced directly from original negatives, photos. Jackson, Webster, Grant, Lee, Carnegie, Barnum; Lincoln; Battle Smoke, Death of Rebel Sniper, Atlanta Just After Capture. Lively commentary. 368pp. 8⅜ x 11¼. **23021-X Pa. $8.95**

TRAVELS OF WILLIAM BARTRAM, William Bartram. From 1773-8, Bartram explored Northern Florida, Georgia, Carolinas, and reported on wild life, plants, Indians, early settlers. Basic account for period, entertaining reading. Edited by Mark Van Doren. 13 illustrations. 141pp. 5⅜ x 8½. **20013-2 Pa. $5.00**

THE GENTLEMAN AND CABINET MAKER'S DIRECTOR, Thomas Chippendale. Full reprint, 1762 style book, most influential of all time; chairs, tables, sofas, mirrors, cabinets, etc. 200 plates, plus 24 photographs of surviving pieces. 249pp. 9⅞ x 12¾. **21601-2 Pa. $7.95**

AMERICAN CARRIAGES, SLEIGHS, SULKIES AND CARTS, edited by Don H. Berkebile. 168 Victorian illustrations from catalogues, trade journals, fully captioned. Useful for artists. Author is Assoc. Curator, Div. of Transportation of Smithsonian Institution. 168pp. 8½ x 9½. **23328-6 Pa. $5.00**

THE CURVES OF LIFE, Theodore A. Cook. Examination of shells, leaves, horns, human body, art, etc., in "*the* classic reference on how the golden ratio applies to spirals and helices in nature . . . ."—Martin Gardner. 426 illustrations. Total of 512pp. 5⅜ x 8½. 23701-X Pa. $5.95

AN ILLUSTRATED FLORA OF THE NORTHERN UNITED STATES AND CANADA, Nathaniel L. Britton, Addison Brown. Encyclopedic work covers 4666 species, ferns on up. Everything. Full botanical information, illustration for each. This earlier edition is preferred by many to more recent revisions. 1913 edition. Over 4000 illustrations, total of 2087pp. 6⅛ x 9¼. 22642-5, 22643-3, 22644-1 Pa., Three-vol. set $25.50

MANUAL OF THE GRASSES OF THE UNITED STATES, A. S. Hitchcock, U.S. Dept. of Agriculture. The basic study of American grasses, both indigenous and escapes, cultivated and wild. Over 1400 species. Full descriptions, information. Over 1100 maps, illustrations. Total of 1051pp. 5⅜ x 8½. 22717-0, 22718-9 Pa., Two-vol. set $15.00

THE CACTACEAE,, Nathaniel L. Britton, John N. Rose. Exhaustive, definitive. Every cactus in the world. Full botanical descriptions. Thorough statement of nomenclatures, habitat, detailed finding keys. The one book needed by every cactus enthusiast. Over 1275 illustrations. Total of 1080pp. 8 x 10¼. 21191-6, 21192-4 Clothbd., Two-vol. set $35.00

AMERICAN MEDICINAL PLANTS, Charles F. Millspaugh. Full descriptions, 180 plants covered: history; physical description; methods of preparation with all chemical constituents extracted; all claimed curative or adverse effects. 180 full-page plates. Classification table. 804pp. 6½ x 9¼. 23034-1 Pa. $12.95

A MODERN HERBAL, Margaret Grieve. Much the fullest, most exact, most useful compilation of herbal material. Gigantic alphabetical encyclopedia, from aconite to zedoary, gives botanical information, medical properties, folklore, economic uses, and much else. Indispensable to serious reader. 161 illustrations. 888pp. 6½ x 9¼. (Available in U.S. only) 22798-7, 22799-5 Pa., Two-vol. set $13.00

THE HERBAL or GENERAL HISTORY OF PLANTS, John Gerard. The 1633 edition revised and enlarged by Thomas Johnson. Containing almost 2850 plant descriptions and 2705 superb illustrations, Gerard's *Herbal* is a monumental work, the book all modern English herbals are derived from, the one herbal every serious enthusiast should have in its entirety. Original editions are worth perhaps $750. 1678pp. 8½ x 12¼. 23147-X Clothbd. $50.00

MANUAL OF THE TREES OF NORTH AMERICA, Charles S. Sargent. The basic survey of every native tree and tree-like shrub, 717 species in all. Extremely full descriptions, information on habitat, growth, locales, economics, etc. Necessary to every serious tree lover. Over 100 finding keys. 783 illustrations. Total of 986pp. 5⅜ x 8½. 20277-1, 20278-X Pa., Two-vol. set $11.00

"OSCAR" OF THE WALDORF'S COOKBOOK, Oscar Tschirky. Famous American chef reveals 3455 recipes that made Waldorf great; cream of French, German, American cooking, in all categories. Full instructions, easy home use. 1896 edition. 907pp. 6⅝ x 9⅜. 20790-0 Clothbd. $15.00

COOKING WITH BEER, Carole Fahy. Beer has as superb an effect on food as wine, and at fraction of cost. Over 250 recipes for appetizers, soups, main dishes, desserts, breads, etc. Index. 144pp. 5⅜ x 8½. (Available in U.S. only) 23661-7 Pa. $2.50

STEWS AND RAGOUTS, Kay Shaw Nelson. This international cookbook offers wide range of 108 recipes perfect for everyday, special occasions, meals-in-themselves, main dishes. Economical, nutritious, easy-to-prepare: goulash, Irish stew, boeuf bourguignon, etc. Index. 134pp. 5⅜ x 8½. 23662-5 Pa. $2.50

DELICIOUS MAIN COURSE DISHES, Marian Tracy. Main courses are the most important part of any meal. These 200 nutritious, economical recipes from around the world make every meal a delight. "I . . . have found it so useful in my own household,"—*N.Y. Times*. Index. 219pp. 5⅜ x 8½. 23664-1 Pa. $3.00

FIVE ACRES AND INDEPENDENCE, Maurice G. Kains. Great back-to-the-land classic explains basics of self-sufficient farming: economics, plants, crops, animals, orchards, soils, land selection, host of other necessary things. Do not confuse with skimpy faddist literature; Kains was one of America's greatest agriculturalists. 95 illustrations. 397pp. 5⅜ x 8½. 20974-1 Pa.$3.95

A PRACTICAL GUIDE FOR THE BEGINNING FARMER, Herbert Jacobs. Basic, extremely useful first book for anyone thinking about moving to the country and starting a farm. Simpler than Kains, with greater emphasis on country living in general. 246pp. 5⅜ x 8½. 23675-7 Pa. $3.50

PAPERMAKING, Dard Hunter. Definitive book on the subject by the foremost authority in the field. Chapters dealing with every aspect of history of craft in every part of the world. Over 320 illustrations. 2nd, revised and enlarged (1947) edition. 672pp. 5⅜ x 8½. 23619-6 Pa. $7.95

THE ART DECO STYLE, edited by Theodore Menten. Furniture, jewelry, metalwork, ceramics, fabrics, lighting fixtures, interior decors, exteriors, graphics from pure French sources. Best sampling around. Over 400 photographs. 183pp. 8⅜ x 11¼. 22824-X Pa. $6.00

ACKERMANN'S COSTUME PLATES, Rudolph Ackermann. Selection of 96 plates from the *Repository of Arts*, best published source of costume for English fashion during the early 19th century. 12 plates also in color. Captions, glossary and introduction by editor Stella Blum. Total of 120pp. 8⅜ x 11¼. 23690-0 Pa. $4.50

SECOND PIATIGORSKY CUP, edited by Isaac Kashdan. One of the greatest tournament books ever produced in the English language. All 90 games of the 1966 tournament, annotated by players, most annotated by both players. Features Petrosian, Spassky, Fischer, Larsen, six others. 228pp. 5⅜ x 8½. 23572-6 Pa. $3.50

ENCYCLOPEDIA OF CARD TRICKS, revised and edited by Jean Hugard. How to perform over 600 card tricks, devised by the world's greatest magicians: impromptus, spelling tricks, key cards, using special packs, much, much more. Additional chapter on card technique. 66 illustrations. 402pp. 5⅜ x 8½. (Available in U.S. only) 21252-1 Pa. $4.95

MAGIC: STAGE ILLUSIONS, SPECIAL EFFECTS AND TRICK PHOTOGRAPHY, Albert A. Hopkins, Henry R. Evans. One of the great classics; fullest, most authorative explanation of vanishing lady, levitations, scores of other great stage effects. Also small magic, automata, stunts. 446 illustrations. 556pp. 5⅜ x 8½. 23344-8 Pa. $6.95

THE SECRETS OF HOUDINI, J. C. Cannell. Classic study of Houdini's incredible magic, exposing closely-kept professional secrets and revealing, in general terms, the whole art of stage magic. 67 illustrations. 279pp. 5⅜ x 8½. 22913-0 Pa. $4.00

HOFFMANN'S MODERN MAGIC, Professor Hoffmann. One of the best, and best-known, magicians' manuals of the past century. Hundreds of tricks from card tricks and simple sleight of hand to elaborate illusions involving construction of complicated machinery. 332 illustrations. 563pp. 5⅜ x 8½. 23623-4 Pa. $6.00

MADAME PRUNIER'S FISH COOKERY BOOK, Mme. S. B. Prunier. More than 1000 recipes from world famous Prunier's of Paris and London, specially adapted here for American kitchen. Grilled tournedos with anchovy butter, Lobster a la Bordelaise, Prunier's prized desserts, more. Glossary. 340pp. 5⅜ x 8½. (Available in U.S. only) 22679-4 Pa. $3.00

FRENCH COUNTRY COOKING FOR AMERICANS, Louis Diat. 500 easy-to-make, authentic provincial recipes compiled by former head chef at New York's Fitz-Carlton Hotel: onion soup, lamb stew, potato pie, more. 309pp. 5⅜ x 8½. 23665-X Pa. $3.95

SAUCES, FRENCH AND FAMOUS, Louis Diat. Complete book gives over 200 specific recipes: bechamel, Bordelaise, hollandaise, Cumberland, apricot, etc. Author was one of this century's finest chefs, originator of vichyssoise and many other dishes. Index. 156pp. 5⅜ x 8. 23663-3 Pa. $2.75

TOLL HOUSE TRIED AND TRUE RECIPES, Ruth Graves Wakefield. Authentic recipes from the famous Mass. restaurant: popovers, veal and ham loaf, Toll House baked beans, chocolate cake crumb pudding, much more. Many helpful hints. Nearly 700 recipes. Index. 376pp. 5⅜ x 8½. 23560-2 Pa. $4.50

THE AMERICAN SENATOR, Anthony Trollope. Little known, long unavailable Trollope novel on a grand scale. Here are humorous comment on American vs. English culture, and stunning portrayal of a heroine/villainess. Superb evocation of Victorian village life. 561pp. 5⅜ x 8½.
23801-6 Pa. $6.00

WAS IT MURDER? James Hilton. The author of *Lost Horizon* and *Goodbye, Mr. Chips* wrote one detective novel (under a pen-name) which was quickly forgotten and virtually lost, even at the height of Hilton's fame. This edition brings it back—a finely crafted public school puzzle resplendent with Hilton's stylish atmosphere. A thoroughly English thriller by the creator of Shangri-la. 252pp. 5⅜ x 8. (Available in U.S. only)
23774-5 Pa. $3.00

CENTRAL PARK: A PHOTOGRAPHIC GUIDE, Victor Laredo and Henry Hope Reed. 121 superb photographs show dramatic views of Central Park: Bethesda Fountain, Cleopatra's Needle, Sheep Meadow, the Blockhouse, plus people engaged in many park activities: ice skating, bike riding, etc. Captions by former Curator of Central Park, Henry Hope Reed, provide historical view, changes, etc. Also photos of N.Y. landmarks on park's periphery. 96pp. 8½ x 11. 23750-8 Pa. $4.50

NANTUCKET IN THE NINETEENTH CENTURY, Clay Lancaster. 180 rare photographs, stereographs, maps, drawings and floor plans recreate unique American island society. Authentic scenes of shipwreck, lighthouses, streets, homes are arranged in geographic sequence to provide walking-tour guide to old Nantucket existing today. Introduction, captions. 160pp. 8⅞ x 11¾. 23747-8 Pa. $6.95

STONE AND MAN: A PHOTOGRAPHIC EXPLORATION, Andreas Feininger. 106 photographs by *Life* photographer Feininger portray man's deep passion for stone through the ages. Stonehenge-like megaliths, fortified towns, sculpted marble and crumbling tenements show textures, beauties, fascination. 128pp. 9¼ x 10¾. 23756-7 Pa. $5.95

CIRCLES, A MATHEMATICAL VIEW, D. Pedoe. Fundamental aspects of college geometry, non-Euclidean geometry, and other branches of mathematics: representing circle by point. Poincare model, isoperimetric property, etc. Stimulating recreational reading. 66 figures. 96pp. 5⅝ x 8¼.
63698-4 Pa. $2.75

THE DISCOVERY OF NEPTUNE, Morton Grosser. Dramatic scientific history of the investigations leading up to the actual discovery of the eighth planet of our solar system. Lucid, well-researched book by well-known historian of science. 172pp. 5⅜ x 8½. 23726-5 Pa. $3.50

CATALOGUE OF DOVER BOOKS

TONE POEMS, SERIES II: TILL EULENSPIEGELS LUSTIGE STREICHE, ALSO SPRACH ZARATHUSTRA, AND EIN HELDENLEBEN, Richard Strauss. Three important orchestral works, including very popular *Till Eulenspiegel's Marry Pranks,* reproduced in full score from original editions. Study score. 315pp. 9⅜ x 12¼. (Available in U.S. only)
23755-9 Pa. $8.95

TONE POEMS, SERIES I: DON JUAN, TOD UND VERKLARUNG AND DON QUIXOTE, Richard Strauss. Three of the most often performed and recorded works in entire orchestral repertoire, reproduced in full score from original editions. Study score. 286pp. 9⅜ x 12¼. (Available in U.S. only)
23754-0 Pa. $7.50

11 LATE STRING QUARTETS, Franz Joseph Haydn. The form which Haydn defined and "brought to perfection." *(Grove's).* 11 string quartets in complete score, his last and his best. The first in a projected series of the complete Haydn string quartets. Reliable modern Eulenberg edition, otherwise difficult to obtain. 320pp. 8⅜ x 11¼. (Available in U.S. only)
23753-2 Pa. $7.50

FOURTH, FIFTH AND SIXTH SYMPHONIES IN FULL SCORE, Peter Ilyitch Tchaikovsky. Complete orchestral scores of Symphony No. 4 in F Minor, Op. 36; Symphony No. 5 in E Minor, Op. 64; Symphony No. 6 in B Minor, "Pathetique," Op. 74. Bretikopf & Hartel eds. Study score. 480pp. 9⅜ x 12¼.
23861-X Pa. $10.95

THE MARRIAGE OF FIGARO: COMPLETE SCORE, Wolfgang A. Mozart. Finest comic opera ever written. Full score, not to be confused with piano renderings. Peters edition. Study score. 448pp. 9⅜ x 12¼. (Available in U.S. only)
23751-6 Pa. $11.95

"IMAGE" ON THE ART AND EVOLUTION OF THE FILM, edited by Marshall Deutelbaum. Pioneering book brings together for first time 38 groundbreaking articles on early silent films from *Image* and 263 illustrations newly shot from rare prints in the collection of the International Museum of Photography. A landmark work. Index. 256pp. 8¼ x 11.
23777-X Pa. $8.95

AROUND-THE-WORLD COOKY BOOK, Lois Lintner Sumption and Marguerite Lintner Ashbrook. 373 cooky and frosting recipes from 28 countries (America, Austria, China, Russia, Italy, etc.) include Viennese kisses, rice wafers, London strips, lady fingers, hony, sugar spice, maple cookies, etc. Clear instructions. All tested. 38 drawings. 182pp. 5⅜ x 8.
23802-4 Pa. $2.50

THE ART NOUVEAU STYLE, edited by Roberta Waddell. 579 rare photographs, not available elsewhere, of works in jewelry, metalwork, glass, ceramics, textiles, architecture and furniture by 175 artists—Mucha, Seguy, Lalique, Tiffany, Gaudin, Hohlwein, Saarinen, and many others. 288pp. 8⅜ x 11¼.
23515-7 Pa. $6.95

THE COMPLETE BOOK OF DOLL MAKING AND COLLECTING, Catherine Christopher. Instructions, patterns for dozens of dolls, from rag doll on up to elaborate, historically accurate figures. Mould faces, sew clothing, make doll houses, etc. Also collecting information. Many illustrations. 288pp. 6 x 9. 22066-4 Pa. $4.50

THE DAGUERREOTYPE IN AMERICA, Beaumont Newhall. Wonderful portraits, 1850's townscapes, landscapes; full text plus 104 photographs. The basic book. Enlarged 1976 edition. 272pp. 8¼ x 11¼. 23322-7 Pa. $7.95

CRAFTSMAN HOMES, Gustav Stickley. 296 architectural drawings, floor plans, and photographs illustrate 40 different kinds of "Mission-style" homes from *The Craftsman* (1901-16), voice of American style of simplicity and organic harmony. Thorough coverage of Craftsman idea in text and picture, now collector's item. 224pp. 8⅛ x 11. 23791-5 Pa. $6.00

PEWTER-WORKING: INSTRUCTIONS AND PROJECTS, Burl N. Osborn. & Gordon O. Wilber. Introduction to pewter-working for amateur craftsman. History and characteristics of pewter; tools, materials, step-by-step instructions. Photos, line drawings, diagrams. Total of 160pp. 7⅞ x 10¾. 23786-9 Pa. $3.50

THE GREAT CHICAGO FIRE, edited by David Lowe. 10 dramatic, eyewitness accounts of the 1871 disaster, including one of the aftermath and rebuilding, plus 70 contemporary photographs and illustrations of the ruins—courthouse, Palmer House, Great Central Depot, etc. Introduction by David Lowe. 87pp. 8¼ x 11. 23771-0 Pa. $4.00

SILHOUETTES: A PICTORIAL ARCHIVE OF VARIED ILLUSTRATIONS, edited by Carol Belanger Grafton. Over 600 silhouettes from the 18th to 20th centuries include profiles and full figures of men and women, children, birds and animals, groups and scenes, nature, ships, an alphabet. Dozens of uses for commercial artists and craftspeople. 144pp. 8⅜ x 11¼. 23781-8 Pa. $4.50

ANIMALS: 1,419 COPYRIGHT-FREE ILLUSTRATIONS OF MAMMALS, BIRDS, FISH, INSECTS, ETC., edited by Jim Harter. Clear wood engravings present, in extremely lifelike poses, over 1,000 species of animals. One of the most extensive copyright-free pictorial sourcebooks of its kind. Captions. Index. 284pp. 9 x 12. 23766-4 Pa. $8.95

INDIAN DESIGNS FROM ANCIENT ECUADOR, Frederick W. Shaffer. 282 original designs by pre-Columbian Indians of Ecuador (500-1500 A.D.). Designs include people, mammals, birds, reptiles, fish, plants, heads, geometric designs. Use as is or alter for advertising, textiles, leathercraft, etc. Introduction. 95pp. 8¾ x 11¼. 23764-8 Pa. $3.50

SZIGETI ON THE VIOLIN, Joseph Szigeti. Genial, loosely structured tour by premier violinist, featuring a pleasant mixture of reminiscenes, insights into great music and musicians, innumerable tips for practicing violinists. 385 musical passages. 256pp. 5⅝ x 8¼. 23763-X Pa. $4.00

THE PHILOSOPHY OF HISTORY, Georg W. Hegel. Great classic of Western thought develops concept that history is not chance but a rational process, the evolution of freedom. 457pp. 5⅜ x 8½. **20112-0 Pa. $4.50**

LANGUAGE, TRUTH AND LOGIC, Alfred J. Ayer. Famous, clear introduction to Vienna, Cambridge schools of Logical Positivism. Role of philosophy, elimination of metaphysics, nature of analysis, etc. 160pp. 5⅜ x 8½. (Available in U.S. only) **20010-8 Pa. $2.00**

A PREFACE TO LOGIC, Morris R. Cohen. Great City College teacher in renowned, easily followed exposition of formal logic, probability, values, logic and world order and similar topics; no previous background needed. 209pp. 5⅜ x 8½. **23517-3 Pa. $3.50**

REASON AND NATURE, Morris R. Cohen. Brilliant analysis of reason and its multitudinous ramifications by charismatic teacher. Interdisciplinary, synthesizing work widely praised when it first appeared in 1931. Second (1953) edition. Indexes. 496pp. 5⅜ x 8½. **23633-1 Pa. $6.50**

AN ESSAY CONCERNING HUMAN UNDERSTANDING, John Locke. The only complete edition of enormously important classic, with authoritative editorial material by A. C. Fraser. Total of 1176pp. 5⅜ x 8½. **20530-4, 20531-2 Pa., Two-vol. set $16.00**

HANDBOOK OF MATHEMATICAL FUNCTIONS WITH FORMULAS, GRAPHS, AND MATHEMATICAL TABLES, edited by Milton Abramowitz and Irene A. Stegun. Vast compendium: 29 sets of tables, some to as high as 20 places. 1,046pp. 8 x 10½. **61272-4 Pa. $14.95**

MATHEMATICS FOR THE PHYSICAL SCIENCES, Herbert S. Wilf. Highly acclaimed work offers clear presentations of vector spaces and matrices, orthogonal functions, roots of polynomial equations, conformal mapping, calculus of variations, etc. Knowledge of theory of functions of real and complex variables is assumed. Exercises and solutions. Index. 284pp. 5⅝ x 8¼. **63635-6 Pa. $5.00**

THE PRINCIPLE OF RELATIVITY, Albert Einstein et al. Eleven most important original papers on special and general theories. Seven by Einstein, two by Lorentz, one each by Minkowski and Weyl. All translated, unabridged. 216pp. 5⅜ x 8½. **60081-5 Pa. $3.50**

THERMODYNAMICS, Enrico Fermi. A classic of modern science. Clear, organized treatment of systems, first and second laws, entropy, thermodynamic potentials, gaseous reactions, dilute solutions, entropy constant. No math beyond calculus required. Problems. 160pp. 5⅜ x 8½. **60361-X Pa. $3.00**

ELEMENTARY MECHANICS OF FLUIDS, Hunter Rouse. Classic undergraduate text widely considered to be far better than many later books. Ranges from fluid velocity and acceleration to role of compressibility in fluid motion. Numerous examples, questions, problems. 224 illustrations. 376pp. 5⅝ x 8¼. **63699-2 Pa. $5.00**

THE SENSE OF BEAUTY, George Santayana. Masterfully written discussion of nature of beauty, materials of beauty, form, expression; art, literature, social sciences all involved. 168pp. 5⅜ x 8½. **20238-0 Pa. $3.00**

ON THE IMPROVEMENT OF THE UNDERSTANDING, Benedict Spinoza. Also contains *Ethics, Correspondence,* all in excellent R. Elwes translation. Basic works on entry to philosophy, pantheism, exchange of ideas with great contemporaries. 402pp. 5⅜ x 8½. **20250-X Pa. $4.50**

THE TRAGIC SENSE OF LIFE, Miguel de Unamuno. Acknowledged masterpiece of existential literature, one of most important books of 20th century. Introduction by Madariaga. 367pp. 5⅜ x 8½. **20257-7 Pa. $4.50**

THE GUIDE FOR THE PERPLEXED, Moses Maimonides. Great classic of medieval Judaism attempts to reconcile revealed religion (Pentateuch, commentaries) with Aristotelian philosophy. Important historically, still relevant in problems. Unabridged Friedlander translation. Total of 473pp. 5⅜ x 8½. **20351-4 Pa. $6.00**

THE I CHING (THE BOOK OF CHANGES), translated by James Legge. Complete translation of basic text plus appendices by Confucius, and Chinese commentary of most penetrating divination manual ever prepared. Indispensable to study of early Oriental civilizations, to modern inquiring reader. 448pp. 5⅜ x 8½. **21062-6 Pa. $5.00**

THE EGYPTIAN BOOK OF THE DEAD, E. A. Wallis Budge. Complete reproduction of Ani's papyrus, finest ever found. Full hieroglyphic text, interlinear transliteration, word for word translation, smooth translation. Basic work, for Egyptology, for modern study of psychic matters. Total of 533pp. 6½ x 9¼. (Available in U.S. only) **21866-X Pa. $5.95**

THE GODS OF THE EGYPTIANS, E. A. Wallis Budge. Never excelled for richness, fullness: all gods, goddesses, demons, mythical figures of Ancient Egypt; their legends, rites, incarnations, variations, powers, etc. Many hieroglyphic texts cited. Over 225 illustrations, plus 6 color plates. Total of 988pp. 6⅛ x 9¼. (Available in U.S. only) **22055-9, 22056-7 Pa., Two-vol. set $16.00**

THE STANDARD BOOK OF QUILT MAKING AND COLLECTING, Marguerite Ickis. Full information, full-sized patterns for making 46 traditional quilts, also 150 other patterns. Quilted cloths, lame, satin quilts, etc. 483 illustrations. 273pp. 6⅞ x 9⅝. **20582-7 Pa. $4.95**

CORAL GARDENS AND THEIR MAGIC, Bronsilaw Malinowski. Classic study of the methods of tilling the soil and of agricultural rites in the Trobriand Islands of Melanesia. Author is one of the most important figures in the field of modern social anthropology. 143 illustrations. Indexes. Total of 911pp. of text. 5⅝ x 8¼. (Available in U.S. only) **23597-1 Pa. $12.95**

DRAWINGS OF WILLIAM BLAKE, William Blake. 92 plates from Book of Job, *Divine Comedy, Paradise Lost,* visionary heads, mythological figures, Laocoon, etc. Selection, introduction, commentary by Sir Geoffrey Keynes. 178pp. 8⅛ x 11. 22303-5 Pa. $4.00

ENGRAVINGS OF HOGARTH, William Hogarth. 101 of Hogarth's greatest works: *Rake's Progress, Harlot's Progress, Illustrations for Hudibras, Before and After, Beer Street and Gin Lane,* many more. Full commentary. 256pp. 11 x 13¾. 22479-1 Pa. $12.95

DAUMIER: 120 GREAT LITHOGRAPHS, Honore Daumier. Wide-ranging collection of lithographs by the greatest caricaturist of the 19th century. Concentrates on eternally popular series on lawyers, on married life, on liberated women, etc. Selection, introduction, and notes on plates by Charles F. Ramus. Total of 158pp. 9⅜ x 12¼. 23512-2 Pa. $6.00

DRAWINGS OF MUCHA, Alphonse Maria Mucha. Work reveals draftsman of highest caliber: studies for famous posters and paintings, renderings for book illustrations and ads, etc. 70 works, 9 in color; including 6 items not drawings. Introduction. List of illustrations. 72pp. 9⅜ x 12¼. (Available in U.S. only) 23672-2 Pa. $4.00

GIOVANNI BATTISTA PIRANESI: DRAWINGS IN THE PIERPONT MORGAN LIBRARY, Giovanni Battista Piranesi. For first time ever all of Morgan Library's collection, world's largest. 167 illustrations of rare Piranesi drawings—archeological, architectural, decorative and visionary. Essay, detailed list of drawings, chronology, captions. Edited by Felice Stampfle. 144pp. 9⅜ x 12¼. 23714-1 Pa. $7.50

NEW YORK ETCHINGS (1905-1949), John Sloan. All of important American artist's N.Y. life etchings. 67 works include some of his best art; also lively historical record—Greenwich Village, tenement scenes. Edited by Sloan's widow. Introduction and captions. 79pp. 8⅜ x 11¼. 23651-X Pa. $4.00

CHINESE PAINTING AND CALLIGRAPHY: A PICTORIAL SURVEY, Wan-go Weng. 69 fine examples from John M. Crawford's matchless private collection: landscapes, birds, flowers, human figures, etc., plus calligraphy. Every basic form included: hanging scrolls, handscrolls, album leaves, fans, etc. 109 illustrations. Introduction. Captions. 192pp. 8⅞ x 11¾. 23707-9 Pa. $7.95

DRAWINGS OF REMBRANDT, edited by Seymour Slive. Updated Lippmann, Hofstede de Groot edition, with definitive scholarly apparatus. All portraits, biblical sketches, landscapes, nudes, Oriental figures, classical studies, together with selection of work by followers. 550 illustrations. Total of 630pp. 9⅛ x 12¼. 21485-0, 21486-9 Pa., Two-vol. set $15.00

THE DISASTERS OF WAR, Francisco Goya. 83 etchings record horrors of Napoleonic wars in Spain and war in general. Reprint of 1st edition, plus 3 additional plates. Introduction by Philip Hofer. 97pp. 9⅜ x 8¼. 21872-4 Pa. $4.00

THE DEPRESSION YEARS AS PHOTOGRAPHED BY ARTHUR ROTHSTEIN, Arthur Rothstein. First collection devoted entirely to the work of outstanding 1930s photographer: famous dust storm photo, ragged children, unemployed, etc. 120 photographs. Captions. 119pp. 9¼ x 10¾.
23590-4 Pa. $5.00

CAMERA WORK: A PICTORIAL GUIDE, Alfred Stieglitz. All 559 illustrations and plates from the most important periodical in the history of art photography, *Camera Work* (1903-17). Presented four to a page, reduced in size but still clear, in strict chronological order, with complete captions. Three indexes. Glossary. Bibliography. 176pp. 8⅜ x 11¼.
23591-2 Pa. $6.95

ALVIN LANGDON COBURN, PHOTOGRAPHER, Alvin L. Coburn. Revealing autobiography by one of greatest photographers of 20th century gives insider's version of Photo-Secession, plus comments on his own work. 77 photographs by Coburn. Edited by Helmut and Alison Gernsheim. 160pp. 8⅛ x 11. 23685-4 Pa. $6.00

NEW YORK IN THE FORTIES, Andreas Feininger. 162 brilliant photographs by the well-known photographer, formerly with *Life* magazine, show commuters, shoppers, Times Square at night, Harlem nightclub, Lower East Side, etc. Introduction and full captions by John von Hartz. 181pp. 9¼ x 10¾. 23585-8 Pa. $6.95

GREAT NEWS PHOTOS AND THE STORIES BEHIND THEM, John Faber. Dramatic volume of 140 great news photos, 1855 through 1976, and revealing stories behind them, with both historical and technical information. Hindenburg disaster, shooting of Oswald, nomination of Jimmy Carter, etc. 160pp. 8¼ x 11. 23667-6 Pa. $5.00

THE ART OF THE CINEMATOGRAPHER, Leonard Maltin. Survey of American cinematography history and anecdotal interviews with 5 masters—Arthur Miller, Hal Mohr, Hal Rosson, Lucien Ballard, and Conrad Hall. Very large selection of behind-the-scenes production photos. 105 photographs. Filmographies. Index. Originally *Behind the Camera.* 144pp. 8¼ x 11. 23686-2 Pa. $5.00

DESIGNS FOR THE THREE-CORNERED HAT (LE TRICORNE), Pablo Picasso. 32 fabulously rare drawings—including 31 color illustrations of costumes and accessories—for 1919 production of famous ballet. Edited by Parmenia Migel, who has written new introduction. 48pp. 9⅜ x 12¼. (Available in U.S. only) 23709-5 Pa. $5.00

NOTES OF A FILM DIRECTOR, Sergei Eisenstein. Greatest Russian filmmaker explains montage, making of *Alexander Nevsky,* aesthetics; comments on self, associates, great rivals (Chaplin), similar material. 78 illustrations. 240pp. 5⅜ x 8½. 22392-2 Pa. $4.50

YUCATAN BEFORE AND AFTER THE CONQUEST, Diego de Landa. First English translation of basic book in Maya studies, the only significant account of Yucatan written in the early post-Conquest era. Translated by distinguished Maya scholar William Gates. Appendices, introduction, 4 maps and over 120 illustrations added by translator. 162pp. 5⅜ x 8½.
23622-6 Pa. $3.00

THE MALAY ARCHIPELAGO, Alfred R. Wallace. Spirited travel account by one of founders of modern biology. Touches on zoology, botany, ethnography, geography, and geology. 62 illustrations, maps. 515pp. 5⅜ x 8½.
20187-2 Pa. $6.95

THE DISCOVERY OF THE TOMB OF TUTANKHAMEN, Howard Carter, A. C. Mace. Accompany Carter in the thrill of discovery, as ruined passage suddenly reveals unique, untouched, fabulously rich tomb. Fascinating account, with 106 illustrations. New introduction by J. M. White. Total of 382pp. 5⅜ x 8½. (Available in U.S. only) 23500-9 Pa. $4.00

THE WORLD'S GREATEST SPEECHES, edited by Lewis Copeland and Lawrence W. Lamm. Vast collection of 278 speeches from Greeks up to present. Powerful and effective models; unique look at history. Revised to 1970. Indices. 842pp. 5⅜ x 8½. 20468-5 Pa. $8.95

THE 100 GREATEST ADVERTISEMENTS, Julian Watkins. The priceless ingredient; His master's voice; 99 44/100% pure; over 100 others. How they were written, their impact, etc. Remarkable record. 130 illustrations. 233pp. 7⅞ x 10 3/5. 20540-1 Pa. $5.95

CRUICKSHANK PRINTS FOR HAND COLORING, George Cruickshank. 18 illustrations, one side of a page, on fine-quality paper suitable for watercolors. Caricatures of people in society (c. 1820) full of trenchant wit. Very large format. 32pp. 11 x 16. 23684-6 Pa. $5.00

THIRTY-TWO COLOR POSTCARDS OF TWENTIETH-CENTURY AMERICAN ART, Whitney Museum of American Art. Reproduced in full color in postcard form are 31 art works and one shot of the museum. Calder, Hopper, Rauschenberg, others. Detachable. 16pp. 8¼ x 11.
23629-3 Pa. $3.00

MUSIC OF THE SPHERES: THE MATERIAL UNIVERSE FROM ATOM TO QUASAR SIMPLY EXPLAINED, Guy Murchie. Planets, stars, geology, atoms, radiation, relativity, quantum theory, light, antimatter, similar topics. 319 figures. 664pp. 5⅜ x 8½.
21809-0, 21810-4 Pa., Two-vol. set $11.00

EINSTEIN'S THEORY OF RELATIVITY, Max Born. Finest semi-technical account; covers Einstein, Lorentz, Minkowski, and others, with much detail, much explanation of ideas and math not readily available elsewhere on this level. For student, non-specialist. 376pp. 5⅜ x 8½.
60769-0 Pa. $4.50

UNCLE SILAS, J. Sheridan LeFanu. Victorian Gothic mystery novel, considered by many best of period, even better than Collins or Dickens. Wonderful psychological terror. Introduction by Frederick Shroyer. 436pp. 5⅜ x 8½. 21715-9 Pa. $6.00

JURGEN, James Branch Cabell. The great erotic fantasy of the 1920's that delighted thousands, shocked thousands more. Full final text, Lane edition with 13 plates by Frank Pape. 346pp. 5⅜ x 8½. 23507-6 Pa. $4.50

THE CLAVERINGS, Anthony Trollope. Major novel, chronicling aspects of British Victorian society, personalities. Reprint of Cornhill serialization, 16 plates by M. Edwards; first reprint of full text. Introduction by Norman Donaldson. 412pp. 5⅜ x 8½. 23464-9 Pa. $5.00

KEPT IN THE DARK, Anthony Trollope. Unusual short novel about Victorian morality and abnormal psychology by the great English author. Probably the first American publication. Frontispiece by Sir John Millais. 92pp. 6½ x 9¼. 23609-9 Pa. $2.50

RALPH THE HEIR, Anthony Trollope. Forgotten tale of illegitimacy, inheritance. Master novel of Trollope's later years. Victorian country estates, clubs, Parliament, fox hunting, world of fully realized characters. Reprint of 1871 edition. 12 illustrations by F. A. Faser. 434pp. of text. 5⅜ x 8½. 23642-0 Pa. $5.00

YEKL and THE IMPORTED BRIDEGROOM AND OTHER STORIES OF THE NEW YORK GHETTO, Abraham Cahan. Film *Hester Street* based on *Yekl* (1896). Novel, other stories among first about Jewish immigrants of N.Y.'s East Side. Highly praised by W. D. Howells—Cahan "a new star of realism." New introduction by Bernard G. Richards. 240pp. 5⅜ x 8½. 22427-9 Pa. $3.50

THE HIGH PLACE, James Branch Cabell. Great fantasy writer's enchanting comedy of disenchantment set in 18th-century France. Considered by some critics to be even better than his famous *Jurgen*. 10 illustrations and numerous vignettes by noted fantasy artist Frank C. Pape. 320pp. 5⅜ x 8½. 23670-6 Pa. $4.00

ALICE'S ADVENTURES UNDER GROUND, Lewis Carroll. Facsimile of ms. Carroll gave Alice Liddell in 1864. Different in many ways from final Alice. Handlettered, illustrated by Carroll. Introduction by Martin Gardner. 128pp. 5⅜ x 8½. 21482-6 Pa. $2.50

FAVORITE ANDREW LANG FAIRY TALE BOOKS IN MANY COLORS, Andrew Lang. The four Lang favorites in a boxed set—the complete *Red, Green, Yellow* and *Blue* Fairy Books. 164 stories; 439 illustrations by Lancelot Speed, Henry Ford and G. P. Jacomb Hood. Total of about 1500pp. 5⅜ x 8½. 23407-X Boxed set, Pa. $15.95

CATALOGUE OF DOVER BOOKS